Graphics Programming
in Turbo C®++

Graphics Programming
in Turbo C®++

BEN EZZELL

Addison-Wesley Publishing Company, Inc.
Reading, Massachusetts   Menlo Park, California   New York
Don Mills, Ontario   Wokingham, England   Amsterdam   Bonn
Sydney   Singapore   Tokyo   Madrid   San Juan

Many of the designations used by manufacturers and sellers to distinguish their products are claimed as trademarks. Where those designations appear in this book and Addison-Wesley was aware of a trademark claim, the designations have been printed in intitial capital letters.

Library of Congress Cataloging-in-Publication Data

Ezzell, Ben.
   Graphics programming in Turbo C + + / Ben Ezzell.
      p.   cm.
   Includes index.
   ISBN 0-201-57023-8
   1. Computer graphics. 2. Turbo C + + (Computer program) I. Title.
T385.E983   1990
006.6′6765 — dc20   90-46175

ISBN: 0-201-57023-8

Production Editor: Amorette Pedersen
Cover Design by Doliber Skeffington Design
Set in 11-point Times by Benchmark Productions

2 3 4 5 6 7 8 9 - MW - 94 93 92 91
Second printing, January 1991

In the 17th century, during an outbreak of the plague, the great universities of England were closed and their students dispersed to safer places. It was during this educational hiatus that a young man was inspired by the sight of a falling apple. He realized not merely a theory accounting for the motions of the planets, but a method of calculation by which otherwise irreducible solutions could be determined. Integral calculus was born.

Sir Isaac Newton's calculus presumed that space was continuous and that such theoretical subdivisions could be carried out ad infinitum. This is a presumption which, three centuries later, is seriously questioned by quantum mechanics and violated by fractal mathematics.

For most purposes Newtonian physics and mathematics serve us well and remind us that valued originality is not the hallmark of the classroom, but is more often found in the eyes of the dreamer.

This volume is dedicated to:

Sir Isaac Newton
Dreamer and Mathematician
1642 — 1727

Had you lived three centuries later and played with our toys, what further wonders might you have shown us?

Table of Contents

Graphics, once limited to children's games and for entertaining CEOs and board members, are now serious business. Graphics are the heart and soul of everything from computer typesetting (which is how this book was produced) to computer aided design (the CAD in CAD/CAM), to fractal mathematics and experimental chemistry, and a thousand other equally diverse fields.

Graphics are more than toys, graphics are also code intensive, often requiring far more code for the graphics execution than for the bulk of the application.

However you feel about computer graphics, they are here and they are increasing in popularity. Ofter, they are the only reasonable solution to application requirements.

Topics and Objectives

Because the subject of graphics programming is not a simple one and covers considerable ground, this book is divided into four sections:

- *Part One: Introduction to Graphics Programming* covers the basic graphics functions supplied by Turbo C++ as well as examples of how existing library functions can be extended to provide special features.

■ *Part Two: Using Turbo C++ Graphics* covers the graphics library functions and the extensions demonstrated will be used in a variety of applications ranging from business graphs to simple animation to demonstrations of how various capabilities may be employed.

Graphics applications differ widely in subject and type but one perennial favorite is business graphics as a means of converting figures into forms that can be easily interpreted. At the same time, however, business graphics are relatively simple and rarely require any interactive capabilities.

Because it often helps to be able to print out hard copy of graphics application screens, EP_GRAPH and LJ_GRAPH provide drivers for dot-matrix and laser printer outputs.

■ *Part Three: Advanced Graphics Programming*, object-oriented graphics will be introduced together with a number of graphics objects that can be used in various future applications, including a mouse object, graphic button objects, scrollbars, and icons.

Some graphics applications require varying degrees of interactive capability and virtually demand a mouse as the primary input device. Therefore, this section will discuss implementing an object-oriented mouse interface.

In many cases, graphics have become the preferred user interaction—in some cases becoming a semiliterate interface offering pictorial rather than text options for the user. In other cases, such as graphics buttons and scrollbars, graphics control elements are more appropriate than text controls. Icon images can be used for a variety of applications ranging from the inane to the sublime.

■ *Part Four: Fractals and Other Strange Phenomena*, fractal mathematics will be introduced in this section, along with one or two graphic/mathematical diversions.

Introducing Object Graphics

This book is an introduction to graphics programming in general as well as to object-oriented graphics. This volume is not an introduction to object-oriented programming and assumes some knowledge both of C and C++ programming in general.

If you desire a more extensive instruction in C++ and object-oriented practices, I recommend *Turbo C++ Programming: An Object-Oriented Approach* (also available from Addison-Wesley Publishing).

If you are a novice to C programming I'll try to show you at least the basics of graphics programming as well as a variety of interesting object-oriented possibilities.

Part One

Introduction to Graphics Programming

When the first microcomputers appeared, an 8-bit CPU and buss architecture with 16K of RAM was fairly standard, clock speeds of 2 Megahertz were considered fast, and video displays handling 80 characters and 25 lines were the absolute tops. If you wanted graphics displays, a ROM-based graphics character set was your only alternative to the familiar ASCII characters. Few provisions were offered for direct access to the video memory and CPU and system memory limitations made what access was available difficult to use.

This early world was divided into two parts: serious computers that concentrated on efficient memory usage and fast processing speeds, and "game-oriented" systems that sacrificed much of their capability in favor of elaborate monochrome or color graphics capabilities.

Later, with more powerful CPUs, operating systems, and faster speeds, greater degrees of freedom became possible. To use Heath/Zenith's Z-100 series (the original MS-DOS system) as an example, three banks of video memory were available, each providing 32K or 64K RAM to control the Red, Blue, and Green color guns (total 192K). If your Z-100 had only one of the three banks (by default the green bank), you were limited to a monochrome display or, if you had all three banks of video RAM but only a monochrome monitor, color was simulated as "shades of grey." With a

1

high-resolution color monitor, you had the breathtaking choice of eight colors (black, blue, violet, red, orange, green, yellow, and white).

More importantly, was the fact that you had a pixel-addressable video memory with a display range of 640 pixels horizontal and 225 pixels vertical. For text, the display was 80 characters (columns) by 25 lines, but there was no distinction necessary between text and graphics modes; both were the same. Text characters were 8 pixels wide, 9 pixels high (including distenders—the portions of lowercase characters that extend below the line as with g, j, p, q, and y) and were created by a ROM character set that was written directly to the video RAM.

You could also write (and read) individual pixels in video RAM, intermixing these with standard characters without changing modes or disabling one type of display in favor of another.

IBM's design approach—while using essentially the same CPU, 16-bit architecture, and Microsoft DOS—chose a minimalist hardware configuration. The first IBM PCs were provided with a rather scanty video RAM (about 4K) limited only to non-graphic displays. If you wanted graphics capabilities, the Color Graphics Adapter (CGA) was available as an add-on that provided high-resolution graphics (640x200 pixels) with 2-colors (monochrome) or a low-resolution (320x200), 4-color display using a choice of four, predefined palettes.

In many ways, this was like Henry Ford's famous statement that you could have a Model-T in any color you wanted ... as long as it was black.

Changing the video adapter was a bit easier than repainting a car and a host of third-party developers looked at the price of RAM chips, warmed up their soldering irons, and went into business creating more advanced video cards such as the Hercules, MCGA, and EGA video adapters.

This proliferation of video hardware (which now includes at least 10 different "standard" video adapters) has presented its own problems for the programmer. Each different design of video hardware supports a different set of capabilities, may use different memory addresses, may not support multiple graphics pages (and/or multiple text pages), may support video modes ranging from 320x200 to 1,024x768 pixel displays and ranging from monochrome to 256 color displays. Of course, the initial problem facing every graphics programmer is simply the question of identifying which video adapter is installed in what machine.

One option has always been to ask the end-user, allowing them to select the video mode that will be used. This is a poor choice because even professional programmers are not always certain what hardware they are working with and the average end-user may not know if they have a graphics adapter at all, much less what type or capabilities are present. So, the alternate choice is to have your software query the hardware to determine the present configuration.

If a standard for hardware identification existed, this would be a simple matter. Unfortunately for programmers, the rapid proliferation of video adapter hardware has occurred without any formalized provisions for identification. In a previous book, *Programming The IBM User Interface*, I discussed several tests for determining the presence or absence of CGA/EGA video adapters and some of the problems inherent in identifying hardware.

Happily, the release of Turbo C++ (and Turbo Pascal 5.5) has relieved much of the indecision both in identifying and in supporting and using the various current video adapter cards. Also, judging by Borland's past performance, it seems fairly safe to assume that new, future video adapters will be similarly supported.

Unhappily, this same support for diverse video capabilities has resulted in creating its own confusion over how to use these new tools, what is possible, and what to do with a plethora of new capabilities.

This confusion is precisely the subject of *Graphics Programming in Turbo C++*.

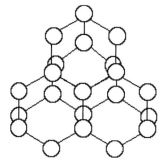

Chapter 1

Graphics Video Adapters

Both Turbo C++ and Turbo Pascal provide comprehensive support for all major video card types currently in use. This book will discuss and illustrate graphics in Turbo C++ only. If you are using Turbo Pascal, corresponding functions are provided, using the same function and procedure names and operating in the same manner.

Contemporary video cards range from the text-only original video systems to the ultra-high resolution IBM-8514 (popular with typesetting or CAD software applications), with a variety of resolutions lying between the two. Obviously, the higher resolution video cards must be matched with monitors that have corresponding pixel resolution. This, however, is a hardware matter and you can simply assume the hardware present corresponds to the identification returned by Turbo C++'s detectgraph function. Any discrepancies in matching video cards and monitors are the end user's responsibility and should not be the programmer's concern.

Video Modes

Every PC, XT, AT, or PS/2 is equipped with some type of video adapter card. Beginning with a basic card, you may have the Monochrome Display Adapter (MDA) which supports text-only display. If this is the case, you will not be able to program or use graphics without upgrading your system.

The first step up is the popular Color Graphics Adapter (CGA) card, while higher resolutions and wider options are provided by the Hercules Monochrome Graphics Adapters, Multi Color Graphics Array (MCGA), and Enhanced Graphics Adapter (EGA) video adapters. For more advanced graphics capabilities, as for typesetting or CAD applications, the AT&T (400-line Graphic Adapter), Variable or Video Graphics Array (VGA), PC-3270, and IBM-8514 video adapters all offer even higher pixel resolutions and color choices.

In Turbo C++, graphics support for all of these is provided in the form of six graphics interface (.BGI) units (ATT, CGA, EGAVGA, HERC, IBM8514, and PC3270) and four graphics fonts (GOTH.CHR, LITT.CHR, SANS.CHR, and TRIP.CHR). As new video graphics cards appear, new .BGI units may be included for support—while new .CHR fonts may be user-created. The graphics support units are not included in the standard memory models (as distributed)—an omission made for the express purpose of speeding compilation time when graphics are not needed. To use the graphics modules, two options exist.

First, Borland has provided TLIB, the Turbo Librarian distributed with Turbo C. Using TLIB, the graphics library (GRAPHICS.LIB) can be incorporated in one or more of the memory model libraries. Using TLIB is explained in more detail in Chapter 9, *Business Graph Displays*.

Second, a project (.PRJ) file can be created for each program, making GRAPHICS.LIB available for linking and allowing your program to load the appropriate .BGI files from disk as needed.

If you are using graphics programming extensively, including GRAPH-ICS.LIB in your standard library is recommended. The BGIOBJ utility can also be used to convert .BGI graphics drivers and .CHR font files to object files, allowing you to link them directly to your program (thus including them directly in your .EXE program).

However, for testing and development, GRAPHICS.LIB is conveniently called as a secondary library and the .BGI and .CHR files are accessed externally.

Including the Graphics Library

If you're using the Turbo C++ command line compiler (TCC.EXE) to compile a source program titled YOURPROG.C, the TCC command would be:

```
tcc yourprog graphics.lib
```

This assumes that YOURPROG.C and GRAPHICS.LIB are in the same directory as TCC and therefore, no path specifications are required.

When using the Turbo C++ integrated compiler (TC.EXE), you need to create and select a project file to instruct the linker to access the external library (GRAPHICS.LIB) in addition to the standard library. This project file is simple and, for this application, requires only a single line:

```
yourprog graphics.lib
```

Here, if GRAPHICS.LIB is located in a different subdirectory from the compiler, you may either specify the path in YOURPROG.PRJ or include the path in the compiler environment configuration (use Alt-O for options menu, then select Environment). In either case, you will have to enter the project name YOURPROG.PRJ (the .PRJ extension is optional and will be assumed if not specified) before selecting the RUN option or compiling your program to disk.

Note that the absence of library functions will not create an error message during compiler execution—only during the second linker pass. As long as the compiler finds the graphics functions correctly defined in the GRAPHICS.H header file (be sure to use *#include <graphics.h>* in your source listing), no error messages will be generated until the linker finds itself unable to actually access the library.

To specify a .PRJ file, enter Alt-P to pop up the Project Menu. Now select the first menu item (**O**pen project...) and either type in the correct project name or use the mouse or arrow keys to select the appropriate .PRJ file.

Remember, if you have TC configured for autosave, the selected project will still be in effect the next time you use C++. The **C**lose project option is used to cancel this selection, allowing you to compile and run a different program. Alternatively, several different project files can be maintained in Turbo C++'s look-up lists.

Disadvantages

Once a program has been compiled (from a project file or using the command line specification), the .EXE program can be distributed along with required external .BGI and .CHR files. These files require about 60K of disk space—not an excessive requirement in terms of storage, however, relying on external files for execution can create difficulties.

First, a call to initgraph must include the drive/path specification of where the .BGI (and .CHR) modules are located. If no path is specified, the current directory is assumed. This routing information is normally supplied by the programmer and, if the required files are not found your program *will* terminate!

Second, if the default (current) path is assumed and all external files are present, but the program is called from another directory or drive, a crash can occur!

Third, never depend on the end-user to be aware of the importance of any external files. They may love your program and guard it jealously, but as soon as space becomes a problem, may ignorantly erase necessary external files.

Alternatively, you can link the .BGI and .CHR files directly into the graphics library, increasing your .EXE program in size by about 30 kilobytes, but making the drivers and fonts part of your .EXE program rather than external files.

Knock, Knock! What's There?

The first step in your graphics program is to initialize the appropriate graphics driver. Table 1-1 shows a list of supported graphics video cards, drivers, and graphics modes.

Table 1-1: Video Modes Supported By Turbo C++

Graphics[1] Driver Constant	Number Value	Graphics Mode(s)	Key[2] Value	Column x Row	Palette[3] or Colors	Video Pages
DETECT	0	requests initgraph to execute autodetection				
CGA	1	CGAC0	0	320 x 200	C0	1
		CGAC1	1	320 x 200	C1	1
		CGAC2	2	320 x 200	C2	1
		CGAC3	3	320 x 200	C3	1
		CGAHI	4	640 x 200	2 colors	1
MCGA	2	MCGAC0	0	320 x 200	C0	1
		MCGAC1	1	320 x 200	C1	1
		MCGAC2	2	320 x 200	C2	1
		MCGAC3	3	320 x 200	C3	1
		MCGAMED	4	640 x 200	2 colors	1
		MCGAHI	5	640 x 480	2 colors	1
EGA	3	EGALO	0	640 x 200	16 colors	4
		EGAHI	1	640 x 350	16 colors	2
EGA64	4	EGA64LO	0	640 x 200	16 colors	1
		EGA64HI	1	640 x 350	4 colors	1
EGAMONO	5	EGAMONOHI	3	640 x 350	2 colors	1-2[4]

Graphics[1] Driver Constant	Number Value	Graphics Mode(s)	Key[2] Value	Column x Row	Palette[3] or Colors	Video Pages
IBM8514[5]	6	IBM8514LO	0	640 x 480	256 colors	1
		IBM8514HI	1	1024 x 768	256 colors	1
HERC	7	HERCMONOHI	0	720 x 348	2 colors	4
ATT400	8	ATT400C0	0	320 x 200	C0	1
		ATT400C1	1	320 x 200	C1	1
		ATT400C2	2	320 x 200	C2	1
		ATT400C3	3	320 x 200	C3	1
		ATT400MED	4	640 x 200	2 colors	1
		ATT400HI	5	640 x 400	2 colors	1
VGA	9	VGALO	0	640 x 200	16 colors	4
		VGAMED	1	640 x 350	16 colors	2
		VGAHI	2	640 x 480	16 colors	1
PC3270	10	PC3270HI	0	720 x 350	2 colors	1

1. The *graphic_drivers* and *graphic_modes* names are constants defined in GRAPH-ICS.H, as are the corresponding numerical values and mode values (see note 2).
2. Mode settings returned by initgraph, detectgraph, or getgraphmode.
3. C0..C3 refer to the predefined 4-color palettes—see setpalette.
4. With 64K on EGAMONO card only one video page is supported; with 256K, two video pages are supported.
5. Autodetection will not correctly recognize the IBM-8514 graphics card. Instead, init-graph or detectgraph will identify the IBM-8514 card as a VGA graphics card that the IBM-8514 will emulate correctly (IBM8514LO is equivalent to VGAHI). To use the higher resolution mode (IBM8514HI, 1024x768 pixels), assign the value IBM8514 (numerical value 6, defined in GRAPHICS.H) to the graphdriver variable before calling initgraph. Do not use detectgraph or DETECT with initgraph. See also text notes on IBM-8514 and setrbgpalette.

detectgraph

Normally, the detectgraph function is called by initgraph, but it can also be called independently.

Example:

```
#include <graphics.h>

int graphdriver = DETECT, graphmode;

main
{
    detectgraph( &graphdriver, &graphmode );
    ......
}
```

If a problem occurs, *graphdriver* returns an error code; otherwise, *graphdriver* identifies the appropriate driver type and *graphmode* returns the highest valid video mode for this driver.

For detectgraph, no driver path is required (refer to initgraph).

The detectgraph function does *not* initialize any graphics settings. Calling detectgraph directly would be done to subsequently use initgraph to call a specific graphics driver or to select a graphics mode which initgraph would not call by default. A different mode can be called after initializing graphics by using the setgraphmode function.

Value returned: *graphdriver* returns driver type or error code; *graphmode* returns highest valid video mode.

Portability: IBM PCs and compatibles only, corresponding functions exist in Turbo Pascal.

initgraph

The initgraph function is provided to set the initial graphics parameter values, load the proper graphics driver, and set the system to the desired graphics mode.

Example:

```
#include <graphics.h>

int graphdriver = DETECT, graphmode;
char driverpath = "";

main
{
    initgraph( &graphdriver, &graphmode,
               driverpath );

    ......

}
```

Setting *graphdriver* as zero instructs initgraph to call *detectgraph(graphdriver, graphmode)* to determine the type (and settings) of the video graphics adapter installed. If an error occurs, *graphdriver* returns an error code indicating the type of error—as shown in Table 1-2.

Table 1-2: Initialization Graphic Error Codes

Error Code	Meaning
−2	Cannot detect graphics card
−3	Cannot locate graphics driver file(s)
−4	Invalid driver (or not recognized)
−5	Insufficient memory to load graphics driver

The detectgraph and graphresult functions return the same error codes. If no error occurs, the internal error code is set to zero, initgraph allocates memory for the appropriate graphics driver, it loads required .BGI file from disk, and it sets the default graphics parameter values. Also, *graphdriver* returns the driver type, while *graphmode* returns the mode setting.

Alternatively, *graphdriver* and *graphmode* can be specified by using the appropriate numerical constants or by using the driver and mode names as defined in <GRAPHICS.H>. In either case, *driverpath* shows the drive and path where the .BGI graphics drivers are located. If *driverpath* is null (as shown in the example) then these files must be located in the default directory. If they are located in a different directory the complete path specification should be shown as:

```
char driverpath = "\\TURBOC\\DRIVERS";
```

Note the use of the double backslash (\\). The backslash character is used to set escape sequences (as in \n for carriage returns or \a for bell). To include a backslash in a string, the \\ is required.

Also, the *driverpath* set by initgraph is also used by settextstyle to search for the character font (.CHR) files. Both .BGI and .CHR files must be located in the same directory.

Value returned: *graphdriver* returns driver type or error code; *graphmode* returns highest valid video mode.

Portability: IBM PCs and compatibles only, corresponding functions exist in Turbo Pascal.

Graphics Error Functions

If a graphics video card is not present, the graphics drivers are not found, or if some other error occurs during detection of initialization, an error code is returned by detectgraph or initgraph. There are, however, other conditions where a graphics error can occur and the graphresult and grapherrormsg functions are provided to test and display appropriate error results and messages.

graphresult

The graphresult function returns a numerical error code set by the last graphics operation that reported an error. This will be an integer value in the range –18..0. Since, when graphresult is called, the error condition is reset to zero, the returned value should be stored in a local variable, then tested for further action.

Example:

```
#include <graphics.h>

int errornumber;

errornumber = graphresult();
```

Value returned: error code (–15..0), see Table 1-3 for interpretation of graphics error messages.

Portability: IBM PCs and compatibles only, corresponding functions exist in Turbo Pascal.

Table 1-3: Graphics Error Messages

Error Code	Graphics Error Constant[1]	Corresponding Error Message String
0	grOk	No error
–1	grNoInitGraph	(BGI) graphics not installed (use initgraph)
–2	grNotDetected	Graphics hardware not detected
–3	grFileNotFound	Device driver file not found (.BGI file)
–4	grInvalidDriver	Invalid device driver file
–5	grNoLoadMem	Not enough memory to load driver
–6	grNoScanMem	Out of memory in scan fill
–7	grNoFloodMem	Out of memory in flood fill
–8	grFontNotFound	Font file not found (.CHR file)
–9	grNoFontMem	Not enough memory to load font
–10	grInvalidMode	Invalid graphics mode for selected driver
–11	grError	Graphics error (generic error)
–12	grIOerror	Graphics I/O error
–13	grInvalidFont	Invalid font file
-14	grInvalidFontNum	Invalid font number
–15	grInvalidDeviceNum	Invalid device number
–18	grInvalidVersion	Invalid version number

1. The *graphics_errors* constants and error messages are defined in GRAPHICS.H. Error values –16..–17 are not assigned.

grapherrormsg

The grapherrormsg function returns a pointer to the appropriate error message string. These strings are defined in the graphics library (GRAPH-ICS.LIB), but a separate error message routine can be created to display a more informative error message.

Example:

```
#include <graphics.h>

int   errornumber;

errornumber = graphresult();
printf(" %s ", grapherrormsg( errornumber ) );
```

Value returned: none.

Portability: IBM PCs and compatibles only, corresponding functions exist in Turbo Pascal.

Other Graphics Mode Functions

With the exceptions of the EGAMONO, HERC, and PC3270 video drivers, each video driver supports two or more video modes that offer varying pixel resolutions or different color palettes. To handle mode inquiries and to change operating modes, Turbo C++ provides several functions.

getgraphmode

The getgraphmode function returns an integer value showing the current (operational) graphics mode that was set by initgraph or setgraphmode.

Example:

```
#include <graphics.h>

int currentmode;

currentmode = getgraphmode();
```

Value returned: current graphics mode.

Portability: IBM PCs and compatibles only, corresponding functions exist in Turbo Pascal.

getmoderange

The getmoderange function is called with an integer value specifying the graphics driver. This may be an integer variable or one of the constants defined in GRAPHICS.H. It returns two values defining the minimum and maximum valid modes supported by the indicated driver.

Example:

```
#include <graphics.h>

int   lomode, himode;

getmoderange( graphdriver, &lomode, &himode );
```

If the value passed as graphdriver is invalid, then both *lomode* and *himode* return −1.

Value returned: maximum and minimum valid modes or −1 error code.

Portability: IBM PCs and compatibles only, corresponding functions exist in Turbo Pascal.

getmaxmode

The getmaxmode function is called without parameters and queries the currently loaded graphics driver directly to return the maximum mode number for the driver.

Example:

```
#include <graphics.h>

int   maxmode;

maxmode = getmaxmode();
```

Unlike getmoderange, getmaxmode works for all drivers, not merely for Borland drivers. The minimum mode number is always 0.

Value returned: maximum valid mode number.

Portability: Turbo C++ only/PC and compatible systems with supported graphics display adapters.

getdrivername

The getdrivername function is called without parameters and returns a pointer to a string with the name of the currently loaded graphics drivers.

Example:

```
#include <graphics.h>

printf( "Driver = %s\n", getdrivername() );
```

Value returned: pointer to string identifying currently loaded graphics driver.

Portability: Turbo C++ only/PC and compatible systems with supported graphics display adapters.

getmodename

The getmodename function is called with an integer value specifying the active graphics mode. This may be an integer variable or one of the constants defined in GRAPHICS.H. It returns a string containing the name of the corresponding graphics mode.

Example:

```
#include <graphics.h>

printf( "Mode is: %s\n",
        getmodename( getgraphmode() ) );
```

The mode names are imbedded in each graphics driver and identify the mode type and specifics about the operating mode. Possible strings returned might be: "320 x 200 CGA P1" or "640 x 480 VGA".

Value returned: string containing corresponding mode name.

Portability: Turbo C++ only/PC and compatible systems with supported graphics display adapters.

graphdefaults

The graphdefaults function resets all graphic settings to their default values—the values originally set by initgraph and defined in GRAPHICS.H. This includes resetting the viewport (graphics window) to the entire screen; moving the current position to (0,0); resetting default palette colors, background color, and drawing color; resetting the default file and pattern styles; and resetting the default text font and justification modes.

Example:

```
#include <graphics.h>

graphdefaults();
```

Value returned: none.

Portability: IBM PCs and compatibles only, corresponding functions exist in Turbo Pascal.

setgraphmode

Graphics mode must have been previously initialized by initgraph and the setgraphmode function must be called with a graphics mode that is valid for the current device driver. Use getgraphmode to find the current mode value or getmoderange to check permissible values. When called, setgraphmode selects a new graphics mode, clearing the screen and resetting all graphics variables to their default values (refer to graphdefaults).

Example:

```
#include <graphics.h>

setgraphmode(modenumber);
```

The setgraphmode function can also be used with the restorecrt function in order to switch back and forth between text and graphics displays. Note that initgraph must have been called before either of these functions can be used.

```
#include <graphics.h>

int  currentmode;

currentmode = getgraphmode();
restorecrtmode();                       /* text mode      */
setgraphmode(currentmode);              /* graphics mode  */
```

If setgraphmode is called with a value that is invalid for the current device driver, graphresult will return a value of −10 (grInvalidMode).

Value returned: none; refer to graphresult for error codes.

Portability: IBM PCs and compatibles only, corresponding functions exist in Turbo Pascal.

restorecrtmode

The restorecrtmode function resets the system video to the original text mode detected by the call to initgraph. This can be used with setgraphmode to alternate between text and graphics displays.

Example:

```
#include <graphics.h>

restorecrtmode();
```

Value returned: none; refer to graphresult for error codes.

Portability: IBM PCs and compatibles only, corresponding functions exist in Turbo Pascal.

closegraph

The closegraph function restores the system to the normal text mode originally detected by initgraph. It also calls _graphfreemem to deallocate memory used by the graphics system for drivers, fonts, and the internal buffer.

Example:

```
#include <graphics.h>

closegraph();
```

If you wish to switch back and forth between text and graphics, use the restorecrtmode and setgraphmode functions. Graphics memory allocation can be changed using the _graphfreemem and _graphgetmem functions.

Value returned: none; refer to graphresult for error codes.

Portability: IBM PCs and compatibles only, corresponding functions exist in Turbo Pascal.

```
/*               FIRSTGRP.C              */
/* demo for initializing and testing */
/*     graphics modes in Turbo C++      */

#ifdef __TINY__
#error Graphics demos will not run in the tiny model.
#endif
```

```
#include    <conio.h>
#include    <stdio.h>
#include    <stdarg.h>
#include    <graphics.h>

char *Fonts[]       = { "Default", "Triplex", "Small",
                        "SansSerif", "Gothic" };
char *LineStyles[]  = { "Solid", "Dotted", "Center",
                        "Dashed", "User Defined" };
char *FillStyles[]  = { "Empty", "Solid", "Line Fill",
                        "Light Slash", "Slash",
                        "Back Slash", "Light Back Slash",
                        "Hatch", "XHatch", "Interleave",
                        "Wide Dot", "Close Dot" };
char *TextDirect[]  = { "Horizontal", "Vertical" };
char *HorizJust[]   = { "Flush Left", "Centered",
                        "Flush Right" };
char *VertJust[]    = { "Bottom", "Centered", "Top" };
int   GraphDriver, GraphMode;
                             /* graphics driver, mode value  */
double AspectRatio;          /* pixel aspect ratio on screen */
int    xasp, yasp;           /* factors for aspect ratio     */
int    MaxX, MaxY;           /* maximum screen resolution     */
int    MaxColors;            /* maximum colors available      */
int    ErrorCode = 0;           /* graphics errors variable  */
struct palettetype  palette;        /* for palette info */

void TestGraphicError()
{
   ErrorCode = graphresult();        /* check the result    */
   if( ErrorCode != grOk )           /* if an error occurs  */
   {                                 /* report error        */
      closegraph();                  /* using text mode     */
      printf(" Graphics System Error: %s\n",
             grapherrormsg( ErrorCode ) );
      exit( 1 );                     /* and exit to DOS      */
} }

void ChangeTextStyle( int font, int direction,
                      int charsize)
{
   graphresult();                            /* clear error code */
```

```
      settextstyle(font, direction, charsize);
      TestGraphicError();                        /* check for errors */
}

void StatusLine( char *msg )
{                             /* display status line at bottom */
   int Height;
   setviewport( 0, 0, MaxX, MaxY, 1 );      /* open viewport */
   setcolor( MaxColors - 1 );        /* start with max color  */
   ChangeTextStyle( DEFAULT_FONT, HORIZ_DIR, 1 );
   settextjustify( CENTER_TEXT, TOP_TEXT );
   setlinestyle( SOLID_LINE, 0, NORM_WIDTH );
   setfillstyle( EMPTY_FILL, 0 );
   Height = textheight( msg );             /* get char height   */
   bar( 0, MaxY-(Height+4), MaxX, MaxY );
   rectangle( 0, MaxY-(Height+4), MaxX, MaxY );
   outtextxy( MaxX/2, MaxY-(Height+2), msg );
   setviewport( 1, Height+5, MaxX-1, MaxY-(Height+5), 1);
}

void DrawBorder()
{      /* draw solid line around current viewport (window) */
   struct viewporttype vp;
   setcolor( MaxColors - 1 );          /* draw color as white */
   setlinestyle( SOLID_LINE, 0, NORM_WIDTH );
   getviewsettings( &vp );
   rectangle( 0, 0, vp.right-vp.left, vp.bottom-vp.top );
}

void ReportWindow( char *header )
{                        /* setup window for graphics report */
   int Height;
   cleardevice();                      /* clear graphics screen */
   setcolor( MaxColors - 1 );
   setviewport( 0, 0, MaxX, MaxY, 1 );      /* set viewport */
   Height = textheight( header );          /* get char height */
   ChangeTextStyle( DEFAULT_FONT, HORIZ_DIR, 1 );
   settextjustify( CENTER_TEXT, TOP_TEXT );
   outtextxy( MaxX/2, 2, header );
   setviewport( 0, Height+4, MaxX, MaxY-(Height+4), 1 );
   DrawBorder();
   setviewport( 1, Height+5, MaxX-1,
```

```
                        MaxY-(Height+5), 1 );
}

void Pause()                                /* wait for key entry  */
{
   static char msg[] = "Press any key...";
   StatusLine( msg );                       /* put msg on screen   */
   if ( kbhit() != 0 ) getch();
   getch();
   cleardevice();                           /* clear the screen    */
}

 /* gprintf is used like printf except the output is */
 /* sent to the screen in graphics mode at the       */
 /* specified co-ordinate, then current position is  */
 /* moved for next line output.                      */
void gprintf( int *xloc, int *yloc, char *fmt, ... )
         /* note ellipsis indicating variable argument ^ list */
{
   va_list  Argptr;                         /* argument list       */
   char Workstr[140];                       /* string for output   */
   struct textsettingstype textinfo;

   va_start( Argptr, fmt );                 /* setup argument list */
   vsprintf( Workstr, fmt, Argptr );
                                            /* create output string */
   outtextxy( *xloc, *yloc, Workstr );
                                            /* print the output    */

   gettextsettings( &textinfo );
                                            /* get output orientation */
   if ( textinfo.direction )
      *xloc += textheight(Workstr) + 2;
                                            /* move CP horiz  */
      else *yloc += textheight(Workstr) + 2;
                                            /* move CP vert   */

   va_end( Argptr );                        /* close argument list */
}

void StepColor()
{             /* steps display colors through valid range */
   int Color;
```

```
    Color = getcolor() - 1;
    if ( !Color ) Color = getmaxcolor();
    setcolor( Color );
}

void ReportStatus()
{                        /* report the current system configuration */
    struct viewporttype        viewinfo;        /* structures */
    struct linesettingstype    lineinfo;        /* for        */
    struct fillsettingstype    fillinfo;        /* inquiries  */
    struct textsettingstype    textinfo;
    struct palettetype         palette;
    int x = 10, y = 4;

    ReportWindow( "Graphic Status Report" );
    getviewsettings( &viewinfo );
                                /* read parameter values   */
    getlinesettings( &lineinfo );
    getfillsettings( &fillinfo );
    gettextsettings( &textinfo );
    getpalette( &palette );
    settextjustify( LEFT_TEXT, TOP_TEXT );
    StepColor();
    gprintf( &x, &y, "Graphics device   : ( %d ) %-10s",
            GraphDriver, getdrivername() );
    StepColor();
    gprintf( &x, &y, "Graphics mode    : ( %d ) %-10s",
            GraphMode, getmodename( GraphMode ) );
    StepColor();
    gprintf( &x, &y, "Screen resolution   : \
                    ( 0, 0, %2d, %2d )",
                    getmaxx(), getmaxy() );
    StepColor();
    gprintf( &x, &y, "Current view port \
                    : ( %2d, %2d, %2d, %2d )",
                    viewinfo.left, viewinfo.top,
                    viewinfo.right, viewinfo.bottom );
    StepColor();
    gprintf( &x, &y, "Clipping       : %s",
                    viewinfo.clip ? "ON" : "OFF" );
    StepColor();
```

```
        gprintf( &x, &y, "Current position (CP) : (%2d,%2d )",
                                            getx(), gety() );
    StepColor();
        gprintf( &x, &y, "Max color / This color : %2d / %2d",
                                    MaxColors, getcolor() );
    StepColor();
        gprintf( &x, &y, "Line thick / style      : %2d / %s",
                        lineinfo.thickness,
                        LineStyles[ lineinfo.linestyle ] );
    StepColor();
        gprintf( &x, &y, "Fill color / style      : %2d / %s",
                        fillinfo.color,
                        FillStyles[ fillinfo.pattern ] );
    StepColor();
        gprintf( &x, &y, "Character size / font  : %2d / %s",
                        textinfo.charsize,
                        Fonts[ textinfo.font ] );
    StepColor();
        gprintf( &x, &y, "Text direction    :    %s",
                        TextDirect[ textinfo.direction ] );
    StepColor();
        gprintf( &x, &y, "Horizontal justify      :    %s",
                        HorizJust[ textinfo.horiz ] );
    StepColor();
        gprintf( &x, &y, "Vertical justify   :    %s",
                        VertJust[ textinfo.vert ] );
    StepColor();
        gprintf( &x, &y, "Aspect Ratio  ( x/y ) \
                : %d / %d = %5.3f",
                        xasp, yasp, AspectRatio );
    Pause();
}

void Initialize()
{           /* initialize graphics system and report errors   */
    GraphDriver = DETECT;              /* request auto-detection  */
    initgraph( &GraphDriver, &GraphMode, "C:\\TC\\BGI" );
    TestGraphicError();               /* check graphics errors   */
    getpalette( &palette );           /* read palette parameters */
    MaxColors = getmaxcolor() + 1;
                                      /* read maximum color range*/
```

```
    MaxX = 380;                         /* set viewport size      */
    MaxY = 174;
    getaspectratio( &xasp, &yasp );
                                        /* read the hardware aspect  */
    AspectRatio = (double)xasp / (double)yasp;
}                                       /* calculate aspect ratio    */
main()
{
    Initialize();                       /* set graphics mode      */
    ReportStatus();                     /* show graphics settings */
    closegraph();                       /* set text mode          */
}
```

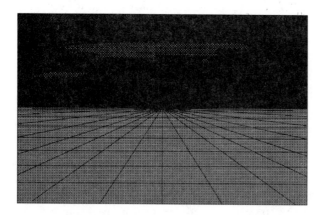

Chapter 2

*Viewport, Screen,
and Page Functions*

Just as windowing and screen management routines are provided for text display modes, similar control features are provided for graphics display modes. These features include the cleardevice and clearviewport functions (graphics equivalents of clrscr), setviewport (equivalent to window), getviewsettings, setactivepage, and setvisualpage.

Not all of these functions have text mode equivalents and there are several text mode functions that are not provided with graphics mode equivalents. Even when a graphics function appears to be similar to the text mode equivalent, it may not operate identically to the text function.

Viewport and Screen Functions

The following graphics functions affect the graphics screen and the viewport.

cleardevice

The cleardevice function erases the entire graphics screen, regardless of viewport settings, and moves the current position (CP) to the screen home (0,0) position. This does not affect the active viewport. The viewport settings are unchanged, but the screen clearing is not limited to the viewport. No values are returned and no error condition is generated.

Example:

```
#include <graphics.h>

cleardevice();
```

While cleardevice is similar to the clrscr text command, where the text function is window sensitive (can be used to clear only the currently active window), the cleardevice command resets the entire *active* graphics screen, but does not affect alternate graphics screens (if any are supported by the graphics hardware present). Remember, text functions such as clrscr do not work in graphics modes and vice versa. Refer also to clearviewport, setactivepage, and setvisualpage.

clearviewport

The clearviewport function erases the current viewport, moving the current position (CP) to the home position (0,0) within the viewpoint setting. Unlike the cleardevice function, clearviewport is limited to a specific area of the screen and operates similarly to the clrscr command with an active window setting.

Example:

```
#include <graphics.h>

clearviewport();
```

Refer also to getviewsettings and setviewport.

setviewport

The setviewport function is roughly equivalent to the text window function and is used to set an active viewport. The coordinates (*xleft, ytop, xright,* and *ybottom*) are absolute screen coordinates and affect only the active graphics page (refer to setactivepage).

Example:

```
#include <graphics.h>

int  xleft, ytop, xright, ybottom, clipflag;

setviewport( xleft, ytop, xright, ybottom, clipflag );
```

The fifth argument passed to setviewport is the *clipflag*. If *clipflag* is non-zero (TRUE), clipping will be in effect and all drawings will be restricted to the current viewport. If *clipflag* is zero, then drawings may extend beyond the viewport perimeters without limitation.

Please note: the viewport limits do not affect the getimage or putimage commands. A pixel image being written to the screen will not be truncated at the viewport perimeter regardless of the *clipflag* setting.

If invalid coordinates are passed to setviewport, graphresult will return a value of –11 (graphics error or generic error) and the previous viewport settings will remain in effect. Both the initgraph and setgraphmode functions initialize the current viewport to the entire graphics screen as defined by the current mode setting.

Refer also to clearviewport and getviewsettings.

getviewsettings

The structured variable *viewport* returns the current graphics window coordinates and the *clipflag* setting. The coordinates returned are absolute screen coordinates.

Example:

```
#include <graphics.h>

struct viewporttype viewport;

getviewsettings( &viewport );
```

The getviewsettings uses a record structure *viewporttype* which is defined in GRAPHICS.H as:

```
struct viewporttype
{
    int left, top, right, bottom;
    int clip;
};
```

Where *clipflag* is non-zero, drawings are truncated at the current viewport margins. Refer to setviewport, clearviewport, initgraph, setgraphmode, and setviewport for further details.

Multiple Graphics Pages

Several graphics video cards offer support for two to four pages of graphics display (most without restricting color or resolution). To use these capabilities, Turbo C++ provides two functions: setactivepage, which selects the active graphics output page and setvisualpage, which selects the graphics page actually appearing on the screen. These are most often used for graphics animation. These commands are valid only with the drivers and modes shown in Table 2-1.

Table 2-1: Graphics Modes Supporting Multiple Pages

Graphics Driver	Driver Value	Graphics Mode	Mode Value	Resolution x-axis x y-axis	Available Colors	Graphics Pages
EGA	3	EGALO	0	640x200	16	4
		EGAHI	1	640x350	16	2
EGAMONO	5	EGAMONOHI	3	640x350	2	4[1]
HERC	7	HERCMONOHI	0	720x348	2	3
VGA	9	VGALO	0	640x200	16	4
		VGAMED	1	640x350	16	2[2]

1. The EGAMono card must have 256K RAM to support multiple video page—some EGAMono cards have only 64K RAM.
2. The VGAHI mode (640x480) supports only *one* graphics page.

Remember, where multiple graphics pages are supported, the graphics pages are numbered from 0. Page zero is active by default. Where multiple graphics pages are not supported, the setactivepage and setvisualpage commands will simply not operate. By default, page zero will remain as the active output page and the active visual page.

Relying on this default behavior is not necessarily the best approach to handling multiple video pages. In many cases, it might be more appropriate to know how many, if any, video pages are available and have your program respond accordingly. The following procedure, VideoPages, returns zero if no alternate video pages are available or an integer value if more than one video page is supported.

```
#include <graphics.h>

int GraphDriver, GraphMode;

int VideoPages(void)
{
   switch( GraphDriver )
   {
      case EGA: switch ( getgraphmode() )
      {
         case EGALO: return( 4 );
         case EGAHI: return( 2 );
      }   break;
      case EGAMONO: return( 0 );            /* see note 1 */
```

```
        case HERC: return( 2 );
        case VGA: switch ( getgraphmode() )
        {
            case VGALO : return( 4 );
            case VGAMED: return( 2 );
            case VGAHI : return( 0 );
        } break;
    }
    return( 0 );                          /* see note 2 */
}
```

1. Some EGAMono cards support four video pages but mode and driver settings do not identify which cards have 256K RAM and which have only 64K RAM. Thus, the best default value returned is 0. This can be changed if your application requires a different response.
2. All remaining drivers and modes identify themselves as supporting single video pages. Newer video cards may require modification of this selection table.

setactivepage

The setactivepage function selects which graphics page (*pagenum*) will be used for output by all graphics functions. This does not affect which graphics page is currently being displayed (refer to setvisualpage) but does allow graphics operations to be directed to an "invisible" page and then displayed either by using the getimage and putimage functions or by changing the displayed page. Use putimage after changing the active page to match the visual page.

Example:

```
#include <graphics.h>

int pagenum;

setactivepage( pagenum );
```

setvisualpage

The setvisualpage function selects the specified graphics page for active display. This is not necessarily the same as the active output graphics page (refer to setactivepage) but is useful for switching the display between different graphics pages. The change is effective immediate (certainly too fast for the eye to follow), and requires only one screen refresh cycle for a complete display change.

Example:

```
#include <graphics.h>

int pagenum;

setvisualpage( pagenum );
```

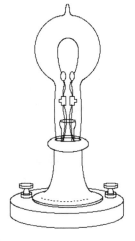

Chapter 3

Graphics Color Selection

In addition to knowing which graphics card and graphics driver to use, you also need to know what palettes or colors are supported.

With the CGA, MCGA, and ATT400 drivers in 320x200 pixel modes, color selections are limited to the four-color, predefined color palettes (C0, C1, C2, and C3). With higher resolutions, some graphics cards offer 16 colors, while others offer either two or four colors. The color selection is independent of the predefined palettes.

Finally, with the IBM-8514, a palette of 256 colors becomes possible, with tint selection from a total of 262,144 shades. The following color and palettes functions are not compatible with the IBM8514 driver. Refer to the IBM-8514 Video Graphics Card.

Color Functions

The following are graphics color functions.

getmaxcolor

The getmaxcolor function returns the maximum valid color number (or palette size −1) for the current graphics mode. This is valid in both high and low resolution modes. In a low resolution (320x200) mode, getmaxcolor will return a value of 3—one less than the number of colors in the predefined palettes. In high resolution modes such as EGAHI, the value returned will be 15 and in monochrome modes such as ATT400HI, a value of 1 will be returned.

Example:

```
#include <graphics.h>

int MaxColors;

MaxColors = getmaxcolor() + 1;
```

Please note that normally the value indicates only the number of separate palette colors that can be used and not the maximum color values. This function is not valid with the IBM8514 driver. Refer also to setcolor.

setcolor

The setcolor function selects the current drawing color or foreground color.

Example:

```
#include <graphics.h>

int forecolor;

forecolor = getmaxcolors();
setcolor( forecolor );
```

In low resolution CGA modes (320x200 pixel) the slected color is the palette color number and not the actual color value. Thus in CGAC2 mode, setcolor(0) selects the background color (refer to setpalette), setcolor(1) selects Green (color value 2), setcolor(2) selects Red (color value 4) and setcolor(3) selects Brown (color value 6).

In high resolution modes, the color values can be either the symbolic names, which are defined in GRAPHICS.H, or the numerical values. If the setpalette or setallpalette functions have been used to change the palette color values, the symbolic color names may not produce expected results.

The current color selected is used for drawing and for graphics text output. The current fillcolor, however, may be different from the current drawing color (see Chapter 13). The colors selected are retrieved from a record of structure *palettetype* as *palette.color[colornumber]*. The structure *palettetype* is defined in GRAPHICS.H as:

```
struct palettetype
{
    unsigned char size;
```

```
     signed    char colors[ MAXCOLORS + 1 ];
};
```

The constant MAXCOLORS is defined as 15. Refer to setpalette for predefined color palettes. See also getcolor and setbkcolor.

getcolor

The getcolor function returns the current drawing (foreground) color.

Example:

```
#include <graphics.h>

int forecolor;

forecolor = getcolor();
```

In low resolution modes using color palettes, the value returned will be the palette number, not the actual color value. In high resolution (16-color) modes, the value returned will correspond to the color values unless the setpalette or setallpalette functions have been used to change the palette values. Refer to setcolor for color values, setpalette for palette colors. See also getbkcolor.

setbkcolor

The setbkcolor function selects the background color values by changing the first entry in the active color palette (*palette.color[0] = backcolor*) to the specified color value. Refer also to setpalette.

Example:

```
#include <graphics.h>

int backcolor;

backcolor = 0;
setbkcolor( backcolor );
```

When setbkcolor is called with a new value, the background color on the entire screen is changed. If this new background color matches the color of an image already on the screen, the image will be invisible, but is *not* lost. When the background color is changed to a contrasting color, the invisible image will become visible.

The *backcolor* argument can be either the symbolic color name or the color value. Table 3-1 shows background color values in GRAPHICS.H.

Table 3-1: Background Color Values

Name	Value	Name	Value
BLACK	0	DARKGREY	8
BLUE	1	LIGHTBLUE	9
GREEN	2	LIGHTGREEN	10
CYAN	3	LIGHTCYAN	11
RED	4	LIGHTRED	12
MAGENTA	5	LIGHTMAGENTA	13
BROWN	6	YELLOW	14
LIGHTGREY	7	WHITE	15

In low resolution (320x200) color palette modes, only the first entry in the palette (*palette.color[0]*) can be changed. Refer to setpalette. In high resolution 16-color modes (EGA/VGA), any or all palette colors can be changed using the setpalette and setallpalette functions. If this is done, the symbolic color names may correspond to unexpected hues.

getbkcolor

The getbkcolor function returns the current background color value.

Example:

```
#include <graphics.h>

int backcolor;

backcolor = getbkcolor();
```

Because the background color is always *palette.color[0]*, the getbkcolor function returns the current background color *value*, not the palette entry number. Refer also to getcolor and setbkcolor.

getpalette

The getpalette function returns the current palette color settings.

Example:

```
#include <graphics.h>

struct palettetype palette;

getpalette( &palette );
```

The getpalette function fills the *palette* structure with current palette information (settings). The structure *palettetype* is defined in GRAPH-ICS.H as:

```
struct palettetype
{
    unsigned char size;
    signed   char colors[ MAXCOLORS + 1 ];
};
```

Palette.size gives the number of colors valid for the current graphics driver and mode, while *palette.color* is an array of *size* of bytes containing the color values for each entry in the palette. Table 3-2 shows color values.

Table 3-2: Color Values

CGA		EGA/VGA	
Name	**Value**	**Name**	**Value**
BLACK	0	EGA_BLACK	0
BLUE	1	EGA_BLUE	1
GREEN	2	EGA_GREEN	2
CYAN	3	EGA_CYAN	3
RED	4	EGA_RED	4
MAGENTA	5	EGA_MAGENTA	5
BROWN	6	EGA_BROWN	20
LIGHTGREY	7	EGA_LIGHTGREY	7
DARKGREY	8	EGA_DARKGREY	56
LIGHTBLUE	9	EGA_LIGHTBLUE	57
LIGHTGREEN	10	EGA_LIGHTGREEN	58
LIGHTCYAN	11	EGA_LIGHTCYAN	59
LIGHTRED	12	EGA_LIGHTRED	60
LIGHTMAGENTA	13	EGA_LIGHTMAGENTA	61
YELLOW	14	EGA_YELLOW	62
WHITE	15	EGA_WHITE	63

Note: most, EGA/VGA graphics cards will accept either the CGA or the EGA/VGA symbolic color names and color values that appear in the preceding list. CGA graphics cards, however, may respond unexpectedly to the EGA/VGA color values.

Refer to setallpalette and setpalette.

setpalette

The setpalette function provides a means of changing individual color values in the palette array.

Example:

```
#include <graphics.h>

int palette_index, color;

setpalette( palette_index, color );
```

With any of the 320x200 pixel video graphics modes (CGA, MCGA, or AT&T), color selections are limited to predefined 4-color palettes: C0, C1, C2, and C3. In each palette, the background color (*palette.color[0]*) can be user-defined, but colors 1..3 cannot be changed. In every other graphics mode, all colors can be redefined. Table 3-3 shows predefined palettes and colors.

Table 3-3: Predefined Palettes and Colors

Palette	Color0	Color1	Color2	Color3
C0	BLACK	LIGHTGREEN	LIGHTRED	YELLOW
C1	BLACK	LIGHTCYAN	LIGHTMAGENTA	WHITE
C2	BLACK	GREEN	RED	BROWN
C3	BLACK	CYAN	MAGENTA	LIGHTGREY

The IBM-8514 graphics card and IBM8514 driver support a color palette of 256 colors chosen from 262,144 (256K) color values. No symbolic constants are defined for this driver, but the IBM-8514 card can also emulate VGA modes. Refer to the IBM-8514 Video Graphics Card for further details.

setallpalette

The setallpalette function provides a means of assigning an entire new palette of colors as the active palette.

Example:

```
#include <graphics.h>

struct palettetype newpalette;

setallpalette( &newpalette );
```

The setallpalette function assigns *newpalette* as the current palette with all new color assignments effective immediately. The colors for *newpalette* must be assigned using setpalette.

In low resolution (320x200) graphics modes using the predefined color palettes, the setallpalette command is not valid since only the background palette color is assignable. Note that changing graphics modes, as from CGAC0 to CGAC2, to change color palettes erases (resets) the graphics screen. Refer also to getpalette.

IBM-8514 Video Graphics Card

Special provisions are supplied to support the IBM-8514 video graphics card's 256/256K palette/color capabilities.

setrbgpalette

The setrbgpalette routine is provided for use with the IBM-8514 graphics card and IBM8514 driver.

Example:

```
#include <graphics.h>

int  colornum, redval, blueval, greenval;

setrbgpalette( colornum, redval, blueval, greenval );
```

The detectgraph function will not identify the IBM-8514 card correctly but will instead identify this hardware configuration as VGA compatible. The VGA driver is recommended for maximum compatibility (see init-graph) when the extended resolution of the IBM8514HI mode is not required.

No symbolic constants are defined for this driver. Instead, each color is defined by three, 6-bit values for the red, green, and blue components.

The *colornum* argument sets the palette color (0..255) to be defined by the *redval*, *blueval*, and *greenval* arguments. Only the six most significant bits from the low byte of each color argument are used (values from 0 to 252 in steps of four). For example, arguments of 252, 253, 254, and 255 are treated identically since the six most significant bits are the same.

The other palette manipulation routines in the graphics library are invalid with the IBM8514 driver in the IBM8514HI (1023x768 pixel) mode. This includes setallpalette, setpalette, and getpalette. Also, the floodfill routine is not valid with this driver and mode.

Chapter 4

Screen Position Functions

Graphics Screen Functions

In graphics modes, the familiar 80 by 25 screen coordinates are replaced by pixel coordinates and may vary, depending on hardware, from 320 horizontal by 200 vertical, to as high as 1,024 horizontal by 768 vertical. Newer and higher resolutions are appearing almost daily.

Because of the variety of screen resolutions, most graphics programs begin by checking the hardware for the appropriate drivers. They then use functions such as getmaxx and getmaxy to determine the screen size, adjusting subsequent operations to fit within these screen limits.

getmaxx and getmaxy

The getmaxx and getmaxy functions return the maximum x-axis and y-axis screen coordinate for the current graphics driver and mode.

Example:

```
#include <graphics.h>

int MaxX, MaxY;

MaxX = getmaxx();
MaxY = getmaxy();
```

In EGAHI mode (640x350), for example, getmaxx returns 639 (0..639) and getmaxy returns 349 (0..349). Both are independent of viewport settings. Refer also to getviewsettings, getx, and gety. Similar information is available in text modes using the gettextinfo function.

getx and gety

The getx and gety functions return the current position'shorizontal and vertical pixel coordinates. These coordinates are the position relative to the current viewport. If no viewport has been set, the default viewport includes the entire screen.

Example:

```
#include <graphics.h>

int xpos, ypos;

xpos = getx();
ypos = gety();
```

Refer also to getviewsettings, moverel, and moveto. Similar information is available in text modes using wherex and wherey.

moveto

The moveto function moves the current position (CP) to the absolute screen pixel coordinates specified by (*x*,*y*) and relative to the current viewport settings where (0,0) is the upper-left corner. The resulting CP is *not* limited by the current viewport settings or by the maximum and minimum screen coordinates.

Example:

```
#include <graphics.h>

int x, y;

moveto( x, y );
```

If no viewport settings have been made, the default settings include the entire screen. Refer also to moverel. In text modes, gotoxy provides the equivalent function.

moverel

For graphics applications, a relative move is often handier than an absolute move. Therefore, the moverel function shifts the new current position a relative distance from the old current position using the offset specified by (*xdev,ydev*). The resulting CP is *not* limited by the current viewport settings or by the maximum and minimum screen coordinates.

Example:

```
#include <graphics.h>

int xdev, ydev;

moverel( xdev, ydev );
```

Refer also to moveto.

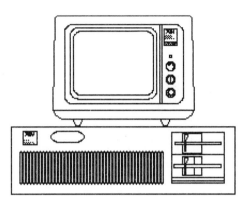

Chapter 5

*Pixel, Drawing,
and Image Functions*

While lines and curves are useful for many drawing applications, some images can only be created by manipulating individual pixels. The line and curve functions, of course, could hardly operate without pixel write procedures. Using pixel functions on a macro scale, entire images can be saved, rewritten, erased, or combined with existing screen images.

Pixel Functions

The following are functions used in the manipulation of pixel write procedures.

putpixel

The putpixel function sets the pixel specified by (*xpos,ypos*) to the color indicated.

Example:

```
#include <graphics.h>

int xpos, ypos, color;

putpixel( xpos, ypos, color );
```

In graphics modes using predefined palettes, *color* must be in the range 0..3, where 0 provides the background color value. In full palette color modes, either the color names defined in GRAPHICS.H or integer color values may be used. Refer also to getpixel.

getpixel

The getpixel function returns the color palette index of the indicated pixel at (x,y). Note: the palette index may or may not correspond to the actual color value.

Example:

```
#include <graphics.h>

int x, y;
color = getpixel( x, y );
```

Refer also to getimage and putpixel.

Line Drawing Functions

Turbo C++ provides three drawing functions for straight lines: line, lineto, and linerel. The coordinate points used for these lines are integer coordinates (positive or negative) that are plotted relative to the current viewport coordinates, but not necessarily restricted to the viewport limits. If the viewport clipflag is non-zero, the lines drawn will be truncated at the viewport borders. If clipflag is zero, lines are truncated only at the limits of the screen though the endpoint coordinates and the resulting current position (CP) may still lie outside the viewport and/or the screen limits.

line

The line function draws a line beginning at the first coordinate pair (*xstart,ystart*) and ending at the second coordinate pair (*xend,yend*). It uses the current drawing color, line style, and thickness. The current position is not changed.

Example:

```
#include <graphics.h>

int xstart, ystart, xend, yend;
line( xstart, ystart, xend, yend );
```

Refer also to linerel and lineto.

lineto

The lineto function draws a line beginning at current position and ending at the coordinates specified (*xpos,ypos*). The current drawing color, line style, and thickness are used and CP is reset to (*xpos,ypos*).

Example:

```
#include <graphics.h>

int xpos, ypos;

lineto(xpos,ypos);
```

Refer also to line and linerel.

linerel

The linerel function draws a line from CP to a point offset from CP by the horizontal and vertical distances specified by (*xdev,ydev*). The line is drawn using the current color, line style, and thickness. CP is updated to (*CPX + xdev, CPY + ydev*).

Example:

```
#include <graphics.h>

int xdev, ydev;

linerel( xdev, ydev );
```

Refer also to line and lineto.

Line Styles

For graphics drawing, two line thicknesses and several line styles are provided. You can also define a custom line style using a 16-pixel pattern. The line thickness and pattern settings are used by arc, bar, bar3d, circle, drawpoly, ellipse, line, linerel, lineto, pieslice, and rectangle.

Turbo C++ (and Turbo Pascal) also provides a new function, setwritemode.

setlinestyle

The setlinestyle function sets the current line width and style.

Example:

```
#include <graphics.h>

unsigned linepattern;
int    style, width;

setlinestyle( style, linepattern, width );
```

The style and width operators (*line_styles* and *thickness*) are enumerated in GRAPHICS.H and shown in Table 5-1.

Table 5-1: Line Styles

Name	Value	Description
SOLID_LINE	0	Solid line (default)
DOTTED_LINE	1	Dotted line
CENTER_LINE	2	Centered dash line
DASHED_LINE	3	Ashed line
USERBIT_LINE	4	User-defined style
NORM_WIDTH	1	1-pixel width (default)
THICK_WIDTH	3	3-pixels width

Note: A line width of 2 can also be assigned, but any value greater than 3 results in a graphics error and causes the line style and width to be set to the default settings.

The remaining argument, *linepattern*, is a 16-bit pattern defining a custom bit pattern to be used for drawing the line. The *linepattern* argument is applicable only if *style = USERBIT_LINE* (numerical value 4). If *style != USERBIT_LINE*, then *linepattern* must still be supplied, but is not used.

When a user-defined pattern is used, each pixel corresponding to a one-bit in the pattern is turned on, while pixels corresponding to a zero-bit are left off. Thus, if *linepattern = 0xFFFF*, a solid line is drawn and, if *linepattern = 0x9999*, a dashed line alternating two pixels on, two pixels off will result. For a long-dashed line, *linepattern = 0xFF00* or *0xF00F* might be used.

If invalid parameters are passed to setlinestyle, graphresult will return a value of –11 (*graphics error* or *generic error*) and the current line style will remain in effect.

Refer also to getlinesettings.

setwritemode

The setwritemode function sets the screen writing mode for line drawing in graphic modes. Two constants are defined: COPY_PUT and XOR_PUT.

Example:

```
#include <graphics.h>

int   writemode;

setwritemode( writemode );
```

The COPY_PUT setting uses the assembly language MOV instruction to overwrite existing screen pixels. The XOR_PUT setting uses the XOR command to combine new lines with existing screen images. If a line is drawn twice using the XOR_PUT setting, the line is erased, and the screen's original appearance is restored.

Note that setwritemode currently works only with line, linerel, lineto, rectangle, and drawpoly.

getlinesettings

The getlinesettings function returns *lineinfo* with the current line style, pattern (*upattern*), and thickness.

Example:

```
#include <graphics.h>

struct linesettingstype lineinfo;

getlinesettings( &lineinfo );
```

The structure *linesettingstype* is defined in GRAPHICS.H as:

```
struct linesettingstype
{
    int linestyle;
    unsigned upattern;
    int thickness;
};
```

Refer to setlinestyle for styles and thickness.

Rectangles, Bar Graphs, and Polygons

While any of the following geometric forms can be created using the line drawing function, it is more convenient to have functions providing faster handling for common shapes.

rectangle

The rectangle function draws a square or rectangle as defined by the corner coordinates passed as arguments.

Example:

```
#include <graphics.h>

int xleft, ytop, xright, ybottom;

rectangle( xleft, ytop, xright, ybottom );
```

The figure is drawn using the current line style, thickness, and color. If one or more corners do not fall within the current viewport limits and the clipflag is set, then only the portion of the figure that fits within the viewport will be created.

Refer also to bar.

bar

The bar function draws a square or rectangle as defined by the corner coordinates passed as arguments.

Example:

```
#include <graphics.h>

int  left, top, right, bottom;

bar( left, top, right, bottom );
```

Unlike the figure created by the rectangle function, the bar figure is not outlined but uses the current fill pattern and fill color (not the drawing color). For an outlined bar, use bar3d with a depth setting of zero.

Refer also to getcolor, getfillsettings, getlinestyle, rectangle, and setfillpattern.

bar3d

The bar3d function outlines a three-dimensional rectangular bar using the current line style and drawing color, and then fills in the faces of the figure using the current fill pattern and fill color.

Example:

```
#include <graphics.h>
```

```
int   left, top, right, bottom, depth, topflag;

bar3d( left, top, right, bottom, depth, topflag );
```

The bar's depth is given in pixels (normally about 25 percent of the width) and is set back at an x/y ratio of 1:1 (approximately 45 degrees adjusted by the screen aspect ratio). If the *topflag* parameter is passed as zero, no top is added to the bar. This allows for bars to be stacked.

A more elaborate figure can be created; each face of the figure can be filled with a different color and/or pattern using the floodfill function. Use the setfillpattern function to select EMPTY_FILL before calling bar3d.

Refer also to bar, getcolor, getfillsettings, getlinestyle, and rectangle.

drawpoly

The drawpoly function draws the outline of a polygon using current color settings and line style.

Example:

```
#include <graphics.h>

int points;
int figure1[] = { 100,100, 110,120, 100,130, 120,125,
         140,140, 130,120, 140,110, 120,115, 100,100 };
int figure2[] = { 180,100, 210,120, 200,130, 220,125,
         240,140, 230,120, 240,110, 220,115, 220,100 };

points = sizeof ( figure1 ) / ( 2 * sizeof ( int ) );
drawpoly( points, figure1 );
drawpoly( sizeof( figure2 ) / ( 2 * sizeof( int ) ),
         figure2 );
```

The *points* argument gives the number of vertices for the polygon and *poly* points to a sequence of integer pairs, each pair defining the *x,y* coordinates for a vertex of the polygon.

In order to draw a closed figure with *n* vertices, *points = n+1* and the *n*th (final) coordinate pair is equal to the 0th (first) coordinate pair.

In the example, *figure1* defines a four-pointed star. Instead of assigning a constant to *points*, the number of points in the figure is calculated from *sizeof(figure)* divided by two times *sizeof(int)* (because each point requires two integer coordinates). The second figure, *figure2* changes the four-pointed star into an open line figure, but it is created in the same manner.

Refer also to getlinesettings, getcolor, fillpoly, and setgraphbufsize.

fillpoly

The fillpoly function draws the outline of a polygon using current color settings and line style and then fills the polygon using the current fill pattern and fill color.

Example:

```
#include <graphics.h>

int figure1[] = { 75, 0, 100, 50, 150, 75, 100, 100,
                75, 150, 50, 100, 0, 75, 50, 50, 75, 0 };
int figure2[] = { 75, 50, 100, 75, 75,100, 50, 75 };

fillpoly( sizeof(figure1)/(2*sizeof(int) ), figure1 );
fillpoly( sizeof(figure2)/(2*sizeof(int) ), figure2 );
```

The *points* argument gives the number of vertices for the polygon; *poly* points to a sequence of integer pairs, each pair defining the *x,y* coordinates for a vertex of the polygon.

In order to draw a closed figure with *n* vertices, *points = n+1* and the *n*th (final) coordinate pair is equal to the *0*th (first) coordinate pair.

In the example, *figure1* defines a four-pointed star. Instead of assigning a constant to *points*, the number of points in the figure is calculated from *sizeof(figure1)* divided by two times *sizeof(int)* (because each point requires two integer coordinates). The second figure, *figure2*, creates an open square. Note that fillpoly will close the figure by connecting the start and end points, then fill the enclosed region.

Unlike floodfill, the fill algorithm used by fillpoly does not depend on a continuous outline to define the area; therefore, broken line styles are acceptable and will simply fill the area defined by the polygon—which includes overwriting any other figure lying within the new boundary. If an error occurs, graphresult returns –6 (*out of memory in scan fill*).

Refer also to drawpoly, getfillsettings, setfillpattern, getcolor, and setgraphbufsize.

Video Aspect Ratios

Each graphics driver and graphics mode has an associated *aspect ratio*— the ratio between vertical and horizontal pixel sizes and spacing. A figure that appears round on one screen (and graphics card/mode) may appear crushed or elongated when using different graphics hardware.

To be sure that geometric figures appear on the screen as intended, the screen *aspect ratio* should be used to calculate and correct the distortions.

getaspectratio

Each graphics driver and graphics mode has an associated aspect ratio determined by the relative height and width of the pixels.

Example:

```
#include <graphics.h>

int xasp, yasp;
double AspectRatio;

getaspectratio( &xasp, &yasp );
AspectRatio = (double) xasp / (double) yasp;
```

Using an EGA graphics card (*EGAHI*), for example, an aspect ratio of 0.775 is found (*xasp = 7750, yasp = 10000*) since the EGA pixels are roughly $1/3$ taller than they are wide. On the other hand, using a VGA graphics card, the aspect ratio is found to be 1.000 (*xasp = 10000, yasp = 10000*), with the pixels appearing to be square. As you can see, there's a considerable difference between the two screen presentations.

The getaspectratio returns integer values for the x- and y-axis aspects. The aspect ratio is calculated as *xasp/yasp* and is used automatically as a scaling factor with the arc, circle, and pieslice routines in order to normalize the appearance of circles and arcs on the screen. The aspect scaling ratio must be included with the ellipse routine, otherwise, no adjustment is applied. The aspect ratio can also be used with other geometric figures to correct scaling and appearance.

The y-axis aspect factor is normalized to 10,000 and, in general, *xasp <= 10,000* (most screens' pixels are taller than they are wide).

setaspectratio

Each graphics driver and graphics mode has an associated aspect ratio determined by the relative height and width of the pixels, used to ensure that circles appear round.

Example:

```
#include <graphics.h>

int xasp, yasp;

setaspectratio( xasp, yasp );
```

If circles appear elliptical, the monitor may be out of alignment and require mechanical (electronic) adjustment. Adjustment can be accomplished by using the setaspectratio function (Turbo C version 2.0 or later) to change the aspect ratio.

Circles, Curves, and Arcs

Curves are the hardest figures to create, requiring relatively complex calculations to determine the points composing them. The functions circle, ellipse, and arc offer great convenience in creating curved figures.

The circle function creates a complete circle, while arc and ellipse are called with start and end angles and may produce complete (closed) curves or only partial arcs.

The getarccoords function returns the start, end, and center coordinates of the last call to arc or ellipse, allowing lines to be drawn to the ends of arcs. The pieslice function uses a combination of these capabilities to create an arc with lines drawn from the end points to the center.

The start and end angles for arc, ellipse, and pieslice are given in degrees, with 0° and 360° at the right, 90° at the top, 180° at the right, and 270° at the bottom.

To draw a closed arc or ellipse, specify a start angle of 0° and an end angle of 360°. Angles greater than 360° can be used as arguments, but will be reduced to 0°..360°. For example, a starting angle of 300° and an end angle of 450° will draw an arc from the 300° point to the 90° point. The same arc can be drawn by specifying 300° and 90° as the start and end points. There is no inherent requirement for the end angle to be greater than the start angle, although allowing angles greater than 360° can simplify many programming procedures.

The arc, circle, ellipse, and pieslice functions do not use the current line style. All curves are drawn as solid lines using the current drawing color.

circle

The circle function draws a complete arc from 0° to 360°. The circle is drawn using the current drawing color and radius specified (in pixels) and is centered at the given screen coordinates.

Example:

```
#include <graphics.h>

int xcenter, ycenter, radius;

circle( xcenter, ycenter, radius );
```

Unlike ellipse, circle is called with a single radius argument. Therefore, the screen aspect ratio is automatically applied to adjust the results for producing a correct (circular) appearance.

Refer also to arc, ellipse, getaspectratio, and pieslice.

arc

The arc function draws a circular curve with the specified radius between the angles specified and centered at the given *x* and *y* coordinates.

Example:

```
#include <graphics.h>

int  xcenter, ycenter, startangle, endangle, radius;

arc( xcenter, ycenter, startangle, endangle, radius );
```

The start and end angles are in degrees (0..360). The center coordinates and the radius are both in pixels. The current drawing color and line style are used. Correction for the screen aspect ratio is handled automatically.

Refer also to circle, ellipse, getaspectratio, and pieslice.

ellipse

The ellipse function is similar to arc except in that separate radii are specified for the x- and y-axes. Figure 5-1 shows angles running counter-clockwise.

Example:

```
#include <graphics.h>

int xcenter, ycenter, startangle, endangle,
    xradius, yradius;

ellipse( xcenter, ycenter, startangle, endangle,
        xradius, yradius );
```

or

```
ellipse( xcenter, ycenter, startangle, endangle,
        xradius, yradius * AspectRatio );
```

The elliptic arc is centered at the given *x* and *y* coordinates, beginning and ending at the specified angles and using the current drawing color. For a complete (closed) ellipse, use a start angle of 0° and an end angle of 360°.

Unlike arc and circle, correction for the screen aspect ratio is not applied automatically. If proportional radii, rather than specific pixel distances are required, the y-axis distance should be adjusted as *yradius * AspectRatio*.

Refer also to arc, circle, fillellipse, pieslice, and sector.

Figure 5-1: Drawing Arc Angles

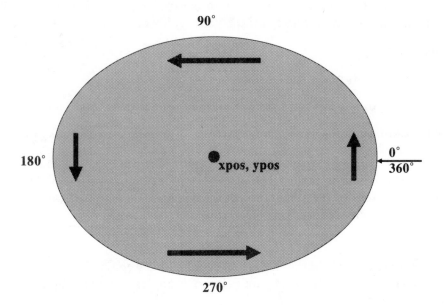

The angles for arc, ellipse, and pieslice run counterclockwise (widershins) beginning with 0°/360° at the right, 90° at the top, 180° at the left, and 270° at the bottom.

getarccoords

The getarccoords function returns the end point and center coordinates of the last call to arc or ellipse.

Example:

```
#include <graphics.h>

struct arccoordstype  arcinfo;

getarccoords( &arcinfo );
```

The structure *arccoordstype* is defined in GRAPHICS.H as:

```
struct arccoordstype
{
    int x, y;
    int xstart, ystart, xend, yend;
};
```

The info structure defines the center point (*x,y*) coordinates of the arc, the starting point coordinates, *xstart,ystart* (these are pixel coordinates, not the angle), and the end point (*xend,yend*) of the arc. These values are used by the pieslice function and can be used to draw chords, radii, or other lines meeting the ends of the arc.

If the circle function was the last curve function called, then getarccoords will return the center coordinates of the circle and the (*xstart,ystart*) and (*xend,yend*) coordinates will be the 0° position on the circle.

fillellipse

The fillellipse function (Turbo C version 2.0 or later) draws an ellipse using xcenter, ycenter as the center point, and xradius and yradius as the horizontal and vertical axes. It fills the ellipse with the current fill color and fill pattern.

Example:

```
#include <graphics.h>

int xcenter, ycenter, xradius, yradius;

fillellipse( xcenter, ycenter, xradius, yradius );
```

Unlike the ellipse function, start and end angle arguments are not supported and an elliptical arc cannot be drawn.

Refer also to arc, circle, ellipse, pieslice, and sector.

pieslice

The pieslice function creates an arc, draws lines from the end points to the center point, and then fills in the completed pieslice.

Example:

```
#include <graphics.h>

int xcenter, ycenter, startangle, endangle, radius;
```

```
pieslice( xcenter, ycenter, startangle, endangle,
          radius );
```

The figure outline is drawn using the current drawing color and current line style for the radius lines. It is then filled using the current fill pattern and fill color. Screen aspect ratio adjustment is automatic.

Refer also to arc, circle, ellipse, getaspectratio, and sector.

sector

The sector function creates an elliptical arc, draws lines from the end points to the center point, and then fills in the completed figure.

Example:

```
#include <graphics.h>

int xcenter, ycenter, startangle, endangle,
    xradius, yradius;

sector( xcenter, ycenter, startangle, endangle,
        xradius, yradius );
```

The sector outline is drawn using the current drawing color and current line style for the radius lines, and is then filled using the current fill pattern and fill color. Screen aspect ratio adjustment is automatic.

Refer also to arc, circle, ellipse, fillellipse, floodfill, getaspectratio, and pieslice.

Fill Patterns and Fill Colors

Several functions are provided to handle fill patterns, to fill enclosed areas and to create custom fill patterns. These include floodfill, getfillpattern, getfillsettings, setfillpattern, and setfillstyle.

floodfill

The floodfill function fills a bounded region defined by the specified *bordercolor* (normally this will be the current drawing color). The (*xpoint,ypoint*) coordinates specify some point to be filled within the area, using the current fill pattern and fill color.

Example:

```
#include <graphics.h>

int xpoint, ypoint, bordercolor;

floodfill( xpoint, ypoint, bordercolor );
```

If the start point is outside a bounded region, the exterior region (limited by the borders set by viewport) will be filled. If any break occurs in the line defining the region, then the fill will leak. Only a very small break is required.

For future compatibility, fillpoly, instead of floodfill, is recommended wherever possible. If an error occurs, graphresult will return a value of –7 (*out of memory in floodfill*).

See also fillpoly, getfillsettings, getlinesettings, and setgraphbufsize.

setfillpattern

The setfillpattern function selects an 8x8, user-defined fill pattern in the specified color.

Example:

```
#include <graphics.h>

int color;
char diamond[8] = { 0x10, 0x38, 0x7C, 0xFE,
                    0x7C, 0x38, 0x10, 0x00 };

setfillpattern( diamond, color );
```

In the example, *diamond* is a sequence of eight bytes, each corresponding to eight pixels in the pattern. One bits turn on pixels, zero bits turn off pixels. The example pattern *diamond* creates a small, 7x7 diamond pattern with a one-pixel border at right and bottom.

After setfillpattern is called to establish the user-defined pattern, setfillstyle must be called to make USER_FILL (12) the current pattern.

A few other possible patterns are:

```
char checker[8] = { 0xAA, 0x55, 0xAA, 0x55,
                    0xAA, 0x55, 0xAA, 0x55 };
char chains1[8] = { 0x6F, 0x40, 0xA0, 0xA0,
                    0xA0, 0x40, 0x6F, 0x00 };
char chains2[8] = { 0x3C, 0xC3, 0xA0, 0x90,
                    0x90, 0xA0, 0x3C, 0xC3 };
```

Refer to getfillpattern, getfillstyle, and setfillstyle.

setfillstyle

The setfillstyle function sets the current fill pattern and fill color.

Example:

```
#include <graphics.h>

setfillstyle( SOLID_FILL, GREEN );
```

Note that *fill* color and *drawing* color are separate and may have different values. Fill patterns are defined in GRAPHICS.H as shown in Table 5-2.

Table 5-2: Fill Patterns

Pattern Name	Value	Description
EMPTY_FILL	0	Background color
SOLID_FILL	1	Solid fill
LINE_FILL	2	Fill with ————————
LTSLASH_FILL	3	Fill with ////
SLASH_FILL	4	Fill with ////, thick
BKSLASH_FILL	5	Fill with \\\\ , thick
LTBKSLASH_FILL	6	Fill with \\\\
HATCH_FILL	7	Light crosshatch
XHATCH_FILL	8	Heavy crosshatch
INTERLEAVE_FILL	9	Interleaving lines
WIDE_DOT_FILL	10	Wide-spaced dots
CLOSE_DOT_FILL	11	Close-spaced dot
USER_FILL	12	User-defined pattern

All patterns except EMPTY_FILL use the current fill color. Pattern 12 (USER_FILL) can only be called after setfillpattern has established a user-defined fill pattern.

See also fillpoly, floodfill, getfillpattern, and getfillstyle.

getfillpattern

The getfillpattern function copies a user-defined fill pattern, set by setfillpattern, to the memory space occupied by *fillpatterninfo*.

Example:

```
#include <graphics.h>

char fillpatterninfo[8];

getfillpattern( &fillpatterninfo );
```

Refer also to setfillpattern.

getfillsettings

The getfillsettings function returns information in fillinfo about the current fillpattern settings.

Example:

```
#include <graphics.h>

struct fillsettingtype fillinfo;

getfillsettings( &fillinfo );
```

The structure *fillsettingtype* is defined in GRAPHICS.H as:

```
struct fillsettingtype
{
    int pattern;          /* predefined pattern numbers only */
    int color;
};
```

Refer also to getfillpattern, setfillpattern, and setfillstyle.

The Internal Graphics Buffer

Several of the graphics functions can return error messages indicating insufficient buffer memory to accomplish their tasks. When this happens, the setgraphbufsize function can be used to allocate additional buffer memory.

setgraphbufsize

Several of the graphics routines use a memory buffer created by initgraph via _graphgetmem. The default buffer size is 4K (4,096 bytes), but this can be decreased to save space or increased if more buffer memory is required.

Example:

```
#include <graphics.h>

unsigned bufsize, oldbufsize;

oldbufsize = setgraphbufsize( bufsize );
```

The setgraphbufsize function must be called *before* calling initgraph. The setbufgraphsize function returns the original buffer size.

Image Manipulation

In addition to drawing functions, procedures are supplied for copying, erasing, duplicating, and manipulating screen images. These are essential for any type of animation. They are useful in image replication for less elaborate applications.

imagesize

The imagesize function returns the size in bytes required to store the bit image specified by the screen coordinates.

Example:

```
#include <graphics.h>

unsigned size;

size = imagesize(ulx, uly, lrx, lry);
```

If the size required for the image is greater than or equal to 64K, a value of 0xFFFF (unsigned 65535 or signed −1) is returned.

Refer also to getimage and putimage.

getimage

The getimage function saves the pixel image from the screen area that is specified by the four parameters.

Example:

```
#include <graphics.h>

void far *bitimage;
int xleft, ytop, xright, ybottom;
unsigned  size;

size = imagesize( xleft, ytop, xright, ybottom );
bitimage = far malloc( size );
getimage( xleft, ytop, xright, ybottom, bitimage);
```

The initsize function is used to calculate the memory required and the malloc function allocates memory for image storage (memory allocation must be less than 64K).

Refer also to imagesize and putimage.

putimage

The putimage function writes a previously saved bit image to the screen with the upper-left corner of the image appearing at (*xleft,ytop*).

Example:

```
#include <graphics.h>

void far *bitimage;
int xleft, ytop, ops;

putimage( xleft, ytop, bitimage, ops );
```

The *ops* parameter controls how each image pixel (color) is combined with the existing screen pixels. The *ops* options are enumerated in GRAPH-ICS.H in *putimage_ops* as shown in Table 5-3.

Table 5-3: Image Put Options

Name	Value	Description
COPY_PUT	0	Image is copied to screen, replacing existing pixels
XOR_PUT	1	Image is eXclusive-OR'd with existing pixels
OR_PUT	2	Image is inclusive-OR'd with existing pixels
AND_PUT	3	Image is ANDed with existing pixels
NOT_PUT	4	Copies the inverse bit-image to the screen

The program PUT-DEMO.C will demonstrate how the various putimage options operate. PUT-DEMO is written for color monitors (EGA or VGA preferred), but can be adapted to run on monochrome systems, though the color overlay effects will not be as visible or may be markedly different.

I suggest running the program as it stands, then experimenting with different color values and fill patterns.

COPY_PUT   Each pixel in the image is mapped directly to the screen, thereby replacing any existing image pixels. This includes image pixels that are blank (background). An entirely blank image can be used to erase other images or portions of the screen. More often, however, the XOR_PUT option is used to "unmap" an existing image.

XOR_PUT   Each existing screen pixel's value is eXclusively OR'd with the corresponding image byte and then the result is written back to the screen. When an image is XOR'd with a existing screen image, the result is a composite of the two.

Notice in PUT-DEMO.C that the LIGHTCYAN pixels (1011) XOR'd with the BLUE (0001) background become LIGHTGREEN (1010), while LIGHTRED XOR'd with BLUE (0001) becomes LIGHTCYAN (1011) and the results appear cleanly against the background image.

If the same image is then XOR'd a second time, it cancels itself bit by bit, and the original screen is restored. This option is particularly useful for animation where an image needs to be placed over an existing screen, then erased again to leave the original screen in place. This put-option will be used heavily in the ANIMATON.C demo (see Chapter 10).

OR_PUT   This might also be called EITHER/OR since each image byte is OR'd with corresponding screen pixels and the result is written back to the screen. Remember, each bit in each pixel is OR'd with the bits in the image, so the result is a color composite of the background and the image.

In PUT-DEMO.C, notice how LIGHTCYAN pixels (1011) OR'd with BLUE (0001) remain LIGHTCYAN (1011), while LIGHTRED (1100) OR'd with the BLUE (0001) background becomes LIGHTMAGENTA (1101).

AND_PUT   Here, only the bits that are on in both the screen pixel and the image byte are on in the result. Notice how the blank background in the Star image wipes out both the Box outline and the fill color, except where the Star image actually overlays the Box. Also, the LIGHTRED (1100) AND'd with LIGHTBLUE (1001) becomes DARKGREY (1000).

NOT_PUT   This is essentially the same as COPY_PUT except that the image is bit-inverted—all BLACK (0000) pixels in the image become WHITE (1111) and so on. The background image is overwritten and lost.

Refer also to imagesize and getimage.

```
/*===================================================*/
/* PUT-DEMO.C = Demonstration of putimage options */
/*===================================================*/

#ifdef __TINY__
#error Graphics demos will not run in the tiny model.
#endif

#include <conio.h>
#include <stdio.h>
#include <stdlib.h>
#include <alloc.h>
#include <graphics.h>
```

```
int    GraphDriver,          /* graphics device driver      */
       GraphMode,            /* graphics mode value         */
       MaxColors,            /* maximum colors available    */
       ErrorCode = 0;        /* reports any graphics errors */
void  *Star, *Box;           /* image pointers              */

void *SaveImage( int left,  int top,
                 int right, int bottom )
{
   void    far *image;       /* local image pointer         */

   image = far malloc( imagesize( left,  top,
                                  right, bottom ) );
   getimage( left, top, right, bottom, image );
                                  /* save the image    */
   putimage( left, top, image, XOR_PUT );
                                  /* erase the image   */
   return( image );               /* return image ptr */
}

void CreateImages()
{
   int  pstar[] = { 100,100, 110,120, 100,130, 120,125,
         140,140, 130,120, 140,110, 120,115, 100,100 };
   int  pbox[]  = { 100,100, 100,140, 140,140, 140,100,
                    100,100 };

   setcolor( LIGHTRED );
   setfillstyle( LINE_FILL, LIGHTCYAN );
   fillpoly( sizeof(pstar)/(2*sizeof(int)), pstar );
   Star = SaveImage( 100, 100, 140, 140 );

   setcolor( LIGHTGREEN );
   setfillstyle( SOLID_FILL, LIGHTBLUE );
   fillpoly( sizeof(pbox)/(2*sizeof(int)), pbox );
   Box  = SaveImage( 100, 100, 140, 140 );

   setcolor( WHITE );

   putimage(   10,  10,  Star,  COPY_PUT  );
   outtextxy(  60,  25,  "+" );
   putimage(   80,  10,  Box,   COPY_PUT  );
   putimage(  200,  10,  Box,   COPY_PUT  );
```

```
    putimage(  200,   10,   Star,   COPY_PUT   );
    outtextxy( 130,   25,           "COPY_PUT" );

    putimage(   10,   60,   Star,   COPY_PUT   );
    outtextxy(  60,   75,   "+"                );
    putimage(   80,   60,   Box,    COPY_PUT   );
    putimage(  200,   60,   Box,    COPY_PUT   );
    putimage(  200,   60,   Star,   AND_PUT    );
    outtextxy( 130,   75,         " AND_PUT"   );

    putimage(   10,  110,   Star,   COPY_PUT   );
    outtextxy(  60,  125,   "+"                );
    putimage(   80,  110,   Box,    COPY_PUT   );
    putimage(  200,  110,   Box,    COPY_PUT   );
    putimage(  200,  110,   Star,   NOT_PUT    );
    outtextxy( 130,  125,         " NOT_PUT"   );

    putimage(  310,   10,   Star,   COPY_PUT   );
    outtextxy( 360,   25,   "+"                );
    putimage(  380,   10,   Box,    COPY_PUT   );
    putimage(  500,   10,   Box,    COPY_PUT   );
    putimage(  500,   10,   Star,   OR_PUT     );
    putimage(  500,   10,   Star,   XOR_PUT    );
    outtextxy( 430,   15,         " OR_PUT"    );
    outtextxy( 430,   25,         "    and "   );
    outtextxy( 430,   35,         " XOR_PUT"   );

    putimage(  310,   60,   Star,   COPY_PUT   );
    outtextxy( 360,   75,   "+"                );
    putimage(  380,   60,   Box,    COPY_PUT   );
    putimage(  500,   60,   Box,    COPY_PUT   );
    putimage(  500,   60,   Star,   OR_PUT     );
    outtextxy( 430,   75,         " OR_PUT"    );

    putimage(  310,  110,   Star,   COPY_PUT   );
    outtextxy( 360,  125,   "+"                );
    putimage(  380,  110,   Box,    COPY_PUT   );
    putimage(  500,  110,   Box,    COPY_PUT   );
    putimage(  500,  110,   Star,   XOR_PUT    );
    outtextxy( 430,  125,         " XOR_PUT"   );
}

void Initialize()
```

```
{                  /* initialize graphics system and report errors */
   GraphDriver = DETECT;          /* request auto-detection */
   initgraph( &GraphDriver, &GraphMode, "C:\\TC\\BGI" );
   ErrorCode = graphresult();          /* test init results */
   if ( ErrorCode != grOk )          /* if error occurred */
   {
      printf( " Graphics System Error: %s\n",
              grapherrormsg( ErrorCode ) );
      exit( 1 );
   }
   MaxColors = getmaxcolor() + 1;          /* max color range */
}

void Pause()                  /* wait for key to be pressed */
{
   if( kbhit() ) getch();
   getch();
}

main()
{
   Initialize();                    /* set graphics mode   */
   CreateImages();                  /* create and save images   */
   Pause();
   closegraph();                    /* restore text mode   */
}
```

Chapter 6

ABCDE
FGHIJK
LMNOP
QRSTU
VWXYZ

Graphics Text Functions

Once a graphics mode has been set, the conventional text displays are no longer available, and labels and text information can only be displayed using graphics text displays.

In graphics modes, however, graphics text display operates quite differently from conventional text display. For example, the conventional character screen positions (column and row coordinates) no longer apply and an individual character can appear almost anywhere on the screen. Special provisions are required to track the screen display position, deciding where the next display line should appear and writing graphics text to the screen. These include the outtext and outtextxy functions.

Because character sizes are varied, different vertical and horizontal justifications are offered and because text can be displayed in both vertical and horizontal orientations, the line offset and display positions become confusing. These variable settings are controlled by settextstyle, settextjustify, and setusercharsize.

With these variables and complications in mind, several functions are provided to make it easier to keep track of display positions, font sizes, and string widths. These include gettextsettings, textheight, and textwidth.

To display program variables and other changing data, as well as string constants, graphics equivalents for the conventional text functions are needed. These capabilities will be discussed in Chapter 8, with the erasestr, printf, and gprintc functions offering examples of advanced graphics text handling functions.

With Turbo C++ (and Turbo Pascal), the installuserfont function allows new graphics fonts and user-created fonts to be incorporated in your programs. See Chapter 15, *The Turbo Font Editor*.

Text Functions

The first task is to be able to write to the screen while in graphics mode:

outtext

The outtext function displays a string in the viewport, beginning at CP.

Example:

```
#include <graphics.h>

outtext( "Display string for viewport" );
```

The current font selection, drawing color, character size, text orientation (direction), and justification are used.

If horizontal justification is LEFT_TEXT and direction is HORIZ_DIR (default settings for graphics text display), then CP's *x*-axis coordinate is advanced by *textwidth(textstring)*. Otherwise the CP is not altered.

Refer to gettextsettings, gprintf, gprintc, outtextxy, setcolor, settextsettings, textheight, and textwidth.

outtextxy

The outtextxy function displays a string in the viewport, beginning at the coordinates specified by (*x,y*) relative to the viewport settings.

Example:

```
#include <graphics.h>

int  x, y;

outtextxy( x, y, "Display string for viewport" );
```

The current font selection, drawing color, character size, text orientation (direction), and justification are used. The current position's (CP) coordinates are not affected.

Refer also to gettextsettings, gprintf, gprintc, outtext, setcolor, settextsettings, textheight, and textwidth.

The outtext and outtextxy functions provide the basic text I/O handling in graphics modes. More advanced graphics text I/O and text formatting capabilities will be demonstrated shortly using gprintf and gprintc.

Graphics Text Styles, Justification, and Sizing

Where conventional text modes offer the display equivalent of a typewritten page, graphics text modes come closer to providing a typeset display. This enhancement is capable of changing fonts, selecting different horizontal and vertical justifications, changing character sizes, and even running text displays vertically instead of horizontally.

settextstyle

The function settextstyle sets the current graphics text *font*, the *direction* for the text display (horizontal or vertical), and the *charsize*.

Example:

```
#include <graphics.h>

int font, direction, charsize;

settextstyle( font, direction, charsize );
```

Table 6-1 shows the standard *font_names* as defined in GRAPHICS.H.

Table 6-1: Graphics Text Fonts

Name[1]	Value	Description
DEFAULT_FONT	0	Bit-mapped 8x8 font
TRIPLEX_FONT	1	Stroked triplex font
SMALL_FONT	2	Stroked small font
SANS_SERIF_FONT	3	Stroked sans-serif font
GOTHIC_FONT	4	Stroked gothic font

1. For additional fonts, see Chapter 15, *The Turbo Font Editor*.

The DEFAULT_FONT is built into the graphics system. Of the other fonts, only one is kept in memory at any time. The .CHR files for the selected font must be located in the directory or subdirectory indicated by initgraph as *driverpath* before it can be loaded.

Multiple fonts, however, can be linked to your program using the BGIOBJ utility (see *Linking Graphics Drivers and Fonts* in Chapter 7). In this case, the registerbgifont function is used to select the font required.

By default graphics text direction is horizontal, but it can be set to vertical (rotated 90° counterclockwise). The two graphics text directions are defined in GRAPHICS.H, as shown in Table 6-2.

Table 6-2: Graphics Text Directions

Name	Value	Description
HORIZ_DIR	0	Left to right (default)
VERT_DIR	1	Bottom to top

In vertical orientation, the text string begins at the bottom and runs up. No provisions currently exist for a string display running down the page or for an inverted string (upside down, running right to left), but these could be created using the image rotation techniques that will be demonstrated in Chapter 12.

For bit-mapped font(s) *charsize* may be 0..10. Values zero and one display 8x8 pixel rectangles, value two displays a 16x16 pixel rectangle, and so on, up to 10 times normal size. For stroked fonts *charsize = 0* magnifies the stroked font by the default factor of 4 or by the user-defined size factors set by setusercharsize. The maximum valid *charsize* is 10. If invalid values are passed to settextjustify, graphresult will return −11 (*general error*) and the current text settings will remain unchanged.

Refer also to settextjustify, textheight, and textwidth.

installuserfont

The installuserfont (Turbo C version 2.0) function loads a .CHR (stroked) font that is not built into the BGI system, and returns a font ID number which can be passed to settextstyle to select the font.

Example:

```
#include <graphics.h>

int   USER_FONT = 0;

USER_FONT =
    installuserfont( "\FontPath\FontName.CHR" );
```

Up to 20 external fonts can be installed at any time. If the internal font table is full, a value of -11 (*grError*) is returned.

settextjustify

The settextjustify function selects horizontal and vertical text justification.

Example:

```
#include <graphics.h>

int  hjustify, vjustify;

settextjustify( hjustify, vjustify );
```

The default values are LEFT_TEXT, TOP_TEXT (0,2) and the justification terms *text_just* are defined in GRAPHICS.H as shown in Table 6-3.

Table 6-3: Text Justification Terms

(Horizontal Justify)		(Vertical Justify)	
Name	**Value**	**Name**	**Value**
LEFT_TEXT	0	BOTTOM_TEXT	0
CENTER_TEXT	1	CENTER_TEXT	1
RIGHT_TEXT	2	TOP_TEXT	2

For horizontal justification, LEFT_TEXT displays the text string to the right starting at CP, CENTER_TEXT displays the text string centered right/left at CP, and RIGHT_TEXT displays the text string to the left, ending at CP.

For vertical justification, BOTTOM_TEXT aligns the bottom of the character string with CP. CENTER_TEXT aligns the center of the display string at CP. TOP_TEXT aligns the top of the string with CP.

When justification is set as LEFT_TEXT and *direction* = HORIZ_DIR, the current position's x setting is advanced after a call to outtext or gprintf by textwidth(string). Figure 6-1 shows several options for text alignment.

Refer also to settextstyle.

setusercharsize

The setusercharsize function provides user-defined character magnification for stroked fonts only. This does not function with the DEFAULT_FONT characters. The font adjustment parameters are active only if settextstyle has been called to set *charsize = 0*.

Example:

```
#include <graphics.h>

int xmult, xdiv, ymult, ydiv;

setusercharsize( xmult, xdiv, ymult, ydiv );
```

Figure 6-1: Text Justification

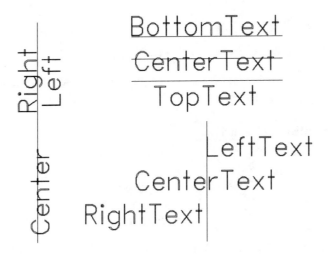

Several options for text alignment are supported. Notice that the CENTER_TEXT line (vertical orientation at left) is centered according to the total font height. This includes blank header space above the characters. All alignments include this header space, as well as a brief margin following the end of a string (or a single character).

When setusercharsize is called to select custom character scaling, the resulting width is defined as *xmult/xdiv* and the resulting height as *ymult/ydiv*.

To create a display with characters scaled to a height of three (24 pixels) and twice as wide as they are tall (48 pixels), setusercharsize would be called with:

```
xmult = 6;   xdiv = 1;
ymult = 3;   ydiv = 1;
setusercharsize( xmult, xdiv, ymult, ydiv );
```

Alternatively, for tall and narrow characters,

```
xmult = 3;   xdiv = 2;
ymult = 6;   ydiv = 1;
```

would produce characters 12 pixels wide and 48 pixels tall.

Refer also to gettextsettings.

Text Settings Information

With the variety of choices in fonts, text direction, and vertical and horizontal justification, it is helpful to determine what the current settings are and how wide and how tall a text string is using the current settings. For these applications, three functions are provided: gettextsettings, textheight, and textwidth.

gettextsettings

The gettextsettings function fills *textinfo* with the current text font, direction, size, and horizontal and vertical justification.

Example:

```
#include <graphics.h>

struct textsettingstype textinfo;

gettextsettings( &textinfo );
```

The structure *textsettingstype* is defined in GRAPHICS.H as:

```
struct textsettingstype
{
    int font;        int direction;
    int charsize;
    int horiz;       int vert;
};
```

Refer also to outtext, textheight, textwidth, and settextstyle.

textheight and textwidth

The textheight function returns the height of a string in pixels, using the current font size, scaling factors, and text direction. This may be the height of a single character or the height of an entire string. When a single character is used, an uppercase character is customary even though the information returned is based on calculated size, rather than actual display size (for instance, a "u" will return the same size as "U").

Example:

```
#include <graphics.h>

int charheight, charwidth;
```

```
charheight = textheight( "Text String" );
charwidth = textwidth( "Text String" );
```

The textwidth function returns the width of a string in pixels, using the current font size, scaling factors, and text direction. This may be the width of a single character or, more often, the width of an entire string.

                                                         Chapter 7

                                                 The Graphics Library

Turbo C++ supplies a graphics function library (GRAPHICS.H) as a supplement to the standard memory model libraries, providing libraries that are memory model specific. When using Turbo C's Integrated Development Environment (TC.EXE) the appropriate memory model is loaded automatically, corresponding to the memory model selected (see menu under Options/Compiler/Model).

   The graphics library, however, is separate and is not automatically included at compile time. For this reason, there are two other options when using graphics functions with Turbo C++: using .PRJ files or incorporating GRAPHICS.LIB in one or more of the standard libraries.

   Remember that the graphics header file must be called in each module of your source code before any graphics functions can be used. Thus, the source line *#include <graphics.h>*, should appear in all code modules. Also, the graphics functions will not work using the TINY memory model because of limited memory. Larger memory models make more memory available for your program.

Graphics Using .PRJ Files

The simplest method of including the graphics library at compile time (using TC.EXE, the Integrated Development Environment) is to use a .PRJ

                                                                               75

file. For example, in a program named PROGNAME.C, you would create a project file, *PROGNAME.PRJ*, which includes the line:

```
progname graphics.lib
```

To compile, you select the pull-down Project menu and enter the project name *PROGNAME* (the extension .PRJ is optional and will be assumed by default). Now select Compile (Alt-C) and proceed.

With the release of Turbo C version 2.0, a new option (Option/Linker/Graphics Library) instructs the linker to automatically search the graphics library without requiring a project file.

Or, using the command line version of Turbo C++ (TCC.EXE), you would simply include the graphics library in your command:

```
tcc progname graphics.lib
```

Remember, you must specify that the graphics library is to be included or you will find an astonishing number of errors reported by the linker.

Adding GRAPHICS.LIB to the Standard Libraries

As an alternative to using .PRJ files or calling GRAPHICS.LIB from the command line, Turbo C++ provides an option that instructs the linker to automatically search for the Graphics Library. Use the Options/Linker/Graphics library menu settings.

The graphics library can also be incorporated into one or more of the standard libraries using TLIB.EXE, the Turbo object code librarian.

To add the graphics library to a specific memory model, the Cx.LIB file and GRAPHICS.LIB file should be in the same directory/subdirectory before entering the command: *tlib cx +graphics.lib<CR>*, where *cx* identifies the specific memory model to use.

If you prefer to add the graphics library to all of the memory model libraries, you might create a .BAT file reading:

```
tlib cs +graphics.lib
tlib cc +graphics.lib
tlib cm +graphics.lib
tlib cl +graphics.lib
tlib ch +graphics.lib
```

The disadvantage of incorporating the graphics library is that you get a slightly longer compile time on non-graphic programs. But this is a minor matter and hardly rates as an inconvenience.

You might want to link the graphics drivers and graphics fonts *before* incorporating the graphics library.

Linking Graphics Drivers and Fonts

By default, Turbo C++ (and Turbo Pascal) use dynamically linked graphics drivers (*.BGI files) and graphics fonts (*.CHR files). Using external drivers and fonts offers two advantages: limited compiled program size, and; flexibility for adding new drivers and fonts at later dates. There are, however, two decided disadvantages to depending on external files for operation.

First, when using external drivers and fonts, the drive and directory path where the external utilities are located must be specified by the programmer at compile time (see initgraph in Chapter 1). If the specified path or drive is changed at a later time, then the program must be recompiled with the new information.

Second, while the .BGI and .CHR files can be distributed with your compiled program, these extra files are subject to accidental erasure and other hazards, any of which can result in a dissatisfied user.

There is an alternative. Link the drivers and fonts directly as a part of the graphics library so that no external files are required and the drivers and fonts will be a part of the .EXE code produced by the C compiler. At this point, the graphics library can be added to the standard libraries using a .PRJ file or linked by a command line specification as detailed previously.

However, in order to link the driver and font files, the BGIOBJ utility must first be called to convert the .BGI and .CHR files to .OBJ files.

The BGIOBJ utility is invoked as:

```
bgiobj <source>
```

It produces an object file with the same name as *source* but the extension .OBJ. Thus, CGA.BGI produces CGA.OBJ and TRIP.CHR produces TRIP.OBJ. Once the .OBJ file(s) are created, TLIB is invoked:

```
tlib graphics +cga +trip
```

This adds the CGA driver and TRIP font to GRAPHICS.LIB. Note: the extensions .LIB and .OBJ are understood and do not need to be specified.

You can also use the following two .BAT files. ADD-DRVR.BAT file for adding graphics drivers to GRAPHICS.LIB:

```
bgiobj cga
bgiobj egavga
```

```
bgiobj herc
bgiobj att
bgiobj pc3270
bgiobj ibm8514
tlib graphics +cga +egavga +herc +att +pc3270 +ibm8514
```

ADD-FONT.BAT file for adding graphics fonts to GRAPHICS.LIB:

```
bgiobj trip
bgiobj litt
bgiobj sans
bgiobj goth
tlib graphics +trip +litt +sans +goth
```

Using the Linked Drivers and Fonts

There is one other requirement to use graphics drivers and fonts after linking with the graphics library that does not appear when using external drivers and fonts: the driver(s) and/or font(s) must be registered *before* calling initgraph.

Several of these functions appear in both near and far versions (as register... and registerfar...). The registerfar... functions and the /F option provide more memory for your programs by registering drivers and fonts at *far* segment addresses.

registerbgidriver and registerfarbgidriver

The registerbgidriver function is used to register a linked-in graphics driver.

Example:

```
#include <graphics.h>

if ( registerbgidriver( <DRIVER_name> ) < 0 ) exit(1);
```

If the specified graphics driver is not found, a negative error code is returned. Otherwise, the internal driver number is returned. Table 7-1 gives more detailed information on graphics drivers.

Table 7-1: Graphics Drivers

Normal Driver File	Far Symbolic Name[1]	Symbolic Name
CGA.BGI	CGA_driver	CGA_driver_far
EGAVGA.BGI	EGAVGA_driver	EGAVGA_driver_far

Normal Driver File	Far Symbolic Name[1]	Symbolic Name
HERC.BGI	Herc_driver	Herc_driver_far
ATT.BGI	ATT_driver	ATT_driver_far
PC3270.BGI	PC3720_driver	PC3720_driver_far
IBM8514.BGI	IBM8514_driver	IBM8514_driver_far

1. See next section, *Linker Error With Drivers and Fonts* for explanation on registerfarbgidriver and *far* driver symbolic names.

```
/*=====================================*/
/* DRIVER.C == call RegisterDrivers() */
/*=====================================*/

#include <graphics.h>

void RegisterDrivers()
{
   if( registerbgidriver(CGA_driver) < 0      ) exit(1);
   if( registerbgidriver(EGAVGA_driver) < 0  ) exit(1);
   if( registerbgidriver(Herc_driver) < 0     ) exit(1);
   if( registerbgidriver(ATT_driver) < 0      ) exit(1);
   if( registerbgidriver(PC3270_driver) < 0  ) exit(1);
   if( registerbgidriver(IBM8514_driver) < 0 ) exit(1);
}

main()
{
   RegisterDrivers();
   Initialize();
   ....
   closegraph();
}
```

Portability: IBM PCs and compatibles only, corresponding functions exist in Turbo Pascal.

registerbgifont and registerfarbgifont

The registerbgifont function is used to register a linked, stroked font character set.

Example:

```
#include <graphics.h>

if ( registerbgifont( name_font ) < 0 ) exit(1);
```

If the specified font is not found, a negative error code is returned; otherwise, the registered font number is returned. Table 7-2 shows the graphics fonts.

Table 7-2: Graphics Fonts

Normal Font File	Far Symbolic Name[1]	Symbolic Name
TRIP.CHR	triplex_font	triplex_font_far
LITT.CHR	small_font	small_font_far
SANS.CHR	sanserif_font	sanserif_font_far
GOTH.CHR	gothic_font	gothic_font_far

1. See the next section, *Linker Error With Drivers and Fonts* for explanation on registerfarbgifont and *far* font symbolic names.

```
/*===================================*/
/* FONTS.C == call RegisterFonts() */
/*===================================*/

#include <graphics.h>

void RegisterFonts()
{
   if( registerbgifont( triplex_font  ) < 0 ) exit(1);
   if( registerbgifont( small_font    ) < 0 ) exit(1);
   if( registerbgifont( sanserif_font ) < 0 ) exit(1);
   if( registerbgifont( gothic_font   ) < 0 ) exit(1);
}

main()
{
   RegisterDrivers();
   RegisterFonts();
   Initialize();
   ....
   closegraph();
}
```

Portability: IBM PCs and compatibles only, corresponding functions exist in Turbo Pascal.

Linker Errors with Drivers and Fonts

It is possible for a linker error to occur when using linked graphics drivers and fonts. The error message, *Segment exceeds 64K*, will appear; a problem which is most likely to occur with tiny, small, or compact memory models.

When BGIOBJ creates .OBJ files, they all use the same memory segment, _TEXT. If too many files are linked and the segment exceeds the 64K size limit, then an error will occur.

If this happens, the /F option should be used with BGIOBJ to create new memory segments of the form FILENAME_TEXT, leaving the default segment free for other applications. Doing so will have two effects.

First, an F will be appended to the .OBJ filenames. Thus CGA.BGI would produce CGAF.OBJ instead of CGA.OBJ and the TLIB commands would need to be altered accordingly. Note: the source filenames must also be seven characters or less in length to allow for this addition.

Second, the public names have *far* appended and the registerfarbgidriver and registerfarbgifont functions will be needed in the RegisterDrivers and RegisterFonts routines.

```
if( registerfarbgidriver(Herc_driver_far)<0 ) exit(1);
if( registerfarbgifont(triplex_font_far) <0 ) exit(1);
```

Custom Graphics Memory Management

Customizing the graphics memory management procedures is possible. However, this should not be attempted lightly. The following two functions are included here solely for completeness.

_graphfreemem

Normally _graphfreemem is called by closegraph to deallocate the memory reserved for drivers, fonts, and internal buffers. By default, _graphfreemem calls the free function. However, custom memory management can be created by defining a new _graphfreemem. The new _graphfreemem function must be declared matching the standard function.

Example:

```
#include <graphics.h>

unsigned  size;
int *memptr;

_graphfreemem( &memptr, size );
```

Refer also to _graphgetmem.

_graphgetmem

Normally _graphgetmem is called by initgraph to allocate memory space
for graphic drivers, graphic character fonts, and internal buffers. By default, _graphgetmem uses the malloc function to set memory allocation.
Custom memory management can be created by defining a new
_graphgetmem function. The new _graphgetmem function must be de-
clared matching the standard function.

Example:

```
#include <graphics.h>

unsigned  size;

_graphgetmem( size );
```

Refer also to _graphfreemem.

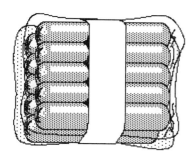

Chapter 8

Combining Text with Graphics

While some early computer designs did not differentiate between text and graphics, contemporary MS-DOS systems do not permit mapping the ROM-based character set(s) directly into a graphics display. To overcome this limitation, both Turbo C++ and Turbo Pascal provide a default bit-mapped graphics character set which is a replacement for the ROM character set. The set includes the extended ASCII characters that provide foreign characters such as the English pound sign, the Japanese yen sign, the accented vowels, and the graphics and math characters.

These extended ASCII characters were not included in all stroked fonts and attempts to print extended character codes using stroked fonts are often ignored. Later versions and the graphics fonts distributed with the Turbo Font Editor (see Chapter 15 for details) do include extended ASCII character set equivalents. These graphics character fonts are not merely replacements for the ROM-based characters. Text displays can be much more elaborate in graphics modes.

Four fancy stroked typefaces—Gothic, Sans Serif, Triplex (Roman), and Small—are supplied. String character positions can be adjusted by pixel instead of character positions. Both the default and the stroked typefaces can be enlarged up to 10 times the normal size; the stroked typefaces can be made taller or wider, and strings may be set flush left, centered, or flush right and displayed vertically as well as horizontally.

While the default font is a fixed width font (all characters are the same basic width), the stroked fonts are proportional (that is, a capital "W" is proportionally wider than a lowercase "i"). Character placement and string spacing reflect these properties, providing a better appearance than typewriter style text.

But there are limitations. The two principal output functions, outtext and outtextxy, each write a string to screen—outtext using the default CP and outtextxy accepting a screen position for the text output. Both of these functions accept only a string for output; there is no direct provision for printing variables or building strings for output as supported in text modes by the printf and cprintf functions. It is possible to create analogous functions to serve these same purposes.

The gprintf function

The gprintf function has been used in most of the demo programs and a slightly different version of gprintf appears in the BGIDEMO program originally distributed with Turbo C version 1.5. In neither case, however, has the operation of the gprintf function been explained in detail.

The gprintf function is used like printf to accept a variable number of arguments and to combine these in creating a string that is output to the screen. Unlike printf, gprintf is called with output coordinates, is usable only in the graphics mode, and does not function in the text mode. Depending on the text direction (horizontal or vertical), either the xloc or yloc coordinate is returned with the appropriate offset so that the next string printed can be appropriately aligned.

The first trick is to accept a variable argument list and then to use this list to create the appropriate output string. This is provided in the declaration of gprintf and in the local variables:

```
void gprintf( int *xloc, int *yloc, char *fmt, ... )
{
    va_list  argptr;
```

The first two arguments passed to gprintf are the output coordinates: the x- and y-axis location. The third argument, *char *fmt,* is a pointer to a string that may be an alphanumeric set of characters or a format string. A format string includes format specifications for subsequent arguments.

The ellipsis (...) ends the argument list and indicates that an undetermined number of arguments may, or may not, be included. The actual number of arguments passed in each call to gprintf is determined by the number of format specifications included in **fmt.*

If your actual argument list is longer than the number of arguments required by the format specifications, no error message will appear and the excess arguments will be ignored. On the other hand, if there is a shortage of arguments, the compiler will issue an error message accordingly.

The *va_list* data type is shown in stdarg.h and declares an array containing information needed to access the argument list.

The remaining local variables are *str[140]*, a buffer string of 140 characters to hold the eventual output string; *textinfo* which will be used to check the text direction; and *pos_adj*, which is initially equal to **xloc*.

```
char     str[140];
struct   textsettingstype  textinfo;
int      pos_adj = *xloc;
```

The va_start function initializes the argument pointer array (*argptr*) to point to *fmt*, the format string, which is the last *fixed* parameter passed to gprintf. The va_start function must be called before any call to va_arg or va_end.

```
va_start( argptr, fmt );
vsprintf( str, fmt, argptr );
```

The vsprintf function behaves very much like the familiar printf except that output goes to a null-terminated (ASCIIZ) string buffer (*str*)that uses the va_arg array and the argument format instructions in *fmt*. It is the programmer's responsibility to ensure that the *str* buffer is large enough to hold the created string. If no optional arguments (except the string *fmt* itself) are passed to gprintf, then *str* equals *fmt*.

Once the output string is created in the *str* buffer, gettextsettings gets the current text justification and direction instructions.

```
gettextsettings( &textinfo );
```

Next, outtextxy writes *str* to the screen in graphics mode, using *pos_adj* and **yloc* to determine the string output position. The graphics string is written using the current text style, font, drawing color, and text justification settings.

```
outtextxy( pos_adj, *yloc, str );
switch ( textinfo.direction )
{
   case HORIZ_DIR: *yloc += textheight( str ) + 2;
                   break;
```

```
    case VERT_DIR: *xloc += textheight( str ) + 2;
};
```

With the screen output finished, *textinfo.direction* is tested again to decide whether to update the x-axis or y-axis coordinate in order to be ready for the next screen output. In graphics text output, including a \n in the format string to end the output string with a carriage_return/line_feed combination would be ineffective. Instead, gprintf automatically provides the graphics analog of a line feed by updating the appropriate x-axis or y-axis position coordinate.

```
    va_end( argptr );
}
```

Lastly, va_end is called to close the pointer to the argument list. This is basic housekeeping that follows any call to va_start. Failure to close with this function might cause unexpected behavior in subsequent operations.

The gprintc function

The gprintc function operates similar to gprintf, but with one important difference. When a string is written to the screen in text modes, any existing text at the output position is overwritten. In graphics modes this is not the case and, when gprintf is used, the output text is written over the existing screen image. Only the pixels that actually comprise the string characters are written; the background pixels remain unchanged. Depending on the existing screen image, the resulting output may not be legible. This can be true when a new graphics string is written over an existing graphics string.

To correct this problem without erasing and recreating the entire screen, gprintc is provided and it includes a call to the erasestr function.

```
    void gprintc( int *xloc, int *yloc, char *fmt, ... )
    {
        . . . . .
        gettextsettings( &textinfo );
        erasestr( *xloc, *yloc, str );
        . . . . .
        outtextxy( pos_adj, *yloc, str );
        . . . . .
    }
```

Other than calling erasestr with the position information and a copy of the formatted output string, gprintc operates the same as gprintf.

The gprintxy function

Both the gprintf and gprintc functions require the x- and y-axis coordinates to be passed, as pointers, to variables so that the changed coordinates can be returned for the next string output. This is not always convenient, however, so the gprintxy function is also included in GPRINT.I.

The gprintxy function differs in accepting the screen coordinates that are passed as values but otherwise acts the same as gprintc. Thus, gprintxy can be called as:

```
gprintxy( 10, 10,
        "Something to print with a number %d ",
        number );
```

while the same call to gprintc would require:

```
int   x = 10,  y = 10;
gprintc( &x,  &y,
        "Something to print with a number %d ",
        number );
```

In many applications this difference will not matter. At other times, such as in a quick graphics line display for debugging, the gprintxy function can provide a tremendous convenience.

The erasestr function

The erasestr function is provided to erase the appropriate area of the screen before writing a string to the screen. This is intended to remove a block of graphics background that would interfere with the string image. This function can also be used to erase a string or portion of a string if necessary.

From gprintc, erasestr is called with the x-axis and y-axis coordinates that will be used to position the output string.

```
void erasestr( int xloc, int yloc, char *str )
{
```

While the *textinfo* structure has already been accessed from gprintc, this information is not directly available to erasestr. Instead of passing the data in the call to erasestr, a local information structure is loaded with the justification settings and text output direction.

```
struct  textsettingstype  textinfo;
int     xdim, ydim;
```

```
void     *textimage;
gettextsettings( &textinfo );
```

The x and y dimensions of the output string are assigned to the appropriate variables according to the text output direction. For horizontal output, the *xloc* variable is decreased to provide a one-pixel offset for the erase area. For vertical output, the *yloc* variable is increased for the same reason.

```
switch ( textinfo.direction )
{
    case HORIZ_DIR: xdim = textwidth( str );
                    ydim = textheight( str );
                    xloc- -;        break;
    case  VERT_DIR: ydim = textwidth( str );
                    xdim = textheight( str );
                    yloc++;
}
```

In the next steps, the *xloc* variable is adjusted according to the horizontal justification setting.

```
switch( textinfo.horiz )
{
    case   LEFT_TEXT:                        break;
    case CENTER_TEXT: xloc -= xdim / 2;   break;
    case  RIGHT_TEXT: xloc -= xdim;
}
```

The *yloc* variable is adjusted using the vertical justification setting.

```
switch( textinfo.vert )
{
    case BOTTOM_TEXT: yloc -= ydim;       break;
    case CENTER_TEXT: yloc -= ydim / 2;  break;
    case    TOP_TEXT: ;
}
```

Before any attempt is made to erase a screen area, two tests are done to make sure that the *xloc* and *yloc* coordinates fall within the valid screen area. If the *xloc* or *yloc* coordinates fall outside the screen area, then nothing would be erased from the screen. this is because the subsequent calls to the getimage and putimage functions would be attempting to use coordinates that did not exist in video memory.

If necessary, *xloc* and *yloc* are adjusted to ensure they lie within the screen limits and, at the same time, the *xdim* and *ydim* offsets are changed to compensate appropriately.

```
while( xloc < 0 ) { xloc++; xdim- -; }
while( yloc < 0 ) { yloc++; ydim- -; }
```

Now it's time to actually erase a block of screen. The first step is to allocate memory for *textimage* according to the screen area that will be cleared. The function imagesize uses the *xloc*, *yloc*, *xdim*, and *ydim* variables to return an unsigned integer indicating the number of bytes required for the selected image.

```
textimage = far malloc(
                imagesize( xloc, yloc, xdim, ydim ) );
```

Next, getimage is called to store the screen area image in *textimage*, then putimage returns the image using the *XOR_PUT* option to clear it. This leaves a blank screen in the desired area.

```
getimage( xloc, yloc, xloc + xdim, yloc + ydim,
          textimage );
putimage( xloc, yloc, textimage, XOR_PUT );
```

Lastly, the free function is used to release the memory allocated for *textimage*. The *textimage* pointer variable cannot be referenced outside of the erasestr function. Memory that has been allocated locally, however, remains allocated until it is specifically released. It must be released while the *textimage* pointer is still available, before exiting erasestr.

```
    free( textimage );
}
```

When erasestr is called again, a new block of memory will be allocated and a new *textimage* pointer assigned. If memory was repeatedly allocated without being released, the system memory would be quickly exhausted and subsequent calls would produce error results.

The erase_block function

The screen area could have been erased by rewriting the individual pixels using the background color as an alternative to using the image functions.

```
void erase_block( int left,  int top,
                  int right, int bottom )
```

```
{
    int   i, j, k = getbkcolor();

    for ( i=left; i<=right; i++ )
        for ( j=top; j<=bottom; j++ )
            putpixel( i, j, k );
}
```

This second option does save the small amount of memory which is allocated in the preceding erasestr function. The trade-off, however, is that this approach is slower in execution than when using the getimage and putimage functions.

Alternative Applications

I mentioned that the erasestr function could also be used to erase a string or portion of a string. This statement was only half true. It can be used to erase an existing string, however, erasing a portion of a string is slightly less practical since erasestr has not been specifically designed for it.

Both of these applications can be accomplished, but there are a couple of prerequisites that must be recognized. First, the text style, fonts, and justification must be the same as when the string was originally written. Second, the original drawing color must be in effect. Third, the screen coordinates where the original string was written must be known. And fourth, the string itself must be known. If any of these first three items have changed, an attempt to erase an existing string or a portion of an existing string will have unexpected results.

In graphics modes, there is no convenient method of "reading" a text string back from the screen, as can be done in text modes.

The first operation is to erase an existing string. Assuming that the text settings and color are correct and that the original screen coordinates are known, it is a simple operation. Just call erasestr directly using the x and y screen coordinates and the string. The appropriate area of the screen will be XOR'd with itself, leaving the screen blank and ready for a rewrite.

In the second application, erasing a portion of a string, the easiest method is to begin by erasing the entire string and then to rewrite the desired portion of the string. While several elaborate schemes could be constructed for erasing specific graphics characters or substrings, all of these would require far more processing and time.

Word processing is not the topic of this book and using graphics fonts and text display is hardly the simplest method of programming a word processor or similar application. However, you may find it necessary to employ text-editing procedures along with a graphics application. If so, here are a few hints:

- The best approach is to treat the screen image as a mapped copy of the actual text array in memory, using some indexing scheme to identify a correspondence between a line of text in memory and its graphics position on the screen.

- If the bitmapped DEFAULT_FONT is used, the screen position for any character is relatively easy to calculate because all characters are fixed width. If the stroked fonts are being used, then the textwidth function is the best method of deciding where a particular string should end.

- Also, the screen cannot be scrolled up or down in the usual manner. While it would be possible to use getimage and putimage to move a major portion of the screen image, you might find the memory requirements are excessive. If so, a simpler method is to move some smaller portion of the screen, using multiple moves to shift as much of the screen as necessary. A similar technique can be used for left and right scrolling.

```
/*========================================================*/
/*                 Listings for GPRINT.I                  */
/* ERASESTR: Used to erase a portion of the screen */
/* before a new string is written to the screen or */
/* simply to remove a string from the screen       */
/*========================================================*/
void erasestr( int xloc, int yloc, char *str )
{
    struct textsettingstype   textinfo;
    int      xdim, ydim;
    void     *textimage;                      /* image pointer  */
    gettextsettings( &textinfo );             /* check settings */
    switch ( textinfo.direction )             /* get dimensions */
    {
        case HORIZ_DIR: xdim = textwidth( str );
                        ydim = textheight( str );
                        xloc- -; break;
        case VERT_DIR : ydim = textwidth( str );
                        xdim = textheight( str );
                        yloc++;
```

```
      }
      switch( textinfo.horiz )                    /* adjust horizontal */
      {
         case    LEFT_TEXT:                             break;
         case CENTER_TEXT:  xloc -= xdim / 2;   break;
         case  RIGHT_TEXT:  xloc -= xdim;
      }
      switch( textinfo.vert )                     /* adjust vertical   */
      {
         case BOTTOM_TEXT:  yloc -= ydim;          break;
         case CENTER_TEXT:  yloc -= ydim / 2;   break;
         case    TOP_TEXT:  ;
      }
      while( xloc<0 ) { xloc++; xdim- -; }       /* if offscreen */
      while( yloc<0 ) { yloc++; ydim- -; }       /* move back    */
      textimage = malloc(
                     imagesize( xloc, yloc, xdim, ydim ) );
      getimage( xloc, yloc, xloc+xdim, yloc+ydim,
               textimage );
      putimage( xloc, yloc, textimage, XOR_PUT );
      free( textimage );              /* release memory allocated */
}                                            /* end EraseStr */


   /*=================================================*/
   /* GPRINTF: Used like PRINTF except the output is  */
   /* sent to the screen in graphics mode at the      */
   /* specified co-ordinate. Depending on text dir-   */
   /* ection, xloc or yloc coordinate is returned     */
   /* offset according to the string (font) height.   */
   /*=================================================*/

void gprintf( int *xloc, int *yloc, char *fmt, ... )
{
   va_list argptr;                    /* argument list pointer   */
   char    str[140];                  /* buffer to build string  */
   struct textsettingstype  textinfo;
   int    pos_adj = *xloc;            /* default position        */
   va_start( argptr, fmt );           /* init va_ functions      */
   vsprintf( str, fmt, argptr );      /* add to str buffer       */
   gettextsettings( &textinfo );         /* check settings       */
   outtextxy( pos_adj, *yloc, str );     /* write string         */
```

```
   switch ( textinfo.direction )             /* adjust next    */
   {
      case HORIZ_DIR: *yloc += textheight( str ) + 2;
                      break;
      case  VERT_DIR: *xloc += textheight( str ) + 2;
   };
   va_end( argptr );                      /* close va_ functions  */
}                                              /* end GPRINTF    */


  /*===================================================*/
  /* GPRINTC: Used like GPRINTF except the area where  */
  /* the text will be written to the screen is first   */
  /* reset to the background color.                    */
  /*===================================================*/
void gprintc( int *xloc, int *yloc, char *fmt, ... )
{
   va_list argptr;                  /* argument list pointer   */
   char    str[140];                /* buffer to build string  */
   struct  textsettingstype  textinfo;
   int     pos_adj = *xloc;            /* default position    */

   va_start( argptr, fmt );            /* init va_ functions */
   vsprintf( str, fmt, argptr );       /* add to str buffer  */
   gettextsettings( &textinfo );       /* check settings     */
   erasestr( *xloc, *yloc, str );        /* erase the area */
   outtextxy( pos_adj, *yloc, str );     /* write string    */
   switch ( textinfo.direction )
   {                                      /* adjust for next */
      case HORIZ_DIR: *yloc += textheight( str ) + 2;
                      break;
      case  VERT_DIR: *xloc += textheight( str ) + 2;
   };
   va_end( argptr );                   /* close va_ functions  */
}                                         /* end GPRINTC   */
```

```
/*=====================================================*/
/* GPRINTXY: Used like GPRINTC except the area where */
/* screen coordinates are passed by value rather     */
/* than passed by address pointer.                   */
/*=====================================================*/

void gprintxy( int xloc, int yloc, char *fmt, ... )
{
   va_list argptr;                  /* argument list pointer */
   char    str[140];                /* buffer to build string */
   struct  textsettingstype  textinfo;
   va_start( argptr, fmt );         /* init va_ functions */
   vsprintf( str, fmt, argptr );    /* add to str buffer  */
   gettextsettings( &textinfo );
   erasestr( xloc, yloc, str );     /* erase the area     */
   outtextxy( xloc, yloc, str );    /* write string       */
   va_end( argptr );                /* close va_ function */
}                                    /* end GPRINTXY       */
           /* ===== end GPRINT.I ===== */


   /*=====================================================*/
   /*                  PRN_DEMO.C                        */
   /* show horizontal and vertical text justification */
   /*=====================================================*/

#ifdef __TINY__
#error GRAPHICS will not run in the tiny model.
#endif

#include <dos.h>
#include <math.h>
#include <conio.h>
#include <stdio.h>
#include <stdlib.h>
#include <stdarg.h>
#include <graphics.h>
#include "gprint.i"              /* added graph print functions */

int     GraphDriver;             /* graphics device driver */
int     GraphMode;               /* graphics mode value    */
int     MaxX, MaxY;              /* max screen resolution  */
int     MaxColors;               /* max available colors   */
```

```c
int        ErrorCode = 0;              /* report graphic errors */
struct    palettetype    palette;      /* read palette info */

void Initialize()
{
   GraphDriver = DETECT;               /* request auto-detect  */
   initgraph( &GraphDriver, &GraphMode, "C:\\TC\BGI" );
   ErrorCode = graphresult();          /* read init results    */
   if ( ErrorCode != grOk )            /* if error during init */
   {
       printf(" Graphics System Error: %s\n",
               grapherrormsg( ErrorCode ) );
       exit( 1 );
   }
   getpalette( &palette );             /* read the palette */
   MaxColors = getmaxcolor() + 1;      /* read max colors  */
   MaxX = getmaxx();                   /* set viewport size */
   MaxY = getmaxy();
}

void StatusLine( char *msg )
{
   int height;
   setcolor( MaxColors - 1 );          /* set color to white */
   settextstyle( DEFAULT_FONT, HORIZ_DIR, 1 );
   settextjustify( CENTER_TEXT, TOP_TEXT );
   height = textheight( "H" );         /* determine height  */
   rectangle( 0, MaxY-(height+4), MaxX, MaxY );
   outtextxy( MaxX/2, MaxY-(height+2), msg );
}

void Pause()
{
   static char msg[] = "Press any key ...";
   StatusLine( msg );        /* put msg at bottom of screen */
   while( kbhit() ) getch();
   getch();
}

main()
{
   int i, xax = 50, yax = 100;
```

```
Initialize();
setfillstyle( CLOSE_DOT_FILL, BLUE );
bar( 0, 0, MaxX, MaxY );
if( MaxColors > 4 ) setcolor(RED);
line( 0, yax, getmaxx()/3, yax );
settextstyle( 3, VERT_DIR, 3 );
if( MaxColors > 4 ) setcolor(GREEN);
line( xax, yax-100, xax, yax+100 );
if( MaxColors > 4 ) setcolor(WHITE);
settextjustify( LEFT_TEXT, CENTER_TEXT );
gprintc( &xax, &yax, "LEFT_TEXT" );

xax = 100;
if( MaxColors > 4 ) setcolor(GREEN);
line( xax, yax-100, xax, yax+100 );
if( MaxColors > 4 ) setcolor(WHITE);
settextjustify( CENTER_TEXT, CENTER_TEXT );
gprintc( &xax, &yax, "CENTER_TEXT" );

xax = 150;
if( MaxColors > 4 ) setcolor(GREEN);
line( xax, yax-100, xax, yax+100 );
if( MaxColors > 4 ) setcolor(WHITE);
settextjustify( RIGHT_TEXT, CENTER_TEXT );
gprintc( &xax, &yax, "RIGHT_TEXT" );
if( MaxColors > 4 ) setcolor(GREEN);

xax = 450;
line( xax, yax-100, xax, yax+100 );
settextstyle( 3, HORIZ_DIR, 3 );

yax = 30;
if( MaxColors > 4 ) setcolor(RED);
line( xax-200, yax, xax+200, yax );
if( MaxColors > 4 ) setcolor(WHITE);
settextjustify( CENTER_TEXT, BOTTOM_TEXT );
gprintc( &xax, &yax, "BOTTOM_TEXT" );

yax = 40;
if( MaxColors > 4 ) setcolor(RED);
line( xax-200, yax, xax+200, yax );
if( MaxColors > 4 ) setcolor(WHITE);
```

```
settextjustify( CENTER_TEXT, TOP_TEXT );
gprintc( &xax, &yax, "TOP_TEXT" );

yax = 100;
if( MaxColors > 4 ) setcolor(RED);
line( xax-200, yax, xax+200, yax );
if( MaxColors > 4 ) setcolor(WHITE);
settextjustify( LEFT_TEXT, CENTER_TEXT );
gprintc( &xax, &yax, "LEFT_TEXT" );

yax = 130;
if( MaxColors > 4 ) setcolor(RED);
line( xax-200, yax, xax+200, yax );
if( MaxColors > 4 ) setcolor(WHITE);
settextjustify( CENTER_TEXT, CENTER_TEXT );
gprintc( &xax, &yax, "CENTER_TEXT" );

yax = 160;
if( MaxColors > 4 ) setcolor(RED);
line( xax-200, yax, xax+200, yax );
if( MaxColors > 4 ) setcolor(WHITE);
settextjustify( RIGHT_TEXT, CENTER_TEXT );
gprintc( &xax, &yax, "RIGHT_TEXT" );

Pause();
closegraph();                    /* return system to text mode   */
}
```

Part Two

Using Turbo C++ Graphics

In the first section of this book, I discussed the various Turbo C++ graphics commands and briefly illustrated some of them. In Part Two, these commands will be used to create graphics and utilities and to demonstrate how various procedures and applications can be created.

The demonstrations will include combining text and graphics, creating two- and three-dimensional graph displays for business applications, simple animation techniques, turtle graphics, image manipulation with rotations in two and three dimensions, image file storage, using a mouse with graphics displays, and creating custom graphics fonts. Since programs must operate on a variety of hardware with varying resolutions and color capabilities, techniques for adapting to various hardware will be shown.

Caveat

Most of these demonstrations have been created specifically for use with EGA or higher resolution graphics hardware using a color monitor. When practical, additional code has been included for adaptation to CGA or monographic equipment, however, some modification of the source codes may be necessary for lower resolution modes.

While lower resolution and monochrome equipment is graphics-capable, 640x350 color provides a good minimum standard for demonstrating graphics applications. If these applications and demonstrations were written to operate only under the limitations of the lowest common resolutions and color capabilities, a great deal of real capability would necessarily be ignored.

The EGA vertical resolution of 350 pixels provides space to show far more detail than is possible with 200 pixels (though the 1,024 vertical resolution of the IBM-8514 would be nice). A palette of 16 colors certainly shows more visual information than monochrome. The utilities demonstrated here will make use of these capabilities whenever possible, even though they are not universally available.

Since VGA monitors are becoming increasingly common—and are making a strong bid to become the new standard—wherever practical, provisions have been included to optimize graphic examples for VGA resolutions.

Also, while Turbo C++ supports both conventional and object-oriented programming, the demo programs in Part Two use conventional programming practices only, even though many of these could be converted to object-oriented practices. Object-graphic practices are reserved for Part Three: *Advanced Graphics Programming*.

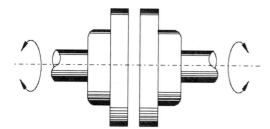

Chapter 9

Business Graph Displays

Business applications often require graphic displays to show sales figures, financial information, stock price fluctuations, and other types of numerical data. A graph display makes information easier to understand than a column of figures and a graph offers convenient visual comparisons making trends, irregularities, and shifts much more obvious than the numbers themselves. Graph displays are far more impressive than mere alphanumerical displays. Given the vagaries of human nature, this last consideration, a visually impressive display, usually outweighs the first two.

The business graphs demonstrated here have been created with visual appeal in mind, using colors and fill patterns where possible. In some cases they have been designed to be more visually impressive than visually informative. Granted, this is a purely subjective distinction, but it is also one that you will need to be aware of when creating graphs and selecting the styles of display, patterns, and colors.

A Cautionary Note

When creating a graph display, restraint is the best virtue. It is possible not only to include too much information in a graph, but also for the resulting graphic display to be rendered unintelligible because of an excess of artistic style, information, or cross-correlation.

The first purpose of a graph is to present information in a manner and style that shows correlations between figures. This primary function should not be overshadowed and defeated by colors, patterns, labels, logos, or other elements intended to make the information eye-catching. Concentrate on the information first, the entertainment second.

The Business Graph Demos

While there are at least several hundred types and styles of business graphs possible, five basic graph displays will be illustrated in this chapter: pie graphs, bar graphs, multiple bar graphs, 3-D bar graphs, and line graphs. (To print graph displays, see Chapter 14.)

The first four graph types have been combined in a single demo program, while the line graph demo is created separately. Each of the first four graph styles will present the same data, but in a different format. The demo program will pause after each graph, waiting for a keystroke. The last graph demo (3-D graphs) will show several displays with different depths, pausing after each display.

The data used for the demo have been written as two arrays: one of *integer* and one of *char*. In actual practice, this information would be read from external sources such as spreadsheet data, database files, internally created data arrays, or from data files created by your own program(s).

```
int Accounts[4][9] =
    { 1985, 133, 35, 33, 17, 29, 15, 17, 32,
      1986, 122, 41, 30, 25, 18, 24, 43, 21,
      1987, 111, 65, 57, 14, 17, 39, 32, 17,
      1988, 100, 60, 70, 12, 16, 13, 17, 12 };
char *AccTypes[9] =
    { "   ", "Motor", "Acsry", "Reprs", "Govmt",
      "Lease", "Tires", "Paint", "Misc" };
```

The dummy data sets shown are an anonymous corporation's income figures for four years, broken into eight categories. You may experiment with the graph displays by changing the figures in any fashion.

The Pie Graph Displays

Four pie graphs (see Figure 9-1), one for each year's data, are created using the function Draw_Pie_Graphs. Three parameters are used, the first specifying the array index for the year, the second and third specifying the *x* and *y* screen positions where the pie graph will be centered.

```
void Draw_Pie_Graphs()
{
    int  Y1 = getmaxy() * 0.275,
         Y2 = getmaxy() * 0.725;

    cleardevice();
    graphdefaults();
    rectangle( 0, 0, MaxX, MaxY );
    Pie_Graph( 0, 150, Y1 );
    Pie_Graph( 1, 450, Y1 );
    Pie_Graph( 2, 150, Y2 );
    Pie_Graph( 3, 450, Y2 );
}
```

As accommodation for different vertical resolutions, the y-axis positions for the pie graphs are calculated, not absolute. This display is valid for CGA, however, EGA or higher resolutions with color are recommended.

When Pie_Graph is called, several local variables are established: total is initialized as zero and will be used to determine the total value of all data elements so that the slices can be apportioned correctly; m is initialized as 135 and will be used to position the year label; s and t are initialized as zero and will be used for start and end angles for each slice.

```
void Pie_Graph( int dataset, int x, int y )
{
    int i, m = 135, r, s = 0, t = 0, HJust, VJust;
    int total = 0;
    int Blank_Line = 0x0000;
    int CapColor;
    struct arccoordstype arcrec;
```

The *Blank_Line* variable is also initialized as zero and will be used to draw an invisible line for positioning labels around the pie graph. The elaboration of 0x0000 is not necessary, a simple 0 would suffice. To define a less empty line style, a four-digit hexadecimal specification is necessary and this form has been followed here.

In the first step, all of the items for the current year (dataset) are totalled and the radius, r, is set to $1/4$ of the total.

```
    for( i=1; i<=8; i++ )
        total += Accounts[dataset][i];
    r = total / 4;
```

Figure 9-1: Multiple Pie Graphs

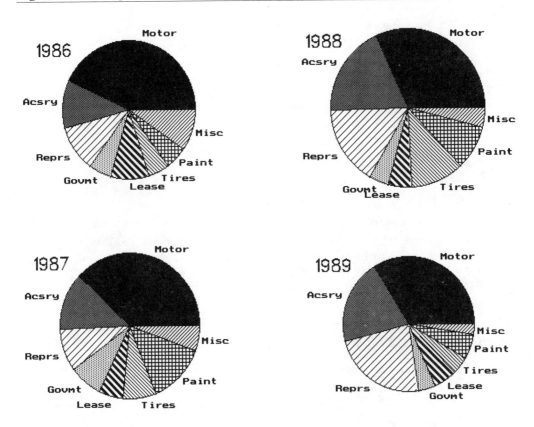

Pie Graphs show a four-year financial breakdown for a fictitious company. The graph was created by GRAPHALL.C in color on a VGA screen and captured directly as a .PCX image. For formal reports, however, this same image could be downloaded to a laserjet printer in GREYSCALE mode using the LJ_GRAPH utility.

Since there are only eight items for each year, the actual integer can be used in the loop. In other applications, the number of elements might vary and a different method of controlling the loop may be preferred. This could be using an index element, *Elements*:

```
for( i=1; i<=Elements; i++ )
```

Or, by calculating the number of elements:

```
for( i=1;
     i<=(sizeof(Accounts)/years*sizeof(integer));
     i++ )
```

Now that there's a radius, you can put a label for the year on the screen (before drawing the pie graph). Instead of arbitrarily positioning the label—and having to create a new label position for each data set—it is preferable to be able to calculate the position.

You could calculate a position since you know the radius (*r*). There is, however, a more elegant method that will be used repeatedly as the pie graph is drawn. When Pie_Graph was called, the *m* variable was initialized at 135, an angle that will be toward the top left of the eventual pie graph.

The line style is set to *Blank_Line*, which was previously defined as 0x0000, and the fill style is set to 0 (EMPTY_FILL), and fill color to 0 (BLACK).

```
setlinestyle( USERBIT_LINE, Blank_Line, NORM_WIDTH );
setfillstyle( 0, 0 );
```

Next, the pieslice function is called with the *x* and *y* center coordinates to draw a pie slice beginning at the angle *m* and ending at the angle *m+1* with a radius of *r+10*. A minimum angle width of one degree is required. Also, using a radius 10 pixels greater than the one that will be used for the pie graph, yields a position outside the eventual graph image.

```
pieslice( x, y, m, m+1, r+10 );
                    /* must have ONE DEGREE minimum width */
getarccoords( &arcrec );
```

The pie slice drawn in this case will be invisible, but it does yield a screen position that can be retrieved by calling getarccoords. Before doing anything with this information the current color, text style, direction, and justification need to be set.

```
if( MaxColors > 4 ) setcolor( WHITE );
settextstyle( SANS_SERIF_FONT, HORIZ_DIR, 2 );
settextjustify( RIGHT_TEXT, BOTTOM_TEXT );
```

Now, the gprintf function can be called with the *xend* and *yend* coordinates in *arcrec* and the year data, which is the 0th element in each *Accounts[dataset]*, is written to the screen.

```
gprintf( &arcrec.xend, &arcrec.yend,
         "%d", Accounts[dataset][0] );
```

Remember, getarccoords returns a data record that contains the start and end *x* and *y* screen coordinates for the last call to any of the arc, circle, ellipse, or pieslice functions.

This particular method of calculation to determine an appropriate screen position for a label, will be used several times while the pie graph is being drawn in order to position a label correctly for each pie slice. Before proceeding, the default text style is selected and, if practical, the drawing color is reset.

```
settextstyle( DEFAULT_FONT, HORIZ_DIR, 1 );
if( MaxColors > 4 ) setcolor( EGA_YELLOW );
```

At this point, the actual pie slices are drawn, again using a loop for a known number of data elements:

```
for( i=1; i<=8; i++ )
{
```

The fill style and color are arbitrarily changed for each slice. In this application, on a monochrome system, the fill color setting can be ignored, though the drawing color is not so inconsequential. Also, the line settings are reset to a solid line before a new pie slice is created.

```
setfillstyle( i, i );
if( MaxColors > 4 ) setcolor( WHITE );
setlinestyle( SOLID_LINE, 0, NORM_WIDTH );
```

The end angle for the pie slice is calculated as the proportional angle. As you will notice, all of the calculations are being carried out as double values for accuracy, with the final result being returned to an integer value since the pieslice function does not accept float or double. Also, the calculated value has been incremented by 0.5, before truncation, to round the results to the nearest integer instead of the next lowest integer.

```
t += (int) ( 360 * (double) Accounts[dataset][i]
                / (double) total + 0.5 );
```

If any angle is returned greater than 360 degrees—an error that is unlikely except on the final slice—then the value is arbitrarily fixed at 360 to prevent a confusing display. Likewise, if the last pie slice does not complete the circle, if *t* is less than 360, then a correction is made to keep the pie graph neatly finished. This type of error is not unlikely when a number of angles are calculated, each being rounded to the nearest integer value. However, the cumulative error should not exceed one degree per slice. In this example, a maximum error of eight degrees is possible.

```
if( t > 360 ) t = 360;
if( i == 8 ) if( t < 360 ) t = 360;
```

Depending on your application, you may wish to arrange matters so that the correction is either added to the largest individual slice or apportioned among the various slices.

Next, the actual pie slice is created using the x and y center coordinates, the start angle s, the end angle t, and the radius r.

```
pieslice( x, y, s, t, r );
```

Now it is time to reset the line style to *Blank_Line* and to reset the fill style and fill color to EMPTY_FILL and BLACK. Also, the working *CapColor* is set to the bright equivalent of the fill color used for the last pie slice ($i+8$) and, if practical, the drawing color is set to *CapColor*.

```
setlinestyle( USERBIT_LINE, Blank_Line, NORM_WIDTH );
setfillstyle( 0, 0 );
CapColor = i+8;
if( CapColor > WHITE ) CapColor = DARKGREY;
if( MaxColors > 4 ) setcolor( CapColor );
```

At this point, the program is repeating the same operation that was used to position the year number before this pie graph was started, but with a slight difference. The angle m becomes the mid-angle between the start and end angles of the current pie slice and, again, an invisible pie slice is drawn and getarccoords returns the screen coordinates for the endpoints.

```
m = ( t - s ) / 2 + s;
pieslice( x, y, m, m+1, r+5 );
getarccoords( &arcrec );
```

The next step arranges the vertical and horizontal text justification settings so that the label for the current pie slice will be positioned outside the pie graph. Also, outtextxy is called to write the label *AccTypes[i]* to the screen.

```
if( arcrec.xend > x ) HJust = LEFT_TEXT;
                  else HJust = RIGHT_TEXT;
```

```
if( arcrec.yend > y ) VJust = TOP_TEXT;
               else VJust = BOTTOM_TEXT;
settextjustify( HJust, VJust );
outtextxy( arcrec.xend, arcrec.yend, AccTypes[i] );
```

Finally, the current end angle becomes the start angle for the next pie slice and the loop continues.

```
    s = t;
}   }
```

Exploded Pie Graphs

The technique that was used to position the labels for the pie graph can also be used to produce an exploded pie graph—a pie graph in which one or more segments are offset from the center to emphasize a specific segment. In order to keep the symmetry of the overall pie graph, the offset should be at the proper angle, the mid-angle of the slice.

The following example code will provide a five-pixel radius offset by first creating an invisible pie slice.

```
setlinestyle( USERBIT_LINE, Blank_Line, NORM_WIDTH );
setfillstyle( 0, 0 );
m = ( t - s ) / 2 + s;
pieslice( x, y, m, m+1, 5 );
getarccoords( &arcrec );
```

Then the fill style and drawing colors are reset.

```
setfillstyle( i, i );
if( MaxColors > 4 ) setcolor( WHITE );
setlinestyle( SOLID_LINE, 0, NORM_WIDTH );
```

And the offset pie slice is created, centered on the *arcrec* coordinates of the invisible slice.

```
pieslice( arcrec.xend, arcrec.yend, s, t, r );
```

The label for this slice will also require its position to be calculated with the additional five units radius in order to be proportionally located.

Bar Graph

While pie graphs are visually more impressive, bar graphs offer a clear visual comparison of magnitude. Most often, bar graphs are drawn vertically, as in the demonstration program, but they can also be presented horizontally.

While the Pie_Graph function does not compensate for horizontal resolutions less than 640 pixels, the function Bar_Graph (see Figure 9-2) adjusts the graphic presentation to fit both the vertical and horizontal resolutions of the screen and graphics mode in use. It begins by setting width to *MaxX* and height to *MaxY*.

```
void Bar_Graph( )
{
   int width = MaxX, height = MaxY, left = 0, top = 0;
   int i, j, hstep, vstep, bottom, x, y, barhigh;
```

Now a viewport (window) is created, leaving a margin at the top for the labels that will later be written along the side. Then *width* is decremented by 30 to leave space for amount labels. The horizontal graph step (*hstep*) is calculated from the width variable to provide for 32 columns, and the vertical step (*vstep*) is calculated from the height variable. Finally, the *bottom* variable is set to six times the vertical step.

```
   setviewport( left, top+5,
                left+width, top+height+5, 0 );
   width -= 30;
   hstep = width/32;
   vstep = height/6;
   bottom = vstep*6;
```

In this particular instance, the graph is being divided vertically into six increments, each increment to be 25 units (which might be dollars, pounds, yen in hundreds, thousands or similar units). In an application where the range of values is not known in advance, you might prefer your program to test for the highest value that will be displayed and then create graph increments accordingly, numbering the vertical scale marks as appropriate. (See the Line_Graph function for an example.)

Horizontally, the bars will be grouped in units of four, placing each type of entry, from each of the four year's data, together. Vertical markers are drawn every fourth *hstep*:

```
   if( MaxColors > 4 ) setcolor( GREEN );
   for( i=0; i<=hstep*32; i+=hstep*4 )
      line( i, 0, i, vstep*6 );
```

Horizontal scale lines are drawn for each *vstep*:

```
if( MaxColors > 4 ) setcolor( CYAN );
for( i=0; i<=bottom; i+=vstep )
   line( 0, i, hstep*32, i );
```

With the scaling grid completed, the *bottom* variable is moved up one pixel so that the bars will not overwrite the base of the grid:

```
bottom- -;
```

Now the drawing color, text style, and fonts are set and the unit increments (the horizontal lines) are labeled beginning with 150 at the top, and decreasing in steps of 25 until 0 is reached at the bottom.

Figure 9-2: Bar Graphs

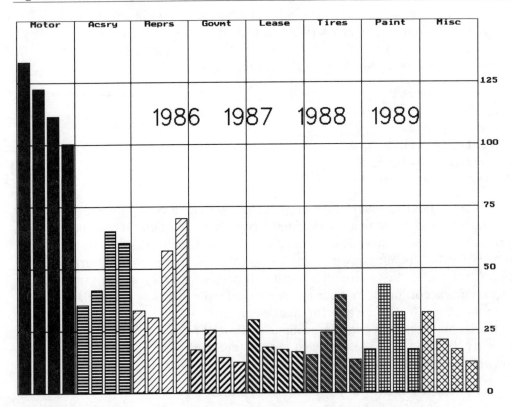

Bar graphs show a four-year financial breakdown for a fictitious company. The graph was created by GRAPHALL.C in color on a VGA screen and captured directly as a .PCX image.

```
if( MaxColors > 4 ) setcolor( WHITE );
settextstyle( DEFAULT_FONT, HORIZ_DIR, 1 );
settextjustify( CENTER_TEXT, CENTER_TEXT );
for ( i=0; i<7; i++ )
{
   x = hstep*32 + 15;
   y = i*vstep;
   gprintf( &x, &y, "%d", 150-i*25 );
}
```

Now, with the background grid complete, it's time to create the bars themselves. The height of the bar will be calculated as a vertical offset from *bottom*, scaled as 25 units per vertical step.

```
for ( i=1; i<=8; i++ )
{
   for ( j=0; j<4; j++ )
   {
      barhigh = bottom - Accounts[j][i]
                  * (double) vstep / (double) 25;
```

If the current video system is color capable in high resolution, then a new outline color (drawing color) and fill color are used for each year's bar. Otherwise, only the fill style is changed and the draw and fill colors are kept as WHITE (*MaxColors-1*).

```
      if( MaxColors > 4 ) setcolor( j+1 );
      if( MaxColors > 4 ) setfillstyle( i, j+1 );
                  else setfillstyle( i, MaxColors-1 );
```

Even though a two-dimensional graph is being created, the bar3d function is used, but with a depth of 0 specified. The bar function does not draw an outline, but only creates a bar using the fill style and color. The bar3d function provides an outline in the current drawing color and creates a better appearance. Alternatively, the rectangle function could be called to draw an outline and then bar called to fill in the area. The effects would have been identical, but slower.

```
      bar3d( (i-1)*hstep*4 + j*hstep + 2,          barhigh,
             (i-1)*hstep*4 + j*hstep + hstep-2, bottom,
             0, 0 );
   }                                    /* end of loop for j */
```

As the last step within this loop, after each set of four bars for the four years' data have been drawn, the drawing color is reset to WHITE and a label is written at the top of the bar graph column.

```
    if( MaxColors > 4 ) setcolor( WHITE );
    outtextxy( i*hstep*4-hstep*2, 5, AccTypes[i] );
}                                      /* end of loop for i */
```

Finally, if high resolution and color are supported, then the four year numbers are added to the screen, with the colors corresponding to the drawing color and fill color used for each bar. If the system is monochrome, there is little purpose in this unless you simply want to show the years. You might, however, modify the code to draw a small block next to each year number, using the corresponding year's fill style.

```
    if( MaxColors > 4 )
    {
        x = MaxX/2;
        y = MaxY/4;
        settextstyle( DEFAULT_FONT, HORIZ_DIR, 2 );
        for (i=0; i<4; i++)
        {
            setcolor(i+1);
            gprintf( &x, &y, "%d", Accounts[i][0] );
            x += textwidth(" ");
}  }  }
```

Multiple Bar Graphs

Combining several years' data in a single bar graph allows for convenient comparison between different years (see Figure 9-3). However, it also makes the comparison between the different categories within each year as well as viewing each year as a whole, difficult. There are times when separate graphs for each year are more useful (and sometimes more impressive) than a single, combined graph. The Draw_Multi_Graphs function creates four graphs on a single screen, one for each year's data.

```
void Draw_Multi_Graphs()
{
    Multi_Bar_Graph( 0, 0, 0 );
    Multi_Bar_Graph( 1, MaxX/2, 0 );
    Multi_Bar_Graph( 2, 0, MaxY/2 );
    Multi_Bar_Graph( 3, MaxX/2, MaxY/2 );
}
```

Figure 9-3: Multiple Bar Graphs

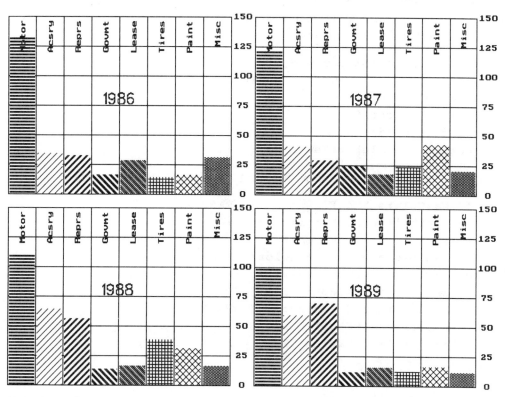

Multiple bar graphs show a four-year financial breakdown for a fictitious company. The graph was created by GRAPHALL.C in color on a VGA screen and captured directly as a .PCX image.

Like Bar_Graph, the function Multi_Bar_Graph adjusts the graphic presentation to fit both the vertical and horizontal resolutions of the screen and graphics mode in use, beginning by setting width to *MaxX/2* and height to *MaxY/2-13*. The height setting includes a 13-pixel margin and the width setting includes a 30-pixel margin allowing for better visual appearance.

```
void Multi_Bar_Graph( int dataset, int left, int top )
{
    int    width  = MaxX/2-30;
    int    height = MaxY/2-13;
    int    i, hstep, vstep, bottom, x, y;
    double   scale;
```

The viewport and scaling factors are set up essentially the same as in the Bar_Graph function, except that only eight bars will be arranged horizontally. Also a vertical scaling factor is calculated as the variable scale, instead of executing a separate scaling calculation each time.

```
setviewport( left, top+5,
              left+width, top+height+5, 0 );
hstep = width/8;
vstep = height/6;
tom = vstep*6;
scale = (double) vstep / 25;
```

A background grid is written with scale factors along the right margin.

```
if( MaxColors > 4 ) setcolor( GREEN );
for( i=0; i<=hstep*8; i+=hstep )
    line( i, 0, i, vstep*6 );
if( MaxColors > 4 ) setcolor( CYAN );
for( i=0; i<=bottom; i+=vstep )
    line( 0, i, hstep*8, i );
if( MaxColors > 4 ) setcolor( WHITE );
settextstyle( DEFAULT_FONT, HORIZ_DIR, 1 );
settextjustify( CENTER_TEXT, CENTER_TEXT );
for( i=0; i<7; i++ )
{
    x = hstep*8 + 15;
    y = i*vstep;
    gprintf( &x, &y, "%d", 150-i*25 );
}
```

The graph is created for the selected year's data and is similar to Bar_Graph, but has one principal difference. Because single bars will need to be labeled and are not wide enough for horizontal text labels, the vertical text direction is selected. The labels will be centered horizontally over each bar and flush against a point that is five pixels below the top of the viewport.

If you are using an EGA or higher resolution system, you should notice that the labels appear clearly in white even though some partially overlie a colored bar. This is also the reason why the bar function, instead of the bar3d function, was used: because an outline might have made the overlying captions more difficult to read. In monochrome modes, however, this becomes a major problem. An alternative will be shown momentarily.

```
settextstyle( DEFAULT_FONT, VERT_DIR, 1 );
settextjustify( CENTER_TEXT, TOP_TEXT );
for( i=0; i<=7; i++ )
{
   if( MaxColors > 4 ) setfillstyle( i+1, i+1 );
      else setfillstyle( i+1, MaxColors-1 );
   bar( i*hstep+2,
        bottom-scale*Accounts[dataset][i+1]-1,
        (i+1)*hstep-2,   bottom-1 );
   outtextxy( i*hstep+hstep/2, 5, AccTypes[i+1] );
}
```

As a last step, the year's data is written to each graph:

```
settextstyle( SANS_SERIF_FONT, HORIZ_DIR, 2 );
settextjustify( CENTER_TEXT, BOTTOM_TEXT );
x = width/2;
y = height/2-4;
gprintf( &x, &y, "%d", Accounts[dataset][0] );
}
```

Improving the Monochrome Display

As mentioned, there is a problem with monochrome display modes where
a label overwrites a bar, resulting in the label not being legible. There is,
however, a simple method you can use with a monochrome display. First,
in the function Multi_Bar_Graph, add a variable declaration for a pointer
to caption.

```
void    *caption;
```

Viewport, text, and color settings are made as before and the background
grid lines are drawn. Then, in the loop before drawing the bar, the erasestr
function (defined in Chapter 8 and included in gprint.i) is called to erase
the area where the label will be written and the label is sent to the screen.

```
for( i=0; i<=7; i++ )
{
   x = i*hstep+hstep/2;
   y = 5;
   erasestr( x, y, AccTypes[i+1] );
   outtextxy( x, y, AccTypes[i+1] );
```

Next, memory space is allocated for the caption:

```
caption = malloc(
    imagesize( x, y, textheight( AccTypes[i+1] ),
                      textwidth( AccTypes[i+1] ) ) );
```

Because horizontal justification was set to CENTER_TEXT, x is offset by half the string height of *AccTypes[i+1]* to ensure that the correct image area is read.

```
x -= textheight(AccTypes[i+1])/2;
```

Now the getimage function reads the label image from the screen as caption, then putimage uses the XOR_PUT option to erase the label momentarily.

```
getimage( x, y,
          x+textheight(AccTypes[i+1]),
          y+textwidth(AccTypes[i+1]),
          caption );
putimage( x, y, caption, XOR_PUT );
```

The bar is drawn as before:

```
if( MaxColors > 4 ) setfillstyle( i+1, i+1 );
              else setfillstyle( i+1, MaxColors-1 );
bar( i*hstep+2,
     bottom-scale*Accounts[dataset][i+1]-1,
     (i+1)*hstep-2,    bottom-1 );
```

And then putimage is called again with the XOR_PUT option to eXclusively-OR the *caption* image with the screen image. The result is that the portion of the label which overlies a bar is now a visible black on white instead of an invisible white on white.

```
putimage( x, y, caption, XOR_PUT );
```

Finally, the memory allocated to caption is released.

```
free( caption );
}
```

This same modification can be used with color displays but the effects may not be what you expect. Remember, eXclusively-ORing WHITE with

WHITE produces BLACK, but eXclusively-ORing WHITE with BLUE produces YELLOW.

Incidentally, if you are using an EGA/VGA system, delete the line in the Initialize function in the GRAPHALL.C demo that reads:

```
GraphDriver = DETECT;
```

Add the instructions:

```
GraphDriver = CGA;
GraphMode = CGAHI;
```

This will force your system to emulate a CGA system and demonstrate the difficulties in a monochrome display. This is also a good way to test your programs to see how they will execute on a CGA system, without having to move your program to another computer.

Three-Dimensional Graphs

While Turbo C++ provides the bar3d function for a three-dimensional bar graph (see Figure 9-4), creating a 3-D graph display is more complicated.

In its simplest form, a 3-D bar graph is simply a flat bar graph with the bars drawn using bar3d to provide an illusion of depth, but with only a single horizontal row of bars. At some point you're probably going to want to use the three-dimensional effect to display several rows of bars with the illusion of depth in the arrangement of the rows, as well as in the bars themselves. This creates further complexity.

First, the 3-D bars created by bar3d can be generated with different depths. Second, for best appearance, a three-dimensional graph requires a three-dimensional setting, with scaling lines and an overall appearance of depth corresponding to the depth aspect of the individual bars. Third, everything must be tied together in an consistent whole, rather than appearing to be merely an assemblage of scattered parts.

In a purely rational sense, a 3-D bar graph is not as informative as a series of flat bar graphs. Visually, it is difficult to discern the relative heights of the various bars and how a specific bar aligns with the background scale lines. The more important consideration here is that the three-dimensional graph is visually very impressive.

The same data that has been presented in the form of pie and bar graphs, will now be displayed in the form of four rows and eight ranks of three-dimensional columns against a scaled three-dimensional field. Also, Graphs_3D will show the same graph data using a series of *ZAxis* depths in steps of five, from 15 to 40 pixels.

The *XAxis* and *YAxis* variables, which will be the horizontal and vertical scale increments, are assigned values scaled to fit within the current screen size limits, while *XOrg* and *YOrd* provide the screen origin point for all three axes. The graph width (*XWidth*) and height (*YHeight*) are now set to multiples of *XAxis* and *YAxis*, which will remain constant. *ZDepth* will be recalculated for each graph display as the *ZAxis* increment size is changed.

```
void Graphs_3D()
{
    XAxis = MaxX/13;
    YAxis = MaxY/14;
    XOrg = MaxX/3;
    YOrg = MaxY/2;
    XWidth = 8 * XAxis;
    YHeight = 6 * YAxis;
    scale = (double) YAxis / 25;
```

Figure 9-4: Three-Dimensional Bar Graphs

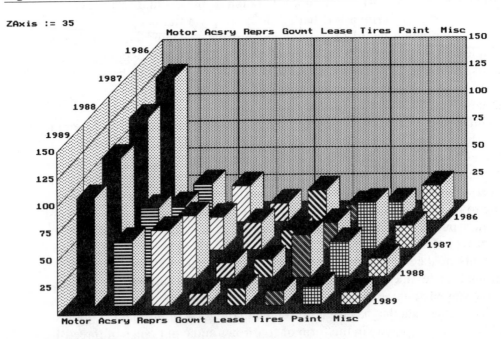

The 3-D bar graph shows a four-year financial breakdown for a fictitious company. The graph was created by GRAPHALL.C in color on a VGA screen and captured directly as a .PCX image.

Graphs_3D loops as long as the display produced by the *ZAxis* value does not exceed the screen limits.

```
for( ZAxis=15; (YOrg+4*ZAxis)<MaxY; ZAxis+=5 )
   Three_D_Graph();
}
```

The Three_D_Graph function creates each graph display, first clearing the screen and setting the z-axis depth for the current *ZAxis*.

```
void Three_D_Graph()
{
   int x, y;
   cleardevice();
   ZDepth  = 4 * ZAxis;
```

A caption is displayed in the upper left corner of screen, showing the current *ZAxis* size; the display background is created by Graph_Field; and the scale lines for each axis are labeled by Show_Labels. The bar graph elements are drawn by the Show_Accounts function. The program pauses for a keystroke before creating the next graph display.

```
   settextjustify( LEFT_TEXT, TOP_TEXT );
   setcolor( MaxColors - 1 );
   x = 10;    y = 10;
   gprintf( &x, &y, "ZAxis = %d", ZAxis );
   Graph_Field();
   Show_Labels();
   Show_Accounts();
   Pause();
}
```

The elements of the overall graph display have been broken down into separate tasks to reduce a complex program to manageable proportions.

The Graph_Field Function

The first of these tasks is the Graph_Field function, which creates a three-dimensional backdrop for the graph, complete with grid lines for all three axes. If color is supported, the Fill_Plane function is used to create three solid planes, rather like three sides of a box, in blue, red, and yellow. These planes will form the background for the display. Fill_Plane is simply a convenient enhancement of the fillpoly function and will be explained in a moment.

```
void Graph_Field()
{
   int i;
   if ( MaxColors > 4 )
   {
      Fill_Plane( XOrg, YOrg, XOrg+XWidth, YOrg,
                  XOrg+XWidth, YOrg-YHeight, XOrg,
                  YOrg-YHeight, SOLID_FILL, LIGHTBLUE );
      Fill_Plane( XOrg, YOrg, XOrg-(ZDepth/AspR),
                  YOrg+ZDepth, XOrg-(ZDepth/AspR),
                  YOrg+ZDepth-YHeight, XOrg,
                  YOrg-YHeight, SOLID_FILL, LIGHTRED );
      Fill_Plane( XOrg, YOrg, XOrg+XWidth, YOrg,
                  XOrg+XWidth-(ZDepth/AspR), YOrg+ZDepth,
                  XOrg-(ZDepth/AspR), YOrg+ZDepth,
                  SOLID_FILL, YELLOW );

   }
```

Next, three lines are drawn from the screen origin point at *XOrg/YOrg*. If the background planes were created, these lines delineate the planes. If the system is using a monochrome display, these axes lines and the following grid lines will serve to create the backdrop.

```
line( XOrg, YOrg, XOrg+XWidth, YOrg );        /* X-axis */
line( XOrg, YOrg, XOrg,  YOrg-YHeight );       /* Y-axis */
line( XOrg, YOrg, XOrg-ZDepth/AspR, YOrg+ZDepth );
                                              /* Z-axis */
```

Notice the z-axis line (above) is adjusted for the screen aspect ratio, *AspR*. This same adjustment will appear in all positioning calculations involving the z-axis to keep the z-axis angle constant (approximately 45°) for all screen resolutions.

```
                                /*   X-axis grid lines */
   if ( MaxColors > 4 ) setcolor(GREEN);
   for ( i = XOrg+XAxis; i <= XOrg+XWidth; i += XAxis )
   {
      line( i, YOrg, i, YOrg-YHeight );
      line( i, YOrg, i-ZDepth/AspR, YOrg+ZDepth  );
   }
                                /*   Y-axis grid lines */
   if ( MaxColors > 4 ) setcolor(CYAN);
```

```
for ( i = YOrg-YAxis; i >= YOrg-YHeight; i -= YAxis )
{
   line( XOrg, i, XOrg+XWidth, i );
   line( XOrg, i, XOrg-ZDepth/AspR, i+ZDepth );
}
                                     /*   Z-axis grid lines */
if ( MaxColors > 4 ) setcolor(RED);
for (i = ZAxis; i <= ZDepth; i += ZAxis)
{
   line( XOrg-i/AspR, YOrg+i,
         XOrg-i/AspR+XWidth,  YOrg+i );
   line( XOrg-i/AspR, YOrg+i,
         XOrg-i/AspR, YOrg-YHeight+i );
}  }
```

The Fill_Plane Function

The Fill_Plane function is simply a convenient method of passing a set of calculated points to be assigned to an integer array (*polygon*), before calling the fillpoly function. This is faster than using the floodfill function and is used several times in this demonstration program to fill large or small areas with either solid colors or patterns. The color value passed (*FColor*) is tested for validity and defaults to WHITE if monochrome graphics are being used.

```
void Fill_Plane( int X1, int Y1, int X2, int Y2,
                 int X3, int Y3, int X4, int Y4,
                 int FStyle, int FColor )
{
   int polygon[10];

   polygon[0] = polygon[8] = X1;
   polygon[1] = polygon[9] = Y1;
   polygon[2] = X2;          polygon[3] = Y2;
   polygon[4] = X3;          polygon[5] = Y3;
   polygon[6] = X4;          polygon[7] = Y4;
   if ( MaxColors < 4 ) FColor = MaxColors - 1;
   setfillstyle( FStyle, FColor );
   fillpoly( 5, polygon );
}
```

The Show_Labels Function

The Show_Labels function displays labels for all three axes of the display, beginning with the vertical magnitude scales along both sides of the display. The right side positions are relatively easy to calculate since they are simply stepped from the *YOrg* position with an x-axis offset equal to *XOrg + XWidth + 15*.

The left side, however, requires both a y-axis offset, which is easily calculated as *ZDepth - i * YAxis*, and an x-axis offset (left from *XOrg*), which is slightly more complicated, but is calculated as *XOrg - ZDepth / AspR - 15*. Remember, the *ZDepth* variable is plotted at an angle so the actual screen offset must be calculated using the screen aspect ratio *AspR* to maintain the 45° screen angle for the z-axis.

```
void Show_Labels()
{
   int i, j, k, l, m;
   settextjustify(CENTER_TEXT,CENTER_TEXT);

   j = XOrg + XWidth + 15;
   l = XOrg - ZDepth / AspR - 15;
   for( i=1; i<7; i++ )
   {
      k = YOrg - i * YAxis;
      gprintf( &j, &k, "%d", i*25 );
      m = YOrg + ZDepth - i * YAxis;
      gprintf( &l, &m, "%d", i*25 );
   }
```

AccTypes labels are written horizontally across the graph's top and bottom:

```
   if ( MaxColors > 4 ) setcolor(LIGHTBLUE);
   j = XOrg + 25;
   l = j - ( ZDepth / AspR );
   m = YOrg + ZDepth + 8;
   k = YOrg - YHeight - 8;
   for( i=1; i<=8; i++ )
   {
      outtextxy( j, k, AccTypes[i] );
      outtextxy( l, m, AccTypes[i] );
      j += 50;
      l += 50;
   }
```

The year dates are written at an angle along the z-axis:

```
if( MaxColors > 4 ) setcolor(LIGHTGREEN);
for( i=0; i<=3; i++ )
{
   j = XOrg - ( i * ZAxis + ZAxis / 2 ) / AspR + 2;
   m = YOrg + i * ZAxis + ZAxis / 2;
   k = m - YHeight;
   l = j + XWidth;
   settextjustify( LEFT_TEXT, TOP_TEXT );
   gprintf( &l, &m, "%4d", Accounts[i][0] );
   settextjustify( RIGHT_TEXT, BOTTOM_TEXT );
   gprintf( &j, &k, "%4d", Accounts[i][0] );
}  }
```

The Show_Accounts Function

The bars for each year could have been drawn using a double loop and incrementing the colors for each year. Instead, four separate loops are used here, permitting the assignment of specific colors for each bar.

```
void Show_Accounts()
{
   int    i;

   if( MaxColors > 4 ) setcolor( EGA_YELLOW );
   for( i=1; i<=8; i++ )
      Add_Bar( i-1, 0, Accounts[0][i] * scale,
               LIGHTCYAN,   CYAN  );
   for( i=1; i<=8; i++ )
      Add_Bar( i-1, 1, Accounts[1][i] * scale,
               LIGHTRED,    RED   );
   for( i=1; i<=8; i++ )
      Add_Bar( i-1, 2, Accounts[2][i] * scale,
               LIGHTBLUE,   BLUE  );
   for( i=1; i<=8; i++ )
      Add_Bar( i-1, 3, Accounts[3][i] * scale,
               LIGHTGREEN, GREEN );
}
```

The Add_Bar Function

The Add_Bar function is used to create and to position the three-dimensional graph bars. The *BarWidth* and *BarDepth* variables that set the size of the bar are initialized as half the x-axis and z-axis step sizes. Making each bar smaller than the spacing between the bars offers a better visual effect. Taller bars do not completely hide smaller bars that lie behind them.

```
void Add_Bar( int left, int bottom, int height,
              int Color1, int Color2 )
{
   int top, right;
   int BarWidth = XAxis / 2;
   int BarDepth = ZAxis / 2;

   if ( MaxColors < 4 )
   {
      Color1 = MaxColors - 1;
      Color2 = MaxColors - 1;
   }
```

The fill style for each bar is incremented from left to right. This helps to make the bars easier to distinguish if the display is in monochrome.

```
   setfillstyle( left+1, Color1 );
```

The left and bottom variables began as integers in the 1..8 and 1..4 ranges describing step positions, but are now converted to the actual screen offset positions while *right* and *top* provide the remaining corner parameters.

```
   left = XOrg + ( left * XAxis )
               - ( ( ( bottom + 0.75 * ZAxis / XAxis )
                  * ZAxis ) / AspR );
   bottom = YOrg + ( ( bottom + 0.75 ) * ZAxis );
   right = left + BarWidth;
   top = bottom - height;
```

At this point, the bar3d function could be used to create the display bars for this graph. There is one flaw in this: the z-axis angle produced by bar3d does not always match the z-axis angle produced by the screen aspect. For this reason, bar3d is called with a 0 depth and the Fill_Plane function is called to create each bar's side and top.

```
   bar3d( left, top, right, bottom, 0, 0 );
   Fill_Plane( right, top,
               right+BarDepth/AspR, top-BarDepth,
               right+BarDepth/AspR, bottom-BarDepth,
```

```
                 right, bottom,
                 CLOSE_DOT_FILL, Color1 );
   Fill_Plane( left, top, right, top,
                 right+BarDepth/AspR, top-BarDepth,
                 left+BarDepth/AspR, top-BarDepth,
                 SOLID_FILL, Color2 );
}
```

If you would like to experiment, comment out the two Fill_Plane calls, set bar3d's depth as *BarDepth/AspR*, and change the final parameter from 0 to 1, in order to put a top on the bar.

The Line Graph Display

The previous demos used the same data set for each graph form. Line graphs, however, are normally used to show six or fewer data sets, with each containing a large number of sequential data points. For demonstration, four data sets will be used, each containing 20 sequential data points. For convenience, as with the previous demo, the data points are contained in a 4 by 20 matrix though, in actual practice, the data would probably be read from some external source or generated within the program.

```
int Accounts[4][20] =
    { 119, 121, 132, 140, 141, 139, 142, 135, 133, 123,
      121, 120, 124, 111, 109, 119, 122, 132, 140, 142,
       97,  99, 100, 107, 119, 123, 137, 148, 159, 160,
      168, 172, 167, 155, 159, 163, 165, 155, 151, 148,
       59,  73,  66,  49,  40,  39,  41,  45,  46,  52,
       56,  59,  60,  56,  51,  54,  55,  53,  72,  75,
       13,  15,  16,  19,  22,  20,  17,  18,  19,  21,
       24,  26,  28,  27,  22,  20,  19,  23,  25,  24 };
int  Years[5] = { 1984, 1985, 1984, 1987, 1988 };
char *AccTypes[4] =
    { "GenMec", "UnvEle", "StrOil", "NrtMfr" };
```

To make the graph visually impressive, a set of four graphic images (see Figure 9-5) will be used in the plot and the procedure Create_Images is used to construct them. In other circumstances, you might prefer to create a series of images separately and to store these as disk files, calling the various images as required. Also, the ICONEDIT utility could be used to create appropriate images.

```
void   *grimage[3];
main()
{
   Initialize();                        /* set graphics mode*/
   Create_Images();
   Line_Graph();
   Pause();
   closegraph();                        /* restore text mode*/
}
```

Figure 9-5: Line Graphs

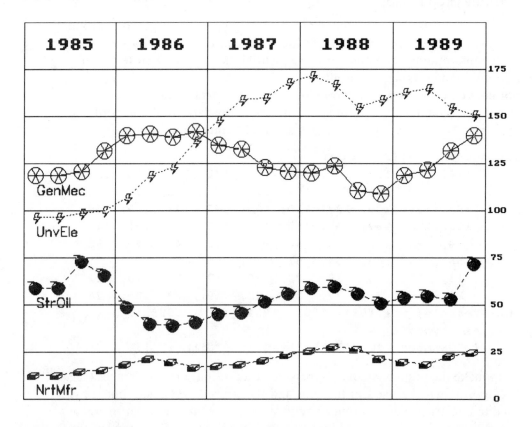

The line graph shows four stocks with bit-images added to deliniate points on the graph. Bit images could also be created (mono or color) using the IconEdit utility demonstrated later in this book. The present graph was created by GRAPHALL.C in color on a VGA screen and captured directly as a .PCX image.

The Create_Images Function

This function is used to generate and save a series of graphic images that will be used to emphasize points on the line graph. The array *figure* is a set of points describing a small stylized lightning bolt.

```
void Create_Images()
{
  int i;
  int figure[] = { 10,   5, 15,   5, 12, 10, 17, 10,
                   10, 18, 12, 13,  8, 13, 10,   5 };
```

The wheel or gear image is created from a series of small pie segments. Please realize that any small arc figure will be grainy. If you need a more detailed figure, it would be best to create an integer bit image after designing your figure on graph paper.

```
if( MaxColors > 4 ) setcolor(2);
for( i=0; i<=5; i++ )
   pieslice( 10, 10, i*60, (i*60)+60, 10 );
grimage[0] = malloc( imagesize( 0, 0, 20, 20 ) );
getimage( 0, 0, 20, 20, grimage[0] );
putimage( 0, 0, grimage[0], XOR_PUT );
```

The lightning bolt image uses the data points in figure and the fillpoly function with the fill style set to EMPTY_FILL.

```
setfillstyle( EMPTY_FILL, 0 );
if( MaxColors > 4 ) setcolor(3);
fillpoly( sizeof(figure)/(2*sizeof(int)), figure );
grimage[1] = malloc( imagesize( 0, 0, 20, 20 ) );
getimage( 0, 0, 20, 20, grimage[1] );
putimage( 0, 0, grimage[1], XOR_PUT );
```

The oil drop image is created in outline by the arc and ellipse functions. Then floodfill is called, using SOLID_FILL and the current (drawing) color, to complete the image.

```
if( MaxColors > 4 ) setcolor(4);
setfillstyle( SOLID_FILL, getcolor() );
arc( 10, 10, 105, 360, 8 );
ellipse( 0,  5, 300, 90, 8, 3 );
ellipse( 3, 10,   0, 90, 16, 8 );
floodfill( 10, 10, getcolor() );
```

```
grimage[2] = malloc( imagesize( 0, 0, 20, 20 ) );
getimage( 0, 0, 20, 20, grimage[2] );
putimage( 0, 0, grimage[2], XOR_PUT );
```

The box image is the simplest of the four, and uses the bar3d function to create a small cube.

```
if( Max Colors > 4 ) setcolor(5);
bar3d( 0, 10, 10, 15, 5, 1 );
grimage[3] = malloc( imagesize( 0, 0, 20, 20 ) );
getimage( 0, 0, 20, 20, grimage[3] );
putimage( 0, 0, grimage[3], XOR_PUT );
}
```

In each case, memory is allocated for the image using malloc and imagesize. The getimage stores the screen image and putimage uses the XOR_PUT option to erase the screen for the next drawing. (See Chapter 12 for further details on image manipulation.)

The Line_Graph function begins by testing the data to find the highest value that requires plotting (*MaxVal*) and the viewport (window) is set to provide a top margin so there is space for labels.

```
void Line_Graph()
{
   int width = getmaxx(), height = getmaxy(),
       left = 0, top = 0, i, j, hstep, vstep, vsteps,
       bottom, x, y, MaxVal = 0;
   double   scale;

   for( i=0; i<4; i++ )
      for( j=0; j<20; j++ )
         if( Accounts[i][j] > MaxVal )
            MaxVal = Accounts[i][j];
   setviewport( left, top+5,
                left+width, top+height+5, 0 );
```

Next, vertical and horizontal steps are set to fit with the current screen resolution and with *MaxVal*.

```
width -= 30;
hstep = width / 20;
vsteps = ( MaxVal / 25 ) + 2;
vstep = height / vsteps;
```

```
bottom = vstep * vsteps;
scale  = (double) vstep / (double) 25;
```

A series of vertical bars is drawn to mark off the years and each year is labeled.

```
if ( MaxColors > 4 ) setcolor( GREEN );
for( i=0; i<=hstep*32; i+=hstep*4 )
    line( i, 0, i, vstep*vsteps );
if( MaxColors > 4 ) setcolor( WHITE );
settextjustify( CENTER_TEXT, CENTER_TEXT );
settextstyle( DEFAULT_FONT, HORIZ_DIR, 2 );
for( i=0; i; i++ )
{
    x = i * hstep * 4 + 2 * hstep;
    y = vstep / 2;
    gprintf( &x, &y, "%d", Years[i] );
}
```

Then a set of horizontal bars are drawn and labeled with amounts in steps of 25 to complete the graph background grid.

```
settextjustify( CENTER_TEXT, CENTER_TEXT );
for( i=0; i<=bottom; i+=vstep )
{
    if( MaxColors > 4 ) setcolor( BLUE );
    line( 0, i, hstep*20, i );
    if( MaxColors > 4 ) setcolor( WHITE );
    x = hstep*20 + 15;
    y = i;
    gprintf( &x, &y, "%d", ((bottom-i)/vstep)*25 );
}
```

Each set of data is plotted separately, using a different color and line style. This plot begins by setting the current position relative to the first horizontal graph position (*hstep/2+3*) and the adjusted vertical position (*bottom - scale*Accounts[i][0]+8*) and calling outtext to put a label on the screen. Then the CP is set to the actual first plot position.

```
settextjustify( LEFT_TEXT, TOP_TEXT );
for( i=0; i<4; i++ )
{
    setlinestyle( i, 0, 3 );
```

```
        if( MaxColors > 4 ) setcolor(i+2);
        moveto( hstep/2+3, bottom-scale*Accounts[i][0]+8 );
        outtext( AccTypes[i] );
        moveto( hstep/2, bottom-scale*Accounts[i][0] );
```

The data plot begins with the appropriate image (symbol) centered on the plot position. Then a line is drawn to the next graph position. When the loop is finished, a final symbol is added at the end plot position.

```
        for ( j=1; j<20; j++ )
        {
            putimage( getx()-10, gety()-10,
                        grimage[i], XOR_PUT );
            lineto( hstep/2+j*hstep,
                    bottom-scale*Accounts[i][j] );
        }
        putimage( getx()-10, gety()-10,
                    grimage[i], XOR_PUT );
    }  }
```

If you would prefer a simpler display, instead of the putimage functions, a three by three dot could also be used to show the plot position.

```
    for( x = -1; x <= 1; x++ )
        for( y = -1; y <= 1; y++ )
            putpixel( getx(), gety(), getcolor() );
```

```
    /*===========================================*/
    /*     GRAPHALL.C == multiple graph demos    */
    /*===========================================*/

#ifdef __TINY__
#error Graphics demos will not run in the tiny model.
#endif

#include <conio.h>
#include <stdio.h>
#include <stdlib.h>
#include <stdarg.h>
#include <graphics.h>
```

```
#include "gprint.i"

int     GraphDriver;                 /* graphics device driver */
int     GraphMode;                     /* graphics mode value */
int     MaxColors;                  /* maximum colors available */
int     ErrorCode = 0;           /* reports any graphics errors */
double  AspR;                           /* screen aspect ratio */
int     XWidth, YHeight, ZDepth;
int     XAxis, YAxis, ZAxis;
int     XOrg, YOrg, MaxX, MaxY;
double  scale;
int     Accounts[4][9] =
        { 1985, 133, 35, 33, 17, 29, 15, 17, 32,
          1986, 122, 41, 30, 25, 18, 24, 43, 21,
          1987, 111, 65, 57, 14, 17, 39, 32, 17,
          1988, 100, 60, 70, 12, 16, 13, 17, 12   };
char    *AccTypes[9] =
        { "    ", "Motor", "Acsry", "Reprs", "Govmt",
          "Lease", "Tires", "Paint", "Misc"          };

void Initialize()
{           /* initialize graphics system and report errors */
   int xasp, yasp;
   GraphDriver = DETECT;          /* request auto-detection   */

   initgraph( &GraphDriver, &GraphMode, "C:\\TC\\BGI" );
   ErrorCode = graphresult();         /* test init results    */
   if ( ErrorCode != grOk )          /* if error during init */
   {
      printf(" Graphics System Error: %s\n",
              grapherrormsg( ErrorCode ) );
      exit( 1 );
   }
   MaxColors = getmaxcolor() + 1;       /* max color range */
   getaspectratio(&xasp,&yasp);
   AspR = (double) xasp / (double) yasp;
   MaxX = getmaxx();
   MaxY = getmaxy();
}

void Pause()
{
```

```
    if( kbhit() ) getch();
    getch();
}

void Pie_Graph( int dataset, int x, int y )
{
    int     i, m = 135, r, s = 0, t = 0, HJust, VJust;
    int     total = 0;
    int     Blank_Line = 0x0000;
    int     CapColor;
    struct  arccoordstype  arcrec;

    for( i=1; i<=8; i++ )
       total += Accounts[dataset][i];
    r = total / 4;
    setlinestyle( USERBIT_LINE, Blank_Line, NORM_WIDTH );
    setfillstyle( 0, 0 );
    pieslice( x, y, m, m+1, r+10 );
                    /* must have a minimum width of one degree */
    getarccoords( &arcrec );
    if( MaxColors > 4 ) setcolor( WHITE );
    settextstyle( SANS_SERIF_FONT, HORIZ_DIR, 2 );
    settextjustify( RIGHT_TEXT, BOTTOM_TEXT );
    gprintf( &arcrec.xend, &arcrec.yend,
            "%d", Accounts[dataset][0] );
    settextstyle( DEFAULT_FONT, HORIZ_DIR, 1 );
    if( MaxColors > 4 ) setcolor( EGA_YELLOW );
    for( i=1; i<=8; i++ )
    {
        setfillstyle( i, i );
        if( MaxColors > 4 ) setcolor( WHITE );
        setlinestyle( SOLID_LINE, 0, NORM_WIDTH );
        t += (int) ( 360 * (double) Accounts[dataset][i]
                        / (double) total + 0.5 );
        if( t > 360 ) t = 360;
        if( i == 8 ) if( t < 360 ) t = 360;
        pieslice( x, y, s, t, r );
        setlinestyle( USERBIT_LINE,
                    Blank_Line, NORM_WIDTH );
        setfillstyle( 0, 0 );
        CapColor = i+8;
```

```
            if( CapColor > 15 ) CapColor = 7;
            if( MaxColors > 4 ) setcolor( CapColor );
            m = ( t - s ) / 2 + s;
            pieslice(x, y, m, m+1, r+5 );        /* 1° minimum width */
            getarccoords( &arcrec );
            if( arcrec.xend > x) HJust = LEFT_TEXT;
                            else HJust = RIGHT_TEXT;
            if( arcrec.yend > y) VJust = TOP_TEXT;
                            else VJust = BOTTOM_TEXT;
            settextjustify( HJust, VJust );
            outtextxy( arcrec.xend, arcrec.yend, AccTypes[i] );
            s = t;
    }   }

void Draw_Pie_Graphs()
{
    int   Y1 = getmaxy() * 0.275,
          Y2 = getmaxy() * 0.725;

    cleardevice();
    graphdefaults();
    rectangle( 0, 0, MaxX, MaxY );
    Pie_Graph( 0, 150, Y1 );
    Pie_Graph( 1, 450, Y1 );
    Pie_Graph( 2, 150, Y2 );
    Pie_Graph( 3, 450, Y2 );
}

void Bar_Graph( )
{
    int   width = MaxX, height = MaxY, left = 0, top = 0;
    int   i, j, hstep, vstep, bottom, x, y, barhigh;

    cleardevice();
    graphdefaults();
    setviewport( left, top+5,
                    left+width, top+height+5, 0 );
    width -= 30;
    hstep = width/32;
    vstep = height/6;
    bottom = vstep*6;
    if( MaxColors > 4 ) setcolor( GREEN );
```

```
for( i=0; i<=hstep*32; i+=hstep*4 )
   line( i, 0, i, vstep*6 );
if( MaxColors > 4 ) setcolor( CYAN );
for( i=0; i<=bottom; i+=vstep )
   line( 0, i, hstep*32, i );
bottom- -;
if( MaxColors > 4 ) setcolor( WHITE );
settextstyle( DEFAULT_FONT, HORIZ_DIR, 1 );
settextjustify( CENTER_TEXT, CENTER_TEXT );
for( i=0; i<7; i++ )
{
   x = hstep*32 + 15;
   y = i*vstep;
   gprintf( &x, &y, "%d", 150-i*25 );
}
for( i=1; i<=8; i++ )
   for( j=0; j<4; j++ )
   {
      barhigh = bottom - Accounts[j][i]
                  * (double) vstep / (double) 25;
      if( MaxColors > 4 ) setcolor( j+1 );
      if( MaxColors > 4 ) setfillstyle( i, j+1 );
         else setfillstyle( i, MaxColors-1 );
      bar3d( (i-1)*hstep*4 + (j*hstep) + 2, barhigh,
            (i-1)*hstep*4 + (j*hstep) + hstep-2,
            bottom, 0, 0 );
      if( MaxColors > 4 ) setcolor( WHITE );
      outtextxy( i*hstep*4-hstep*2, 5, AccTypes[i] );
   }
if( MaxColors > 4 )
{
   x = MaxX/2;
   y = MaxY/4;
   settextstyle( DEFAULT_FONT, HORIZ_DIR, 2 );
   for( i=0; i; i++ )
   {
      setcolor(i+1);
      gprintf( &x, &y, "%d", Accounts[i][0] );
      x += textwidth("    ");
   }
}  }  }
```

```
void Multi_Bar_Graph( int dataset, int left, int top )
{
   int    width  = MaxX/2-30;
   int    height = MaxY/2-13;
   int    i, hstep, vstep, bottom, x, y;
   double scale;

   setviewport( left, top+5,
                left+width, top+height+5, 0 );
   hstep = width/8;
   vstep = height/6;
   bottom = vstep*6;
   scale = (double) vstep / 25;
   if( MaxColors > 4 ) setcolor( GREEN );
   for( i=0; i<=hstep*8; i+=hstep )
      line( i, 0, i, vstep*6 );
   if( MaxColors > 4 ) setcolor( CYAN );
   for( i=0; i<=bottom; i+=vstep )
      line( 0, i, hstep*8, i );
   if( MaxColors > 4 ) setcolor( WHITE );
   settextstyle( DEFAULT_FONT, HORIZ_DIR, 1 );
   settextjustify( CENTER_TEXT, CENTER_TEXT );
   for( i=0; i<7; i++ )
   {
      x = hstep*8 + 15;
      y = i*vstep;
      gprintf( &x, &y, "%d", 150-i*25 );
   }
   settextstyle( DEFAULT_FONT, VERT_DIR, 1 );
   settextjustify( CENTER_TEXT, TOP_TEXT );
   for( i=0; i<=7; i++ )
   {
      if( MaxColors > 4 ) setfillstyle( i+1, i+1 );
         else setfillstyle( i+1, MaxColors-1 );
      bar( i*hstep+2,
           bottom-scale*Accounts[dataset][i+1]-1,
           (i+1)*hstep-2, bottom-1 );
      outtextxy( i*hstep+hstep/2, 5, AccTypes[i+1] );
   }
   settextstyle( SANS_SERIF_FONT, HORIZ_DIR, 2 );
   settextjustify( CENTER_TEXT, BOTTOM_TEXT );
```

```
   x = width/2;
   y = height/2-4;
   gprintf( &x, &y, "%d", Accounts[dataset][0] );
}

void Draw_Multi_Graphs()
{
   cleardevice();
   graphdefaults();
   Multi_Bar_Graph( 0, 0,       0      );
   Multi_Bar_Graph( 1, MaxX/2, 0       );
   Multi_Bar_Graph( 2, 0,       MaxY/2 );
   Multi_Bar_Graph( 3, MaxX/2, MaxY/2 );
}

void Fill_Plane( int X1, int Y1, int X2, int Y2,
                 int X3, int Y3, int X4, int Y4,
                 int FStyle, int FColor  )
{
   int polygon[10];

   polygon[0] = polygon[8] = X1;
   polygon[1] = polygon[9] = Y1;
   polygon[2] = X2;          polygon[3] = Y2;
   polygon[4] = X3;          polygon[5] = Y3;
   polygon[6] = X4;          polygon[7] = Y4;
   if( MaxColors  4 ) FColor = MaxColors - 1;
   setfillstyle(FStyle,FColor);
   fillpoly( 5, polygon );
}

void Graph_Field()
{
   int i;

   if( MaxColors > 4 )
   {
      Fill_Plane( XOrg, YOrg, XOrg+XWidth, YOrg,
                  XOrg+XWidth, YOrg-YHeight, XOrg,
                  YOrg-YHeight, SOLID_FILL, LIGHTBLUE );
      Fill_Plane( XOrg, YOrg, XOrg-(ZDepth/AspR),
                  YOrg+ZDepth, XOrg-(ZDepth/AspR),
```

```
                         YOrg+ZDepth-YHeight, XOrg,
                         YOrg-YHeight, SOLID_FILL, LIGHTRED );
        Fill_Plane( XOrg, YOrg, XOrg+XWidth, YOrg,
                    XOrg+XWidth-(ZDepth/AspR), YOrg+ZDepth,
                    XOrg-(ZDepth/AspR), YOrg+ZDepth,
                    SOLID_FILL, YELLOW );
    }
    line( XOrg, YOrg, XOrg+XWidth, YOrg );           /*  X-axis */
    line( XOrg, YOrg, XOrg,Y Org-YHeight );          /*  Y-axis */
    line( XOrg, YOrg, XOrg-ZDepth/AspR, YOrg+ZDepth );
                                                     /*  Z-axis */
    if( MaxColors > 4 ) setcolor(GREEN);
                                     /* X-axis position lines */
    for( i=XOrg+XAxis; i<=XOrg+XWidth; i+=XAxis )
    {
        line( i, YOrg, i, YOrg-YHeight );
        line( i, YOrg, i-ZDepth/AspR, YOrg+ZDepth );
    }
    if ( MaxColors > 4 ) setcolor(CYAN);
                                     /* Y-axis position lines */
    for( i=YOrg-YAxis; i>=YOrg-YHeight; i-=YAxis )
    {
        line( XOrg, i, XOrg+XWidth, i );
        line( XOrg, i, XOrg-ZDepth/AspR, i+ZDepth );
    }
    if( MaxColors > 4 ) setcolor(RED);
                                     /* Z-axis position lines */
    for( i=ZAxis; i<=ZDepth; i+=ZAxis )
    {
        line( XOrg-i/AspR, YOrg+i,
              XOrg-i/AspR+XWidth, YOrg+i );
        line( XOrg-i/AspR, YOrg+i,
              XOrg-i/AspR, YOrg-YHeight+i );
    }
} }

void Show_Labels()
{
    int i, j, k, l, m;

    settextjustify( CENTER_TEXT, CENTER_TEXT );
    j = XOrg + XWidth + 15;
    l = XOrg - ZDepth / AspR - 15;
```

```
for ( i=1; i<7; i++ )
{
    k = YOrg - i * YAxis;
    gprintf( &j, &k, "%d", i*25 );
    m = YOrg + ZDepth - i * YAxis;
    gprintf( &l, &m, "%d", i*25 );
}
if ( MaxColors > 4 ) setcolor(LIGHTBLUE);
j = XOrg + 25;
l = j - ( ZDepth / AspR );
m = YOrg + ZDepth + 8;
k = YOrg - YHeight - 8;
for( i=1; i<=8; i++ )
{
    outtextxy( j, k, AccTypes[i] );
    outtextxy( l, m, AccTypes[i] );
    j += 50;
    l += 50;
}
if( MaxColors > 4 ) setcolor(LIGHTGREEN);
for ( i=0; i<=3; i++ )
{
    j = XOrg - ( i * ZAxis + ZAxis / 2 ) / AspR + 2;
    m = YOrg + i * ZAxis + ZAxis / 2;
    k = m - YHeight;
    l = j + XWidth;
    settextjustify( LEFT_TEXT, TOP_TEXT );
    gprintf( &l, &m, "%4d", Accounts[i][0] );
    settextjustify( RIGHT_TEXT, BOTTOM_TEXT );
    gprintf( &j, &k, "%4d", Accounts[i][0] );
} }

void Add_Bar( int left, int bottom, int height,
              int Color1, int Color2 )
{
    int    top, right;
    int    BarWidth = XAxis / 2;
    int    BarDepth = ZAxis / 2;

    if( MaxColors < 4 )
    {
```

```
         Color1 = MaxColors - 1;
         Color2 = MaxColors - 1;
      }
   setfillstyle( left+1, Color1 );
   left = XOrg + ( left * XAxis )
            - ( ( ( bottom + 0.75 * ZAxis / XAxis )
                 * ZAxis ) / AspR );
   bottom = YOrg + ( ( bottom + 0.75 ) * ZAxis );
   right = left + BarWidth;
   top = bottom - height;
   bar3d( left, top, right, bottom, 0, 0 );
   Fill_Plane( right, top,
                 right+BarDepth/AspR, top-BarDepth,
                 right+BarDepth/AspR, bottom-BarDepth,
                 right, bottom, CLOSE_DOT_FILL, Color1 );
   Fill_Plane( left, top, right, top,
                 right+BarDepth/AspR, top-BarDepth,
                 left+BarDepth/AspR, top-BarDepth,
                 SOLID_FILL, Color2 );
}

void Show_Accounts()
{
   int  i;

   if( MaxColors > 4 ) setcolor( EGA_YELLOW );
   for( i=1; i<=8; i++ )
      Add_Bar( i-1, 0, Accounts[0][i] * scale,
                 LIGHTCYAN,   CYAN  );
   for( i=1; i<=8; i++ )
      Add_Bar( i-1, 1, Accounts[1][i] * scale,
                 LIGHTRED,    RED   );
   for( i=1; i<=8; i++ )
      Add_Bar( i-1, 2, Accounts[2][i] * scale,
                 LIGHTBLUE,   BLUE  );
   for( i=1; i<=8; i++ )
      Add_Bar( i-1, 3, Accounts[3][i] * scale,
                 LIGHTGREEN, GREEN );
}

void Three_D_Graph()
{
```

```
      int  x,  y;

      cleardevice();
      ZDepth  = 4 * ZAxis;
      settextjustify( LEFT_TEXT,  TOP_TEXT );
      setcolor( getmaxcolor() );
      x = 10;    y = 10;
      gprintf( &x,  &y,  "ZAxis = %d",  ZAxis );
      Graph_Field();
      Show_Labels();
      Show_Accounts();
      Pause();
}

void Graphs_3D()
{
      cleardevice();
      graphdefaults();
      XAxis = MaxX/13;
      YAxis = MaxY/14;
      ZAxis = 10;
      XOrg  = MaxX/3;
      YOrg  = MaxY/2;
      XWidth  = 8 * XAxis;
      YHeight = 6 * YAxis;
      scale = (double) YAxis / 25;
      for( ZAxis=15; (YOrg+4*ZAxis)<MaxY; ZAxis+=5 )
          Three_D_Graph();
}

main()
{
      Initialize();                         /*  set graphics mode   */
      Draw_Pie_Graphs();
      Pause();
      Bar_Graph();
      Pause();
      Draw_Multi_Graphs();
      Pause();
      Graphs_3D();
      closegraph();                         /*  restore text mode   */
}
```

```
/*===============================================*/
/*                 LINEGRAF.C                    */
/* sample LINE-GRAPH with Turbo C++ graphics */
/*===============================================*/

#ifdef __TINY__
#error Graphics demos will not run in the tiny model.
#endif

#include <conio.h>
#include <stdio.h>
#include <stdlib.h>
#include <stdarg.h>
#include <graphics.h>

#include "gprint.i"

int    GraphDriver;                /* graphics device driver   */
int    GraphMode;                  /* graphics mode value      */
int    MaxColors;                  /* maximum colors available */
int    ErrorCode = 0;              /* report graphics errors   */
void   *grimage[3];
int    Accounts[4][20] =
    { 119, 121, 132, 140, 141, 139, 142, 135, 133, 123,
      121, 120, 124, 111, 109, 119, 122, 132, 140, 142,
       97,  99, 100, 107, 119, 123, 137, 148, 159, 160,
      168, 172, 167, 155, 159, 163, 165, 155, 151, 148,
       59,  73,  66,  49,  40,  39,  41,  45,  46,  52,
       56,  59,  60,  56,  51,  54,  55,  53,  72,  75,
       13,  15,  16,  19,  22,  20,  17,  18,  19,  21,
       24,  26,  28,  27,  22,  20,  19,  23,  25,  24 };
int  Years[5] = { 1984, 1985, 1984, 1987, 1988 };
char *AccTypes[4] =
    { "GenMec", "UnvEle", "StrOil", "NrtMfr" };

void Initialize()
{           /* initialize graphics system and report errors */
   GraphDriver = DETECT;                /* request auto-detection */
   initgraph( &GraphDriver, &GraphMode, "C:\\TC\\BGI" );
   ErrorCode = graphresult();           /* test init results   */
   if( ErrorCode != grOk )              /* if error during init */
   {
```

```
        printf( " Graphics System Error: %s\n",
                grapherrormsg( ErrorCode ) );
        exit( 1 );
    }
    MaxColors = getmaxcolor() + 1;
}

void Pause()
{
    if( kbhit() ) getch();
    getch();
}

void Line_Graph()
{
    int    width = getmaxx(), height = getmaxy(),
           left = 0, top = 0, i, j, hstep, vstep,
           vsteps, bottom, x, y, MaxVal = 0;
    double  scale;

    for( i=0; i<4; i++ )
        for( j=0; j<20; j++ )
            if( Accounts[i][j] > MaxVal )
                MaxVal = Accounts[i][j];
    setviewport( left, top+5,
                 left+width, top+height+5, 0 );
    width -= 30;
    hstep  = width / 20;
    vsteps = ( MaxVal / 25 ) + 2;
    vstep  = height / vsteps;
    bottom = vstep * vsteps;
    scale  = (double) vstep / (double) 25;
    if( MaxColors > 4 ) setcolor( GREEN );
    for( i=0; i<=hstep*32; i+=hstep*4 )
        line( i, 0, i, vstep*vsteps );
    if( MaxColors > 4 ) setcolor( WHITE );
    settextjustify( CENTER_TEXT, CENTER_TEXT );
    settextstyle( DEFAULT_FONT, HORIZ_DIR, 2 );
    for( i=0; i<5; i++ )
    {
        x = i * hstep * 4 + 2 * hstep;
        y = vstep / 2;
```

```
            gprintf( &x, &y, "%d", Years[i] );
        }
    settextjustify( CENTER_TEXT, CENTER_TEXT );
    for( i=0; i<=bottom; i+=vstep )
    {
        if( MaxColors > 4 ) setcolor( BLUE );
        line( 0, i, hstep*20, i );
        if( MaxColors > 4 ) setcolor( WHITE );
        x = hstep*20 + 15;
        y = i;
        gprintf( &x, &y, "%d", ((bottom-i)/vstep)*25 );
    }
    settextjustify( LEFT_TEXT, TOP_TEXT );
    for( i=0; i<4; i++ )
    {
        setlinestyle( i, 0, 3 );
        if ( MaxColors > 4 ) setcolor(i+2);
        moveto( hstep/2+3, bottom-scale*Accounts[i][0]+8 );
        outtext( AccTypes[i] );
        moveto( hstep/2, bottom-scale*Accounts[i][0] )

            /* instead of putimage, create a  */
            /* 'dot' around the plot position */
/*      for( x = -1; x <= 1; x++ )                          */
/*      for( y = -1; y <= 1; y++ )                          */
/*      putpixel( getx()+x, gety()+y, getcolor() );         */

        putimage( getx()-10, gety()-10,
                  grimage[i], XOR_PUT );
        lineto( hstep/2+j*hstep,
                bottom-scale*Accounts[i][j] );
    }
    putimage( getx()-10, gety()-10, grimage[i], XOR_PUT );
}

void Create_Images()
{
    int i;
    int figure[] = { 10,  5, 15,  5, 12,10, 17,10,
                     10,18, 12,13,  8,13, 10,  5 };

    setfillstyle(EMPTY_FILL,0);                /* wheel/gear */
```

```
    if( MaxColors > 4 ) setcolor(2);
    for( i=0; i<=5; i++ )
        pieslice( 10,10, i*60, (i*60)+60, 10 );
    grimage[0] = malloc( imagesize( 0, 0, 20, 20 ) );
    getimage( 0, 0, 20, 20, grimage[0] );
    putimage( 0, 0, grimage[0], XOR_PUT );
    if( MaxColors > 4 ) setcolor(3);
                                                /* lightning bolt */
    fillpoly( sizeof(figure)/(2*sizeof(int) ), figure );
    grimage[1] = malloc( imagesize( 0, 0, 20, 20 ) );
    getimage( 0, 0, 20, 20, grimage[1] );
    putimage( 0, 0, grimage[1], XOR_PUT );
    if ( MaxColors > 4 ) setcolor(4);
                                                    /* oil drop */

    setfillstyle(SOLID_FILL,getcolor());
    arc( 10,  10, 105, 360, 8 );
    ellipse(  0,  5, 300, 90,  8, 3 );
    ellipse(  3, 10,   0, 90, 16, 8 );
    floodfill( 10, 10, getcolor() );
    grimage[2] = malloc( imagesize( 0, 0, 20, 20 ) );
    getimage( 0, 0, 20, 20, grimage[2] );
    putimage( 0, 0, grimage[2], XOR_PUT );
    if( MaxColors > 4 ) setcolor(5);
                                                    /* box */

    bar3d( 0, 10, 10, 15, 5, 1 );
    grimage[3] = malloc( imagesize( 0, 0, 20, 20 ) );
    getimage( 0, 0, 20, 20, grimage[3] );
    putimage( 0, 0, grimage[3], XOR_PUT );
}

main()
{
    Initialize();                       /*  set graphics mode   */
    Create_Images();
    Line_Graph();
    Pause();
    closegraph();                       /*  restore text mode   */
}
```

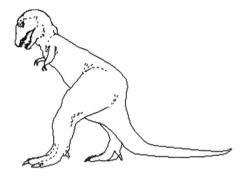

Chapter 10

Simple Graphics Animation

The word animation might first bring to mind cartoon images from Saturday morning TV. Or you might settle on advertising animation where a computer is able to eat a stick of gum or to drink a soda by plugging into the bottle. Or you may be an aficionado of the arcade graphic animations where, for a quarter, swarms of saucers, ninjas, and fantasy monsters present themselves for electronic combat.

These are all animations and are computer generated in whole or in part. Graphic animation, however, is not a product of the computer age. Over a century ago, the zeoscope combined a series of pictures to create a moving animation. Graphic images appeared in the margins of books where the pages could be riffled to create a moving picture. Decades of cartoons have been created by combining carefully hand-drawn images to create masterpieces ranging from Wile E. Coyote and Roadrunner to Fantasia.

Today, much of the cartoon animation drugery is handled by computer graphics programs, but the animation processes used may still be categorized as two types: combined images and morphological images.

Combined images are images built up from a stockpile or library of image parts as used in the demo program ANIMATE1.C. In this very simple demo, "George" is created first as a head and torso image. This initial image is saved, then additions are made to create a second image with one arm swinging forward and the other back. By combining these simple images,

George is able to saunter through the maze, swinging his arms as he walks in a moderately convincing graphic animation.

More complex actions, such as picking up an object or doing a broad-jump, require a different set of images and the program that allows George to walk has only a very simple set of rules and responses.

The second type of animation is the morphological image: the image that is created in response to a set of programming rules instead of being selected from a series of stored images. In the second animation demo ANIMATE2.C, a simple stick figure (in this case limited to a head and two legs) will walk along a cluttered plane. However, instead of a series of images, each figure is created from a simple set of links describing a basic skeleton with hinge points and each follows a limited set of response rules.

In a sense, this figure is a robot who can walk without falling over and, as Samuel Johnson once said of dancing dogs, the fascination lies not in it being done well, but merely that it can be done at all. Essentially the same is true of the robot—it walks, if not well.

Unlike the series of prewritten images, however, the robot image can be programmed to respond to a variety of situations and to create images to adapt to different circumstances. There are, however, drawbacks. The programmer must create decision trees and loops to adapt to the varying circumstances and the calculations required for each image are more extensive than those required to simply place the appropriate image in the correct screen position.

Image Animation

Depending on your hardware graphics card, your system may support two or more pages of graphics video memory with the zero page being the default both for visual display and for graphics mode operations. In Turbo C++, the setvisualpage and setactivepage provide access to the alternate video pages, if supported by the hardware. The setactivepage function selects which video graphics page will be written to by all graphics operations. The setvisualpage function selects which graphics video page is actually displayed.

Remember, the active page and the visual page are not necessarily the same page. Graphics operations can be carried out on any supported page whether it is visible or not and any supported page can be switched to active (visible) display instantly. The actual time required to switch visual pages is less than $1/50$ of a second (varying according to hardware capabilities).

The demo program ANIMATE1.C will begin by switching the active graphics page (assuming your graphics card supports alternate video pages) to go "backstage," and create a series of images out of sight. Once this is finished and our actor is ready, the active graphics page will be reset to match the active visual page and a maze will be drawn on screen with George appearing at the upper left of the maze. At this point, the cursor controls (or a mouse) can be used to walk George through the maze.

This is not a case of dragging an image across the screen. As George moves in different directions, the image is animated using a series of three poses to create the appearance of a man walking as seen from above. Since these operations can be carried out quickly, the screen action is slowed, using the delay function, to approximate a realistic walking pace. The program begins with definitions that will control the movement directions:

```
#define   RIGHT   0
#define   LEFT    1
#define   UP      2
#define   DOWN    3
```

A second set controls George's poses as he moves:

```
#define   NSTEP   0
#define   LSTEP   1
#define   RSTEP   2
```

Two arrays of pointers for the graphics images will be used:

```
void   *Flash[3];
void   *Man[4][3];
```

The first array (Flash) will be used to provide a visual response whenever George runs into something, while the second array (Man) provides three different poses of George facing in four directions.

The program begins by using the Initialize function to set up the graphics screen mode; then, because creating the images will require a few seconds, it writes a message to the active screen display before calling setactivepage to switch to an alternate video page as the active graphics page.

```
main()
{
    Initialize();                        /*   set graphics mode   */
    outtextxy(10,10," One Moment Please ");
    setactivepage( 1 );
```

If your hardware does not support alternate video pages, this selection command will be ignored and the graphics images will be visible during their construction. The time required is the same in either case, but it is a bit more elegant to keep the nuts and bolts assembly work out of sight. If you are curious, this selection can be commented out to allow the image creation process to proceed in plain view.

The CreateImages function constructs the graphics images that will be used, then the active video graphics page is reset to the default page and the screen is cleared. Alternatively, the setvisualpage function could be used to change the visual (displayed) graphics video page to match the active video page. The results would be the same.

```
CreateImages();
setactivepage( 0 );
clearviewport();
```

Now the maze for the game is created on screen and the game proceeds.

```
CreateMaze();
StartGame();
```

The ClearImages function is used before exiting to release the memory allocated to store the several graphics images. In this particular application, memory release is not absolutely necessary since exiting the program will take care of this, but it is still good practice to provide for proper memory management.

```
ClearImages();
closegraph();
}
```

CreateImages

The CreateImages function creates and saves a series of graphic images, beginning with a series of integer arrays (*pflash#* and *##arm_#*) that describe elements used in the images.

```
void CreateImages()
{
    int   i, j, MaxColor = getmaxcolor();
    int pflash1[] = { 100, 40, 110, 60, 100, 70, 120,
        65, 140, 80, 130, 60, 140, 50, 120, 65, 100, 40 };
    int pflash2[] = { 120, 40, 110, 55,  90, 60, 110,
        65, 120, 80, 130, 65, 150, 60, 130, 65, 120, 40 };
     int pflash3[] = { 140, 40, 130, 60, 140, 70, 120,
        65, 100, 80, 110, 60, 100, 50, 120, 55, 140, 40 };
     int bkarm_u[] = { 100, 62, 102, 68, 105, 70,
                       108, 69, 109, 65 };
```

```
int ftarm_u[] = { 140, 62, 143, 52,
                  130, 47, 125, 52 };
int bkarm_r[] = { 121,145, 128,147, 130,150,
                  129,153, 125,154 };
int ftarm_r[] = { 117,176, 106,176,
                  100,165, 107,160 };
```

The randomize function is used to seed the random number generator. Then the drawing color, fill style, and fill color are selected randomly for each of the *pflash#* images.

```
randomize();
setcolor( random( MaxColor ) + 1 );
setfillstyle( random(11) + 1, random(MaxColor) + 1 );
```

This initial image (see Figure 10-1) consists of four ellipses. The head is an ellipse with a vertical radius of 12 and a horizontal radius of eight. Each shoulder is an ellipse with a vertical radius of eight and a horizontal radius of 12, with centers offset four pixels right and left. Last, the nose is a small ellipse with a vertical radius of four and a horizontal radius of two.

This image will be inverted (top to bottom) to create the downfacing image, but instead of rotating for right and left facing images, these will be created by transposing the axis coordinates and radii and using *AspR* (aspect resolution) to adjust the X/Y resolution.

When calling the fillpoly function, instead of having to know the size of the integer array for each polygon, the size passed to fillpoly is calculated as *sizeof(pflash#)* divided by two times *sizeof(int)* because two integer values are required for each polygon point.

```
fillpoly( sizeof( pflash1 )/( 2 * sizeof( int ) ),
          pflash1 );
```

The SaveImage function will be described in a moment, but in brief, it returns a pointer to a memory image. The four parameters describe the screen coordinates for the image to be saved.

```
Flash[0] = SaveImage( 100, 40, 140, 80 );
```

Essentially, the same sequence of operations is repeated for the *pflash2* and *pflash3* arrays.

George's images begin with a series of ellipses to create two heads with noses and shoulders; one head with the long axis horizontal, the other vertical. The floodfill function fills in the images using SOLID_FILL for the heads and HATCH_FILL for the shoulders.

Figure 10-1: Basic Figure Animation—Initial Image

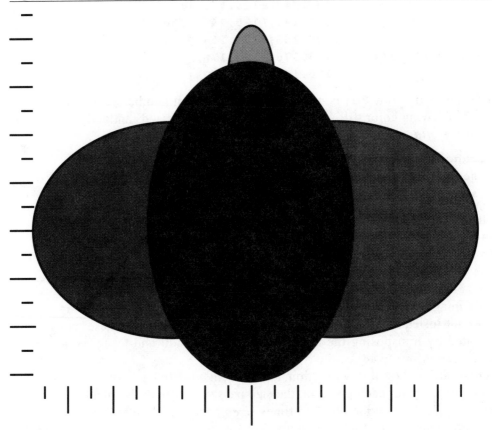

This initial image consists of four ellipses. The head is an ellipse with a vertical radius of 12 and a horizontal radius of eight. Each shoulder is an ellipse with a vertical radius of eight and a horizontal radius of 12, with the centers offset four pixels right and left. Last, the nose is a smaller ellipsis with a vertical radius of four and a horizontal radius of two.

This image will be inverted (top to bottom) to create the downfacing image, but instead of rotating for right and left facing images, these will be created by transposing the axis coordinates and radii and using AspR (aspect resolution) to adjust the X/Y resolution.

```
setcolor( MaxColor );
setfillstyle( SOLID_FILL, MaxColor );
ellipse(   120,  60,   0, 360, 10, 10 );
floodfill( 120,  60, MaxColor );
ellipse(   220, 160,   0, 360, 13,  7 );
```

```
floodfill( 220, 160, MaxColor );
ellipse(   120,  51,   0, 180,  3,  3 );
ellipse(   207, 160,  90, 270,  3,  2 );
setfillstyle( HATCH_FILL, MaxColor );
ellipse(   128,  60, 270,  90, 12,  6 );
floodfill( 135,  60, MaxColor );
ellipse(   112,  60,  90, 270, 12,  6 );
floodfill( 105,  60, MaxColor );
ellipse(   220, 154,   0, 180,  8,  9 );
floodfill( 220, 150, MaxColor );
ellipse(   220, 166, 180, 360,  8,  9 );
floodfill( 220, 170, MaxColor );
```

In lieu of duplicating efforts to draw separate heads facing left and right, and up and down, two of the existing images are mapped, pixel by pixel, to create matching reversed images.

```
for( i=100; i<=145; i++ )
   for( j= 45; j<= 70; j++ )
      putpixel( 345-i, 120-j, getpixel( i, j ) );
for( i=204; i<=235; i++ )
   for( j=145; j<=175; j++ )
      putpixel( 345-i, j, getpixel( i, j ) );
```

The four end products are saved as individual images.

```
Man[UP][NSTEP]    = SaveImage( 100,  45, 140,  70 );
Man[DOWN][NSTEP]  = SaveImage( 205,  50, 245,  75 );
Man[LEFT][NSTEP]  = SaveImage( 203, 140, 234, 180 );
Man[RIGHT][NSTEP] = SaveImage( 111, 140, 142, 180 );
```

So far, four stationary images have been created. Now two of these will be used as the basis for further images by adding arms to the bodies (see Figure 10-2). In Figure 10-2 arms are added to the initial image, then the image will be rotated up/down and right/left to create two pairs of movement images. The right/left facing image will have arms added, then run through the same pixel transformation.

The end results will be 12 images in sets of three (stationary, right arm forward, left arm forward) facing four directions (up, right, left, and down) for movement through the maze.

While this is extremely simple animation, the basic principles required for greater elaborations are fully demonstrated. The fillstyle is set to CLOSE_DOT_FILL and fillpoly is called to add the two arms to the image.

```
setfillstyle( CLOSE_DOT_FILL, MaxColor );
putimage( 100, 45, Man[ UP ][ NSTEP ], COPY_PUT );
fillpoly( sizeof( bkarm_u )/( 2 * sizeof(int) ),
          bkarm_u );
fillpoly( sizeof( ftarm_u )/( 2 * sizeof(int) ),
          ftarm_u );
putimage( 100, 45, Man[ UP ][ NSTEP ], OR_PUT );
```

Figure 10-2: Basic Figure Animation—Secondary Image

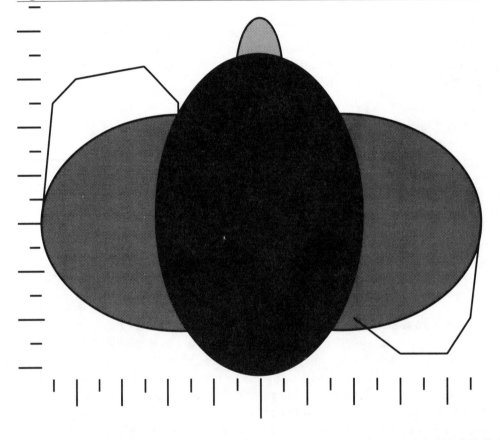

The initial image is modified to create two arms, one swung slightly forward and the other slightly back in the manner of a person walking. The next step will be to fill in the arm images before, again, inverting this secondary image (top to bottom) to create the downfacing image. The left and right facing images will be created in the same fashion as previously.

Note that putimage has been called twice; first with the COPY_PUT option and the second time with the OR_PUT option. Using COPY_PUT the image is written to the screen, replacing any existing pixels at the image location. Next, the fillpoly function is used to add arms as new elements to this screen image.

There is, however, a minor problem with fillpoly (see Figure 10-3). The fillpoly function does not follow the existing outlines when adding the fill pattern. Instead, fillpoly calculates the area by assuming a line between the first point plotted and the last, and fills everything within the polygon area. This is also a portion of the original image—and this is not desired. The line shading on the arms of George in Figure 10-3 shows the area of the original image that will be overwritten by fillpoly. Instead of trying to close the polygon in a way that avoids this overwrite, the putimage function is called a second time using OR_PUT, to restore the overwritten pixels.

The first call to putimage could be omitted since it has no effect on the operations carried out by fillpoly and the final call to putimage will insert the head and body image. The first call, however, was used to line up the arms correctly and was left in the code to allow you to examine the results produced by the interaction with fillpoly.

At this point, the image has one arm in front of the body and the other swung back. Now, it will be transposed to create three other images; one also facing up but with the arms reversed; the other two facing down with the left and right arms alternately in front and in back.

```
for( i=100; i<=145; i++ )
  for( j= 45; j<= 70; j++ )
  {
    putpixel( 345-i,      j, getpixel( i, j ) );
    putpixel( 345-i, 220-j, getpixel( i, j ) );
    putpixel(      i, 220-j, getpixel( i, j ) );
  }
```

The final four images are saved individually:

```
Man[UP] [LSTEP]    = SaveImage( 100,  45, 145,  70 );
Man[UP] [RSTEP]    = SaveImage( 200,  45, 245,  70 );
Man{DOWN][LSTEP] = SaveImage( 100, 150, 145, 175 );
Man[DOWN][RSTEP] = SaveImage( 200, 150, 245, 175 );
```

Figure 10-3: Basic Figure Animation—Secondary Image

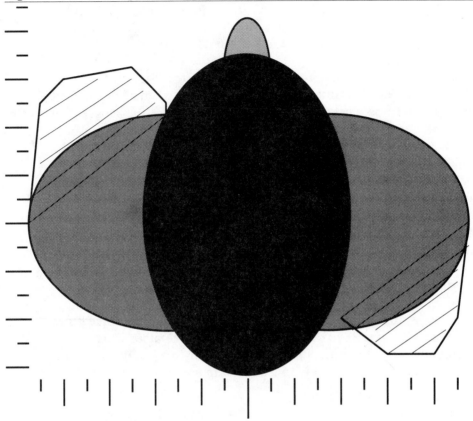

The fillpoly function is excellent for creating the arms for the image ... but it also has one minor problem because fillpoly does not take into account existing borders. Instead the entire polygon area is draw and portions of the existing shoulder images are overwritten and need to be restored before the image is completed.

Next, using the original left-facing image, the same process is repeated, arms are added and the result is transposed three ways, to create the final set of images.

```
putimage( 100, 140, Man[ LEFT ][ NSTEP ], COPY_PUT );
fillpoly( sizeof( bkarm_r )/( 2 * sizeof(int) ),
          bkarm_r );
fillpoly( sizeof( ftarm_r )/( 2 * sizeof(int) ),
          ftarm_r );
putimage( 100, 140, Man[ LEFT ][ NSTEP ], OR_PUT );
```

```
for ( i=100; i<=132; i++)
    for ( j=144; j<=177; j++)
    {
        putpixel( 345-i,      j, getpixel( i, j ) );
        putpixel( 345-i, 220-j, getpixel( i, j ) );
        putpixel(      i, 220-j, getpixel( i, j ) );
    }
    Man[LEFT][RSTEP] = SaveImage( 100, 144, 132, 177 );
    Man[LEFT][LSTEP] = SaveImage( 100,  43, 132,  76 );
    Man[RIGHT][LSTEP]= SaveImage( 213,  43, 245,  76 );
    Man[RIGHT][RSTEP]= SaveImage( 213, 144, 245, 177 );
}
```

SaveImage

The SaveImage function is called with four parameters specifying the corners of a rectangle on the screen. SaveImage uses the imagesize function to calculate the memory necessary and uses the function malloc to allocate memory for the image area specified, also assigning a local pointer image to the memory location.

```
void *SaveImage( int left, int top,
                 int right, int bottom )
{
    void  *image;
    image = malloc( imagesize( left,  top,
                               right, bottom ) );
```

The getimage function transfers the screen image to the memory area pointed at by *image*, then putimage uses the XOR_PUT option to erase the screen image. Finally, the image pointer is returned to the calling function.

```
    getimage( left, top, right, bottom, image );
    putimage( left, top, image, XOR_PUT );
    return( image );
}
```

At this point, memory has been allocated for the graphic image, the screen image information has been written to this memory location, and the pointer to the location has been returned in order to be assigned to the appropriate pointer variable (so the local pointer *image* can be forgotten).

CreateMaze

The CreateMaze function writes a maze to the screen. The maze elements are described as a series arrays of integers specifying pairs of points.

```
void CreateMaze()
{
    int i, j;
    int maze1[] = { 200, 40,  50, 40,  50,160, 100,160 };
    int maze2[] = { 100,  80, 100,120, 200,120, 200,240 };
       .

       .

       .
    int maze16[] = { 550,120, 550,200, 450,200,
                     450,280, 550,280 };
    int maze17[] = { 500,240, 600,240 };
    struct viewporttype vp;
```

This maze data could be retrieved from an external file or even generated by an appropriate algorithm. For purposes of demonstration, it is easiest to provide the data as shown.

The viewport (window) is set to the entire screen—in this case, EGA or higher resolution is assumed—and a brief instruction is written at the bottom.

```
    setcolor( MaxColors - 1 );
    setviewport(0,0,639,349,1);          /*Set draw color white*/
    settextstyle( DEFAULT_FONT, HORIZ_DIR, 1 );
    outtextxy(  20, 330, "Use Arrow Keys to move "
                "'George' or <Q>uit to exit program" );
```

Now the viewport is reduced in size and a border is drawn around the area.

```
    setviewport(0,0,600,320,1);
    setlinestyle( SOLID_LINE, 0, NORM_WIDTH );
    getviewsettings( &vp );
    rectangle( 0, 0, vp.right - vp.left,
                     vp.bottom - vp.top );
```

The final step is to draw the walls of the maze and to add labels for the start and finish points.

```
    outtextxy( 10, 20, "START" );
    drawpoly( sizeof( maze1  )/(2*sizeof(int) ), maze1  );
```

```
drawpoly( sizeof( maze2  )/(2*sizeof(int) ), maze2  );
   .
   .
   .
drawpoly( sizeof( maze16 )/(2*sizeof(int) ), maze16 );
drawpoly( sizeof( maze17 )/(2*sizeof(int) ), maze17 );
outtextxy( 550, 300, "FINISH" );
}
```

In this case, the drawpoly function is used instead of fillpoly because you only want lines drawn without fill to be added. The operation is otherwise the same as described in the Create_Images function.

No record of the maze construction nor of the position of the walls is necessary; the program will not depend on any such record for operation. Instead, the screen image itself will be tested to decided if movements are valid or not.

StartGame

Now, it is time for the actual game control, which begins with the Start-Game function. Initially, StartGame calls the Put_Image function to put George on the screen at the start coordinates, then reads the keyboard (or a mouse) to direct George's movements on the screen. Only five keys will be accepted as input: the UP, DOWN, RIGHT, and LEFT arrow keys and Q for quit.

```
void StartGame()
{
    har ch;
    int  Quit = 0;
    Move = LastMove = RIGHT;
    Put_Image( NSTEP );
```

The *Quit* variable was initialized as zero (a Boolean false). Until *Quit* is true, the *while* loop will continue.

```
    while ( !Quit )
    {
        ch = getch();
        if ( ch == 0x00 )
        {
```

If the first key read is a NULL one of the function keys was pressed and a second character code is read to decide which key. The four arrow keys (cursor keys) control George's movements, each calling the Move_Image function with the appropriate direction as a parameter.

```
ch = getch();
switch( ch )
{
    case 'M' : Move_Image( RIGHT );    break;
    case 'K' : Move_Image( LEFT );     break;
    case 'H' : Move_Image( UP );       break;
    case 'P' : Move_Image( DOWN );
}   }
```

Note that both Q and q are accepted as valid inputs. If *Quit* increments, then *Quit* becomes a Boolean true and the *while* loop exits.

```
        else if (ch == 'Q' || ch == 'q') Quit++;
}    }
```

Move_Image

The Move_Image function is called with an argument *NextStep*, which specifies the direction for George to move. First, Put_Image is called to erase the current screen image. The *Move* variable, which controls direction and selects the set of images used, takes the value *NextStep* and Put_Image is called again to put George back on the screen, but facing in the correct direction.

```
void Move_Image( int NextStep )
{
    int i, XFake, YFake, XStep, YStep, XFlash, YFlash;
    Put_Image( NSTEP );
    Move = NextStep;
    Put_Image( NSTEP );
```

Before the two calls to Put_Image, George may have been facing the same direction as he will be after the calls but, rather than writing a test for direction, it is simple enough to erase the existing image and restore the desired image.

Depending on the direction of movement, several variables: *XFake*, *YFake*, *XStep*, *YStep*, *XFlash*, and *YFlash* are assigned values that might be subsequently needed. It's easiest, however, to use one *switch* statement to set all six variables for the proper directions and then not worry about them anymore.

```
switch( Move )
{
    case RIGHT:    XFake  = 5;    YFake  = 0;
                   XStep  = 5;    YStep  = 0;
                   XFlash = 5;    YFlash = 0;    break;
    case  LEFT:    XFake  = -5;   YFake  = 0;
                   XStep  = -5;   YStep  = 0;
                   XFlash = 2;    YFlash = 0;    break;
    case   UP:     XFake  = 0;    YFake  = -5;
                   XStep  = 0;    YStep  = -4;
                   XFlash = 0;    YFlash = 2;    break;
    case  DOWN:    XFake  = 0;    YFake  = 5;
                   XStep  = 0;    YStep  = 4;
                   XFlash = 0;    YFlash = 0;
}
```

The call to the Test_Move function decides if George can move in the direction requested.

```
if( !Test_Move() )
{
```

If Test_Move returns a Boolean false, then Put_Image erases the stationary image, increments the position by *XFake* or *YFake* (one of these is always zero), places the stepping image (LSTEP) on the screen, and calls FlashImage.

```
Put_Image( NSTEP );
XPos += XFake;
YPos += YFake;
Put_Image( LSTEP );
FlashImage( XPos+XFlash, YPos+YFlash );
```

Now, the LSTEP image is erased, the position coordinates are returned to their previous values, and the NSTEP image is restored.

```
Put_Image( LSTEP );
XPos -= XFake;
Pos -= YFake;
Put_Image( NSTEP );
}
```

In this manner, George takes a half step forward and bumps into the wall of the maze. Flashing stars are superimposed cartoon-style (with sound effects) and, finally, George steps back and waits for the next instruction.

If Test_Move returns true, then George is free to move forward. This begins by erasing the stationary image (NSTEP) and incrementing the position coordinates.

```
else
{
   Put_Image( NSTEP );
   XPos += XStep;
   YPos += YStep;
```

In order to make the illusion of movement as smooth as possible, George's *LastMove* is tested to decide on which foot he should now be leading. Actually, George's feet are never seen, only the illusion of his arms swinging as he walks. If the sequence of his movements were not coordinated, the results would look very awkward indeed. Since *LastMove* will be either 1 or 2 (LSTEP or RSTEP), only a simple Boolean test is required.

```
if( LastMove != LSTEP )
{
```

Each time an arrow key is pressed (or a mouse sends the equivalent signal), George is going to take several steps on the screen. Instead of writing all the individual instructions necessary for each step and each position adjustment, a loop will run calls through to the Take_Step function to make George walk forward, with his last step the same as his first in this sequence and ending in the NSTEP (stationary) position.

```
for( i=1; i<=2; i++ )
{
   Take_Step( XStep, YStep, LSTEP );
   Take_Step( XStep, YStep, NSTEP );
   Take_Step( XStep, YStep, RSTEP );
   Take_Step( XStep, YStep, NSTEP );
}
Take_Step( XStep, YStep, LSTEP );
Put_Image( NSTEP );
delay( TimeOut );
}
```

The *XStep* and *YStep* variables have already been assigned the appropriate offsets for the movement direction (*Move*). Each call to Take_Step places the appropriate image on the screen, waits momentarily, erases the image; and then increments the position coordinates.

If *LastMove* was LSTEP, then George starts off with RSTEP, running through the same sequences.

```
else
{
    for( i=1; i<=2; i++ )
    {
        Take_Step( XStep, YStep, RSTEP );
        Take_Step( XStep, YStep, NSTEP );
        Take_Step( XStep, YStep, LSTEP );
        Take_Step( XStep, YStep, NSTEP );
    }
    Take_Step( XStep, YStep, RSTEP );
    Put_Image( NSTEP );
    delay( TimeOut );
}       }
```

The Test_Move function is the key decision mechanism for this game. It reads the screen pixels in the direction requested to decide if George is free to move. The *switch(Move)* directive decides which test is appropriate for the selected direction.

```
int Test_Move()
{
    int i;
```

Since the *XPos/YPos* coordinates are at the upper-left corner of the image, different offsets and ranges need to be tested for each direction. The test itself is very simple: if any pixel tested is not zero (BLACK), then a zero value (FALSE) is immediately returned. The function exits returning a false result.

```
switch( Move )
{
    case RIGHT: for ( i = XPos+47; i <= XPos+96; i++ )
                 if ( getpixel( i, YPos+5 ) )
                    return( 0 );  break;
    case  LEFT: for ( i = XPos; i >= XPos-50; i- - )
                 if ( getpixel( i, YPos+5 ) )
                    return( 0 );  break;
    case    UP: for ( i = YPos; i >= YPos-40; i- - )
```

```
                      if ( getpixel( XPos+5, i ) )
                          return( 0 );   break;
          case   DOWN: for ( i = YPos+37; i <= YPos+76; i++ )
                      if ( getpixel( XPos+5, i ) )
                          return( 0 );

    }
```

If no non-BLACK pixels were encountered by the selected test, then a one (TRUE) is returned and George is free to move forward.

```
    return( 1 );
}
```

In other applications, different test types may be required. This test is merely the most practical and serves nicely in the application. In other situations, however, you may find that you need to test for a specific color value, test several pixels for a condition, or test against a separate "map" for responses based on information that is not visible on the screen. You may even use a combination of all of these.

The Take_Step Function

The Take_Step function is the principal movement function in this demo program and is called with three parameters. The x and y arguments are the horizontal and vertical movement increments that will determine the next screen image position. The *Step* argument is passed to Put_Image in order to control which image (NSTEP, LSTEP, or RSTEP) will be used and to set the value for *LastMove*.

```
void Take_Step( int x, int y, int Step )
{
    Put_Image( Step );
    delay( TimeOut );
    Put_Image( Step );
    XPos += x;
    YPos += y;
    if( Step ) LastMove = Step;
}
```

The first call to Put_Image places the appropriate image on the screen and, after a time delay, the second call erases the image. Note also that the position is incremented only after the image is erased.

Put_Image

The Put_Image function places the desired image on the screen using the XOR_PUT option. If the image indicated by *Move* and *Step* is already on the screen, then XOR_PUT erases the image. If there is another image already on the screen, then the new image overlies the existing image without erasing it. If the current image is being XOR'ed with itself, then the original image is restored.

```
void Put_Image( int Step )
{
   int    x = XPos, y = YPos;
   switch( Move )
   {
      case RIGHT:
      case  LEFT:  x+=8;  break;
      case    UP:
      case  DOWN:  y+=5;
   }
   putimage( x, y, Man[ Move ][ Step ], XOR_PUT );
}
```

For left- and right-facing images, the x-axis position is offset by eight pixels; for up and down, the y-axis is offset by five pixels. This does not affect the *XPos* and *YPos* screen coordinates, but simply improves positioning of the images within the maze walls.

FlashImage

The FlashImage function is called—following the finest cartoon traditions—when George runs into a wall. This function overwrites George's image with a series of irregular colored stars and adds random sound effects. Each flash is popped onto the screen, the sound effect is activated, and the flash is XOR'd with itself and a new sound effect is generated.

The three flash images are cycled three times, but no time delay is used; therefore, the resulting screen image is a very brief multicolored star or series of stars that vanish before they are completely seen.

```
void FlashImage( int x, int y )
{
   int i, j, k;
   for( i=1; i<=3; i++ )
      for( j=0; j<3; j++ )
```

```
for( k=0; k<2; k++ )
{
    putimage( x, y, Flash[j], XOR_PUT );
    sound( random(100) + 100 );
}
nosound();
}
```

Before the function exits, the nosound function is called to cancel the last generated sound. Remember, each generated sound continues until a new sound command is called or until the nosound function is called to explicitly terminate the sound effects.

ClearImages

The final function used in this demonstration is the ClearImages function, which uses the free function to release the memory allocated for the various images.

```
void ClearImages()
{
    int i, j;
    for( i=0; i<=2; i++ )      free( Flash[i] );
    for( i=0; i<=3; i++ )
        for( j=0; j<=2; j++ ) free( Man[i][j] );
}
```

Once your program exits, these memory allocations should be released by a call to closegraph. It is good practice to explicitly release the memory allocated to the images. In other applications, it may be advantageous to use the free function to release memory that was used for one application and make it available for another.

Morphological Animation

While conventional animation techniques that use precreated images are fine for arcade games and simpler applications, the programmer is required to provide in advance for all contingencies and to individually create each of the required images. The alternative is to create rules for the construction of an image and then have the computer draw each image as needed, rearranging them according to the situation's requirements.

In the second animation demo, ANIMATE2.C, Elmer is a stylized stick figure consisting of a triangular body and two legs. This is not a precreated image, however, but is drawn and erased according to a moderately simple series of program rules. The legs are links with defined limits of freedom and fixed lengths—literally, a skeleton much like your own.

In the demo, Elmer will stand up, then walk across the screen from left to right. To accomplish this, a total of more than 5,000 images will be written or erased. Standing up requires some 242 images and each step requires a series of 243 images.

The disadvantage to this approach is: first, that Elmer requires a great deal of calculation; second, the rules for Elmer's motion and position are complex; and third, the more complex the image, the greater the required processing time. These disadvantages can be overcome by various methods. Movement rules can be simplified to minimize calculation and math co-processors will cut the time required for the calculations. The calculated image can be combined in part with stored images to reduce the complexity of calculations. The big advantage is that the programmer can create rules and decision trees to govern the images and positions and can design these in a manner to provide flexibility that fixed images cannot emulate. The present demo does not have a complex set of responses, but the basic requirements are here. You are invited to try your hand at expanding this program and creating a more complex set of adaptations.

Warning: If you don't enjoy math, you are going to hate morphological animation! There are no easy solutions and you have to look at rules that require serious number crunching and a bit of skull work. Thus warned, it's time to take a look at how image morphology is handled.

ANIMATE2.C begins with two constants: PI which will be used to convert angles from degrees to radians, and BRIEF which will provide a time delay constant. BRIEF can be increased or decreased according to the speed of your system.

```
const    double  PI = 3.1415;
const    int     BRIEF = 5;
```

A series of global variables will be used for the action points and to define the relations between the several portions of Elmer's anatomy.

```
int  rcolor, lcolor,               /*right and left leg colors */
     urangle, ulangle,          /*upper right & left leg angles */
     lxknee, lyknee, rxknee, ryknee,      /*coords for knees */
     lrangle, llangle,          /*lower right & left leg angles */
     lxfoot, lyfoot, rxfoot, ryfoot,       /*coords for feet */
     ujoint, ljoint,          /*length of upper and lower legs */
     xpos,   ypos;                  /*body coords (center) */
```

Before getting into these special functions, a brief digression. In C, the conventional trigonometry functions accept angle arguments in radians, while Turbo C++'s graphics functions are configured to use arguments in degrees. For this application, it is more convenient to use angles in degrees even though the conventional trigonometric functions will be used. For this reason, the function rad is created to convert an angle expressed in degrees to an angle expressed in radians.

```
double rad( int degrees )
{
    return( PI * degrees / 180 );
}
```

For convenience, the functions rsin and rcos are provided to calculate the sin and cos values for angles in degrees. Note also that an integer argument (degrees) returns a double (decimal fraction) result.

```
double rsin( int degrees )
{
    return sin( rad( degrees ) );
}

double rcos( int degrees )
{
    return cos( rad( degrees ) );
}
```

The main program begins by using the same Initialize function as previous programs, then it sets initial values for the variables that describe Elmer's structure and beginning position.

```
main()
{
    int    i;

    Initialize();
    urangle = 30;    ulangle = 30;
    lrangle = 0;     llangle = 0;
    ujoint = 30;     ljoint = 30;
    lxfoot = 30;     lyfoot = ryfoot = 150;
    rcolor = BLUE;   lcolor = RED;
```

The Create_Field function draws a plane for Elmer to walk on and provides a few background structures for demonstration. Start_Walker puts Elmer on the screen in his beginning configuration (a folded squat),

Raise_Walker allows Elmer to stand up, and then Walk_Right is looped for the 20 steps necessary for Elmer to cross the screen.

```
Create_Field();
Start_Walker();
Raise_Walker();
for( i=1; i<=20; i++ ) Walk_Right();
Pause();
closegraph();                    /*    restore text mode    */
}
```

In main, initial values were set for several of Elmer's definitions, but these may not be correct. Some of the values are better established by calculation than by a programmer's entry. This is another way of saying that it's easier to let the computer figure out how Elmer fits together, than to run out the angles and formulas on your pocket calculator and type them in. After all, why do it the hard way?

To begin, the position of the left foot is predefined and the left knee is directly above the foot (as per the defined length of the lower leg).

```
void Start_Walker()
{
    lxknee = lxfoot;
    lyknee = lyfoot-ljoint;
```

With the lower left leg and knee in position, the body coordinates are calculated according to the angle from vertical (*ulangle*) and the length of the upper joint (*ujoint*). The the calculation used is fast, but inaccurate. An accurate calculation of the coordinate position can be made with the formula:

```
ptx = (ptx * cos( angle ) + pty * sin( angle ) );
pty = (pty * cos( angle ) + ptx * sin( angle ) );
```

Now the body coordinates are calculated:

```
xpos = lxfoot + rsin( ulangle ) * ujoint;
ypos = lyfoot + rcos( ulangle ) * ujoint - ljoint;
```

The calculations continue down the right leg until the right knee and right foot are positioned.

```
rxfoot = xpos + rsin( urangle ) * ujoint;
rxknee = rxfoot;
ryknee = ryfoot - ljoint;
```

```
    Body_Image( MaxColors-1 );
}
```

The last step is to put Elmer on the screen by calling Body_Image. The Body_Image function is called both to draw Elmer on the screen and, with a color value of 0, to erase Elmer again.

```
void Body_Image( int color )
{
    int i, j, left, right, top, bottom;

    setcolor( color );
    if( color ) setcolor(lcolor);
```

Beginning with the left leg, CP is set to the proper coordinates and a knot is drawn for Elmer's foot. A line is then drawn up to the knee and another knot is added for the knee.

```
    moveto( lxfoot, lyfoot );
    Plot_Knot();
    lineto( lxknee, lyknee );
    Plot_Knot();
```

The line continues up to the hip, changes color for the right leg, and works back down to the right foot.

```
    lineto( xpos, ypos );
    if( color ) setcolor(rcolor);
    lineto( rxknee, ryknee );
    Plot_Knot();
    lineto( rxfoot, ryfoot );
    Plot_Knot();
```

The last task is drawing the body. Because Elmer's body doesn't bend or shift, a simple set of line commands are used for this part of his anatomy.

```
    if( color ) setcolor( MaxColors-1 );
    bottom = ypos+10;
    top    = ypos-5;
    left   = xpos-11;
    right  = xpos+11;
    line( xpos,  ypos, left,  top    );
    line( xpos,  ypos, right, top    );
    line( xpos,  ypos, xpos,  bottom );
    line( left,  top,  right, top    );
```

```
line( left,   top,   xpos,   bottom );
line( right,  top,   xpos,   bottom );
}
```

The Body_Image function is called more than 5,000 times to draw Elmer in different ways as he moves. To speed operations, draw this portion of the body once, save the screen image, and use put_image with the XOR_PUT.

The Plot_Knot function draws a 3x3 pixel knot to define Elmer's feet and knees.

```
void Plot_Knot()
{
    int  i,  j,  k = getcolor();

    for( i=-1; i<=1; i++ )
        for( j=-1; j<=1; j++ )
            putpixel( getx()+i, gety()+j, k );
}
```

The Raise_Walker function takes Elmer from his initial squatting position to an erect posture. When Elmer was first set up, his upper leg angle (*ulangle*) was initialized at 30 degrees. Now, he'll straighten up in one-degree steps, with new knee and hip positions calculated for each one-degree change, until he is fully erect with an upper leg angle of 150 degrees. Because both legs are assumed to be moving in the same way and at the same time, calculations are greatly simplified.

```
void Raise_Walker()
{
    while( ulangle<=150 )
    {
        ulangle++;
        Body_Image( 0 );
        lxknee = xpos - rsin( ulangle ) * ujoint;
        lyknee = ypos - rcos( ulangle ) * ujoint;
        lrangle = llangle =
            180 *atan2((lxfoot-lxknee),(lyfoot-lyknee))/PI;
        lxknee = lxfoot - rsin( llangle ) * ljoint;
        rxknee = rxfoot + rsin( lrangle ) * ljoint;
        ryknee = lyknee = lyfoot-rcos(llangle)*ljoint;
        ypos = lyknee + rcos( ulangle ) * ujoint;
        Body_Image( 15 );
```

```
      delay( BRIEF * 10 );
  }
```

The right and left angles are then equalized and, in case of any remaining
error, the lower angles (*lrangle* and *llangle*) are set to zero.

```
  urangle = ulangle;
  lrangle = llangle = 0;
}
```

Now that Elmer is standing, the Walk_Right function will be used to
move him across the screen. When you try complicating Elmer's responses,
you may wish to break this function into a series of functions for calculating each movement element independently.

```
void Walk_Right()
{
  int     i;
```

The first element here involves swinging the right foot (the lower right
leg) up 30 degrees:

```
  for( i=1; i<=30; i++ )
  {
    Body_Image( 0 );
    lrangle++;
    rxfoot = rxknee + rsin( lrangle ) * ljoint;
    ryfoot = ryknee + rcos( lrangle ) * ljoint;
    Body_Image( MaxColors-1 );
    delay(BRIEF);
  }
```

Now that Elmer has his foot up, the left leg is ready to bend down until
the right foot is back on the ground (or approximately so). Since Elmer
weighs nothing, he doesn't have to worry about falling over and can
balance without any adjustments. In other applications it might be advis-
able to provide for a counter movement to better simulate natural motion.
To keep this demo program simple, however, gravity is replaced by levity.

Again, the calculations begin with one foot (the left), go up to the hip,
and then down to the right foot.

```
  for( i=1; i<=30; i++ )
  {
    Body_Image( 0 );
    llangle++;
```

```
   lxknee = lxfoot + rsin( llangle ) * ljoint;
   lyknee = lyfoot - rcos( llangle ) * ljoint;
   xpos = lxknee + rsin( ulangle ) * ujoint;
   ypos = lyknee + rcos( ulangle ) * ujoint;
   rxknee = xpos + rsin( urangle ) * ujoint;
   ryknee = ypos - rcos( urangle ) * ujoint;
   rxfoot = rxknee + rsin( lrangle ) * ljoint;
   ryfoot = ryknee + rcos( lrangle ) * ljoint;
   Body_Image( MaxColors-1 );
   delay(BRIEF);
}
```

Now it's time to straighten up the right leg, with the left leg moving to compensate:

```
for( i=1; i<=30; i++ )
{                   /*bring right leg back to standing*/
   Body_Image( 0 );
   lrangle- -;
   rxknee = rxfoot - rsin( lrangle ) * ljoint;
   ryknee = ryfoot - rcos( lrangle ) * ljoint;
   xpos = rxknee - rsin( urangle ) * ujoint;
   ypos = ryknee + rcos( urangle ) * ujoint;
   lxknee = xpos - rsin( ulangle ) * ujoint;
   lyknee = ypos - rcos( ulangle ) * ujoint;
   lxfoot = lxknee - rsin( llangle ) * ljoint;
   lyfoot = lyknee + rcos( llangle ) * ljoint;
   Body_Image( MaxColors-1 );
   delay(BRIEF);
}
```

Finally, the left leg swings back to the standing position to complete Elmer's step:

```
for( i=1; i<=30; i++ )
{                   /*    bring left leg back to standing    */
   Body_Image( 0 );
   llangle- -;
   lxfoot = lxknee - rsin( llangle ) * ljoint;
   lyfoot = lyknee + rcos( llangle ) * ljoint;
   Body_Image( MaxColors-1 );
   delay(BRIEF);
}
```

At this point, the coordinates and angles of each foot have been recalculated about 120 times and, inevitably, a certain amount of error has accumulated in the process. If you observe the resulting figure carefully, you may note that Elmer's right foot is slightly above the ground plane where he started and the left leg is approximately one pixel farther off the ground than the right.

As he continues across the screen, if no correction is made, he will slowly walk up the screen as well as right.

If these positions were critical, the optimum choice would be to redesign the calculation path—specifically, redesign the loop conditions. For this application, however, a simple corrective Ground_Image function is quite sufficient to keep Elmer's feet firmly on the ground.

```
    Ground_Image();
}
```

The Ground_Image function simply allows gravity to take charge for a moment and pull Elmer back down to the ground by adjusting the five critical vertical coordinates.

```
void Ground_Image()
{
   while( !getpixel( lxfoot, lyfoot+3 ) )
   {
      Body_Image( 0 );
      lyknee++;    ryknee++;
      lyfoot++;    ryfoot++;
      ypos++;
      Body_Image( MaxColors-1 );
}  }
```

This completes the initial task of taking Elmer for a walk.

Retaining a Background Image

When you run this demo, you will notice that Elmer walks across a plane that is cluttered by a set of boxes. Given the simplicity of the program, Elmer is quite oblivious to this clutter and, as Elmer's image is successively redrawn, the boxes are erased by the image of his leg.

Without going into the problem of having Elmer see these obstacles and climb over them (though this is a good place for you to experiment with decision and response rules), there are two ways to avoid having the background image erased.

One approach is to save an image of the background and, instead of using the Body_Image function with a BLACK color value to erase Elmer, simply use the putimage function with the COPY_PUT option to restore the background and erase Elmer at the same time. You can then draw Elmer's new image for the next step.

To do this, you will need three new global variables:

```
int      PositionTop, PositionLeft;
void     *Background;
```

The Walk_Right function would be changed to:

```
void Walk_Right()
{
    int      i;
    for( i=1; i<=30; i++ )
    {
        Erase_Image();                     /* replaces Body_Image(0);*/
        lrangle++;
        rxfoot = rxknee + rsin( lrangle ) * ljoint;
        ryfoot = ryknee + rcos( lrangle ) * ljoint;
        Get_Background();          /*  to restore background */
        Body_Image( MaxColors-1 );
        delay(BRIEF);
    }
    ...
}
```

The key to the operation is the Get_Background function, which would be written like this:

```
void Get_Background()
{
    int left, top, right, bottom = 150;

    if( lxfoot < lxknee ) left = lxfoot-5;
                    else left = lxknee-5;
    if( rxfoot > rxknee ) right = rxfoot+5;
                    else right = rxknee+5;
    if( lyknee < ypos ) top = ypos-7;
                    else top = lyknee-5;
    PositionTop = top;
    PositionLeft = left;
    Background = malloc(imagesize(left,top,right,bottom));
```

```
    getimage( left, top, right, bottom, Background );
}
```

The *left* and *right* variables are tested for the maximum extent of Elmer's image, and *top* for the height. Of course, a slight margin has been added on all sides and, for simplicity, *bottom* is fixed. *PositionTop* and *Position-Left* are global variables for saving the corner coordinates.

The Erase_Image function uses putimage to restore the background using COPY_PUT, then releases the memory allocated to *Background*. Remember, if memory is allocated repeatedly without being released, you will quickly run out of it!

```
void Erase_Image()
{
    putimage( PositionLeft, PositionTop,
              Background, COPY_PUT );
    free( Background );
}
```

Also remember, the Get_Background function must be called for the first time *before* Elmer is initially placed on the screen, but *after* Elmer's feet and knees have been calculated (see the Start_Walker function).

XOR_Line

A second option is to create an XOR_Line function. This is the equivalent of the line function in Turbo C++ but, instead of writing the pixel values directly to the screen, each calculated line pixel is XOR'd with the existing screen pixel. To do this, the first step is to calculate the line. XOR_Line is called exactly the same as the line function.

```
void XOR_Line( int x1, int y1, int x2, int y2 )
{
    int    i, j, k = getcolor();
    int    x = 10, y = 10;
    double slope;
```

The line calculation begins by testing the endpoints to find if the greater distance is on the x-axis or the y-axis.

```
    if( abs(x1-x2) > abs(y1-y2) )
    {
```

The endpoints are then tested for order and, if the first point is greater than the second, both the x- and y-axis coordinates are swapped. This is done for simplicity of calculation, the final loop always proceeding from the lesser to greater value. Both coordinate pairs are exchanged so the line will retain the correct result.

```
if( x1 > x2 )
{
    i = x1;    x1 = x2;    x2 = i;
    i = y1;    y1 = y2;    y2 = i;
}
```

The variable *j* takes the x-axis difference and *slope* is calculated for the line.

```
j = x2-x1;
slope = (double) (y2-y1)/j;
```

Last, a loop proceeds through the x-axis range of the line and a y-axis point corresponding to each x-axis point is calculated from the slope value. The results are passed to the XOR_Plot function.

```
    for( i=1; i<=j; i++ )
        XOR_Plot( x1+i, y1+(int)(i*slope), k );
}
else
{
```

The second case, where the y-axis distance is greater than the x-axis distance, proceeds in exactly the same way, but with an x-axis point calculated for each y-axis point.

```
    if( y1 > y2 )
    {
        i = y1;    y1 = y2;    y2 = i;
        i = x1;    x1 = x2;    x2 = i;
    }
    j = y2-y1;
    slope = (double) (x2-x1)/j;
    for( i=1; i<=j; i++ )
        XOR_Plot( x1+(int)(i*slope), y1+i, k );
} }
```

The XOR_Plot function uses the putpixel function to rewrite the screen but XOR's the specified color value with the pixel's present value.

```
void XOR_Plot( int x, int y, int color )
{
    putpixel( x, y, color ^ getpixel( x, y ) );
}
```

XOR equivalents for the lineto and linerel functions are also easily created and, if the same line is drawn a second time using an XOR function, then the first line is erased. The original background is left intact.

To use these in the ANIMATE2.C demo program, change all occurrences of Body_Image(0) to Body_Image(MaxColors −1) or simply change the Body_Image function to ignore or to remove the color argument.

Of course, there is one minor drawback to this approach: the XOR_Line function shown is considerably slower than Turbo C++'s line function. If you intend to use this extensively and speed is a consideration, you should write your XOR line equivalents in assembly language and optimize speed of operation.

If you have Turbo C version 2.0, the setwritemode function can be used for this same purpose and executes with no particular loss of speed.

```
/*=========================================================*/
/* ANIMATE1.C  Simple Animation using Turbo-C Graphics*/
 /*images and maze image are created for EGA or higher*/
/*resolutions - CGA requires image / maze adjustments */
/* though present demo will run as is on CGA systems   */
/*=========================================================*/

#ifdef __TINY__
#error Graphics demos will not run in the tiny model.
#endif

#include <conio.h>
#include <stdio.h>
#include <stdlib.h>
#include <stdarg.h>
#include <graphics.h>

#define  RIGHT   0
#define  LEFT    1
#define  UP      2
#define  DOWN    3

#define  NSTEP   0
```

```
#define    LSTEP   1
#define    RSTEP   2

int        GraphDriver;              /*    graphics device driver */
int        GraphMode;               /*       graphics mode value */
int        MaxColors;               /* maximum colors available */
int        ErrorCode = 0;           /*   reports graphics errors */
int        XPos = 3, YPos = 3;              /* initial position */
int        Move, LastMove;          /* movement directions      */
void       *Flash[3];               /* flash when hitting walls */
void       *Man[4][3];              /* images to run thru maze  */
unsigned   TimeOut = 100;

void Initialize()
{            /* initialize graphics system and report errors */
   GraphDriver = DETECT;            /*    request auto-detection */
   initgraph( &GraphDriver, &GraphMode, "C:\\TC\\BGI" );
   ErrorCode = graphresult();              /* test init results */
   if ( ErrorCode != grOk )         /* if error during init */
   {
      printf( "Graphics System Error: %s\n",
              grapherrormsg( ErrorCode ) );
      exit( 1 );
   }
   MaxColors = getmaxcolor() + 1;          /* max color range */
}

void *SaveImage( int left, int top, int right, int bottom )
{
   void   *image;

   image = malloc(imagesize(left,top,right,bottom));
   getimage( left, top, right, bottom, image );     /* save */
   putimage( left, top, image, XOR_PUT );           /* erase */
   return( image );                          /* return ptr */
}

void CreateImages()
{
   int   i, j, MaxColor = getmaxcolor();
   int   pflash1[] = { 100, 40, 110, 60, 100, 70, 120,
         65, 140, 80, 130, 60, 140, 50, 120, 65, 100, 40 };
   int   pflash2[] = { 120, 40, 110, 55,  90, 60, 110,
```

```
       65, 120, 80, 130, 65, 150, 60, 130, 65, 120, 40 };
int   pflash3[] = { 140, 40, 130, 60, 140, 70, 120,
       65, 100, 80, 110, 60, 100, 50, 120, 55, 140, 40 };
int   bkarm_u[] = { 100, 62, 102, 68, 105, 70,
                         108, 69, 109, 65 };
int   ftarm_u[] = { 140, 62, 143, 52,
                         130, 47, 125, 52 };
int   bkarm_r[] = { 121,145, 128,147, 130,150,
                         129,153, 125,154 };
int   ftarm_r[] = { 117,176, 106,176,
                         100,165, 107,160 };

randomize();
setcolor( random( MaxColor ) + 1 );
setfillstyle( random(11)+1, random(MaxColor)+1 );
fillpoly( sizeof(pflash1)/(2*sizeof(int)), pflash1 );
Flash[0] = SaveImage( 100, 40, 140, 80 );

setcolor( random( MaxColor ) + 1 );
setfillstyle( random(11)+1, random(MaxColor)+1 );
fillpoly( sizeof(pflash2)/(2*sizeof(int)), pflash2 );
Flash[1] = SaveImage(  90, 40, 150, 80 );

setcolor( random( MaxColor ) + 1 );
setfillstyle( random(11)+1, random(MaxColor)+1 );
fillpoly( sizeof(pflash3)/(2*sizeof(int)), pflash3 );
Flash[2] = SaveImage( 100, 40, 140, 80 );

setcolor( MaxColor );
setfillstyle( SOLID_FILL, MaxColor );
ellipse(   120,  60,   0, 360, 10, 10 );
                               /*   draw and fill heads   */
floodfill( 120,  60, MaxColor );
ellipse(   220, 160,   0, 360, 13,  7 );
floodfill( 220, 160, MaxColor );
ellipse(   120,  51,   0, 180,  3,  3 );
                               /*   now tack on noses   */
ellipse(   207, 160,  90, 270,  3,  2 );
setfillstyle( HATCH_FILL, MaxColor );
                               /*   change fill style   */
ellipse(   128,  60, 270,  90, 12,  6 );
                               /*   add shoulders   */
floodfill( 135,  60, MaxColor );
```

```
ellipse(   112,   60,   90, 270,  12,   6 );
floodfill( 105,   60, MaxColor );
ellipse(   220, 154,    0, 180,   8,   9 );
floodfill( 220, 150, MaxColor );
ellipse(   220, 166,  180, 360,   8,   9 );
floodfill( 220, 170, MaxColor );

for ( i=100; i<=145; i++)
   for ( j= 45; j<= 70; j++)
      putpixel( 345-i, 120-j, getpixel( i, j ) );

for ( i=204; i<=235; i++)
   for ( j=145; j<=175; j++)
      putpixel( 345-i, j, getpixel( i, j ) );

Man[UP][NSTEP]    = SaveImage( 100,  45, 140,  70 );
Man[DOWN][NSTEP]  = SaveImage( 205,  50, 245,  75 );
Man[LEFT][NSTEP]  = SaveImage( 203, 140, 234, 180 );
Man[RIGHT][NSTEP] = SaveImage( 111, 140, 142, 180 );

setfillstyle( CLOSE_DOT_FILL, MaxColor );

putimage( 100, 45, Man[UP][NSTEP], COPY_PUT );

                                         /*   add arms    */
fillpoly( sizeof(bkarm_u)/(2*sizeof(int)), bkarm_u );
fillpoly( sizeof(ftarm_u)/(2*sizeof(int)), ftarm_u );

        /* fillpoly fills calculated outline between end */
        /* points — may overwrite part of original image */
        /* and boundary — restore original using OR_PUT  */
putimage( 100, 45, Man[UP][NSTEP], OR_PUT );

for ( i=100; i<=145; i++)
   for ( j= 45; j<= 70; j++)
   {
      putpixel( 345-i,       j, getpixel( i, j ) );
                            /*   rotate left/right   */
      putpixel( 345-i, 220-j, getpixel( i, j ) );
                            /*   and invert to   */
      putpixel(     i, 220-j, getpixel( i, j ) );
                            /*   face down ...   */
   }

                            /*   save all images   */
```

```
Man[UP][LSTEP]    = SaveImage( 100,   45, 145,   70 );
Man[UP][RSTEP]    = SaveImage( 200,   45, 245,   70 );
Man[DOWN][LSTEP]  = SaveImage( 100, 150, 145, 175 );
Man[DOWN][RSTEP]  = SaveImage( 200, 150, 245, 175 );

putimage( 100, 140, Man[LEFT][NSTEP], COPY_PUT );
fillpoly( sizeof(bkarm_r)/(2*sizeof(int)), bkarm_r );
                                     /*  add arms       */
fillpoly( sizeof(ftarm_r)/(2*sizeof(int)), ftarm_r );
putimage( 100, 140, Man[LEFT][NSTEP], OR_PUT );


for ( i=100; i<=132; i++)
    for ( j=144; j<=177; j++)
    {
        putpixel( 345-i, j, getpixel( i, j ) );
                              /*    rotate up/down   */
        putpixel( 345-i, 220-j, getpixel( i, j ) );
                              /*   and invert to    */
        putpixel( i, 220-j, getpixel( i, j ) );
                              /*   face right ...    */
    }
Man[LEFT][RSTEP]  = SaveImage( 100, 144, 132, 177 );
Man[LEFT][LSTEP]  = SaveImage( 100,  43, 132,  76 );
Man[RIGHT][LSTEP] = SaveImage( 213,  43, 245,  76 );
Man[RIGHT][RSTEP] = SaveImage( 213, 144, 245, 177 );
}

void CreateMaze()
{
    int i, j;
    int  maze1[]  = { 200, 40,  50, 40,  50,160, 100,160 };
    int  maze2[]  = { 100, 80, 100,120, 200,120, 200,240 };
    int  maze3[] = { 0,200, 100,200 };
    int  maze4[] = { 150,160, 150,240, 50,240, 50,280 };
    int  maze5[] = { 150, 80, 300, 80 };
    int  maze6[] = { 250, 80, 250,160 };
    int  maze7[] = { 100,280, 100,320 };
    int  maze8[] = { 150,280, 250,280, 250,240, 300,240 };
    int  maze9[]  = { 250, 40, 350, 40, 350, 80 };
    int  maze10[] = { 200,200, 300,200, 300,120,
```

```
                       400,120, 400, 80, 400,160 };
int   maze11[] = { 300,280, 350,280, 350,160 };
int   maze12[] = { 400,  0, 400, 40 };
int   maze13[] = { 450,120, 450, 40,
                   550, 40, 550, 80 };
int   maze14[] = { 500, 80, 500,160,
                   400,160, 400,240 };
int   maze15[] = { 400,280, 400,320 };
int   maze16[] = { 550,120, 550,200, 450,200,
                   450,280, 550,280 };
int   maze17[] = { 500,240, 600,240 };
struct viewporttype vp;

setcolor( MaxColors - 1 );
                              /*   Set draw color to white   */
setviewport(0,0,639,349,1);
settextstyle( DEFAULT_FONT, HORIZ_DIR, 1 );
outtextxy( 20, 330, "Use Arrow Keys to move 'George'"
                    "or <Q>uit to exit program");

setviewport(0,0,600,320,1);
setlinestyle( SOLID_LINE, 0, NORM_WIDTH );
getviewsettings( &vp );
rectangle( 0, 0, vp.right - vp.left,
                 vp.bottom - vp.top );

outtextxy( 10, 20, "START" );
drawpoly( sizeof(maze1)/(2*sizeof(int)), maze1 );
drawpoly( sizeof(maze2)/(2*sizeof(int)), maze2 );
drawpoly( sizeof(maze3)/(2*sizeof(int)), maze3 );
drawpoly( sizeof(maze4)/(2*sizeof(int)), maze4 );
drawpoly( sizeof(maze5)/(2*sizeof(int)), maze5 );
drawpoly( sizeof(maze6)/(2*sizeof(int)), maze6 );
drawpoly( sizeof(maze7)/(2*sizeof(int)), maze7 );
drawpoly( sizeof(maze8)/(2*sizeof(int)), maze8 );
drawpoly( sizeof(maze9)/(2*sizeof(int)), maze9 );
drawpoly( sizeof(maze10)/(2*sizeof(int)), maze10 );
drawpoly( sizeof(maze11)/(2*sizeof(int)), maze11 );
drawpoly( sizeof(maze12)/(2*sizeof(int)), maze12 );
drawpoly( sizeof(maze13)/(2*sizeof(int)), maze13 );
drawpoly( sizeof(maze14)/(2*sizeof(int)), maze14 );
drawpoly( sizeof(maze15)/(2*sizeof(int)), maze15 );
```

```
    drawpoly( sizeof(maze16)/(2*sizeof(int)), maze16 );
    drawpoly( sizeof(maze17)/(2*sizeof(int)), maze17 );
    outtextxy( 550, 300, "FINISH" );
}

void FlashImage( int x, int y )
{
    int i, j, k;

    for( i=1; i<=3; i++ )
       for( j=0; j<3; j++ )
          for( k=0; k<2; k++ )
          {
               putimage( x, y, Flash[j], XOR_PUT );
               sound( random(100) + 100 );
          }
    nosound();
}


void Put_Image( int Step )
{
    int   x = XPos, y = YPos;

    switch( Move )
    {
       case RIGHT:
       case  LEFT: x+=8;  break;
       case    UP:
       case  DOWN: y+=5;
    }
    putimage( x, y, Man[ Move ][ Step ], XOR_PUT );
}

int Test_Move()
{
    int i;

    switch( Move )
    {
        case RIGHT: for( i = XPos+47; i <= XPos+96; i++ )
                    if( getpixel( i, YPos+5 ) )
                        return( 0 );                    break;
        case  LEFT: for( i = XPos; i >= XPos-50; i- - )
```

```
                        if( getpixel( i, YPos+5 ) )
                            return( 0 );                   break;
         case     UP: for( i = YPos; i >= YPos-40; i- - )
                        if( getpixel( XPos+5, i ) )
                            return( 0 );                   break;
         case   DOWN: for( i = YPos+37; i <= YPos+76; i++ )
                        if( getpixel( XPos+5, i ) )
                            return( 0 );
      }
      return( 1 );
}

void Take_Step( int x, int y, int Step )
{
   Put_Image( Step );
   delay( TimeOut );
   Put_Image( Step );
   XPos += x;
   YPos += y;
   if( Step != NSTEP) LastMove = Step;
}

void Move_Image( int NextStep )
{
   int i, XFake, YFake, XStep, YStep, XFlash, YFlash;

   Put_Image( NSTEP );
   Move = NextStep;
   Put_Image( NSTEP );
   switch( Move )
   {
      case RIGHT: XFake  = 5;    YFake  = 0;
                  XStep  = 5;    YStep  = 0;
                  XFlash = 5;    YFlash = 0;    break;
      case  LEFT: XFake  = -5;   YFake  = 0;
                  XStep  = -5;   YStep  = 0;
                  XFlash = 2;    YFlash = 0;    break;
      case    UP: XFake  = 0;    YFake  = -5;
                  XStep  = 0;    YStep  = -4;
                  XFlash = 0;    YFlash = 2;    break;
      case  DOWN: XFake  = 0;    YFake  = 5;
                  XStep  = 0;    YStep  = 4;
```

```
                        XFlash = 0;    YFlash = 0;
}
if( !Test_Move() )
{
   Put_Image( NSTEP );
   XPos += XFake;
   YPos += YFake;
   Put_Image( LSTEP );
   FlashImage( XPos+XFlash, YPos+YFlash );
   Put_Image( LSTEP );
   XPos -= XFake;
   YPos -= YFake;
   Put_Image( NSTEP );
}
else
{
   Put_Image( NSTEP );
   XPos += XStep;
   YPos += YStep;
   if( LastMove != LSTEP )
   {
      for( i=1; i<=2; i++ )
      {
         Take_Step( XStep, YStep, LSTEP );
         Take_Step( XStep, YStep, NSTEP );
         Take_Step( XStep, YStep, RSTEP );
         Take_Step( XStep, YStep, NSTEP );
      }
      Take_Step( XStep, YStep, LSTEP );
      Put_Image( NSTEP );
      delay( TimeOut );
   }
   else
   {
      for ( i=1; i<=2; i++ )
      {
         Take_Step( XStep, YStep, RSTEP );
         Take_Step( XStep, YStep, NSTEP );
         Take_Step( XStep, YStep, LSTEP );
         Take_Step( XStep, YStep, NSTEP );
```

```
        }
        Take_Step( XStep, YStep, RSTEP );
        Put_Image( NSTEP );
        delay( TimeOut );
}  }  }
void StartGame()
{
    char ch;
    int   Quit = 0;

    Move = LastMove = RIGHT;
    Put_Image( NSTEP );
    while( !Quit )
    {
        ch = getch();
        if( ch == 0x00 )
        {
            ch = getch();
            switch( ch )
            {
                case 'M': Move_Image( RIGHT );  break;
                case 'K': Move_Image( LEFT );   break;
                case 'H': Move_Image( UP );     break;
                case 'P': Move_Image( DOWN );
            }  }
        else if( ch == 'Q' || ch == 'q' ) Quit++;
}  }                                      /*   exit!   */
void ClearImages()
{
    int i, j;

    for( i=0; i<=2; i++ )    free( Flash[i] );
    for( i=0; i<=3; i++ )
        for( j=0; j<=2; j++ ) free( Man[i][j] );
}

main()
{
    Initialize();                  /* set graphics mode      */
    outtextxy(10,10," One Moment Please ");
    setactivepage( 1 );
```

```
        CreateImages();                    /* create and save images */
        setactivepage( 0 );
        clearviewport();
        CreateMaze();                          /* build the maze    */
        StartGame();                           /* now run the demo  */
        ClearImages();                         /* free memory used  */
        closegraph();                          /* restore text mode */
}




        /*=====================================================*/
        /*  ANIMATE2.C == Simple Animation using Turbo-C  */
        /*   Graphics and formula-generated images          */
        /*=====================================================*/
#ifdef __TINY__
#error Graphics demos will not run in the tiny model.
#endif

#include <conio.h>
#include <stdio.h>
#include <stdlib.h>
#include <stdarg.h>
#include <math.h>
#include <graphics.h>

int     GraphDriver;        /* graphics device driver       */
int     GraphMode;          /* graphics mode value          */
int     MaxColors;          /* maximum colors available     */
int     ErrorCode = 0;      /* reports any graphics errors  */

const   double PI = 3.1415;
const   int   BRIEF = 5;           /* change to slow images  */

int   rcolor, lcolor,            /* right and left leg colors */
      urangle, ulangle,          /* up right & left leg angle */
      lxknee, lyknee, rxknee, ryknee,       /* knee coords  */
      lrangle, llangle,        /* lower right/left leg angles */
      lxfoot, lyfoot, rxfoot, ryfoot,       /* feet coords  */
      ujoint, ljoint,          /* length of leg joints */
      xpos,   ypos;            /* body coords (center) */

void Initialize()
```

```c
{                 /* initialize graphics system and report errors */
   GraphDriver = DETECT;              /* request auto-detection */
   initgraph( &GraphDriver, &GraphMode, "C:\\TC\BGI" );
   ErrorCode = graphresult();         /* test init results     */
   if( ErrorCode != grOk )           /* if error during init */
   {
      printf( "Graphics System Error: %s\n",
              grapherrormsg( ErrorCode ) );
      exit( 1 );
   }
   MaxColors = getmaxcolor() + 1;            /* max color range */
}
double rad( int degrees )
{
   return( PI * degrees / 180 );
}

double rsin( int degrees )
{
   return sin( rad( degrees ) );
}

double rcos( int degrees )
{
   return cos( rad( degrees ) );
}

void Pause()
{
   while( kbhit() ) getch();
   getch();
}

void Create_Field()
{
   int   base = 152;

   line( 0, base, 639, base );
   rectangle( 100, base-10, 120, base );
   rectangle( 150, base-15, 175, base );
   rectangle( 255, base-20, 300, base );
   rectangle( 375, base-10, 420, base );
}
```

```
void Plot_Knot()
{
    int i, j, k = getcolor();

    for( i=-1; i<=1; i++ )
        for( j=-1; j<=1; j++ )
            putpixel( getx()+i, gety()+j, k );
}

void Body_Image( int color )
{
    int i, j, left, right, top, bottom;

    setcolor( color );

    if( color ) setcolor(lcolor);
    moveto( lxfoot, lyfoot );
    Plot_Knot();
    lineto( lxknee, lyknee );
    Plot_Knot();
    lineto( xpos, ypos );
    Plot_Knot();
    if( color ) setcolor(rcolor);
    lineto( rxknee, ryknee );
    Plot_Knot();
    lineto( rxfoot, ryfoot );
    Plot_Knot();
    if( color ) setcolor(MaxColors-1);

    bottom = ypos+10;
    top    = ypos-5;
    left   = xpos-11;
    right  = xpos+11;
    line( xpos,  ypos,  left,  top    );
    line( xpos,  ypos,  right, top    );
    line( xpos,  ypos,  xpos,  bottom );
    line( left,  top,   right, top    );
    line( left,  top,   xpos,  bottom );
    line( right, top,   xpos,  bottom );
}

void Start_Walker()
{
    lxknee = lxfoot;
```

```
   lyknee = lyfoot-ljoint;
   xpos = lxfoot + rsin( ulangle ) * ujoint;
   ypos = lyfoot + rcos( ulangle ) * ujoint - ljoint;
   rxfoot = xpos + rsin( urangle ) * ujoint;
   rxknee = rxfoot;
   ryknee = ryfoot-ljoint;
   Body_Image( MaxColors-1 );
}
void Raise_Walker()
{
   while( ulangle<=150 )
   {
      ulangle++;
      Body_Image( 0 );
      lxknee = xpos - rsin( ulangle ) * ujoint;
      lyknee = ypos - rcos( ulangle ) * ujoint;
      lrangle = llangle = 180 *
         atan2((lxfoot-lxknee),(lyfoot-lyknee))/PI;
      lxknee = lxfoot - rsin( llangle ) * ljoint;
      rxknee = rxfoot+rsin(lrangle)*ljoint;
      ryknee = lyknee = lyfoot-rcos(llangle)*ljoint;
      ypos = lyknee+rcos(ulangle)*ujoint;
      Body_Image( 15 );
      delay(BRIEF*10);
   }
   urangle = ulangle;
   lrangle = llangle = 0;
}
void Ground_Image()
{
   while( !getpixel( lxfoot, lyfoot+3 ) )
   {
      Body_Image( 0 );
      lyknee++;     ryknee++;
      lyfoot++;     ryfoot++;
      ypos++;
      Body_Image( MaxColors-1 );
   }  }

void Walk_Right()
```

```
{
    int   i;

    for( i=1; i<=30; i++ )
    {                         /*   swing right foot up 30 degrees   */
        Body_Image( 0 );
        lrangle++;
        rxfoot = rxknee + rsin( lrangle ) * ljoint;
        ryfoot = ryknee + rcos( lrangle ) * ljoint;
        Body_Image( MaxColors-1 );
        delay(BRIEF);
    }

    for( i=1; i<=30; i++ )
    {                         /* adjust left leg to advance foot */
        Body_Image( 0 );
        llangle++;
        lxknee = lxfoot + rsin( llangle ) * ljoint;
        lyknee = lyfoot - rcos( llangle ) * ljoint;
        xpos = lxknee + rsin( ulangle ) * ujoint;
        ypos = lyknee + rcos( ulangle ) * ujoint;
        rxknee = xpos + rsin( urangle ) * ujoint;
        ryknee = ypos - rcos( urangle ) * ujoint;
        rxfoot = rxknee + rsin( lrangle ) * ljoint;
        ryfoot = ryknee + rcos( lrangle ) * ljoint;
        Body_Image( MaxColors-1 );
        delay(BRIEF);
    }

    for( i=1; i<=30; i++ )
    {                         /* bring right leg back to standing */
        Body_Image( 0 );
        lrangle- -;
        rxknee = rxfoot - rsin( lrangle ) * ljoint;
        ryknee = ryfoot - rcos( lrangle ) * ljoint;
        xpos = rxknee - rsin( urangle ) * ujoint;
        ypos = ryknee + rcos( urangle ) * ujoint;
        lxknee = xpos - rsin( ulangle ) * ujoint;
        lyknee = ypos - rcos( ulangle ) * ujoint;
        lxfoot = lxknee - rsin( llangle ) * ljoint;
        lyfoot = lyknee + rcos( llangle ) * ljoint;
        Body_Image( MaxColors-1 );
```

```
      delay(BRIEF);
   }

   for( i=1; i<=30; i++ )
   {                        /* bring left leg back to standing */
      Body_Image( 0 );
      llangle- -;
      lxfoot = lxknee - rsin( llangle ) * ljoint;
      lyfoot = lyknee + rcos( llangle ) * ljoint;
      Body_Image( MaxColors-1 );
      delay(BRIEF);
   }
   Ground_Image();
}

main()
{
   int i;

   Initialize();                        /*    set graphics mode   */

   urangle = 30;    ulangle = 30;       /* initial values for */
   lrangle = 0;     llangle = 0;        /*    charlie (walker) */
   ujoint = 30;     ljoint = 30;
   lxfoot = 30;     lyfoot = ryfoot = 150;
   rcolor = BLUE;   lcolor = RED;

   Create_Field();
   Start_Walker();
   Raise_Walker();
   for( i=1; i<=20; i++ ) Walk_Right();
   Pause();
   closegraph();                        /*    restore text mode   */
}




     /*==========================================*/
     /*    The XOR_Line And XOR_Plot Functions    */
     /*==========================================*/
void XOR_Plot( int x, int y, int color )
{
   putpixel( x, y, color ^ getpixel( x, y ) );
```

```
}
void XOR_Line( int x1, int y1, int x2, int y2 )
{
    int     i, j, k = getcolor();
    int     x = 10, y = 10;
    double slope;
    if( abs(x1-x2) > abs(y1-y2) )
    {
        if( x1 > x2 )
        {
            i = x1;    x1 = x2;    x2 = i;
            i = y1;    y1 = y2;    y2 = i;
        }
        j = x2-x1;
        slope = (double) (y2-y1)/j;
        for( i=1; i<=j; i++ )
            XOR_Plot( x1+i, y1+(int)(i*slope), k );
    }
    else
    {
        if( y1 > y2 )
        {
            i = y1;    y1 = y2;    y2 = i;
            i = x1;    x1 = x2;    x2 = i;
        }
        j = y2-y1;
        slope = (double) (x2-x1)/j;
        for( i=1; i<=j; i++ )
            XOR_Plot( x1+(int)(i*slope), y1+i, k );
}   }
```

Chapter 11

Turtle Graphics

The original concept of Turtle Graphics was proposed by Seymour Papert and co-workers at MIT as a convenient method of creating graphics without requiring an understanding of Cartesian coordinates. This basic vision was a turtle capable of walking along a straight line for a specified distance at a specific angle and drawing a line in its track, rather like the line left by a turtle's tail after coming ashore on a sandy beach.

The basic concept proved popular. On one hand, even relatively young children could use the turtle to program images and; on the other, experienced programmers found turtle graphics an excellent tool capable of creating interesting images using basic algorithms. These algorithms were simpler than those required for similar results using Cartesian coordinates.

The turtle implemented in this chapter is designed to adapt to various screen and video capabilities, handling colors where hardware supported and adjusting movement to match video screen aspect ratios.

The TURTLE.I utility provides 29 functions for complete turtle capabilities. Not all of these are intended for direct use, some are written only to be called by other functions, but the complete source code for all of the functions is included. Of course you are invited to modify or revise these functions for your own "mutant" turtle applications.

While the turtle functions are currently implemented as conventional C graphics, this could be an ideal area for you to experiment with reimplementation as an object turtle.

Just as with other graphics functions, the turtle graphics operate within a window, but the turtle window is independent of your graphics viewport. Separate turtle windows and graphics viewports can be used at one time.

Turtle routines operate on *turtle coordinates*. The home position (at turtle coordinates 0,0) is in the center of the active turtle window, with positive turtle coordinates to the right (x-axis) and upwards (y-axis) and, with negative coordinates to the left (x-axis) and down (y-axis). The *turtle angles* follow mapping conventions and begin with 0° as up or NORTH, 90° to the right or EAST, 180° as down or SOUTH, and 270° as left or WEST. Both 0° and 360° are valid angles but all angles and rotations greater than 360° or less than 0° are translated into the range 0..360°. The four ordinal directions; NORTH, EAST, SOUTH, and WEST, are constants defined in Turtle.I.

As you have probably noticed, the turtle coordinates and angles do not correspond with the angles and coordinates used in the Turbo C++ graphics system or the familiar screen coordinate system. By normal computer conventions (as dictated by the screen address requirements), y-axis values increase from top to bottom while the turtle y-axis values decrease over the same range. At the same time, the Turbo C++ graphics system considers the zero angle to lie horizontally to the right (EAST) with angles increasing counterclockwise, while the turtle angles place zero at the top (NORTH) with the angles increasing in a clockwise direction.

These rotations and directions are not completely arbitrary. The turtle angles and directions follow cultural conventions long established and are almost instinctive like: the compass (or clock) rotates clockwise, graphs increase going up, the king is at the top of the mountain. Alternatively, the rotations and directions that have become familiar to the programmer were forged under different constraints.

Since the basic concept behind the turtle graphics was to design them to be accessible and acceptable to individuals who are not "computer sophisticated," the turtle angles and directions/values were written to follow the common and familiar conventions. For the same reasons, this set of turtle commands continues to follow the earlier standards, the possible dangers of confusing an occasional programmer notwithstanding.

The Turtle Graphic Commands

The turtle graphics utility presumes that Turbo C++ has initialized the graphics system and selected a graphics driver and mode. This done, turtle graphics are initialized by their own function: init_turtle.

init_turtle

Syntax: `init_turtle();`

While turtle graphics do not require any special device drivers or modes aside from those provided by the normal graphics initialization, the init_turtle function does take care of several important tasks, beginning by calling the create_turtle function to draw a turtle cursor and to save an image of the cursor. The init_turtle function also calculates the current screen aspect ratio (*TAsp*), sets up an initial turtle window, and sets several default conditions. These conditions include: pen color is the maximum valid color, the turtle cursor is set to visible, screen wrap is off, the turtle pen is down in drawing position, and the initial heading is NORTH (0).

Correction for screen aspect ratio is automatically applied to the y-axis.

turtle_window

Syntax: `turtle_window( x_center, y_center, width, height );`

The turtle_window function defines an area of the screen as the active turtle graphics window. Unlike the graphics window function (setviewport), turtle_window's first two arguments are the *x* and *y center* coordinates while the last two arguments provide the width and height for the window.

The window is always centered on the home coordinates (position 0,0 in turtle coordinates, but x_center, y_center in absolute screen coordinates) and is initially established to include the entire screen, less a three pixels margin. This default margin is provided to ensure that the putimage function, which handles the turtle cursor, is not called with coordinates that fall outside the valid full screen limits—an error that would prevent the cursor from appearing correctly.

The clear_turtle_screen erases the turtle window; the hide_turtle, show_turtle, no_wrap, wrap, and turtle_delay functions control the turtle display parameters.

clear_turtle_screen

Syntax: `clear_turtle_screen();`

The clear_turtle_screen function borrows the Turbo C++ graphics viewport functions to erase the turtle screen, restoring the original graphics viewport settings afterwards.

hide_turtle and show_turtle

Syntax: `hide_turtle();`
Syntax: `show_turtle();`

The hide_turtle and show_turtle functions disable and enable the turtle cursor display by setting the *visible* flag. In this program, initially, the turtle is visible. Other turtle graphics programs prefer to start the turtle as hidden.

wrap and no_wrap

Syntax: `no_wrap();`
Syntax: `wrap();`

The wrap and no_wrap functions control the turtle response when the turtle window limits are reached. If wrap is in effect, the turtle reaches the window limits and will reenter the window at the opposite border.

If no_wrap is in effect, the turtle is allowed to move beyond the turtle window limits (or even outside the screen limits entirely), but the turtle drawing will not extend beyond the window borders.

turtle_delay

Syntax: `turtle_delay( milliseconds );`

By default, the turtle moves as fast as possible, but speed is not always desired. The turtle_delay function allows you to specify a delay in milliseconds between turtle steps (between pixel movements).

Also, if the turtle is off-screen, outside of the turtle window, the time delay has been disabled. This can prevent long waits for elaborate nothings that take place outside the active turtle window, but it does not otherwise affect the display or the off-screen reference points used for lines.

Turtle Movements

The turtle movements are controlled by three factors: position, distance, and direction. The position functions provide for absolute moves, the distance functions provide for movements a specified distance along the current heading, and the direction functions set the movement headings.

home

Syntax: `home();`

The home function moves the turtle cursor to the home coordinates (0,0) at the center of the turtle window without drawing a line in the process. If a turtle_delay time is in effect, the cursor will be moved immediately, but no further movements will occur until the delay time has elapsed.

set_position

Syntax: `set_position( xaxis, yaxis );`

The set_position function immediately moves the turtle cursor to the turtle coordinates specified. No line is drawn by this move. If a turtle_delay time is in effect, the cursor will be moved immediately, but no further movements will occur until the delay time has elapsed.

forward

Syntax: `forward( distance );`

The forward function is the heart of the turtle graphics. The turtle cursor is moved the distance specified from the current position along the current heading. Movement is in one-pixel steps and, if the turtle pen is down (*draw* = TRUE), a line is drawn using the current *pencolor*. If the turtle pen is up, the turtle cursor is moved (if *visible* = TRUE) without drawing a line. If *visible* is FALSE, the turtle cursor is moved invisibly.

If *distance* is negative, then movement is executed in the direction opposite the current heading. If a turtle_delay time is in effect, movement will halt after each step until the set delay time has elapsed. This movement delay is used regardless of the *draw* or *visible* flag settings.

The forward function uses the rcos and rsin functions to calculate the appropriate x-axis and y-axis distances, and the step_turtle function to accomplish the actual movement.

```
void forward( int distance )
{
   int  i, xdistance, ydistance,
        xorg = xpos, yorg = ypos;
   double slope;
   xdistance = rsin( direction ) * distance;
   ydistance = rcos( direction ) * distance * TAsp;
```

Some turtle drivers do not adjust for screen aspect. In this application, the *TAsp* variable is used to adjust vertical and horizontal movements in order to maintain equal line lengths on the screen in each direction. A movement of 50 units on the x-axis causes the turtle to move 50 pixels. The same distance on the y-axis is adjusted by the aspect ratio for the current graphics driver and mode. Also see the drawstr function.

The next step, after calculating the x and y offsets resulting from the *direction* and *distance*, is a series of decisions beginning by deciding which is greater, the *xdistance* or *ydistance*.

```
if( abs( xdistance ) > abs( ydistance ) )
{
```

When plotting a line, always begin with the axis with greater change, then for each point along this axis, calculate the minor axis position—but begin by calculating the *slope* of the line.

```
slope = (double) ydistance / xdistance;
```

If the *xdistance* is positive, an increasing loop is used and a y-axis position is calculated and plotted for each x-axis position.

```
if( xdistance > 0 )
    for( i=1; i<=xdistance; i++ )
        step_turtle( xorg + i,
                        yorg + (int) ( i * slope ) );
```

Otherwise, a decreasing loop is used, but the calculations are the same.

```
else
    for( i=-1; i>=xdistance; i- - )
        step_turtle( xorg + i,
                        yorg + (int) ( i * slope ) );
}
```

Alternatively, the x-axis positions are calculated along the y-axis.

```
else
{
    slope = (double) xdistance / ydistance;
    if( ydistance > 0 )
        for( i=1; i<=ydistance; i++ )
            step_turtle( xorg + (int) ( i * slope ),
                            yorg + i );
    else
        for( i=-1; i>=ydistance; i- - )
```

```
        step_turtle( xorg + (int) ( i * slope ),
                     yorg + i );
}   }
```

back

Syntax: `back( distance );`

The back function moves the turtle according to the same rules as the forward function, except that movement is in the direction opposite the current heading. If *distance* is negative, then movement is forward.

drawstr

Syntax: `drawstr( int scale, char charstr[150] )`

The drawstr function differs from the forward and back functions in two important respects: first, no correction is applied for the screen aspect ratio and; second, all movements are executed in absolute pixel steps. The reason for this is that attempting to draw small, closed figures using the slope calculations tends to produce a cumulative error when decimal fractions are rounded to integers. The resulting endpoints do not always match the start points, leaving jagged or open corners on the resulting figures. By using absolute pixel movements for small, closed figures, these errors are eliminated and a smooth finished appearance is created.

The drawstr function accepts two parameters, a scale multiplier, and an array of characters describing the turtle movements that create a figure, turtle character, logo, or other drawing. For this type of drawing, turtle movement is restricted to eight directions, the four cardinal directions, and the four diagonals lying between these (see turtle_write for details).

```
void drawstr( int scale,  char charstr[150] )
{
    int  distance, j, k, x, y;
```

A loop steps through the *charstr* array, acting in response to each element in the instruction string:

```
    for( j=0; j<=strlen(charstr); j++ )
    {
        distance = scale;
        switch( charstr[j] )
        {
```

The instruction characters *a..h* set the step direction (see Figure 11-1). As long as either *x* or *y* is not zero, turtle movement will be executed after the switch/case selector is finished. Selecting a direction also causes the turtle to take one step in this direction.

```
case 'a':    x = 0;     y = -1;    break;
case 'b':    x = 1;     y = -1;    break;
case 'c':    x = 1;     y = 0;     break;
case 'd':    x = 1;     y = 1;     break;
case 'e':    x = 0;     y = 1;     break;
case 'f':    x = -1;    y = 1;     break;
case 'g':    x = -1;    y = 0;     break;
case 'h':    x = -1;    y = -1;    break;
```

Figure 11-1: Plot Compass for Turtle Fonts

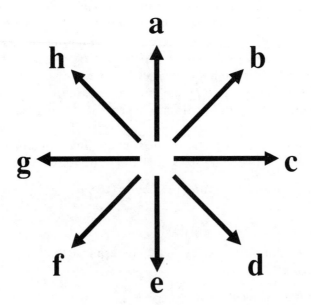

The instruction characters *m* and *p* call the pen_up and pen_down functions after setting both the *x* and *y* step increments to zero so that no turtle movement is executed in response.

```
case 'm':    x = 0;    y = 0;   pen_down();
                                 break;
case 'p':    x = 0;    y = 0;   pen_up();
                                 break;
```

The instruction characters *2..0* continue movement in the active direction, setting the *distance* according to the scale and the multiplier. Because the instruction that set the direction also resulted in one turtle step (with *distance* equal to *scale*), a movement instruction of *1* is ignored entirely. An instruction of *2* is accepted, but no action is taken, leaving the value for *distance* = (2 – 1) * scale (which is already the value of *distance*) so only a break statement is needed. Instructions *3* through *9* multiply distance by one less than the instruction integer and an instruction of *0* is taken as the equivalent of 10, making *distance* equal *scale* times 9 (10–1).

```
        case '2':                                   break;
        case '3':    distance = scale * 2;          break;
        case '4':    distance = scale * 3;          break;
        case '5':    distance = scale * 4;          break;
        case '6':    distance = scale * 5;          break;
        case '7':    distance = scale * 6;          break;
        case '8':    distance = scale * 7;          break;
        case '9':    distance = scale * 8;          break;
        case '0':    distance = scale * 9;          break;
        default :    x = 0;    y = 0;
    }
```

The default case in the switch statement sets null values for the *x* and *y* step values in any case where the instruction character is not recognized; therefore, preventing error movements. This might be applicable if you wanted to delimit your instruction strings using spaces, commas, dashes, or even several characters, simply to make the instructions easier to read.

Finally, the turtle is stepped along the appropriate heading for the distance set.

```
        for( k=1; k<=distance; k++ )
            step_turtle( xpos + x, ypos + y );
}   }
```

set_heading

Syntax: `set_heading( degrees );`

The set_heading function sets the current heading to an absolute value. The argument *degrees* can be any integer value, or the four cardinal directions (NORTH, EAST, SOUTH, and WEST) defined in TURTLE.I can be used.

If a negative value is passed to set_headings or if the variable *degrees* is greater than 360°, then the correct_direction function corrects the heading value to the range 0..360°.

turn_left and turn_right

Syntax: `turn_left( angle );`
Syntax: `turn_right( angle );`

The turn_left function (counterclockwise) decreases the current heading by *angle* degrees. The turn_right function (clockwise) increases the current heading by *angle* degrees. In either function, a negative argument reverses the direction, the current angle is changed and both turn_left and turn_right use the correct_direction function to ensure that the resulting turtle heading remains within the 0..360° range.

Turtle Drawing

The turtle graphics utility provides three functions to control the drawing: set_pen_color to select the turtle drawing color and pen_down and pen_up to lower and raise the pen during movements.

set_pen_color

Syntax: `set_pen_color( color );`

The set_pen_color function selects the turtle drawing color and accepts the color names defined in graphics.h. In monochrome modes (CGAHI for example), the drawing color is limited to BLACK or WHITE. In palette selection modes (CGAC0 for example), the drawing colors are limited to the predefined palette selections. Otherwise, the drawing color may be any valid, supported color.

pen_up and pen_down

Syntax: `pen_down();`
Syntax: `pen_up();`

The pen_up and pen_down functions operate exactly as the function names imply, setting the *draw* flag to FALSE or TRUE respectively. If *draw* is

FALSE (set by pen_up), turtle movements do not draw a line. If *draw* is TRUE (set by pen_down), turtle movements draw a line in the current *pencolor*.

Turtle Information

Functions are also provided to return information about the turtle settings and coordinates.

heading

Syntax: `angle = heading();`

The heading function returns an integer value reporting the current turtle heading.

turtle_where

Syntax: `if( turtle_where() ) ... ;`

The turtle_where function returns a Boolean value: TRUE if the current turtle position is within the turtle window limits, FALSE if the turtle is outside the window limits.

xcor and ycor

Syntax: `xaxis = xcor();`
Syntax: `yaxis = ycor();`

The xcor and ycor functions return the x-axis and y-axis turtle cursor coordinates.

Turtle Graphics Demo (TURTLE.C)

Turtle Graphics are excellent for simple drawing programs or for creating various types of figures or illustrations. They require only a minimum of programming information. In the Turtle demonstration (TURTLE.C), two complex figures are generated as examples, using very simple instructions. Then a series of turtle characters and a logo illustration are created using the turtle_write function.

The maze used in the demo in Chapter 10, could also have been drawn using turtle graphics. A random maze could also be created using turtle graphics and a generation algorithm. In chief, turtle graphics are simply a programming tool, an alternative to the line functions in Turbo C++ graphics, and an entry point for creating complex forms from simple algorithms.

turtle_write

Syntax: `turtle_write( xaxis, yaxis, scale, color, workstr )`

The turtle_write function draws characters defined using a simple instruction set that may be employed to create your own fonts, special characters, logos, or other graphic elements.

The character set used in the turtle demo comprises only eight characters and is designed primarily to demonstrate how a font can be created. In general, turtle characters are similar to the stroked character fonts provided with Turbo Pascal and Turbo C++ (see Chapter 15, *The Turbo Font Editor*) though the character images and methods used here are neither as sophisticated, nor as extensive.

The turtle_write and drawchar functions could be implemented by a variety of methods: the character definitions could be condensed, stored in binary files, or redesigned to include curve calculations (though curves are not provided by the turtle functions) for smooth, rounded characters. The method used was chosen primarily for simplicity and for ease of demonstration. Because curves are not supported, the strokes comprising a character are limited to unit steps in the eight directions shown in Figure 11-1. Figure 11-2 shows two turtle characters, *e* and *i*, diagrammed as vector strokes with the turtle_write instructions.

The beginning and end points for each character are shown as a register mark (a circle enclosing a cross mark). For the character *e*, the complete instruction string reads:

pbama*6b2c4d2e2f2g4edc3bcef2g4h2***pb2a3***mbc2dfg2h***pd7**

Note: italicized instructions are executed pen down, the others pen up.

Each stroke begins as a direction and may be followed by a number 2..0 indicating how many steps are to be executed in this direction. If no number follows the direction key, only one step is executed; thus a 1 would be redundant and is not used. A zero is used for 10 steps and distances greater than 10 steps are coded as multiple instructions. A move right of 16 steps would be coded as *c8c8* rather than *c16*.

In addition to the directions, two other instructions, *p* and *m*, are used. In the instruction string for *e*, the instruction *p* calls pen_up so that the next two move instructions, *ba*, are executed without drawing a line. The instruction *m* calls pen_down and the following instruction groups draw the outside of the character. Next, another pen_up is followed by *b2a3* to position the turtle to draw the eye of the character. The final three instructions, *pd7*, move the turtle, without drawing, to the terminating position.

The turtle ends on the same horizontal as it began, but is one pixel beyond the character, leaving a thin margin on both sides.

The character *i* is coded as: pc*ma9bpamhabdefpemde9g2*pc3. You should be able to follow the coding for these two characters in Figure 11-2. Following are the rest of the characters used in the Turtle demonstration, together with their code strings:

- *l* is coded as: pb*ma7a7bde7e7fh*pdc2
- *r* is coded as: pc*ma9bce2b2c2d2eghg2f2e6g2*pc9
- *t* is coded as: pb2c*ma8g3hbc3a3bde3c3dfg3e7dcdfg2h2*pd2c5

Notice that the character *t* begins at a point inside the left-most extent of the cross bar (as shown by the register mark). This offset provides kerning to allow the character to fit better with other letters, creating a smoother appearance. The *l* and *r* characters are shown in Figure 11-3. The *t* is shown in Figure 11-4.

Figure 11-2: Plot for Characters "e" and "i"

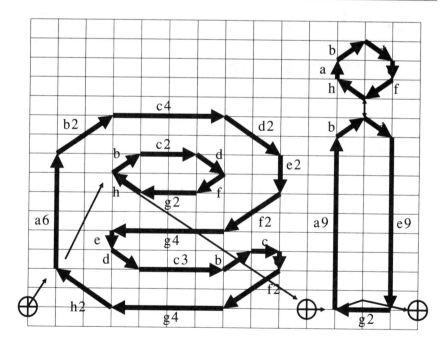

Figure 11-3: Plot for Characters "l" and "r"

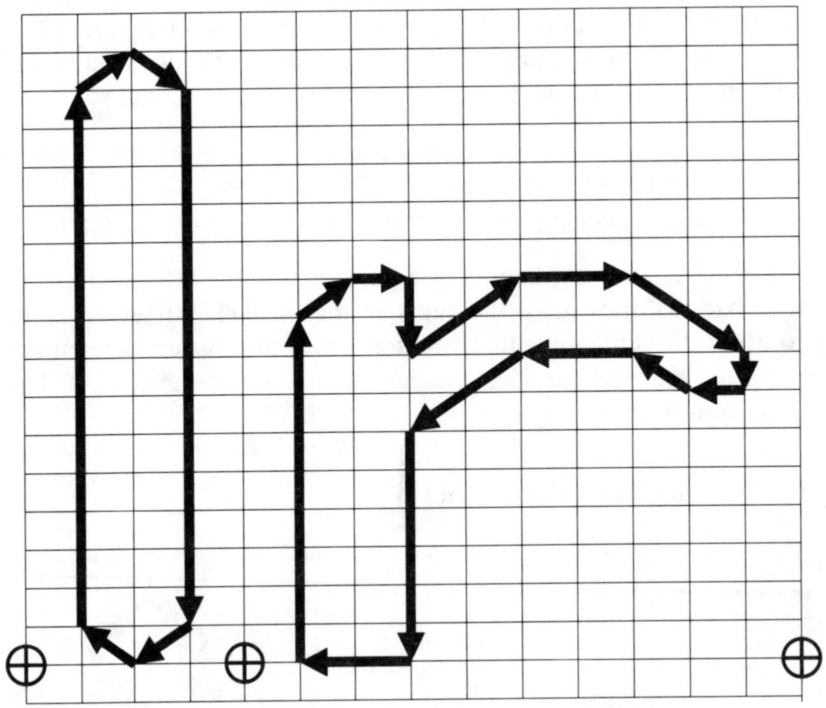

Characters may be kerned left or right and, in many cases, special kerning is assigned to pairs of letters to make them visually fit together. For example, the characters AV are usually kerned to allow the left top of the V to overlap the bottom right of the A. No provision has been made here for pair kerning, but it is frequently used in typesetting.

u is coded as: pba*ma7bde6dc2ba6bde7deghfg4h2*pd2c7

In this case, the character *u* ends immediately at the tail on the right, instead of allowing a pixel margin (see Figure 11-5). Like the kerning on the *t*, this provides a better visual appearance when the character is written as part of a word.

The character *w* is considerably wider than any of the others shown but still receives only a one pixel right and left margin (see Figure 11-6). When written together, as the demo program will show, the characters present a smooth, proportional appearance.

Figure 11-4: Plot for Character "t"

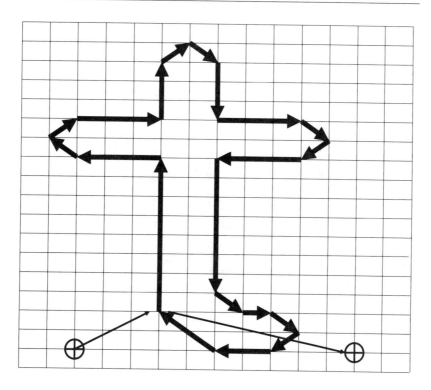

As executed in the demo program, the turtle_write function is called with five arguments: the *x* and *y* screen position (in turtle coordinates), a scaling factor, a color argument, and the string to be written.

```
void turtle_write( int x, int y, int scale,
                   int color, char workstr[100] )
{
    int    i;
    char logostr[125] =
        "pcma8a8b2c8c8c8e8e8f2g8g8g8a8a8c8c8c8"
        "f2g0g0e5b2c0c0a5f2e3g9g9a3g2e5c7c8c7"
        "f2g0g0e5b2c0c0a5f2e3g9g9a3g2e5c8c8c8pcd";
```

Unlike most string functions, *workstr* is not a pointer to a string, but is an array of characters as is the local variable *logostr*. This handling is used because the turtle_write function will treat the various strings as arrays of

Figure 11-5: Plot for Character "u"

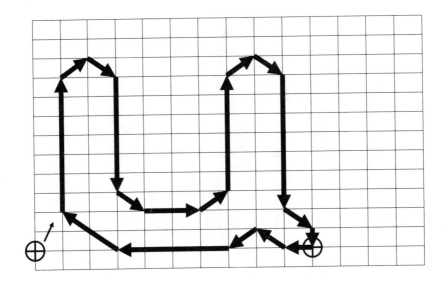

Figure 11-6: Plot for Character "w"

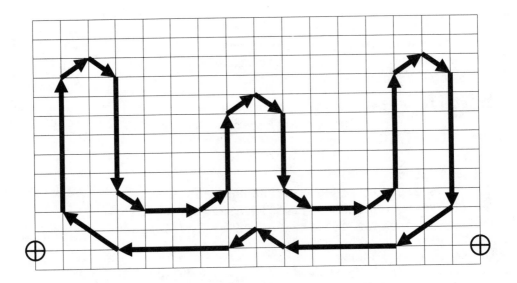

elements and use individual elements as instructions. This could still be managed using pointers, but is simpler as shown.

The *logostr* array is defined in its declaration, but could also have been passed directly to the drawstr function from some other source. This handling was chosen only because it was convenient to the demonstration.

The *color* argument allows passing color settings with the string to be displayed. Also, a negative color value can be passed as an argument and will result in a random color selection for each character drawn.

```
if( color <= MaxColors ) set_pen_color( color );
```

The *scale* factor is a multiplier setting the size of the characters. Negative and zero *scale* factors are not allowed.

```
if( scale <= 0 ) scale = 1;
```

The initial screen position is set (x, y), then a loop runs through the length of the string to be written:

```
set_position( x, y );
for( i=0; i<=strlen(workstr); i++ )
{
    if( color < 0 )
        set_pen_color( random( MaxColors ) + 1 );
```

As the loop proceeds, each element of the string to be written is sent, as a string of stroke instructions, directly to the drawstr function:

```
switch( workstr[i] )
{
    case ' ': drawstr( scale, "pc6");
              break;
    case 'e': drawstr( scale,
              "pbama6b2c4d2e2f2g4edc3bc"
              "ef2g4h2pb2a3mbc2dfg2hpd7" );
              break;
    case 'i': drawstr( scale,
              "pcma9bpamhabdefpemde9g2pc3" );
              break;
    case 'l': drawstr( scale,
              "pbma7a7bde7e7fhpdc2" );
              break;
    case 'r': drawstr( scale,
```

```
                         "pcma9bce2b2c2d2eghg2f2e6g2pc9" );
                         break;
         case 't':  drawstr( scale,
                         "pb2cma8g3hbc3a3bde3c3dfg3"
                         "e7dcdfg2h2pd2c5" );
                         break;
         case 'u':  drawstr( scale,
                         "pbama7bde6dc2ba6bde7deghfg4h2pd2c7");
                         break;
         case 'w':  drawstr( scale,
                         "pbama7bde6dc2ba3bde3dc2b"
                         "a6bde7f2g4hfg4h2pd2c6c7" );
                         break;
   }  }
```

After each line is written, the logo illustration is added.

```
    drawstr( scale, logostr );
}
```

The logo character is a figure known as a double bolix—a bolix is a type of visual paradox—shown in Figure 11-7.

```
logostr = pcma8a8b2c8c8c8e8e8f2g8g8g8a8a8c8c8c8
          f2g0g0e5b2c0c0a5f2e3g9g9a3g2e5c7c8c7
          f2g0g0e5b2c0c0a5f2e3g9g9a3g2e5c8c8c8pcd
```

Unlike most of the letter characters, the logo design could not be drawn in a single, continuous line. Two options were possible: one, to use the pen_up function to move to a new location in order to fill in necessary elements; or two, to simply trace over existing lines as required. Since visually, the two options appear quite similar, the second was chosen and line elements are retraced as required until the figure is completed.

Display logos can also be created using a variety of drawing programs such as PC Paint, Microsoft Paint, GEM Draw, or others, stored as disk files, and subsequently accessed by your program (precise methods vary depending on the utility chosen). A turtle-created logo, however, offers greater flexibility because, as shown in the demo program, a turtle logo can be scaled to size.

Since individual turtle graphic elements can be defined by instruction strings, as shown with the sample alphabet, picture elements can also be created as turtle graphic instructions using either the turtle_write function or via an instruction handler designed to use the forward, back, turn_right, turn_left and set_heading functions if you need more flexible line elements.

Figure 11-7: Plot for Author's Logo

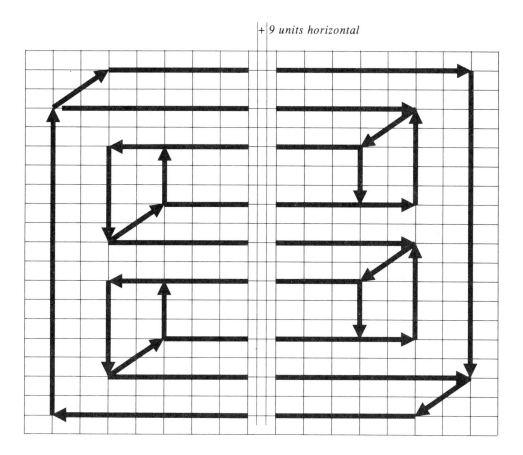

+|*9 units horizontal*

Other Turtle Options

The turtle functions are not designed so much as to be used directly as to be called indirectly by other program applications. Turtle functions could, however, be easily interfaced to a mouse, joystick, or to cursor keys for a drawing utility or combined with various algorithms to trace business data graphs in a moving presentation. They can also be used to create interactive graphic slide shows and to show different relations or connections between display elements in interactive stories or programmed instructions.

You might also experiment with revisions to permit separate x- and y-axis scaling. Currently, the turtle_write function is best suited to create "balloon" or "outline" typefaces. With minor additions to the drawstr function, however, the floodfill function could create solid letters or fill letters using various fillpatterns. Another enhancement might be an option to include color changes in the instruction strings.

The turtle functions are simply a tool set. Feel free to enhance, change and revise these according to your needs and imagination.

Turtle Graphics with Plotters

A color graphics screen can be written to a graphics plotter but the results are neither fast nor satisfactory in all senses. Because both turtle graphics and graphics plotters are stroke (line) oriented, essentially the same functions that are used here to drive the turtle can also be adapted to duplicate the motions (with scaling adjustments, if necessary) on a graphics plotter.

If you need business graph displays in full color for slide and overhead projector applications, keep the turtle graphics and plotter in mind—they suit each other nicely.

```
/*===========================================*/
/*                 TURTLE.I                  */
/* 28 turtle functions for Turbo C graphics  */
/*===========================================*/

#include <math.h>

#define   NORTH    0
#define   EAST     90
#define   SOUTH    180
#define   WEST     270
#define   PI       3.14159
#define   FALSE    0
#define   TRUE     1

double    TAsp;
int       direction, draw, pencolor, timeout, wrapoff,
          xhome, xpos, yhome, ypos, visible = 0,
          left, right, top, bottom;
void      *turtle;
```

```
void      back( int distance );
void      clear_turtle_screen();
void      correct_direction();
void      create_turtle();
void      drawstr( int scale,  char charstr[150] );
void      forward( int distance );
int       heading();
void      hide_turtle();
void      home();
void      init_turtle();
void      no_wrap();
void      pen_down();
void      pen_up();
double    rsin( int degrees );
double    rcos( int degrees );
void      set_heading( int degrees );
void      set_pen_color( int color );
void      set_position( int xaxis, int yaxis );
void      show_turtle();
void      step_turtle( int xmove, int ymove );
void      turn_left( int degrees );
void      turn_right( int degrees );
void      turtle_delay( int time );
int       turtle_where();
void      turtle_window( int xaxis, int yaxis,
                         int width, int height );
void      wrap();
int       xcor();
int       ycor();

void create_turtle()
{
   int  i, j, k = getmaxcolor(), size;
   void *temp;
   size = imagesize( 1, 1, 5, 5 );
   temp = malloc( size );
   getimage( 1, 1, 5, 5, temp );
   putimage( 1, 1, temp, XOR_PUT );
   for( i=1; i<=5; i++ ) putpixel( i, 3, k );
   for( j=1; j<=5; j++ ) putpixel( 3, j, k );
   putpixel( 3, 3, 0 );
```

```
      turtle = malloc( imagesize( 1, 1, 5, 5 ) );
      getimage( 1, 1, 5, 5, turtle );
      putimage( 1, 1, turtle, XOR_PUT );
      putimage( 1, 1, temp, COPY_PUT );
      free( temp );
}

double rsin( int degrees )
{
      return( (double) sin( PI * degrees / 180 ) );
}

double rcos( int degrees )
{
      return( (double) cos( PI * degrees / 180 ) );
}

void clear_turtle_screen()
{
      struct  viewporttype  graphport;
      getviewsettings( &graphport );
      setviewport( left, top, right, bottom, 1 );
      clearviewport();
      setviewport( graphport.left,  graphport.top,
                   graphport.right, graphport.bottom,
                   graphport.clip );
      if( visible )
         putimage( xpos-2, ypos-2, turtle, XOR_PUT );
      home();
}

void correct_direction()
{
      while( direction > 360 ) direction -= 360;
      while( direction < 0 )    direction += 360;
}

void step_turtle( int xstep, int ystep )
{
      if( visible )
         putimage( xpos-2, ypos-2, turtle, XOR_PUT );
      xpos = xstep;
```

```
   ypos = ystep;
   if( !wrapoff )
   {
      if( xpos < left ) xpos += right;
      else if( xpos > right ) xpos -= right;
      if( ypos < top ) ypos += bottom;
      else if( ypos > bottom ) ypos -= bottom;
   }
   if( draw && turtle_where() )
      putpixel( xpos, ypos, pencolor );
   if( visible )
      putimage( xpos-2, ypos-2, turtle, XOR_PUT );
   if( timeout && turtle_where() ) delay( timeout );
}

void drawstr( int scale,  char charstr[150] )
{
   int  distance, j, k, x, y;

   for( j=0; j<=strlen(charstr); j++ )
   {
      distance = scale;
      switch( charstr[j] )
      {
         case 'a':  x = 0;      y = -1;      break;
         case 'b':  x = 1;      y = -1;      break;
         case 'c':  x = 1;      y = 0;       break;
         case 'd':  x = 1;      y = 1;       break;
         case 'e':  x = 0;      y = 1;       break;
         case 'f':  x = -1;     y = 1;       break;
         case 'g':  x = -1;     y = 0;       break;
         case 'h':  x = -1;     y = -1;      break;
         case 'm':  x = 0;      y = 0;
                    pen_down();               break;
         case 'p':  x = 0;      y = 0;
                    pen_up();                 break;
         case '2':                            break;
         case '3':  distance = scale * 2;     break;
         case '4':  distance = scale * 3;     break;
         case '5':  distance = scale * 4;     break;
         case '6':  distance = scale * 5;     break;
```

```
            case '7':   distance = scale * 6;   break;
            case '8':   distance = scale * 7;   break;
            case '9':   distance = scale * 8;   break;
            case '0':   distance = scale * 9;   break;
             default:   x = 0;   y = 0;
        }
        for( k=1; k<=distance; k++ )
            step_turtle( xpos + x, ypos + y );
}  }

void forward( int distance )
{
    int    i, xdistance, ydistance,
            xorg = xpos, yorg = ypos;
    double slope;

    xdistance = rsin( direction ) * distance;
    ydistance = rcos( direction ) * distance * TAsp;
    if( abs( xdistance ) > abs( ydistance ) )
    {
        slope = (double) ydistance / xdistance;
        if( xdistance > 0 )
            for( i=1; i<=xdistance; i++ )
                step_turtle( xorg + i,
                            yorg + (int) ( i * slope ) );
        else
            for( i=-1; i>=xdistance; i- - )
                step_turtle( xorg + i,
                            yorg + (int) ( i * slope ) );
    }
    else
    {
        slope = (double) xdistance / ydistance;
        if( ydistance > 0 )
            for( i=1; i<=ydistance; i++ )
                step_turtle( xorg + (int) ( i * slope ),
                            yorg + i );
        else
            for( i=-1; i>=ydistance; i- - )
                step_turtle( xorg + (int) ( i * slope ),
                            yorg + i );
```

```
}  }
void back( int distance )
{
   forward( distance * -1 );
}

int  heading()
{
   return( direction );
}

void hide_turtle()
{
   if( visible )
      putimage( xpos-2, ypos-2, turtle, XOR_PUT );
   visible = FALSE;
   if( timeout ) delay( timeout );
}

void home()
{
   if( visible )
      putimage( xpos-2, ypos-2, turtle, XOR_PUT );
   xpos = xhome;
   ypos = yhome;
   if( timeout ) delay(timeout);
   if( visible )
      putimage( xpos-2, ypos-2, turtle, XOR_PUT );
}

void no_wrap()
{
   wrapoff = TRUE;
}

void pen_down()
{
   draw = TRUE;
}

void pen_up()
{
```

```
      draw = FALSE;
}

void set_heading( int degrees )
{
   direction = degrees;
   correct_direction();
}

void set_pen_color( int color )
{
   if( color < 0 ) color = 0;
   if( color > getmaxcolor() ) color = getmaxcolor();
   pencolor = color;
   setcolor( pencolor );
}

void set_position( int xaxis, int yaxis )
{
   if( visible )
      putimage( xpos-2, ypos-2, turtle, XOR_PUT );
   xpos = xhome + xaxis;
   ypos = yhome - yaxis;
   if( timeout ) delay(timeout);
   if( visible )
      putimage( xpos-2, ypos-2, turtle, XOR_PUT );
}

void show_turtle()
{
   if( !visible )
      putimage( xpos-2, ypos-2, turtle, XOR_PUT );
   visible = TRUE;
   if( timeout ) delay( timeout );
}

void turn_left( int degrees )
{
   direction += degrees;
   correct_direction();
}

void turn_right( int degrees )
```

```
{
   direction -= degrees;
   correct_direction();
}

void turtle_window( int xaxis, int yaxis,
                    int width, int height )
{
   int  xlimit = getmaxx() - 3,
        ylimit = getmaxy() - 3;

   left = xaxis - ( width / 2 );
   while( left < 3 ) left++;
   right = left + width;
   while( right > xlimit ) right- -;

   top = yaxis - ( height / 2 );
   while( top < 3 ) top++;
   bottom = top + height;
   while( bottom > ylimit ) bottom- -;

   setviewport( left, right, top, bottom, 0 );
   clearviewport();

   xpos = xhome = xaxis;
   ypos = yhome = yaxis;
}

int turtle_where()
{
   if( xpos >= left && xpos <= right &&
       ypos >= top  && ypos <= bottom   )
         return( TRUE );
   else return( FALSE );
}

void turtle_delay( int time )
{
   timeout = time;
}

void wrap()
{
```

```c
      wrapoff = FALSE;
}

int xcor()
{
   return( xpos - xhome );
}

int ycor()
{
   return( -1 * ( ypos - yhome ) );
}

void init_turtle()
{
   int   xasp, yasp, MaxX, MaxY;

   create_turtle();
   getaspectratio( &xasp, &yasp );
   TAsp = (double) xasp / (double) yasp * -1;
   MaxX = getmaxx();
   MaxY = getmaxy();
   turtle_window( MaxX/2, MaxY/2, MaxX, MaxY );
   set_pen_color( getmaxcolor() );
   show_turtle();
   turtle_delay( 0 );
   no_wrap();
   pen_down();
   set_heading( 0 );
}


      /*===========================================*/
      /*  TURTLE.C == Turtle Graphics Demo Program  */
      /*===========================================*/

#ifdef __TINY__
#error Graphics demos will not run in the tiny model.
#endif

#include <conio.h>
#include <stdio.h>
#include <stdlib.h>
```

```c
#include <stdarg.h>
#include <graphics.h>
#include <gprint.i>
#include <fcntl.h>
#include "turtle.i"

int    GraphDriver;
int    GraphMode;
int    MaxColors;
int    ErrorCode = 0;

void Initialize()
{
    GraphDriver = DETECT;
    initgraph( &GraphDriver, &GraphMode, "C:\\TC\\BGI" );
    ErrorCode = graphresult();
    if( ErrorCode != grOk )
    {
        printf( "Graphics System Error: %s\n",
                grapherrormsg( ErrorCode ) );
        delay( 10000 );
        exit( 1 );
    }
    MaxColors = getmaxcolor() + 1;
}

void Pause()
{
    while( kbhit() ) getch();
    getch();
}

void TurtleDemo()
{
    int   i, j;

    turtle_delay(10);
    set_heading( SOUTH );
    pen_up();
    forward( 100 );
    delay( 500 );

    turtle_delay(0);
```

```
    pen_down();
    set_heading( 45 );
    for( i=1; i<=15; i++ )
    {
        set_pen_color( i );
        for( j=1; j<=6; j++ )
        {
            forward(100 + i*3);
            turn_right(59);
    }   }
    home();
    Pause();
    clear_turtle_screen();
    wrap();
    set_position( -100, -100 );
    set_heading( 45 );
    for( i=1; i<=15; i++ )
    {
        set_pen_color( i );
        for( j=1; j<=3; j++ )
        {
            forward( 200 );
            turn_left( 90 );
        }
        forward( 200 );
    }
    home();
    Pause();
}

void turtle_write( int x, int y, int scale,
                   int color, char workstr[100] )
{
    int     i;
    char    logostr[125] =
            "pcma8a8b2c8c8c8e8e8f2g8g8g8a8a8c8c8c8"
            "f2g0g0e5b2c0c0a5f2e3g9g9a3g2e5c7c8c7"
            "f2g0g0e5b2c0c0a5f2e3g9g9a3g2e5c8c8c8pcd";

    if( color <= MaxColors ) set_pen_color( color );
    if( scale <= 0 ) scale = 1;
```

```
    set_position( x, y );
    for( i=0; i<=strlen(workstr); i++ )
    {
        if( color < 0 )
            set_pen_color( random( MaxColors ) + 1 );
        switch( workstr[i] )
        {
            case ' ': drawstr( scale, "pc6");
                        break;
            case 'e': drawstr( scale,
                        "pbama6b2c4d2e2f2g4edc3bc"
                        "ef2g4h2pb2a3mbc2dfg2hpd7" );
                        break;
            case 'i': drawstr( scale,
                        "pcma9bpamhabdefpemde9g2pc3" );
                        break;
            case 'l': drawstr( scale,
                        "pbma7a7bde7e7fhpdc2" );
                        break;
            case 'r': drawstr( scale,
                        "pcma9bce2b2c2d2eghg2f2e6g2pc9" );
                        break;
            case 't': drawstr( scale,
                        "pb2cma8g3hbc3a3bde3c3dfg3"
                        "e7dcdfg2h2pd2c5" );
                        break;
            case 'u': drawstr( scale,
                        "pbama7bde6dc2ba6bde7deghf"
                        "g4h2pd2c7" );
                        break;
            case 'w': drawstr( scale,
                        "pbama7bde6dc2ba3bde3dc2b"
                        "a6bde7f2g4hfg4h2pd2c6c7" );
                        break;
        } }
    drawstr( scale, logostr );
}

void TurtleWriteDemo()
{
    randomize();
```

```
    turtle_delay( 10 );
    turtle_write( -300, -110, 5, MaxColors,
                  "turtle write ");
    turtle_delay( 7 );
    turtle_write( -300,  -20, 4, random(MaxColors)+1,
                  "write turtle ");
    turtle_delay( 5 );
    turtle_write( -300,   55, 3, -1, "turtle write ");
    turtle_delay( 3 );
    turtle_write( -300,  110, 2, -1, "write turtle ");
    turtle_delay( 1 );
    turtle_write( -300,  150, 1, MaxColors,
                  "turtle write turtle write "
                  "turtle write turtle write turtle " );
    home();
    Pause();
}

void main()
{
    Initialize();
    init_turtle();
    show_turtle();
    TurtleDemo();
    TurtleWriteDemo();
    closegraph();
}
```

Chapter 12

Image Files and Manipulation

Creating images is only one aspect of graphics programming and it also helps—in some applications—to be able to store and retrieve images as disk files and to manipulate existing images.

Structure of an Image

When Turbo C++ saves an image of a portion of the screen, the screen image is coded or compressed to minimize memory usage. For example, assume an image that is 41 by 41 pixels in size. If each pixel value was stored as a char value, the image would require 1,681 bytes of memory. In a monographic mode, each pixel location contains only one bit of real information: a Boolean bit indicating that the pixel is on or off. At the other extreme, in EGA/VGA color modes, each pixel contains six bits of information, the RrGgBb color bits (see Chapters 13 and 14 for more detail on color video data). Instead of 1,681 bytes, for an EGA/VGA system, only 1,261 bytes of actual information are required to be saved. For a monochrome image, only 211 bytes are needed.

Turbo C++ goes one step farther and uses a data compression algorithm to minimize the memory requirements, reducing 1,681 EGA/VGA pixels to a mere 990 bytes of image data (about a 42 percent savings over storing the image as char data). In monographic modes, similar compression results in even greater savings.

The data compression and deciphering is automatic and is handled whenever getimage and putimage are called. There is one item of information in the data image that is useful to know about: the first four bytes of data contain the x- and y-axis size of the image coded as *X_lsb*, *X_msb*, *Y_lsb*, *Y_msb*.

For the example proposed, the first four bytes of the image would read *28h*, *00h*, *28h*, *00h* (28h = 40 decimal) with the least_significant_byte first and the most_significant_byte second. Notice also that the size value is not stored as 41, but as 40—a minimum size of one for each axis being a reasonable assumption.

Image Files: Storage and Retrieval

When using graphics images, instead of placing the code description for a series of images in your program, it's often more convenient to create an image or several images once, then store these as external image files, and recall them when necessary for use in your application program.

For example, in the line-graph demo, four images were used to represent four different types of stock or four different types of company. In a real application, this line graph might require dozens or even hundreds of image symbols, though only a few would be needed at any particular time. Instead of including the coding to create each of these in the application program and wasting both the time to draw each image and the memory required to store all of the images, a more efficient approach would be to use a separate image creation utility program, store the images as external files, and then read the image files for each *when and if* it was required by the application. This is simple to accomplish.

As mentioned, because the image size is included in the image (and therefore, in the image file), all you actually need to know in order to retrieve an image, is the filename.

The FILE_IMG.C Demo

The demo program FILE_IMG.C will show how this is accomplished; first, by creating a image (Flash); then by storing it as a diskfile (FLASH.IMG); and, finally, by retrieving FLASH.IMG as Flash2.

FILE_IMG begins by declaring two pointers:

```
void    *Flash, *Flash2;
```

It then initializes the graphics system and calls CreateImage for the actual demonstration. When done, FILE_IMG waits for a key entr, before releasing the memory allocated for the images and then exiting.

```
main()
{
    Initialize();
    CreateImage();
    Pause();
    free(Flash);
    free(Flash2);
    closegraph();
}
```

The CreateImage procedure is adapted from an earlier animation program, using one of the flash images demonstrated.

```
void CreateImage()
{
    int   Size = 0, MaxColor = getmaxcolor();
    int   pflash[] = { 100, 40, 110, 60, 100, 70, 120, 65,
             140, 80, 130, 60, 140, 50, 120, 55, 100, 40};
    randomize();
    setcolor( random( MaxColor ) + 1 );
    setfillstyle( random(11) + 1, random(MaxColor) + 1 );
    fillpoly( sizeof(pflash)/(2*sizeof(int)), pflash );
```

The *Flash* image is created by calling SaveImage, but in this application, SaveImage has been modified slightly to accept a fifth parameter, *Size. Size* is passed by *address* so that the value calculated will be returned for further use. This is not an absolute requirement since the imagesize function can be called at any time, but it is convenient and the size information will be needed by FileImage.

```
    Flash = SaveImage( 100, 40, 140, 80, &Size );
```

The FileImage function is passed the image pointer (*Flash*), the size of the image (*Size* returned by SaveImage), and the filename where the image will be stored.

```
    FileImage( Flash, Size, "FLASH.IMG" );
```

The ReadImage function requires only the filename, returning a pointer to the new image retrieved from the disk. For confirmation, the image retrieved is written to the screen.

```
Flash2 = ReadImage( "FLASH.IMG" );
putimage( 200, 200, Flash2, COPY_PUT );
}
```

The SaveImage procedure operates exactly as before, except for the added parameter, *size*.

```
void *SaveImage( int left, int top, int right,
                 int bottom, unsigned *size )
{
   void  *image;
   *size = imagesize( left, top, right, bottom );
   image = malloc( *size );
   getimage( left, top, right, bottom, image );
   putimage( left, top, image, XOR_PUT );
   return( image );
}
```

The FileImage procedure is the key to storing an image on disk and it accepts three parameters: *image*, a pointer to the image to be written; *size*, the size of the image as calculated by the imagesize function; and the filename.

```
void FileImage( void *image, unsigned size,
                char *filename )
{
```

A file handle (stream) is declared and fileopen assigns the filename and indicates that this is a new file created for write.

```
   FILE  *f1 = fopen( filename, "w" );
```

The fwrite function references the pointer *image* to write *one* data item of *size* bytes to the stream pointed to by *f1*.

```
   fwrite( image, size, 1, f1 );
```

The fflush function is called to flush the stream (*f1*) and fclose closes the file.

```
   fflush( f1 );
   fclose( f1 );
}
```

That's it. The disk file was created, the image written, and the file closed.

Using the ReadImage procedure, retrieving the image from the created file is almost as simple as creating and saving it. In this application only one parameter is required, the filename. Using the filename and opening *fl* for read, and using the local pointer, *tempimage*, to reference the image, ReadImage declares three unsigned integers: *xaxis*, *yaxis,* and *size*. It also declares a file handle, *fl*.

```
void *ReadImage( char *filename )
{
   unsigned xsize, ysize, size;
   FILE    *fl = fopen( filename, "r" );
   void    *tempimage;
```

As mentioned, the screen size of the image is contained in the image data and, therefore, imagesize can be called locally to determine *size*. This is convenient because your program will not know how much memory is needed for an image retrieved from disk and memory *must be* allocated for this purpose.

The first trick is to read the image screen size (*xsize* and *ysize*) from the image data. Since this information is stored in reverse order with the least significant byte of each integer value appearing first and the most significant byte second, the data is read as byte values (type char) and OR'd to create an unsigned integer.

```
   xsize = fgetc( fl ) | (fgetc( fl ) << 8);
   ysize = fgetc( fl ) | (fgetc( fl ) << 8);
```

With these two values, the imagesize function can return *size*.

```
   size = imagesize( 0, 0, xsize, ysize );
```

The image width and height and the memory size are written to the screen simply for demonstration purposes.

```
   gprintxy( 10, 10,
      " xsize = %d, ysize = %d, imagesize = %d ",
                  xsize,       ysize,           size );
```

Once *size* is known, malloc allocates the necessary memory with *tempimage* pointed to the memory address.

```
   tempimage = malloc( size );
```

Since the file pointer is already four bytes into the data, the file pointer must be reset to the start of the file using the rewind function before the actual image can be retrieved.

```
rewind( f1 );
```

This done, the fread function is called in exactly the same manner as the fwrite function was called: the pointer *tempimage* is accessed to read *one* data item of *size* bytes from the stream pointed to by *f1*.

```
fread( tempimage, size, 1, f1 );
```

The fclose function closes down the file and the pointer value *tempimage* is returned to the calling function.

```
close( f1 );
return( tempimage );
}
```

It's done. Only a bit more work was required than when the image file was written. The image file was opened for read, the image screen size data was read, the memory size calculated, and the memory allocated. Then the file was reset to the beginning and *size* bytes of image data were read into *tempimage*. Finally, after the file was closed, the image pointer was returned to the calling function.

Files with Multiple Images

While it is possible to write several images to a single file, it is not recommended (though it may be necessary for some applications). Rather than offering any hard and fast rules for creating multiple image files, here are considerations and suggestions that should help when programming this type of application. They are not guaranteed solutions.

First, will all the images be the same size? Or will there be several different size images in a single file? In either case, the handling can be similar, but if the images are all the same size (exactly the same size!), then positioning the file pointer to seek a specific image becomes simpler. If the images differ only slightly in size, it may be convenient to make them all the size of the largest.

If the images are all different sizes, then retrieval is a matter of reading successive images until the desired item is reached.

Or is it?

How are you going to retrieve the four bytes of information that tell you the screen image size and the size of the data to read? The fseek function offers assistance here but you will need to keep track of your file pointer (file position). Remember, the data has no way to tell you that it is the beginning of an image and there are no reserved flag bytes possible with graphics images—any value could occur in an image.

Second, how are you going to write multiple images to a file? The file append option, used when the file is opened, is the obvious choice. But, when writing the file, should you add a few nulls between items or should you create a specific pattern of bits to insert between entries as a recognizable safety? Actually, if your handling is accurate, such safeties shouldn't be necessary. If your handling isn't accurate, these probably won't help anyway, so your best bet is not to depend on fancy insertions.

If you do need multiple images in a single file, it can be done. And, it can be done easier in C (specifically Turbo C++) than in Pascal or Basic. But it must be done carefully. And consistently.

Think of it as a challenge and have fun.

More Image Manipulation

The second principal topic in this chapter is image manipulation. Previously, in Chapter 10 on animation, images were rotated 180 degrees or flipped left for right, simple, transpositional manipulations in four basic directions. But a mere four directions is a rather limited choice of orientations. What about a true image rotation? The computer is great at crunching numbers and can calculate coordinate transformations without raising a sweat, so why not use this capability?

The demo program, ROTATE.C, will show two types of rotation: direct image rotation and calculated image rotation.

Direct Image Rotation

In direct image rotation, an existing image is rotated pixel by pixel to create a second image, duplicating the first, but with a different orientation.

First, each pixel in the specified image area is tested, to see if it is non-zero. There is no point in rotating background pixels. If the pixel value is not zero—if it does contain visual information—then the pixel's position is read as an x-axis/y-axis offset from a center point. An image is rotated geocentrically (self-centered), but provisions can also be made to rotate an image eccentrically by specifying the necessary zero point coordinates.

In either case, the pixel's position, as an x-axis/y-axis offset, is converted to an angle and a vector distance (the hypotenuse of a right triangle formed by the x and y distances, see *Vector Calculations*). The pixel angle is then incremented by the rotation angle and the vector distance reconverted to an x-axis/y-axis offset that becomes the new pixel position.

Since overwriting the original image would be self-defeating, each rotated pixel offset is plotted from a new center position to create a new, rotated image.

As ROTATE.C will demonstrate, the rotated image is not as smooth as the original. This is due to variations in the calculation that results in small changes in angles (both in the original pixel coordinates and the rotated vector angle) and return fractional values that must finally be reduced to integer coordinates for the actual plot. Basically, the higher the screen resolution, the smoother the rotated image will appear. However, these calculated image rotations cannot be smoothed entirely when carried out on a pixel by pixel basis.

Calculated Image Rotation

The second method of image rotation does not apply to all types of images but, for any image that is generated primarily using the Turbo C++ arc and line functions, the line and arc coordinates can be rotated and a new image generated. These coordinate rotations are carried out in the same manner as for direct image rotation.

One obvious exception exists: the ellipse function cannot be rotated by rotating coordinates since there is no provision for circular elongation except directly along the x-axis or the y-axis. Also, the circle function, which is a special case of the ellipse, is not affected by coordinate rotation.

When coordinate rotation is practical, there are advantages. The resulting images are smoother than those produced by direct image rotation and creating the image is generally faster since fewer calculations are required.

Video Aspect Adjustments

As ROTATE.C will demonstrate (unless you are using a VGA system), the video aspect ratio also needs to be taken into account when rotating either pixels or image element coordinates. In some cases, as with the text legend in the center of the image, the rotated text is clearest when no aspect correction is applied (but the rest of the image is definitely distorted without correction).

The ROTATE.C Demo

The image rotation facilities demonstrated in this program are designed less as "plug-in" utilities than as a demonstration of how image rotation procedures can be created. Four basic methods are shown: direct (pixel) image rotation and calculated image rotation; both with and without video aspect correction.

This demonstration is written primarily for EGA/VGA systems. The demo will run on CGA, but the bottom portion of the display will be off the screen. To begin, the main procedure initializes the graphics system (and sets the video aspect ratio), then calls the Show_Rotation procedure with an angle (in degrees) for rotation. Acceptable values are *0..360*, though values outside of this range will be adjusted to fit.

```
main()
{
    Initialize();
    Show_Rotation( 135 );
    Pause();
    closegraph();
}
```

The Show_Rotation procedure creates a simple screen image and demonstrates rotation using the four methods previously discussed.

```
void Show_Rotation(int degrees)
{
    int   i, j, x = 320, y = 100, Point, radius = 50;

    settextjustify( CENTER_TEXT, TOP_TEXT );
    outtextxy( 320, 10, "Original");
    circle( x, y, radius );
    line( x-radius, y+radius*AspR,
       x+radius, y-radius*AspR );
    line( x+radius, y-radius*AspR,
       x+radius, y-(radius-20)*AspR );
    line( x+radius, y-radius*AspR,
       x+radius-20, y-radius*AspR );
    outtextxy( 320, 100, "Horizontal?" );
```

In the original image, a circle is drawn with an arrow crossing it at an angle of 45° degrees and the question *Horizontal?* is written across the center. This original image has been created in WHITE; but now, two colored circles will be written to the right and left to act as reference marks for the subsequent image rotations.

```
    setcolor(RED);
    x = 160;
```

```
circle( x, y, radius );
setcolor(GREEN);
x = 480;
circle( x, y, radius );
setcolor(WHITE);
```

Two captions are added to show the rotation angle selected:

```
x = 160;   y = 30;
gprintf( &x, &y, "Figure rotated %d degrees",
         degrees );
gprintf( &x, &y, "without aspect correction");
x = 480;   y = 30;
gprintf( &x, &y, "Figure rotated %d degrees",
         degrees );
gprintf( &x, &y, "using aspect correction");
```

Now, the original image is rotated using Rotate_Point to the left and Adj_Rotate_Point to the right.

```
for( i=-50; i<=50; i++ )
   for( j=-50; j<=50; j++ )
   {
      Point = getpixel( 320+i, 100+j );
      if( Point > 0 )
      {
         x = i;
         y = j;
         Rotate_Point( &x, &y, degrees );
         putpixel( 160+x, 100+y, Point );
         x = i;
         y = j;
         Adj_Rotate_Point( &x, &y, degrees );
         putpixel( 480+x, 100+y, Point );
      }
   }
```

On the bottom half of the screen (not visible on CGA systems), two more captions are written for the coordinate rotation demonstrations.

```
x = 160;   y = 180;
gprintf( &x, &y, "Coordinates rotated %d degrees",
         degrees);
gprintf( &x, &y, "without aspect correction");
```

```
x = 480;   y = 180;
gprintf( &x, &y, "Coordinates rotated %d degrees",
         degrees);
gprintf( &x, &y, "using aspect correction");
```

The first coordinate rotation—in red, to the left—is done without using video aspect ratio corrections in the calculations. The *AspR* factor appearing here is the same as was used to correct the original figure, but does not affect the values created by the Rotate_Line function.

As you will notice, the text insertion that was rotated in the first half of this demonstration will not appear in this portion. Turbo C++ does not offer provisions for fractional rotation of the graphics text fonts. Also, except for 90° increments, the graphic text fonts appear distorted even when direct image rotation is used.

```
setcolor( RED );
x = 160;   y = 250;
```

The *x* and *y* coordinates set the center point for the new image, and the original line formulas are repeated using the new reference point.

```
circle( x, y, radius );
Rotate_Line( x, y, degrees,
             x-radius, y+radius*AspR,
             x+radius, y-radius*AspR );
Rotate_Line( x, y, degrees,
             x+radius, y-radius*AspR,
             x+radius, y-(radius-20)*AspR );
Rotate_Line( x, y, degrees,
             x+radius,    y-radius*AspR,
             x+radius-20, y-radius*AspR );
```

The second coordinate rotation—in green, to the right—does use video aspect ratios in the coordinate calculation.

```
setcolor( GREEN );
x = 480;  y = 250;
circle( x, y, radius );
Adj_Rotate_Line( x, y, degrees,
                 x-radius, y+radius*AspR,
                 x+radius, y-radius*AspR );
Adj_Rotate_Line( x, y, degrees,
                 x+radius, y-radius*AspR,
```

```
                       x+radius, y-(radius-20)*AspR );
    Adj_Rotate_Line( x, y, degrees,
                       x+radius, y-radius*AspR,
                       x+radius-20, y-radius*AspR );
}
```

In the Rotate_Line procedure, the *x* and *y* parameters are the center point, *degrees* is the angle for rotation, and *x1*, *y1*, *x2*, and *y2* are the begin and end points for the line to be rotated.

```
void Rotate_Line( int x,   int y,   int degrees,
                  int x1, int y1, int x2, int y2 )
{
```

The begin and end coordinate pairs are converted to offsets relative to the center point coordinates.

```
    x1 -= x;   y1 -= y;
    x2 -= x;   y2 -= y;
```

The offset pairs are rotated using Rotate_Point.

```
    Rotate_Point( &x1, &y1, degrees );
    Rotate_Point( &x2, &y2, degrees );
```

A new line is drawn using the line function and passing parameters as the centerpoint coordinates, plus the x-axis and y-axis offsets returned by the Rotate_Point function.

```
    line( x+x1, y+y1, x+x2, y+y2 );
}
```

The Adj_Rotate_Line procedure works the same way as Rotate_Line, except for calling Adj_Rotate_Point instead of Rotate_Point.

```
void Adj_Rotate_Line( int x,   int y,   int degrees,
                      int x1, int y1, int x2, int y2 )
{
    x1 -= x;   y1 -= y;
    x2 -= x;   y2 -= y;
    Adj_Rotate_Point( &x1, &y1, degrees );
    Adj_Rotate_Point( &x2, &y2, degrees );
    line( x+x1, y+y1, x+x2, y+y2 );
}
```

The Adj_Rotate_Point function is an intermediate procedure calling the Rotate_Point function after adjusting the *Y_Off* (y-axis offset) value using the aspect ratio. In this case, the offset is being normalized to the same effective value it would have if plotted against the x-axis instead of being plotted on the y-axis (or, as if the x and y pixel sizes were the same).

```
void Adj_Rotate_Point( int *X_Off, int *Y_Off,
                       int degrees )
{
   int   X0 = *X_Off;
   int   Y0 = *Y_Off / AspR;
   Rotate_Point( &X0, &Y0, degrees );
```

After Rotate_Point returns the rotated value, the y-axis value (*Y0*) is corrected for the screen aspect ratio.

```
   *X_Off =   X0;
   *Y_Off =   Y0 * AspR;
}
```

Both values (the coordinate pair) are returned to the calling function after rotation. The Rotate_Point function carries out the actual calculations, accepting x-axis and y-axis offset values (which may be positive or negative distances) and the rotation angle in degrees.

```
void Rotate_Point( int *X_Off, int *Y_Off, int degrees )
{
   double   HypLen, R_Angle, O_Angle = 0;
   int      Sign_X = 1,  Sign_Y = 1;
   double   X0 = (double) *X_Off + 0.5,
            Y0 = (double) *Y_Off + 0.5;
```

The offset parameters are accepted as local variables of type double and a decimal fraction of 0.5 is added to each. This fractional adjustment improves the results following calculations by helping smooth the final round-down corrections when the double values are returned as integers.

The angle *degrees* is only accepted as a positive rotation value.

```
   degrees = abs( degrees );
```

Turbo C++'s hypot function conveniently returns a vector distance from the two offset values.

```
   HypLen = hypot( X0, Y0 );
```

The vector angle is calculated, using the offset coordinates, as a value in radians.

```
if( abs(X0) > 0 ) O_Angle = atan2( (-1 * Y0), X0 );
else if( Y0 < 0 ) O_Angle = PI/2;
        else          O_Angle = 3*PI/2;
```

If the absolute value of *X0* is greater than 0, then atan2 returns the angle in radians. Alternatively, if *X0* is zero, then the y-axis offset is the determining factor and the angle can be either *PI/2* or *3*PI/2*, depending on whether the y-axis offset is positive or negative.

In the previous step, the atan2 function returns values from *–PI* to *PI* and the angle (in radians) may have been returned as a negative value. If so, then the value in *O_Angle* is converted to a positive angle.

```
if( O_Angle < 0 ) O_Angle += 2*PI;
```

This conversion makes subsequent calculations easier but does not change the actual vector angle. The value in *degrees* is also converted to a local parameter value in radians:

```
R_Angle = (double) degrees / 180 * PI;
```

Then the original angle (*O_Angle*) is added to the rotation angle (*R_Angle*).

```
R_Angle += O_Angle;
```

If the result is greater than *2*PI*, then *R_Angle* is returned to the normal range (*0..2*PI*).

```
if( R_Angle > 2*PI ) R_Angle -= 2*PI;
```

The next step is to check which quadrant *R_Angle* falls in and assign the necessary vector polarity because the vector coordinates will be calculated as absolute values and the *Sign_X* and *Sign_Y* flags will be used to determine the actual sign of the results. This is done as a correction for the fact that the calculated coordinate values will not match the coordinate values needed for screen positions (see *Vector Calculations*, following).

```
if( ( R_Angle > PI/2 ) & ( R_Angle <= 3*PI/2 ) )
    Sign_X = -1;
if( ( R_Angle > 0 )    & ( R_Angle <= PI ) )
    Sign_Y = -1;
```

Now the vector distance (*HypLen*) and rotated vector angle (*R_Angle*) are returned to the new coordinate values (*X0* and *Y0*). Depending on which half of each quadrant's (see Figure 12-1) *R_Angle* falls in, either *X0* is calculated using the cosine or *Y0* is calculated using the sine of the angle with the other coordinate calculated as the remaining side of a right triangle.

```
if( ( ( R_Angle >=   PI/4 ) &
      ( R_Angle <= 3*PI/4 ) ) |
    ( ( R_Angle >= 5*PI/4 ) &
      ( R_Angle <= 7*PI/4 ) ) )
{
   X0 = HypLen * cos( R_Angle );
   Y0 = sqrt( pow( HypLen, 2 ) - pow( X0, 2 ) );
}
else
{
   Y0 = HypLen * sin( R_Angle );
   X0 = sqrt( pow( HypLen, 2 ) - pow( Y0, 2 ) );
}
```

Last, the absolute values of *X0* and *Y0* are multiplied by their sign and returned as *X_Off* and *Y_Off* coordinates.

```
   *X_Off = abs( X0 ) * Sign_X;
   *Y_Off = abs( Y0 ) * Sign_Y;
}
```

Vector Calculations

You've seen how to rotate a point but haven't received any explanation about it. If your high school or college trig is a bit rusty, you may be wondering about the previous calculations.

First, a reminder about a few facts that you already know, but which you need to keep firmly in the forefront of your mind to understand what's happening here.

With computer graphics, all screen positions are described as *x,y* coordinates beginning with a 0,0 coordinate in the upper left corner of the screen. The upper-left screen position is normally referenced as 1,1 in Turbo C++ or in Turbo Pascal, but to the computer, this is still the 0,0 reference point (and before DOS receives the C or Pascal coordinates they are changed to match this zero-origin system).

Figure 12-1: Sine / Cosine Angle Values

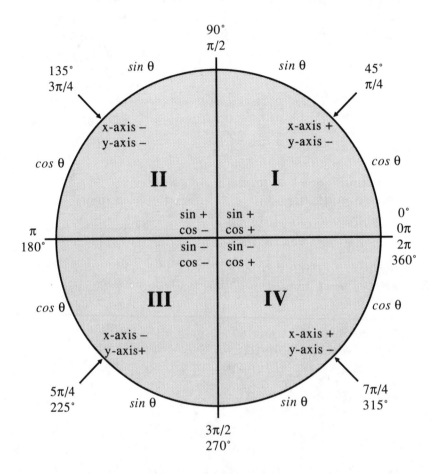

Angle values are shown both in radians and degrees. The signs for the sines and cosines of angles in each quadrant are shown for normal polar coordinates, while the x- and y-axis signs are shown for the screen coordinate system.

In screen coordinates, x-axis values increase from left to right and y-axis values increase from top to bottom. All of this should be very familiar to computer programmers.

In the Cartesian coordinate system (rectangular parallel coordinates), however, the x-axis values also increase from left to right (with negative values left of the 0,0 coordinate) but the y-axis values increase from bottom to top with the negative values on the y-axis lying below the 0,0 coordinate.

Since the Cartesian coordinate system is well established (long predating computers) it has priority and, therefore, all trigonometric conversions from *x,y* coordinate values assume Cartesian values initially. All conversions from polar coordinates (vector angle and magnitude) yield results compatible with the Cartesian system, not the screen coordinate system. Because of this some minor, but important, adaptations will be necessary.

First, in order to rotate an image, a center point for rotation is required. This point becomes a new 0,0 reference point, but has no relationship to the screen origin 0,0 point. This center point reference is quite arbitrary, it is for local (program) reference only and can be anywhere on the screen (or even off the screen, if you desire).

Each rotated point, however, is now referenced in terms of an X and Y offset from this 0,0 coordinate. If the center point is located at screen coordinates 100,145 and the point to be rotated is at screen coordinates 50,175, then the rotation coordinates will be 50,30 (by convention, the *x*-axis coordinate is always given first and, the first coordinate is always the *x*-axis).

In Chapter 10, left-right and mirror image transformations were made quite simply by changing the sign of the offset (relative to a new center coordinate). True rotation, however, cannot be accomplished this easily and requires something other than the x,y coordinate system.

To rotate a point, its *x,y* coordinates must first be converted to a polar vector. A vector consists of two values: an angle and a length and, for these purposes, the angle will always be in the range *0..2*PI (0..360°)* and the length (magnitude) will always be a positive value. Negative vector angles and angles greater than 2*PI are possible and valid, as are negative vector magnitudes. Since these can always be normalized without loss of information, only normalized vectors are used in these calculations (besides, it's easier).

Since engineers were among the principal earlier users of computers—bless their little tinker-toy hearts—to prefer radian angles to degree/minute/second angles, computer trig functions commonly use angles expressed in radians instead of degrees. Both systems begin with a zero angle, 180° equals PI radians, and 360° equals 2*PI radians. Other angles are commonly expressed either as decimal radians or as radian fractions, see Figure 12-1.

Now back to calculating a polar (vector) coordinate from the screen position coordinates. To get the vector magnitude (*HypLen*), C's hypot function is ready made:

```
HypLen = hypot ( X0, Y0 );
```

The atan2 function very conveniently transforms the *x,y* coordinates into a vector angle—with one exception, an x-offset value of 0.

```
if( abs(X0) > ) O_Angle = atan2( (-1 * Y00, X0 );
```

Before covering the exception, however, there is another point to discuss. Notice the −1 in the formula above? The value for *Y0* is precisely opposite in sign to what the atan2 (or atan) functions expect. This is because (see Figure 12-1) the normal math functions treat positive values as 1st Quadrant points. That is, a positive value for *Y0* is expected to be above the 0,0 coordinate—as if the screen 0,0 point was at the bottom left corner of the screen.

Since this is a screen coordinate system, however, a positive vertical value is down and negative is up. Therefore, *Y0* is multiplied by −1 to change its sign before the angle is calculated (this discrepancy between normal and screen coordinates will appear again in these calculations).

The atan2 function is used rather than the atan function because the atan function is limited to angles in the range *−PI/2..PI/2* and requires large values for the x parameter involved. The atan2 function returns values in the range *−PI..PI* and is accurate when the x parameter approaches 0 ... but not helpful when the x parameter equals zero (and the angles could be *PI/2* or *−PI/2*).

If the value of *X0* is zero, then the *Y0* parameter is used to determine the angle:

```
else if( Y0 < 0 )  O_Angle = PI/2;
       else        O_Angle = 3*PI/2;
```

Since atan2 returns the angle in radians in the range *−PI..PI*, the resulting *O_Angle* is normalized for convenience (remember, PI radians = 180°).

```
if( O_Angle < 0 ) O_Angle += 2*PI;
```

The *x,y* coordinates have been converted to a vector angle and magnitude (size, length, distance) that can be rotated. Rotation becomes a simple matter of adding the rotation angle to the vector angle (or subtracting the rotation angle; but here rotation has been limited to the counterclockwise direction). That's it, the vector has been rotated.

This has been the easy part. The vector must be restored to *x,y* coordinates before it can be used, which is the whole point of doing this. What remains seems hard but only requires a bit of care and explanation.

Again, please refer to Figure 12-1. The original angle and the rotation angle have already been summed together as *R_Angle*. If the value of

R_Angle lies in the range *PI/2..3*PI/2*, then the vector is in the 2nd or 3rd quadrants and sign of X will be negative. (*Sign_X* and *Sign_Y* were initialized as +1.)

```
if( ( R_Angle > PI/2 ) & ( R_Angle <= 3*PI/2 ) )
   Sign_X = -1;
```

Likewise, if the value of *R_Angle* lies in the range *0..PI*, the vector angle is in the 1st or 2nd quadrants and the sign of Y will be negative (in the screen coordinate system, which is the only one that counts here).

```
if( ( R_Angle > 0 ) & ( R_Angle <= PI ) )
   Sign_Y = -1;
```

Normally, the sign of the sine of the angle would determine the sign of X. The sign of the cosine of the angle would determine the sign of Y. Except that, first, in the screen coordinate system, this would be correct for X and invalid for Y and; second, the *x,y* results are going to be calculated in a slightly different manner.

If the angle lies in the range *PI/4..3*PI/4* or in the range *5*PI/4..7*PI/4*, then the x-axis value (*X0*) will be calculated using the cosine of the angle and the y-axis value will be calculated as the square root of the difference of the squares of the remaining sides (Pythagorean Theorem).

```
if( ( ( R_Angle >=   PI/4 ) &
      ( R_Angle <= 3*PI/4 ) ) |
    ( ( R_Angle >= 5*PI/4 ) &
      ( R_Angle <= 7*PI/4 ) ) )
{
   X0 = HypLen * cos( R_Angle );
   Y0 = sqrt( pow( HypLen, 2 ) - pow( X0, 2 ) );
}
```

Otherwise, the same calculations are carried out, but using the sine of the angle to find the y-axis value and Pythagoras' rule for the x-axis.

```
else
{
   Y0 = HypLen * sin( R_Angle );
   X0 = sqrt( pow( HypLen, 2 ) - pow( Y0, 2 ) );
}
```

The reason for this is accuracy. By using the sin and cos only within the angle ranges where they yield the greatest accuracy (using sin where the y-axis value is greater than the x-axis value and cos where the x-axis value is greater) and calculating the remaining value using the Pythagorean Theorem, the resulting position coordinates are as accurate as possible and the image rotation smoother. This is also why the local variables, *X0* and *Y0*, are double rather than integer values.

Notice also the italicized *sinθ* and *cosθ* in Figure 12-1 show the ranges where each function yields the greater accuracy.

Since either the x or y value was calculated using the square root function, one of these is a positive value. (Since the square root of a number could be either positive or negative, sqrt always returns a positive value.) If only the sin and cos functions had been used, then the y-axis value could simply be inverted (multiplied by –1) to correct it for the screen coordinate system. This was not the case.

Instead, the absolute values of both *X0* and *Y0* are multiplied by the sign values determined earlier, then returned as screen coordinate integers.

```
*X_Off = abs( X0 ) * Sign_X;
*Y_Off = abs( Y0 ) * Sign_Y;
```

If this is confusing, please refer to the text and to Figure 12-1, remembering that the coordinate values used are screen coordinates, that the y-axis values are negative toward the top of the screen, and that the angle increases in a counterclockwise direction. It really isn't a matter of difficulty, but of careful calculations and making allowance for the differences between the Cartesian coordinate system and the screen coordinate system.

Other Image Rotation Options

When the direct image rotation was demonstrated, each pixel was tested and the background pixels ignored. Further selective rotation could be applied, however, and different color values rotated separately by different angles or in different directions.

Since in EGA/VGA modes the same color hues can be assigned to different palette entries and rotation made on the basis of the palette entry rather than the actual hue, it is practical to rotate one part of an image while leaving another portion, apparently the same color, unaffected.

Including Text Rotations

Earlier, when discussing graphics text options, I pointed out that only two text orientations were supported. Using the direct image rotation possibilities, even upside-down text becomes possible and, with care, some other text angles are practical (though not as convenient) as the directly supported text presentations.

Finally, these are tools for your usage—develop and employ them as you see fit. The possibilities, if not endless, are certainly vast and a bit of imagination should suggest a variety of options.

```c
/*=======================================================*/
/*    FILE_IMG.C == Saving an image as a data file    */
/*=======================================================*/

#ifdef __TINY__
#error Graphics demos will not run in the tiny model.
#endif

#include <conio.h>
#include <stdio.h>
#include <stdlib.h>
#include <stdarg.h>
#include <graphics.h>

#include "gprint.i"

int     GraphDriver;
int     GraphMode;
double  AspectRatio;
int     xasp, yasp;
int     MaxColors;
int     ErrorCode = 0;
void    *Flash, *Flash2;

void Pause()
{
    while( kbhit() ) getch();
    getch();
}

void Initialize()
{
    GraphDriver = DETECT;
    initgraph( &GraphDriver, &GraphMode, "C:\\TC\\BGI" );
    ErrorCode = graphresult();
```

```
   if( ErrorCode != grOk )
   {
      printf(" Graphics System Error: %s\n",
              grapherrormsg( ErrorCode ) );
      exit  ( 1 );
   }
   MaxColors = getmaxcolor() + 1;
   getaspectratio( &xasp, &yasp );
   AspectRatio = (double) xasp / (double) yasp;
}

void *SaveImage( int left,  int top,
                 int right, int bottom, unsigned *size )
{
   void  *image;

   *size = imagesize( left, top, right, bottom );
   image = malloc( *size );
   getimage( left, top, right, bottom, image );
   putimage( left, top, image, XOR_PUT );
   return( image );
}

void FileImage( void *image, unsigned size,
                char *filename )
{
   FILE  *f1 = fopen( filename, "w" );

   fwrite( image, size, 1, f1 );
   fflush( f1 );
   fclose( f1 );
}

void *ReadImage( char *filename )
{
   unsigned xsize, ysize, size;
   FILE    *f1 = fopen( filename, "r" );
   void    *tempimage;

   xsize = fgetc( f1 ) | ( fgetc( f1 ) << 8 );
   ysize = fgetc( f1 ) | ( fgetc( f1 ) << 8 );
   size = imagesize( 0, 0, xsize, ysize );
   gprintxy( 10, 10,
```

```
                   " xsize = %d, ysize = %d, imagesize = %d ",
                        xsize,        ysize,              size );
   tempimage = malloc( size );
   rewind( f1 );
   fread( tempimage, size, 1, f1 );
   fclose( f1 );
   return( tempimage );
}

void CreateImage()
{
   int  Size = 0, MaxColor = getmaxcolor();
   int  pflash[] = { 100, 40, 110, 60, 100, 70, 120, 65,
            140, 80, 130, 60, 140, 50, 120, 55, 100, 40};

   randomize();
   setcolor( random( MaxColor ) + 1 );
   setfillstyle( random(11) + 1, random(MaxColor) + 1 );
   fillpoly( sizeof(pflash)/(2*sizeof(int)), pflash );
   Flash = SaveImage( 100, 40, 140, 80, &Size );
   FileImage( Flash, Size, "FLASH.IMG" );
   Flash2 = ReadImage( "FLASH.IMG" );
   putimage( 200, 200, Flash2, COPY_PUT );
}

main()
{
   Initialize();                            /* set graphics mode */
   CreateImage();                           /* create and save image */
   Pause();
   free( Flash );
   free( Flash2 );
   closegraph();                            /*    restore text mode   */
}



       /*=========================================*/
       /*                ROTATE.C                 */
       /* Rotating an image using Turbo-C Graphics */
       /*=========================================*/

#ifdef __TINY__
```

```
#error Graphics demos will not run in the tiny model.
#endif

#include <conio.h>
#include <math.h>
#include <stdio.h>
#include <stdlib.h>
#include <stdarg.h>
#include <graphics.h>
#include <gprint.i>

const    double  PI = 3.14159254;

int      GraphDriver;              /* graphics device driver    */
int      GraphMode;               /* graphics mode value       */
double   AspR;                    /* screen aspect ratio       */
int      xasp, yasp;              /* factors for aspect ratio */
int      MaxColors;               /* maximum colors available */
int      ErrorCode = 0;           /* reports graphics errors  */

void Initialize()
{               /* initialize graphics system and report errors */
   GraphDriver = DETECT;           /* request auto-detection    */
   initgraph( &GraphDriver, &GraphMode, "C:\\TC\\BGI" );
   ErrorCode = graphresult();      /* test init results         */
   if ( ErrorCode != grOk )        /* if error during init     */
   {
      printf(" Graphics System Error: %s\n",
             grapherrormsg( ErrorCode ) );
      exit( 1 );
   }
   MaxColors = getmaxcolor() + 1;        /* max color range     */
   getaspectratio( &xasp, &yasp );       /* get video aspect   */
   AspR = (double) xasp / (double) yasp;
}                                  /* calculate aspect ratio */

void Pause()
{
   setcolor(WHITE);
   settextjustify( CENTER_TEXT, BOTTOM_TEXT );
   outtextxy( getmaxx()/2, getmaxy(),
             "press any key ..." );
```

```
   while ( kbhit() ) getch();
   getch();
   cleardevice();
}


void Rotate_Point( int *X_Off, int *Y_Off, int degrees )
{
   double  HypLen, R_Angle, O_Angle = 0;
   int     Sign_X = 1,  Sign_Y = 1;
   double  X0 = (double) *X_Off + 0.5,
           Y0 = (double) *Y_Off + 0.5;

   degrees = abs( degrees );         /* positive rotation only */
   HypLen = hypot( X0, Y0 );         /* offset vector distance */
   if( abs(X0) > 0 ) O_Angle = atan2( (-1 * Y0), X0 );
   else if( Y0 < 0 ) O_Angle = PI/2;            /* get angle  */
        else         O_Angle = 3*PI/2;          /* in radians */
   if( O_Angle < 0 ) O_Angle += 2*PI;
                                     /* positive angles only */
   R_Angle = (double) degrees / 180 * PI;
                                     /* convert to radians  */
   R_Angle += O_Angle;              /* add original angle   */
   if( R_Angle > 2*PI ) R_Angle -= 2*PI;
                                     /* test range < 2*PI    */

   if( ( R_Angle > PI/2 ) &         /* 2nd, 3rd quadrant = -X */
       ( R_Angle <= 3*PI/2 ) ) Sign_X = -1;
   if( ( R_Angle > 0 ) &            /* 1st, 2nd quadrant = -Y */
       ( R_Angle <= PI ) )     Sign_Y = -1;
   if( ( ( R_Angle >=   PI/4 ) &
         ( R_Angle <= 3*PI/4 ) ) |
       ( ( R_Angle >= 5*PI/4 ) &
         ( R_Angle <= 7*PI/4 ) ) )
   {
      X0 = HypLen * cos( R_Angle );
      Y0 = sqrt( pow( HypLen, 2 ) - pow( X0, 2 ) );
   }
   else
   {
      Y0 = HypLen * sin( R_Angle );
      X0 = sqrt( pow( HypLen, 2 ) - pow( Y0, 2 ) );
```

```
   }
   *X_Off = abs( X0 ) * Sign_X;          /* return position */
   *Y_Off = abs( Y0 ) * Sign_Y;          /* with adj sign   */
}

void Adj_Rotate_Point( int *X_Off, int *Y_Off,
                       int degrees )
{
   int  X0 = *X_Off;
   int  Y0 = *Y_Off / AspR;              /* normalize aspect */

   Rotate_Point( &X0, &Y0, degrees );         /* and rotate */
   *X_Off =  X0;                   /* return rotated position   */
   *Y_Off =  Y0 * AspR;         /* with aspect ratio restored */
}

void Rotate_Line( int x,  int y,  int degrees,
                  int x1, int y1, int x2, int y2 )
{
   x1 -= x;    y1 -= y;            /* convert coords relative */
   x2 -= x;    y2 -= y;            /* to center of rotation   */
   Rotate_Point( &x1, &y1, degrees );
   Rotate_Point( &x2, &y2, degrees );
   line( x+x1, y+y1, x+x2, y+y2 );
}

void Adj_Rotate_Line( int x,  int y,  int degrees,
                      int x1, int y1, int x2, int y2 )
{
   x1 -= x;    y1 -= y;            /* convert coords relative */
   x2 -= x;    y2 -= y;            /* to center of rotation   */
   Adj_Rotate_Point( &x1, &y1, degrees );
   Adj_Rotate_Point( &x2, &y2, degrees );
   line( x+x1, y+y1, x+x2, y+y2 );
}

void Show_Rotation(int degrees)
{
   int   i, j, x, y, Point, radius = 50;

   settextjustify( CENTER_TEXT, TOP_TEXT );
   outtextxy( 320, 10, "Original");
   x = 320;
```

```
y = 100;
circle( x, y, radius );
line( x-radius, y+radius*AspR,
      x+radius, y-radius*AspR );
line( x+radius, y-radius*AspR,
      x+radius, y-(radius-20)*AspR );
line( x+radius, y-radius*AspR,
      x+radius-20, y-radius*AspR );
setcolor(RED);
x = 160;
circle( x, y, radius );              /* circle for reference */
setcolor(GREEN);
x = 480;
circle( x, y, radius );              /* circle for reference */
setcolor(WHITE);
x = 160; y = 30;
gprintf( &x, &y, "Figure rotated %d degrees",
         degrees);
gprintf( &x, &y, "without aspect correction");
x = 480; y = 30;
gprintf( &x, &y, "Figure rotated %d degrees",
         degrees);
gprintf( &x, &y, "using aspect correction");
for( i=-50; i<=50; i++ )
   for( j=-50; j<=50; j++ )
   {
      Point = getpixel( 320+i, 100+j );
      if( Point > 0 )
      {
         x = i;
         y = j;
         Rotate_Point( &x, &y, degrees );
         putpixel( 160+x, 100+y, Point );
         x = i;
         y = j;
         Adj_Rotate_Point( &x, &y, degrees );
         putpixel( 480+x, 100+y, Point );
   }  }
x = 160;   y = 180;
gprintf( &x, &y, "Coordinates rotated %d degrees",
```

```
                    degrees );
      gprintf( &x, &y, "without aspect correction");
      x = 480;    y = 180;
      gprintf( &x, &y, "Coordinates rotated %d degrees",
                    degrees );
      gprintf( &x, &y, "using aspect correction" );
      setcolor(RED);
      x = 160;    y = 250;
      circle( x, y, radius );
      Rotate_Line( x, y, degrees,
                      x-radius, y+radius*AspR,
                      x+radius, y-radius*AspR );
      Rotate_Line( x, y, degrees,
                      x+radius, y-radius*AspR,
                      x+radius, y-(radius-20)*AspR );
      Rotate_Line( x, y, degrees,
                      x+radius, y-radius*AspR,
                      x+radius-20, y-radius*AspR );
      setcolor( GREEN );
      x = 480;   y = 250;
      circle( x, y, radius );
      Adj_Rotate_Line( x, y, degrees,
                        x-radius, y+radius*AspR,
                        x+radius, y-radius*AspR );
      Adj_Rotate_Line( x, y, degrees,
                        x+radius, y-radius*AspR,
                        x+radius, y-(radius-20)*AspR );
      Adj_Rotate_Line( x, y, degrees,
                        x+radius,    y-radius*AspR,
                        x+radius-20, y-radius*AspR );
}

main()
{
   Initialize();
   Show_Rotation( 90 );
   Pause();
   closegraph();
}
```

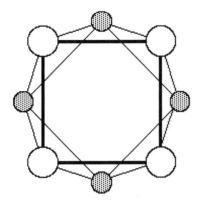

Chapter 13

Colors and Color Selection

Because colors are an inherent part of computer graphics, this chapter is concerned primarily with colors and color selections in EGA/VGA modes and secondarily with CGA and Monochrome systems.

This caveat is not intended as a put down of CGA or Monochrome video modes; it is simply a recognition of the fact that CGA systems have limited color capabilities and Monochrome systems have effectively none.

Video Signal Cues

On Monochrome systems, graphic video output is limited to two bits of information per pixel: a video on/off and an intensity bit (see Table 13-1).

Table 13-1: System Video Attributes

Bit	Monochrome	Color RGBI	Color RrGgBb
0		Blue	Primary Blue
1		Green	Primary Green
2		Red	Primary Red
3	Video		Secondary Blue
4	Intensity	Intensity	Secondary Green
5			Secondary Red

On CGA systems, the RGBI (Red, Green, Blue, and Intensity) color system is used with four bits of information per graphics pixel, but combinations are limited to four, predefined palettes of three colors, plus background color (as shown in Table 13-3). The background color in each palette is BLACK by default, but can be selected from the entire range of 16 colors shown in Table 13-2.

Table 13-2: CGA Color Values

Color DEC	Values Hex	4-Bit Binary	Color Components	Constant/Color Name
0	0	0000	....	BLACK
1	1	0001	...B	BLUE
2	2	0010	..G.	GREEN
3	3	0011	..GB	CYAN
4	4	0100	.R..	RED
5	5	0101	.R.B	MAGENTA
6	6	0110	.RG.	BROWN
7	7	0111	.RGB	LIGHTGREY
8	8	1000	I...	DARKGREY
9	9	1001	I..B	LIGHTBLUE
10	A	1010	I.G.	LIGHTGREEN
11	B	1011	I.GB	LIGHTCYAN
12	C	1100	IR..	LIGHTRED
13	D	1101	IR.B	LIGHTMAGENTA
14	E	1110	IRG.	YELLOW
15	F	1111	IRGB	WHITE

On EGA/VGA systems, the RrGgBb color system uses six bits of information per pixel for a total of 64 colors/hues. The default colors for this palette are shown in Table 13-4.

CGA Colors

For CGA systems, 16 possible colors are supported, as shown in Table 13-2. In text modes, any of these colors can be selected as foreground color, though only the first eight colors are valid as background. Using Turbo C++ graphics, the AT&T driver, modes ATT400C0..ATT400C3, and the MCGA driver, modes MCGAC0..MCGAC3 operate in the same fashion as CGA modes, CGAC0..CGAC3. Similarly, color operation in the CGAHI mode is duplicated by the MCGAMED, MCGAHI, ATT400MED, and ATT400HI modes.

As shown in Table 13-2, each color is defined by four register bits controlling the red, green, and blue hues, and an intensity control. Each hue (color gun) has two settings: low and high intensity. When the Intensity bit is TRUE (ON), all color guns are set high. If Intensity is FALSE, all color guns respond as low.

Table 13-3: Predefined CGA Color Palettes

Palette Color	Color Value	4-Bit Binary	Color Components	Constant/Color Name
	PALETTE NUMBER 0(CGAC0)			
0	0	0000	....	BLACK
1	A	1010	I.G.	LIGHTGREEN
2	C	1100	IR..	LIGHTRED
3	E	1110	IRG.	YELLOW
	PALETTE NUMBER 1(CGAC1)			
0	0	0000	....	BLACK
1	B	1011	I.GB	LIGHTCYAN
2	D	1101	IR.B	LIGHTMAGENTA
3	F	1111	IRGB	WHITE
	PALETTE NUMBER 2(CGAC2)			
0	0	0000	....	BLACK
1	2	0010	..G.	GREEN
2	4	0100	.R..	RED
3	6	0110	.RG.	BROWN
	PALETTE NUMBER 3(CGAC3)			
0	0	0000	....	BLACK
1	3	0011	..GB	CYAN
2	5	0101	.R.B	MAGENTA
3	7	0111	.RGB	LIGHTGREY

BLUE is generated by turning on the Blue gun at low intensity; LIGHT-BLUE also turns on the Blue gun but, because of the Intensity flag, is turned on high and produces a brighter color. In the same fashion, turning on both the Green and Blue guns produces CYAN; adding the Intensity signal produces LIGHTCYAN.

Notice that enabling the Intensity signal alone (with the Red, Green, and Blue guns off), still produces a response from all three of the color guns, though their output is very low, and the result is DARKGREY. You might consider this a bug that has been turned into a feature—and, in all probability, may have originated in exactly this fashion.

In graphics modes, the CGA system supports multiple colors only in four low-resolution, 320x200 pixel modes (C0, C1, C2, and C3). Each of these modes selects one of the predefined 4-color palettes shown in Table 13-3.

By default, the background color in each palette is BLACK, but may be changed to any of the 16 CGA colors (see Table 13-2) using the setbkcolor function. The setpalette and setallpalette functions, used in EGA/VGA modes to change palette colors, are not applicable in CGA modes. There is, however, one exception: the function setpalette(palette_index, color) can be used with a *palette_index* of zero (background) as an alternative to the setbkcolor function.

The CGA colors BLUE (value 1), DARKGREY (value 8), and LIGHT-BLUE (value 9) do not appear in any of the defined palettes. These can, of course, be used as background colors.

CGA High Resolution

In any of the high resolution modes (CGAHI, MCGAMED, or ATT400MED at 640x200 pixels, MCGAHI at 640x480 pixels, or ATT400HI at 640x400 pixels), two colors are supported: a black background and a color foreground. The foreground color is selected from the 16 CGA colors using the setbkcolor function.

This is not an error—due to a quirk in the CGA hardware, the setbkcolor function is used to select the CGAHI foreground color. The background color remains black.

All pixels with a value of 1 are displayed in the foreground color, pixels with a value of 0 remain black.

The IBM8514 and VGA Video Adapters

At the other extreme, the highest color resolution is provided by the IBM-8514 video card and the IBM8514 mode or by the VGA video card using the VGA256.BGI driver (see Appendix E), both of which are supported by the setrgbpalette function.

The setrgbpalette function allows custom color definition for a palette of 256 colors. To maintain compatibility with other video adapters, the first 16 palette entries are predefined by the .BGI drivers to correspond to the default EGA/VGA color palette entries.

All 256 palette entries (numbered 0..255) can be individually defined by three integer color arguments: red, green, and blue. While the arguments passed to the setrgbpalette function are integer values, only the six most-significant bits of the lower (LSB) byte are actually used to set the palette color value (values from 0 to 252 in steps of four. Arguments of 252, 253, 254, and 255 are treated identically since the six most-significant bits are the same and only the two most-significant bits differ).

EGA/VGA Color

EGA/VGA video modes offer a palette of 16 colors selected from a spectrum of 64 possible hues. In actual fact, VGA systems are capable of wider color ranges, having 256 color registers and 256K possible hues. When using Turbo C++ procedures, they are limited to the EGA color range, though they still support the higher resolutions.

The EGA/VGA modes also begin with a default palette of 16 hues. Unlike the CGA color system using 4-bit colors, each EGA/VGA color is defined by a 6-bit value. This is commonly called an RrGgBb color system.

The RrGgBb color system provides two flags (and two signals) for each of the three color guns: a primary Red and secondary red, a primary Blue and secondary blue, and a primary Green and secondary green. (By custom, the primary color is capitalized and the secondary is in lowercase.)

If you prefer, you can think of the RrGgBb system as analogous to the RBGI system except that the secondary colors act as individual intensity flags for each of the primary color guns.

Just as DARKGREY was created in CGA by turning on the Intensity flag but leaving off all of the color flags, EGA_DARKGREY turns on the rgb (intensity) flags while leaving the RGB (primary) color guns turned off. On the other hand, where the CGA system created BROWN by mixing the Red and Green guns, EGA_BROWN is created by mixing the Red color gun with the green intensity flag—effectively by mixing Red with a very low Green to produce a deeper Brown.

Aside from the EGA_BROWN, the default palette colors for EGA/VGA are the same as the CGA colors except that three intensity signals (rgb) are used in place of a single intensity flag—gang-controlling all three color guns. The default colors are shown in Table 13-4.

Table 13-4: EGA/VGA Default Palette

Palette Color	Default Value	6-Bit Binary	Color Values Components	Color Constant/Name
0	0	000000	......	EGA_BLACK
1	1	000001	.....B	EGA_BLUE
2	2	000010	....G.	EGA_GREEN
3	3	000011	....GB	EGA_CYAN

Palette Color	Default Value	6-Bit Binary	Color Values Components	Color Constant/Name
4	4	000100	...R..	EGA_RED
5	5	000101	...R.B	EGA_MAGENTA
6	14	010100	.g.R..	EGA_BROWN
7	7	000111	...RGB	EGA_LIGHTGREY
8	38	111000	rgb...	EGA_DARKGREY
9	39	111001	rgb..B	EGA_LIGHTBLUE
A	3A	111010	rgb.G.	EGA_LIGHTGREEN
B	3B	111011	rgb.GB	EGA_LIGHTCYAN
C	3C	111100	rgbR..	EGA_LIGHTRED
D	3D	111101	rgbR.B	EGA_LIGHTMAGENTA
E	3E	111110	rgbRG.	EGA_YELLOW
F	3F	111111	rgbRGB	EGA_WHITE

A Wider Range of Hues

One of the advantages of EGA/VGA, in addition to being able to use 16 colors in high resolution modes, is being able to select your palette from 64 separate hues. To be frank, some of these 64 colors are not particularly appealing and the precise tone of a particular hue is subject to the color balance adjustments on the monitor used—but beauty is, as always, in the eye and monitor of the beholder.

For an example of the range of color, Table 13-5 shows 11 varieties of yellow, ranging from a color value of 06 which matches the CGA BROWN to a color value of 62 which corresponds to EGA_YELLOW.

Looking at the color components shown in Table 13-5, you will notice all of the yellows include Green and, with two exceptions, blend Red. In one case, color value 18, the color is actually high intensity Green—but, depending on the surrounding colors and background, this may be recognized as either Yellow, Green, or Chartreuse. The precise recognition and label applied to any color is largely a matter of subjective perception.

Table 13-5: EGA Yellows

	Color Values		
Dec	Hex	6-Bit Binary	Secondary and Primary Components
0606h	000	110	...RG.
140Eh	001	110	..bRG.
1812h	010	010	.g..G.
2216h	010	110	.g.RG.
261Ah	011	010	.gb.G.

	Color Values		
Dec	Hex	6-Bit Binary	Secondary and Primary Components
301Eh	011	110	.gbRG.
3826h	100	110	r..RG.
462Eh	101	110	r.bRG.
5436h	110	110	rg.RG.
5537h	110	111	rg.RGB
623Eh	111	110	rgbRG.

Manipulating Color and Hue

In the EGA/VGA color system, specific color values can be created by manipulating the combinations of primary and secondary flags for each color gun. Each of the three color guns has four settings—completely off, low intensity (color off, intensity on), normal (color on, intensity off), and high (color on, intensity on)—for a total of 4^3 or 64 colors.

If you need to manipulate colors directly, these bit-values can be set directly to build a specific color value, then assign the created value to the EGA/VGA palette. For example, suppose that you need three pure greens. Bit 1 controls the Green color gun (bit 0, at the right, is blue) and bit 4 is the Green intensity flag, so the three pure greens, in order of intensity, would be 16 (010 000 or .g. . . .), 2 (000 010 or . . . .G.), and 18 (010 010 or .g. .G.).

The first green (color value 16) is a dark green, appearing almost khaki against some backgrounds. The second (color value 2) is a fairly pure green and corresponds to EGA_GREEN, while the third green (color value 18) is a bright or chartreuse green and, depending on surroundings, appears almost yellow (and is also included in the yellows in Table 13-5).

But there is another green that does not appear among these possibilities. This fourth green is EGA_LIGHTGREEN, color value 58 (111 010 or rgb .G.). In this case, the rgb produces DARKGREY (which, since we're working with light emission and not color absorption/reflection, is also soft white). The dark grey is added to the Green color gun for a lighter green without overbalancing into chartreuse.

To show some of these relationships and to provide a convenient method of examining the variety of possible colors, two demo programs, COL-CUBE.C and COLORS.C, are provided. Please note that both of these demo programs will operate only on EGA/VGA capable systems. No provision has been made to adapt them for CGA system; they are for high resolution color systems only.

The Color Relations Cube

The COLCUBE.C program uses the default color palette to create a doubled cube showing the relationships between the primary and secondary colors.

The physical spectrum, as seen in the rainbow or displayed by a prism, begins with Red, proceeds to Orange, Yellow, Green, Blue, and ends with Violet. To create our computer color spectrum, we have only the Red, Green, and Blue colors to work with. These three primary colors are, however, the three that the eye best perceives and, by combining these as light, the eye perceives colors that are not actually present.

In the case of a TV signal, these same three colors are used to generate everything from subtle ranges of flesh tones to the intense flashing headlines favored by automobile dealers on late-night movie ads. The TV, using analog signals, is able to offer finer gradations and combinations of primary colors than the computer which, in EGA/VGA mode, is limited to four values.

Notice the figure created by COLCUBE.C (see Figure 13-1) has four main axes: red, green, blue, and white (or intensity). The human retina has three types of color receptors believed to correspond to these three primary colors. Color perception is not limited simply to recognition of these three values, but also to the relative intensity of each and the balance between these. A balanced combination of all three colors is perceived as grey or white, depending on overall intensity.

As mentioned, how colors are perceived is affected by other colors surrounding them and COLCUBE shows this effect by swapping the EGA_BLACK and EGA_WHITE colors between palette color 0 (background) and palette color 15.

The COLORS.C Demo

The COLORS.C demo (see Figure 13-2) is simple, beginning with three global variables: *radius* which sets the size for the display circles, *StepForward* which is used as a Boolean flag to determine whether the colors are incremented or decremented, and *palette* which is the color palette structure. The structure type *palettetype* is defined in GRAPHICS.H.

```
int    radius = 30;
int    StepForward = 1;
struct  palettetype  palette;
```

Figure 13-1: Color Cube

Enter <Q> to quit or any key to change colors

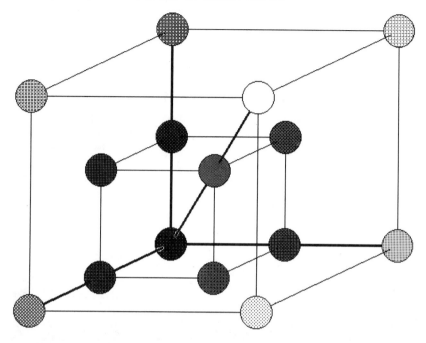

This graphics image was created by COLORCUB.C on a VGA screen and was captured as a .PCX image file before coversion to a greyscale image.

The main procedure starts the graphics system using the same Initialize procedure as virtually all of the other programs in this book. If you haven't figured out how Initialize works by now, there's little point in offering another description of the setup procedures.

The settextjustify and settextstyle procedures pick a font and text justification for the screen display, then write the appropriate messages to the screen.

```
main()
{
    Initialize();
    settextjustify( CENTER_TEXT, CENTER_TEXT );
    settextstyle( SANS_SERIF_FONT, HORIZ_DIR, 1 );
```

```
   outtextxy( 320, 10, "Enter <Q> to quit or any key to
change colors " );
   outtextxy( 100, 250, "Enter <-> for" );
   outtextxy( 100, 270, "reversed step" );
   outtextxy( 540, 250, "Enter <+> for" );
   outtextxy( 540, 270, "forward step" );
```

Next, a special palette is created by the Initialize_Colors procedure. Show_Colors writes 16 colored circles in two rows, Color_Wheel creates a pie chart with the same 16 colors and, with the screen set up and drawn, Step_Colors is ready to show you through the 64 EGA/VGA color values.

```
   Initialize_Colors();
   Show_Colors();
   Color_Wheel();
   Step_Colors();
   closegraph();
}
```

Figure 13-2: Color Range Demo

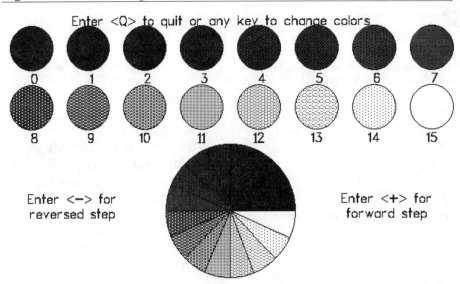

This graphics image was created by COLORCUB.C on a VGA screen and was captured as a .PCX image file before coversion to a greyscale image.

In the Initialize_Colors procedure, instead of using the default EGA/VGA palette colors, the palette entries are reset to color values 0..15—the first 16 colors. The setpalette function assigns the unsigned integer values to the index elements in the *palette* structure.

```
void Initialize_Colors()
{
    int   i;
    for( i=0; i<=15; i++ ) setpalette( i, i );
}
```

The Show_Colors procedure uses a single loop from 0 through 7 to draw 16 circles in two rows across the top portion of the screen.

```
void Show_Colors()
{
    int   i;
    for( i=0; i<=7; i++ )
    {
```

The first row of circles use the first eight palette colors: (*palette.color[0]..palette.color[7]*). At the moment, these are also the first eight possible color values. But it is the palette entry value that is assigned to the screen pixels, not the color value contained by each palette entry.

```
        setfillstyle( SOLID_FILL, i );
        circle( 80*i+40, 50, radius );
        floodfill( 80*i+40, 50, getcolor() );
```

The Label_Colors function labels each colored circle with the color value, not the palette item number.

```
        Label_Colors( i );
```

The second row of circles takes the second set of palette item assignments (*palette.color[8]..palette.color[15]*).

```
        setfillstyle( SOLID_FILL, i+8 );
        circle( 80*i+40, 130, radius );
        floodfill( 80*i+40, 130, getcolor() );
        Label_Colors( i+8 );
}   }
```

The Label_Colors procedure is called with one argument specifying the palette entry number, then reads the value in *palette.colors[i]* and writes this value on the screen next to the colored circle. While the rest of the screen will not be rewritten as colors change, the labels for the specific color values are rewritten each time a palette entry is changed.

```
void Label_Colors( int i )
{
    if( i > 7 )
        gprintxy( 80*i-600, 135+radius, " %d ",
                    palette.colors[i] );
    else gprintxy( 80*i+40,  55+radius, " %d ",
                    palette.colors[i] );
}
```

The Color_Wheel function draws a second display in the form a of pie graph that has 16 slices filled with the 16 palette colors.

```
void Color_Wheel()
{
    int  i;
    for( i=0; i<=15; i++ )
    {
        setfillstyle( SOLID_FILL, 15-i );
        pieslice( 320, 270, i*22.5, (i+1)*22.5, radius*3 );
}  }
```

The last element in this demo is the Step_Colors procedure.

```
void Step_Colors()
{
    int  i, this_color, Done = 0;
    char Ch;
```

The *Done* variable was initialized as 0 (False), setting up a loop condition that will continue until *Done* becomes non-zero. Until then, Step_Colors waits for a keyboard entry.

An entry of Q or q increments *Done* to allow an exit; an entry of − or + selects a direction for the colors to change.

```
    while( !Done )
    {
        Ch = getch();
```

```
if( (toupper(Ch) == 'Q') ) Done++;
if( Ch == '-' ) StepForward = 0;
if( Ch == '+' ) StepForward = 1;
if( !Done )
{
```

Any keyboard entry that has not set the exit condition allows a second loop to increment or decrement the current palette color values. The loop steps through the 16 palette entries with *this_color* taking the value of each palette entry (*palette.colors[i]*) in turn. Then *this_color* is incremented or decremented as appropriate with a final test to ensure that the resulting color value remains within the range 0..63.

```
for( i=0; i<=15; i++ )
{
    this_color = palette.colors[i];
    if( StepForward ) this_color++;
    else              this_color- -;
    if( this_color < 0 )  this_color = 63;
    if( this_color > 63 ) this_color = 0;
```

Finally, setpalette sets *palette.colors[i]* to the new color value, getpalette updates the *palette* record, Label_Colors updates the screen label, and a delay of 30 milliseconds is executed before the loop continues.

```
    setpalette( i, this_color );
    getpalette( &palette );
    Label_Colors( i );
    delay(30);
}   }   }   }
```

When you run this demo, notice the screen colors change *immediately* when a new value is passed to setpalette. If you would like to see a more pronounced demonstration of this effect, increase the value in *delay(30)*, and add another delay before updating the color label on screen.

Remember, the only action required to change a screen color is to assign a new value to the appropriate palette entry. This action will update the entire screen on the next sweep refresh cycle, regardless of window or viewport settings or which video page is currently active.

This speed of change also allows other effects. For example, you could define several palettes as an array of type palette. For example: *struct palettetype alt_palette[10]* declares an array of 10 alternate palettes numbered 0..9. These alternate color palettes can be used to save any array of colors desired.

```
for( i=0; i<=16; i++ )
   palette.colors[i] =
      alt_palette[ new_palette ].colors[i];
```

The loop can assign any of these as *new_palette* to the active *palette* definition. Turbo C++ does not allow the direct assignment of arrays in the form: *palette = alt_palette[new_palette]*. While this assignment will *appear* to work—no error condition occurs and the structure *palette* will contain new values—the screen colors will not change and will continue to use the default palette.

In conclusion, here is a pair of (pun intended) colorful demo programs. Take them apart and play with them for a while. Try a few experiments and see what happens. If nothing else, the results should be interesting.

Also, have a shot at building color values as previously described, these results can also be interesting. And, try using the shift operators (<< and >>) directly on the color values (not on the palette entry numbers). The effects are unusual. Take a bit of time, relax, and play with the color assignments and see what happens. You might find something fascinating or useful, or both.

```
/*=====================================*/
/*               COLORCUB.C            */
/*  Color Chart for EGA Mode/Palettes  */
/*=====================================*/

#ifdef __TINY__
#error Graphics demos will not run in the tiny model.
#endif

#include <conio.h>
#include <stdio.h>
#include <stdlib.h>
#include <stdarg.h>
#include <graphics.h>

#include "gprint.i"

int    GraphDriver;            /* graphics device driver  */
int    GraphMode;              /* graphics mode value     */
```

```
int    MaxColors;                        /* maximum colors available */
int    ErrorCode = 0;                    /* report graphics errors   */
int    radius = 20;
int    xoff[3]  = { 235,   380,   525 };
int    yoff[3]  = { 230,   135,    40 };
int    zxoff[3] = {   0,   -90,  -180 };
int    zyoff[3] = {   0,    30,    60 };
int    Colors;

void Initialize()
{          /* initialize graphics system and report errors */
   GraphDriver = DETECT;              /* request auto-detection */
   initgraph( &GraphDriver, &GraphMode, "C:\\TC\\BGI" );
   ErrorCode = graphresult();            /* test init results */
   if( ErrorCode != grOk )            /* if error during init */
   {
      printf(" Graphics System Error: %s\n",
              grapherrormsg( ErrorCode ) );
      exit( 1 );
}  }

void set_circle( int x, int y, int z, int color )
{
   setfillstyle( SOLID_FILL, color );
   setlinestyle( SOLID_LINE, 0, 1 );
   setcolor( EGA_WHITE );
   circle( xoff[x] + zxoff[z], yoff[y] + zyoff[z],
           radius );
   setcolor( EGA_BLACK );
   circle( xoff[x] + zxoff[z], yoff[y] + zyoff[z],
           radius / 2 );
   floodfill( xoff[x] + zxoff[z] + 1,
              yoff[y] + zyoff[z] + 1, EGA_WHITE );
   setcolor( EGA_LIGHTGREY );
}

void cline( int x1, int y1, int z1,
            int x2, int y2, int z2, int wt )
{
   setlinestyle( SOLID_LINE, 0, wt );
   line( xoff[x1] + zxoff[z1],  yoff[y1] + zyoff[z1],
         xoff[x2] + zxoff[z2],  yoff[y2] + zyoff[z2]  );
```

```
}

void Color_Cube()
{
    setcolor( EGA_RED );
    cline( 0, 0, 0, 1, 0, 0, 3 );
    cline( 1, 0, 0, 2, 0, 0, 3 );
    cline( 1, 0, 0, 1, 1, 0, 1 );
    cline( 1, 0, 0, 1, 0, 1, 1 );
    set_circle( 1, 0, 0, EGA_RED );
    setcolor( EGA_BLUE );
    cline( 0, 0, 0, 0, 1, 0, 3 );
    cline( 0, 1, 0, 0, 2, 0, 3 );
    cline( 0, 1, 0, 1, 1, 0, 1 );
    cline( 0, 1, 0, 0, 1, 1, 1 );
    set_circle( 0, 1, 0, EGA_BLUE );
    setcolor( EGA_GREEN );
    cline( 0, 0, 0, 0, 0, 1, 3 );
    cline( 0, 0, 1, 0, 0, 2, 3 );
    cline( 0, 0, 1, 1, 0, 1, 1 );
    cline( 0, 0, 1, 0, 1, 1, 1 );
    set_circle( 0, 0, 1, EGA_GREEN );
    setcolor( EGA_LIGHTGREY );
    cline( 0, 0, 0, 1, 1, 1, 3 );
    cline( 1, 1, 1, 2, 2, 2, 3 );
    set_circle( 0, 0, 0, EGA_BLACK );
    cline( 0, 1, 1, 1, 1, 1, 1 );
    set_circle( 0, 1, 1, EGA_CYAN );
    cline( 1, 1, 0, 1, 1, 1, 1 );
    set_circle( 1, 1, 0, EGA_MAGENTA );
    cline( 1, 0, 1, 1, 1, 1, 1 );
    set_circle( 1, 0, 1, EGA_BROWN );
    set_circle( 1, 1, 1, EGA_LIGHTGREY );
    setcolor( EGA_LIGHTRED );
    cline( 2, 0, 0, 2, 2, 0, 1 );
    cline( 2, 0, 0, 2, 0, 2, 1 );
    set_circle( 2, 0, 0, EGA_LIGHTRED );
    setcolor( EGA_LIGHTBLUE );
    cline( 0, 2, 0, 0, 2, 2, 1 );
    cline( 0, 2, 0, 2, 2, 0, 1 );
    set_circle( 0, 2, 0, EGA_LIGHTBLUE );
```

```
   setcolor( EGA_LIGHTGREEN );
   cline( 0, 0, 2, 2, 0, 2, 1 );
   cline( 0, 0, 2, 0, 2, 2, 1 );
   set_circle( 0, 0, 2, EGA_LIGHTGREEN );
   cline( 2, 2, 0, 2, 2, 2, 1 );
   set_circle( 2, 2, 0, EGA_LIGHTMAGENTA );
   cline( 0, 2, 2, 2, 2, 2, 1 );
   set_circle( 0, 2, 2, EGA_LIGHTCYAN );
   cline( 2, 0, 2, 2, 2, 2, 1 );
   set_circle( 2, 0, 2, EGA_YELLOW );
   set_circle( 2, 2, 2, EGA_WHITE );
}

void Color_Switch()
{
   int   Done = 0;
   char Ch;
   while( !Done )
   {
      Ch = getch();
      if( (toupper(Ch) == 'Q') ) Done++;
      if( Colors )
      {
         setpalette( 0, EGA_BLACK );
         setpalette( 15, EGA_WHITE );
         Colors = 0;
      }
      else
      {
         setpalette( 0, EGA_WHITE );
         setpalette( 15, EGA_BLACK );
         Colors = 1;
} } }

main()
{
   Initialize();
   Colors = 1;
   outtextxy( 10, 10,
      "Enter <Q> to quit or any key to change colors" );
   Color_Cube();
```

```c
   Color_Switch();
   closegraph();                        /*    restore text mode    */
}                                        /*    end COLCUBE.C    */


      /*==========================================*/
      /*                  COLORS.C                  */
      /*  Color Chart for EGA/VGA Mode/Palettes  */
      /*==========================================*/

#ifdef __TINY__
#error Graphics demos will not run in the tiny model.
#endif

#include <conio.h>
#include <stdio.h>
#include <stdlib.h>
#include <stdarg.h>
#include <graphics.h>

#include "gprint.i"

int    GraphDriver;             /* graphics device driver    */
int    GraphMode;               /* graphics mode value       */
int    MaxColors;               /* maximum colors available  */
int    ErrorCode = 0;           /* reports any graphics errors */
int    radius = 30;
int    StepForward = 1;
struct  palettetype  palette;

void Initialize()
{           /* initialize graphics system and report errors */
   GraphDriver = DETECT;              /* request auto-detection */
   initgraph( &GraphDriver, &GraphMode, "C:\\TC\\BGI" );
   ErrorCode = graphresult();            /* test init results */
   if ( ErrorCode != grOk )          /* if error during init */
   {
      printf(" Graphics System Error: %s\n",
            grapherrormsg( ErrorCode ) );
      exit( 1 );
   }  }
void Label_Colors( int i )
{
```

```
        if( i > 7 )
            gprintxy( 80*i-600, 135+radius, " %d ",
                        palette.colors[i] );
        else gprintxy( 80*i+40,   55+radius, " %d ",
                        palette.colors[i] );
}

void Show_Colors()
{
    int  i;

    getpalette( &palette );
    for( i=0; i<=7; i++ )
    {
        setfillstyle( SOLID_FILL, i );
        circle( 80*i+40, 50, radius );
        floodfill( 80*i+40, 50, getcolor() );
        Label_Colors( i );
        setfillstyle( SOLID_FILL, i+8 );
        circle( 80*i+40, 130, radius );
        floodfill( 80*i+40, 130, getcolor() );
        Label_Colors( i+8 );
}   }

void Color_Wheel()
{
    int  i;
    for( i=0; i<=15; i++ )
    {
        setfillstyle( SOLID_FILL, 15-i );
        pieslice( 320, 270, i*22.5, (i+1)*22.5, radius*3 );
}   }

void Step_Colors()
{
    int  i, Done = 0;
    char Ch;

    while( !Done )
    {
        int  this_color;

        Ch = getch();
        if( (toupper(Ch) == 'Q') ) Done++;
```

```
      if( Ch == '-' ) StepForward = 0;
      if( Ch == '+' ) StepForward = 1;
      if( !Done )
      {
         for( i=0; i<=15; i++ )
         {
            this_color = palette.colors[i];
            if( StepForward ) this_color++;
            else              this_color- -;
            if( this_color < 0 )  this_color = 63;
            if( this_color > 63 ) this_color = 0;
            setpalette( i, this_color );
            getpalette( &palette );
            Label_Colors( i );
            delay(30);
} } } }

void Initialize_Colors()
{
   int  i;

   for( i=0; i<=15; i++ ) setpalette( i, i );
}

main()
{
   Initialize();
   settextjustify( CENTER_TEXT, CENTER_TEXT );
   settextstyle( SANS_SERIF_FONT, HORIZ_DIR, 1 );
   outtextxy( 320, 10,
      "Enter <Q> to quit or any key to change colors " );
   outtextxy( 100, 250, "Enter <-> for" );
   outtextxy( 100, 270, "reversed step" );
   outtextxy( 540, 250, "Enter <+> for" );
   outtextxy( 540, 270, "forward step" );
   Initialize_Colors();
   Show_Colors();
   Color_Wheel();
   Step_Colors();
   closegraph();                       /*   restore text mode   */
}
```

Chapter 14

Graphics Printer Output

Computer graphics are wonderful on screen, but unless you can create these same graphics on paper, they also can be quite frustrating. Pasting a computer terminal into a manuscript is close to impossible.

For text modes, the Shift-PrtSc (Shift-PrintScreen) key command is available to send an ASCII screen to the printer, and several TSR utilities have been created to execute the same task for a graphics screen. These latter, however, have been less than satisfactory. Most work only with specific printers, operate only in specific modes and, when used, may occupy entirely too much resident memory and also prevent other applications from running.

In this chapter, two graphics screen print utilities are created providing monochrome outputs using the Epson (dot-matrix) and LaserJet printers. These graphic output utilities avoid the problems mentioned because they can be tailored for any output device, will adapt to different video modes, and can be incorporated directly into your application program.

Since more people have color monitors on their systems than have color plotters, the LaserJet graphics driver offers, in addition to Portrait and Landscape modes, a Greyscale mode (with two options: normal and inverse grey scales) that translates colors to greys in 16 shades on output.

Please note: all of the graphics output devices shown here are generic drivers. They have been specifically designed to work with most dot-matrix or laserjet devices presently marketed or can be easily adapted to work with any devices that require variant handling codes. The standard devices chosen—Epson MX/FX series dot-matrix and HP LaserJet Series II printers—are also de facto industry standards. Most devices, regardless of manufacturers' trademarks, use essentially the same control codes and operate in basically the same manner.

Two output device types not covered here are the color dot-matrix printers using multicolor ribbons or the multicolor inkjet printers. However, a specialty driver for this type of device is easily created following the pattern of the monochrome examples given here.

Using the Epson Dot-Matrix Printers

The Epson FX-85 printer is used as the standard device for dot-matrix printers. This ensures compatibility with the MX and RX series and, for the most part, with the LX (inkjet) series, as well as the majority of other manufacturers of dot-matrix printers. Most offer graphics modes compatible with the Epson, but you should consult your printer manual for the capabilities of any specific device and adapt the graphics driver as needed.

Because the dot-matrix graphics operations presented here are designed for 9-pin heads, this driver is not directly compatible with the newer dot-matrix printers using 24-pin print heads. Operations, however, are directly analogous and the EP_GRAPH driver may be easily adapted for use with newer printer types.

The FX-85 printer offers eight graphics operation modes as shown in Table 14-1. A word of caution: if you are using an Epson printer (or compatible) with the dip switch selection set to IBM mode, or an IBM dot matrix printer, only graphics modes 0-3 will be available.

Table 14-1: Epson FX-85 Graphics Modes

Mode	Density	Description	Speed
0	Single	60 dpi	16 in/sec
1	Low Speed Double	120 dpi	8 in/sec
2	High Speed Double	120 dpi	16 in/sec[1]
3	Quadruple	240 dpi	8 in/sec[1]
4	CRT 1	80 dpi	8 in/sec[2]
5	One-to-one	72 dpi	12 in/sec[2]
6	CRT II	90 dpi	8 in/sec
7	Dual-Density	144 dpi	3 in/sec[3]

1. Does not print consecutive dots in any one row.
2. Matches screen density of Epson QX-10.
3. Plotter modes: provide one-to-one horizontal dot density.

While Epson provides mode 4 (CRT I) to match the screen (pixel) density of the QX-10 computer monitor, none of these modes offers an exact match for either CGA or EGA/VGA screen modes. Some, however, provide a better match than others, but this also depends on your output orientation.

Portrait Versus Landscape Orientation

Both the laserjet and dot-matrix drivers offer a choice of Landscape or Portrait imaging. The Portrait orientation plots the screen's x-axis across the width of your paper and the y-axis along the length of the paper, producing a half-sheet image. The Landscape orientation matches the long axis of the paper to the screen's x-axis, plotting the screen's y-axis across the width of the paper and producing a single screen image per page. This, in general, is the preferred output orientation.

For each orientation and screen mode, there is a preferred dot-matrix mode to best match the screen image, as shown in Table 14-2.

Table 14-2: Preferred Dot-Matrix Modes for Graphics

Direction	CGA	EGA	VGA
PORTRAIT	3 / 7	1 / 7	1 / 7
LANDSCAPE	0	0	

Three criteria apply in printer mode selection for a graphics screen output. First, the number of dots per inch (dpi) must be high enough to map the screen pixels within the physical page limits. Using a resolution of 60 dpi (mode 0) in Portrait orientation would require a paper width greater than eight inches. For a 13-inch wide printer, 60 dpi would be acceptable for plotting 640 pixels horizontal but, on an eight-inch printer, only 480 pixels would be plotted before the margins were exceeded.

Second, the dots per inch horizontal and the lines per inch vertical must be balanced to achieve an output image close to your screen image. The horizontal dpi can be varied, the vertical cannot (or not easily).

Third, since the image is plotted one to one (one pixel/one dot), the higher the printer density (dots per inch), the smaller the resulting image. For example, mode 3 will plot an entire screen image, in Portrait mode, in a width of only 2.7 inches (and in very distorted proportions).

The modes shown are not dictated by fiat. I suggest that you experiment with your own equipment, try the various modes and see firsthand how each matches output and screen image. In this particular application, a picture is quite literally worth a thousand words.

Remember, the higher the number of dots per inch (dpi), the smaller the resulting image horizontally. If you need both the dense bit imaging and a larger image, for a dot matrix, rewrite the graphics driver to output two (or more) printer dots per screen pixel. See also Greyscaling which uses 16 dots per pixel (at 300 dpi) for color conversion with a laserjet and compare this approach with Epson's mode 3 Quadruple density (240 dpi).

Note also, for CGA modes C0..C3 (low resolution), printer mode 0 works well in Portrait orientation.

Calculating the Dot-Matrix Graphics Character

When the dot-matrix printer is used for normal (alphanumeric) output, an 8-bit character code selects a 9x9 pin pattern from the printer's ROM character sets. In graphics modes, however, only eight of these pins are used and an 8-bit character is sent for each horizontal printhead position with each bit of this character code controlling one of the active pins.

The graphics character is calculated with the top pin controlled by bit 7 of the character, the bottom pin controlled by bit 0. Three examples of graphic character calculations are shown in Figure 14-1.

Figure 14-1: Individual Pin Calculation

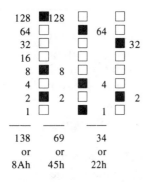

The graphics character code for the dot-matrix print head is calculated as an 8-bit character with bit 7 for the top pin (value 128) and bit 0 for the bottom pin (value 1). The character code sent is the sum of the values for the pins desired to print.

Graphics results are shown in both decimal and hexadecimal codes.

On the dot-matrix, a series of graphics characters prints eight horizontal rows of dots, then the paper is advanced and the print head returned for the next row. Thus, in Portrait mode, each print line accounts for eight screen pixel rows and each character is generated from eight vertical pixels (see Figure 14-2).

In Landscape mode, the print direction and paper advance remain constant but the screen pixels are scanned as horizontal sets of eight pixels with a print line beginning at the top right of the screen and moving down. Subsequent print lines begin by scanning eight horizontal pixels at the top of the screen but with the horizontal scan position moved eight pixels left while final print line scans the left-most portion of the screen (see Figure 14-3).

Figure 14-2: Calculating Bit-Image Characters for the Dot-Matrix

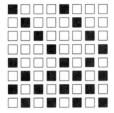

In PORTRAIT mode, the pixels would be read as eight vertical sets (left to right) as 8Ah, 45h, 22h,15h, 8Ah, 45h, 2Ah, and 15h and transmitted in this order.

In LANDSCAPE mode, the pixels would be read as eight horizontal sets (top to bottom) as 11h, 22h, 44h, 88h, 51h, AAh, 55h and AAh and tranmitted in this order. Remember, the high order bit is to the right, the low order bit to the left.

EP_Graph—Dot-Matrix Graphics Driver

To describe the EP_Graph function (dot-matrix driver) as simplicity itself would be demeaning to a very smooth programming function. The EP_Graph function is precisely this: very simple and very smooth.

Before calling EP_Graph, however, I suggest defining two constants that will be used by the calling function to specify the output orientation desired:

```
#define  PORTRAIT   0
#define  LANDSCAPE  1
```

Two parameters are required to call EP_Graph: *Mode* and *Direction*.

```
void EP_Graph( int Mode, int Direction )
{
```

The *Mode* parameter is a provision allowing you test different printer modes. When you've settled on a preferred printer graphics mode, this calling parameter can be eliminated with mode constants supplied in both the *case PORTRAIT* and *case LANDSCAPE* options.

Also, if you prefer to use only Landscape or Portrait orientation, the second parameter (*Direction*) can also be eliminated with the *switch* and *case* provisions rewritten for the preferred option. In either case, a few local variables are required:

```
char   m;
int    i, j, k, Msb, Lsb,
       MaxX = getmaxx(),
       MaxY = getmaxy();
```

The last two variables, *MaxX* and *MaxY*, may duplicate similar declarations elsewhere in your program, but this will not interfere with their local declaration and these values will be needed.

```
setviewport( 0, 0, MaxX, MaxY, 0 );
```

If your calling program has other settings in effect, or if you want other settings in effect, this can be changed or eliminated. If you need to map a smaller area, it can be done by setting the limits to match the desired screen region. Be sure the data width specifications are set to match.

The printer should be set to graphics mode:

```
fprintf( stdprn, "\x1BA%c", 7 );
```

In Turbo C++, *stdprn* is a predefined file corresponding to LPT. If you need a different output port, change this designation accordingly.

Figure 14-3: Mapping Screen to Paper in LANDSCAPE Mode

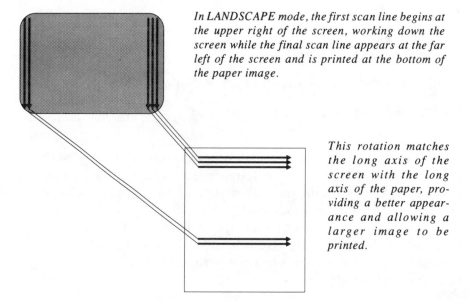

In LANDSCAPE mode, the first scan line begins at the upper right of the screen, working down the screen while the final scan line appears at the far left of the screen and is printed at the bottom of the paper image.

This rotation matches the long axis of the screen with the long axis of the paper, providing a better appearance and allowing a larger image to be printed.

The string \x1BAn instructs the printer to set line spacing as n/72. In this case the *character* 07h specifies 7/72 (about 82 dpi vertical spacing). Valid settings for *n* are 0..85. Next, output orientation is selected as Portrait or Landscape:

```
switch( Direction )
{
    case PORTRAIT:
    {
```

The next step is to give the printer a graphics mode command and to specify how wide each line will be (how many dot positions will be plotted). The *Mode* value was specified when EP_Graphic was called and, in *PORTRAIT* orientation, this width would be the 640 pixels horizontally on the screen (assuming high resolution modes).

However, since the Epson printer can only accept 8-bit data, the 640 dot specification is reduced to two 8-bit arguments: *Lsb* and *Msb*. Since *MaxX* will have a value of 639 returned by getmaxx, the argument used to calculate *Lsb* and *Msb* is incremented by one.

```
Lsb = (MaxX+1) & 0x00FF;
Msb = (MaxX+1) >> 8;
```

A loop begins at the top of the screen. Each loop, however, will plot eight vertical pixels.

```
for( j=0; j<=MaxY/8; j++ )
{
```

The arguments *Mode*, *Lsb*, and *Msb* are passed as char values (unsigned 8-bit integers) with the \x1B* argument indicating that a graphics mode is being selected.

```
fprintf( stdprn, "\x1B*%c%c%c",
         Mode, Lsb, Msb );
```

This graphics mode setting is valid only for one line. After a graphics mode command and line length parameters are sent, the next *x* data bytes (set by the *Lsb* and *Msb* arguments) received are interpreted as graphics pin instructions, regardless of their contents! Thus, the graphics mode settings command initializes each and every graphics data line transmitted to the printer.

Now another loop begins, starting at the left screen margin and progressing across the screen to *MaxX*.

```
for( i=0; i<=MaxX; i++ )
{
```

The character *m* is set to null (0) at the start of each step, then an inner loop steps from *0* through *7* to read eight screen pixels (vertically).

```
m = 0;
for( k=0; k<8; k++ )
{
```

As the inner loop executes, the character *m* is shifted left one bit. If the current pixel is not *0* (black or background palette entry), then *m* is incremented (the rightmost or zero bit is set). As the loop continues and *m* is shifted left, each bit moves up and a new null bit becomes the low-order bit.

```
m <<= 1;
if( getpixel( i, j*8+k ) ) m++;
}
```

After the inner loop is finished, the resulting character is output to the printer.

```
fprintf( stdprn, "%c", m );
}
```

When the line is finished, the CR/LF codes are explicitly sent to the printer to advance the print head to the beginning of the next line.

```
fprintf( stdprn, "\x0D\x0A" );
}   }
```

This process continues until the entire screen has been read, eight pixels at a time—and transferred to the printer in the form of a graphics character.

In the Landscape mode, the process is the same except that a different graphics string length is calculated using *MaxY* instead of *MaxX* and the screen image is read, starting at the top right and moving down and left, eight horizontal pixels at a byte (pun intended).

```
case LANDSCAPE:
{
    Lsb = MaxY & 0x00FF;
```

```
Msb = MaxY >> 8;
for( j=0; j<MaxX; j+=8 )
{
    fprintf( stdprn, "\x1B*%c%c%c",
             Mode, Lsb, Msb );
```

Unlike the Portrait mode, here the screen image is read beginning at the bottom of the screen and working up.

```
for( i=MaxY; i>=0; i- - )
{
    m = 0;
    for( k=0; k<8; k++ )
    {
        m <<= 1;
        if( getpixel( j+k, i ) ) m++;
    }
    fprintf( stdprn, "%c", m );
}
fprintf( stdprn, "\x0D\x0A" );
}  }  }
```

Finally, after the entire screen image has been transmitted to the printer, a formfeed is sent to advance the paper.

```
    fprintf( stdprn,"\f" );
}
```

This completes the image transmission process. Simple.

Using the LaserJet Printer

A graphics screen dump to a laserjet printer is no more difficult than printing to a dot-matrix, but there are differences both in the capabilities of the laserjet and in how the laserjet is treated.

First, the laserjet is capable of printing a finer dot-image than a dot-matrix printer—up to 300 dpi—but most laserjets also support four distinct dot resolutions: 75 dpi, 100 dpi, 150 dpi, and 300 dpi. At 75 dpi, the image dots are 16 times as large (4x4) as the dots produced at 300 dpi and, naturally, only 1/16 as much information can be mapped to a page. Similarly, the 100 dpi and 150 dpi resolutions create dot sizes which are submultiples of the 300 dpi.

Second, the resolution used does not affect the output speed. The time required to generate a graphics output is determined only by the amount of bit information sent to the printer (transmission time) and not by the resolution setting used by the printer to map the information to the page. The same image generated at 300 dpi and at 75 dpi will require the same output time.

Third, the dot resolution selected does not directly affect the relative x-/y-axis spacing. While the x-axis spacing is determined by the dot resolution, the y-axis line spacing is directly under the control of the program. Screen aspect ratios can be matched on output with excellent results and, if desired, deliberate distortions can be introduced.

In sum, since the laserjet labors under fewer *mechanical* constraints than a dot-matrix, the resulting output is capable both of much higher resolution and of more faithful reproduction of the original video screen image.

Because of this lack of mechanical constraints, the laserjet is controlled in a different manner than a dot-matrix with two principal differences in operation. First, each row (or column) of screen pixels is mapped one for one to the laserjet output scan. In Portrait mode, instead of reading successive groups of eight vertical pixels, as was done for the dot matrix, the screen image is read by rows, with each successive eight pixels transmitted as a graphics character and 80 characters creating one row of graphics dots on the page. The dpi resolution is selected and it determines the horizontal spacing between the dots.

Second, since there is no physical printhead involved, each graphics string output must be prefaced with position instructions explaining where on the page the dot image is to appear. However, as mentioned before, this is precisely the element which makes it possible for the aspect of the output image to match the screen image faithfully.

The LaserJet Screen Print Utility

The utility functions in LJ-GRAPH.I provide three modes for transferring your screen image to paper: Landscape, Portrait, and Greyscale. The first two modes, Landscape and Portrait, provide a fast monochrome output in 75 and 100 dpi resolutions. The third mode, Greyscale, translates screen colors into either four (CGA Low Resolution) or 16 (EGA/VGA) shades of grey (see Table 14-3).

As you will note, the Greyscale mode requires a fair amount of time—slightly more than six minutes—to output some 600,000 bytes of information describing a color screen. The image produced is effectively the same resolution and size as in Landscape mode except that each pixel has been mapped to a 16-bit (4x4) grey dot image. The practice and options in grey scaling will be discussed further in this chapter (see *Sixteen and Four Tone Greyscale Palettes*).

The same screen in either Landscape or Portrait mode requires slightly more than one minute. These times will vary, of course, depending on CPU speeds and other machine capabilities but the values given above provide a general rule for time requirements. Three other considerations should be kept in mind.

First, if you do not have a laserjet immediately available, the screen dump output can be redirected to a disk file and then sent directly from disk to a laserjet at a later time using the DOS Print command.

Second, multiple copies of a screen image can be printed without requiring multiple transmission times. Adding a multicopy command to the output print image will be discussed later in this chapter.

Third, *do not* attempt to use the Greyscale mode with CGA monochrome graphics. There is simply no point, the results will be a very pale image and the Landscape mode will produce much more satisfactory results in about 1/6 the time.

Table 14-3: LaserJet Graphic Screen Dump Modes

Mode	Approximate Data	Resolution	Time
LANDSCAPE	50,000 bytes	75 DPI	~1 minute
PORTRAIT	40,000 bytes	100 DPI	~1 minute
GREYSCALE	600,000 bytes	300 DPI	~6 minutes

LaserJet Instruction Codes

Table 14-4 shows a sample series of laserjet graphic output instructions with each command sequence appearing on a separate line and with comments. In actual practice, the command sequences are not separated by any CR/LF sequences unless they happen to appear as graphics dot commands.

Each command sequence begins with the Escape character (^{1}B) followed by a series of ASCII characters that define the command and any parameters included in the command. For example, the sequence ^{1}B*t300R, sets 300 dpi resolution with the parameter *300* sent as a plain-text ASCII sequence and never as a code or value sequence as was used with the dot-matrix codes.

Table 14-4: An Example of LaserJet Output Instructions

1_BE	reset
$^1_B\&l1H$	select paper feed from tray
$1_B\&lOO$	reset 0 origin for printer cursor position
1_B*pOX	cursor position 0 dots horizontal
1_B*pOY	cursor position 0 dots vertical
$1_B*t300R$	300 dpi resolution
$1_B\&a1228.8h1180.8V$	cursor position, horizontal & vertical decipoints
1_B*r1A	start graphics at current cursor
1_B*b23W 0F FF FF FF FF FF FF FF FF FF FF FF FF FF FF FF FF FF FF FF FF FF F8	
	transfer 23 bytes graphic data
1_B*rB	end graphics
$1_B\&a1228.8h1183.2V$	position cursor, horizontal & vertical decipoints
1_B*r1A	start graphics at current cursor
1_B*b23W 01 F0 20 20 20 20 20 20 20 20 20 20 20 20 20 20 20 20 20 20 20 27 80	
	transfer 23 bytes graphic data
1_B*rB	end graphics
.	
.	*(graphics instructions continue)*
.	
1_B*rB 0C	end graphics + form feed (0Ch)
$1_B\&lOO$	reset 0 origin printer cursor position (*default*)
$1_B(8U$	primary symbol set Roman-8 (*default*)
$1_B(sOp10h12vsb3T$	reset primary font values (*defaults*)
$1_B\&l1H$	select paper feed from tray (*default*)

(end of printer instructions)

The DeciPoint Position Instructions

The laserjet supports three separate print cursor position modes: row, dot, and decipoint. For this application, only the decipoint coordinate system will be used.

First, however, a bit of background explanation. Printers (meaning people rather than devices) have traditionally used a pica and point system to measure type sizes with six picas equalling one inch and 12 points to the pica. There are 72 points to the inch and the dot-matrix printer standard also provides for spacing in $1/2$-inch increments.

But the laserjet uses a dot size of $1/300$ of an inch, requiring a finer position increment than a mere point size and the laserjet's dot coordinate system provides this spacing in $1/300$-inch steps.

An even finer degree of positioning, however, is provided by the decipoint coordinates. A decipoint is $1/10$ of a point or $1/720$ of an inch and, to carry precision one degree further, the decipoint measurements also allow a decimal fraction (as 1234.5 decipoints) for a precision of $1/7200$ of an inch.

The decipoint.decimal is the position coordinate system that will be used to control the graphics print positions, which should be sufficient positioning to satisfy even the most finicky programmer.

One other bit of information: the 0,0 coordinate is a position roughly $1/2$ inch down from the top of the page and $1/2$ inch from the left. All decipoint measurements are made from this coordinate location.

Using 300 dpi resolution, each dot is nominally 0.0033... inches in diameter and, converting this measurement to decipoints, yields a basic vertical increment of 2.4 decipoints. For 150 dpi, this increment would be doubled to 4.8; at 100 dpi, becoming 7.2 decipoints and; at 75 dpi, the vertical increment becomes 9.6 decipoints.

These basic printer scan line increments are adjusted according to the screen pixel aspect ratios to ensure that the proportions of the final print image match the screen appearance.

Note also that the printer cursor position command consists of a single instruction preface followed by two values: the *x* and *y* coordinates. Since the h character identifying the preceding as a horizontal decipoint position coordinate is lowercase, the instruction preface does not have to be repeated. The second coordinate is ended with a capital V indicating that the current command sequence is being terminated.

If you look at the next to the last command sequence in Table 14-4, the sequence begins with a single instruction preface (^{1}B(*s*) followed by a series of values and lowercase instruction indicators with the final instruction indicator in uppercase as a terminator. This format is used frequently when several commands sharing the same instruction preface sequence are being sent.

Additional information and explanation on the laserjet printer control sequences can be found in the *LaserJet series II Printer User's Manual*, Appendix A, or in the *LaserJet series II Printer Technical Reference Manual*, both available from Hewlett-Packard.

Writing Graphics Characters to the LaserJet

Before the graphics data is transmitted, the printer cursor position is set using the horizontal and vertical decipoint coordinates, then the ^{1}B**r1A* sequence confirms that graphics output will begin at the cursor setting.

The next command sequence, ^{1}B**b##W*, tells the printer to treat the next ## characters as graphics characters. Just as the 300 dpi resolution figure was sent as plain text instead of using code characters (as was done with the dot-matrix), the number of data characters to be transmitted will also be sent as plain-text ASCII. That is, if 80 graphics characters will follow, then the ## markers will read an ASCII "80" instead of the "P" character which would have been used with the dot-matrix printer. See Figure 14-5 for examples.

As before, information is transmitted in the form of 8-bit characters and for the laserjet, these bit-images are calculated precisely the same as for the dot-matrix images except for the direction and order of screen pixels read for each mode (see Figure 14-4).

While the transmit graphics data command explicitly stated how many bytes (characters) of graphics data would be sent, an end graphics command string is still sent after the data transfer is complete. Granted, this appears redundant, but it is safe and adds little overhead to the data transmitted.

When all of the graphics data have been sent, the final end graphics command will be followed by the character 0Ch, the standard form feed character, instructing the laserjet to eject the page.

The four code sequences following the form feed character are simply housekeeping sequences to reset the laserjet to default values.

Sixteen and Four-Tone Greyscale Palettes

In addition to the direct mapping modes (Landscape and Portrait), the provided Greyscale mode maps each screen pixel on output to a grey 4x4 dot image, the grey value being determined by the palette color number of the screen pixel. This is not a true greyscale conversion, but is an arbitrary map providing 16 greys for EGA/VGA color screens and four greys for CGA low-resolution color screens.

This greyscale conversion is accomplished by setting an output resolution of 300 dpi, then scanning each screen pixel four times and outputting 16 dots (four per line on four lines) for each screen pixel. The resulting print image is the same size and aspect as created by the Landscape mode except that the screen colors are now approximated as shades of grey. There are also flaws in this particular method of greyscaling.

First, since this is an arbitrary grey mapping, the darker colors are assigned the lightest greys and WHITE is printed as an almost solid black. The grey palette result for LIGHTGREY is out of order, being one dot lighter than the grey palette result assigned to DARKGREY (assuming the default EGA/VGA color palette). This light to dark scaling was arbitrarily chosen as normal since it leaves the screen background printed as white.

Figure 14-4: Calculating Bit-Image Characters for the LaserJet

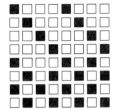

In PORTRAIT mode, the eight horizontal sets of pixels would be read as 88h, 44h, 22h, 11h, 8Ah, 55h, AAh, and 55h. As with the dot-matrix, each set of eight pixels is transmitted as a single graphics character and each set would be transmitted on a separate line.

In LANDSCAPE mode, the pixels would be read as eight vertical sets as 15h, 2Ah, 45h, 8Ah, 15h, 22h, 45h, and 8Ah. Again, each eight pixels are transmitted as a single graphics character and each vertical set shown here would be transmitted on a separate line.

An option is provided to invert the greyscale results such that the background will be printed as black and the WHITE will be plotted as white on the page. This inversion, however, will not correct the minor discrepancy between the grey tones assigned to the LIGHTGREY and DARKGREY default palette entries.

Second, if new colors are assigned to the EGA/VGA palette, the greyscale values will not change to accommodate these colors. If the palette color entry number two is assigned a bright green, it will still be greyscaled according to the palette entry number and not the color value assigned.

Third, the shades of grey provided may not be easily distinguished from each other and two adjacent shades of grey may be almost exactly the same in appearance, depending on the output device and the state of the ink (toner) cartridge used.

These are, however, the closest approximations to 16 shades of grey possible to create within the limitations of the laserjet and the requirement of mapping an entire 640x350 (or larger) graphics screen.

Figure 14-5 shows the grey bit-maps assigned to each palette entry.

LJ-GRAPH.I

The LJ-GRAPH's utility include file contains the Laserjet Graphics driver functions and begins by declaring three constants and one global variable.

```
#define    PORTRAIT   0
#define    LANDSCAPE  1
#define    GREYSCALE  2
int        Negative;
```

Figure 14-5: Bit Patterns for 16-level Greyscale Palette

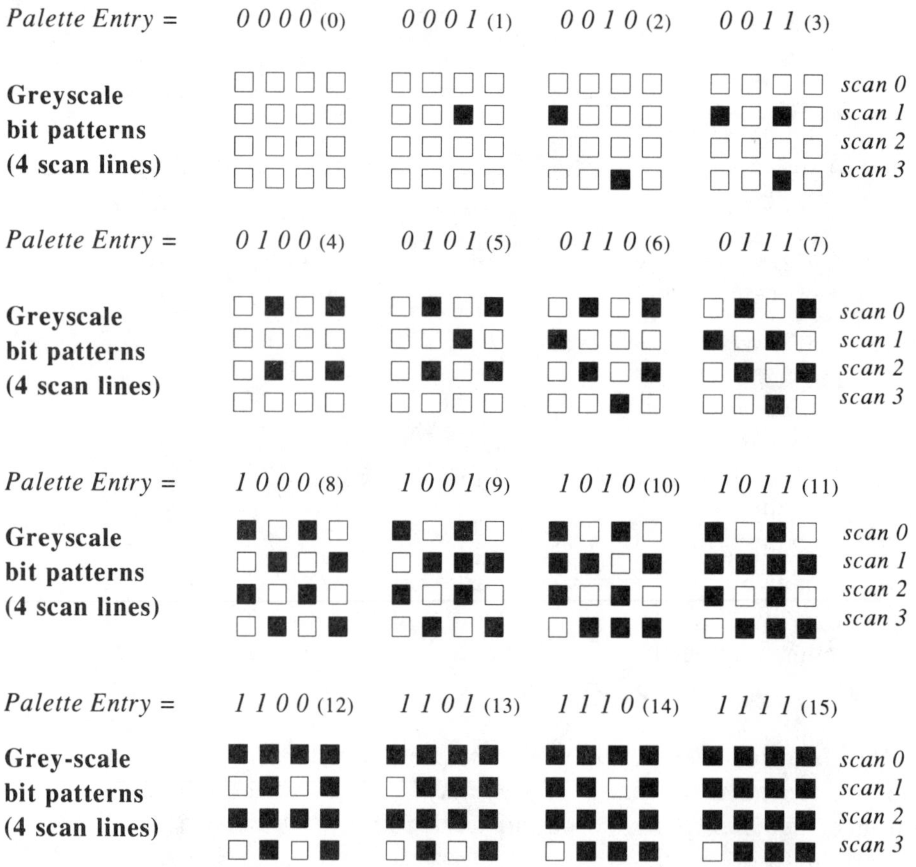

Palette Entry =   *0 0 0 0* (0)   *0 0 0 1* (1)   *0 0 1 0* (2)   *0 0 1 1* (3)

Greyscale
bit patterns
(4 scan lines)

scan 0
scan 1
scan 2
scan 3

Palette Entry =   *0 1 0 0* (4)   *0 1 0 1* (5)   *0 1 1 0* (6)   *0 1 1 1* (7)

Greyscale
bit patterns
(4 scan lines)

scan 0
scan 1
scan 2
scan 3

Palette Entry =   *1 0 0 0* (8)   *1 0 0 1* (9)   *1 0 1 0* (10)   *1 0 1 1* (11)

Greyscale
bit patterns
(4 scan lines)

scan 0
scan 1
scan 2
scan 3

Palette Entry =   *1 1 0 0* (12)   *1 1 0 1* (13)   *1 1 1 0* (14)   *1 1 1 1* (15)

Grey-scale
bit patterns
(4 scan lines)

scan 0
scan 1
scan 2
scan 3

The constants Portrait, Landscape, and Greyscale are provided as a convenience in selecting the desired mode when calling the LJ_Graphic function. The variable *Negative* is used as a flag by the Greyscale function to select normal or inverse greyscale mapping.

The LJ_Graphic function is called with one parameter, *Mode*, selecting Portrait, Landscape, or Greyscale output orientation and resolution. Since your calling program may not provide x and y screen limits and a screen aspect ratio, these are declared as local variable along with the doubles *xprint, yprint,* and *prstep* and the character variables *m* and *resolution*.

```
void LJ_Graphic( int Mode )
{
```

```
int       i, j, k, p, q, xasp, yasp,
          MaxX = getmaxx() + 1,
          MaxY = getmaxy() + 1;
double    xprint, yprint, prstep, AspR;
char      m, resolution[3];
```

Two character strings, *graph_ends* and *graph_init*, are also defined.

Figure 14-6: Bit Patterns for 4-level Greyscale Palette

The argument \x1B is the Escape character (in hexadecimal format) but, if you have the disk version of these programs, Escape will appear on screen as a low-lighted [character (*ctrl-[*). Also, the Escape character (or any control character) can be entered directly by using the Turbo C++ editor's Control-Prefix entry (usually *Alt-P*), then entering the [key.

```
static char graph_init[] =
    "\x1BE\x1B&11H\x1B&1O\x1B*p0X\x1B*p0Y\x1B*t";
static char graph_ends[] = "\x1B*rB";
```

The *graph_init* character string breaks down into several commands as shown in Figure 14-5. The final portion of the string, ¹ᴮ*t, is the preface to the set resolution command which will be completed before the sequence is transmitted.

Now, the LJ_Graphic function checks the screen aspect ratio, then restores the viewport settings to the full screen.

```
getaspectratio( &xasp, &yasp );
AspR = (double) xasp / (double) yasp;
setviewport( 0, 0, MaxX, MaxY, 0 );
```

The switch command uses the *Mode* argument to select the desired output operation.

```
switch( Mode )
{   case PORTRAIT:
    {
```

In Portrait mode, the output x/y coordinates are set using initial *decipoint* values:

```
xprint = 690.0;
yprint = 500.0;
```

The string sequence 100 is copied to the string variable *resolution* and the completed initialization string is sent to the printer.

```
strcpy( resolution, "100" );
fprintf( stdprn, "%s%sR", graph_init,
         resolution );
```

These two commands can be rewritten, if desired, as a single command:

```
fprintf( stdprn, "%s100R", graph_init );
```

This command could also be written as:

```
fprint( stdprn, "%s%3dR", graph_init, 100 );
```

Now the *prstep* variable is set to match the printer aspect ratio to the screen aspect ratio.

```
prstep = 7.2 / AspR;
```

So far, this has all been setup and initialization for the printer and for values used while the graphics loops execute. Now it's time to read the video screen and send the output information to the printer.

Because this is Portrait mode, the loop begins at the top of the screen sends a printer cursor position command, then increments the *yprint* coordinate by the value in *prstep*.

```
for( j=0; j<=MaxY; j++ )
{
    fprintf( stdprn, "\x1B&a%-*.1fh%-*.1fV",
             format( xprint ), xprint,
             format( yprint ), yprint );
    yprint += prstep;
```

Notice that two parameters are used for the x coordinate and two for the y coordinate. The parameter provided by *format(xprint)* is a width statement specifying how many places will be created in the *%-*.1f* number string. C is notorious for formatting floating point numbers in all number to string conversions. Since any leading or trailing spaces would confuse the laserjet, the format function has been created to return an integer value, setting the string format to exclude leading or trailing blanks.

Next, commands are send to start graphics at the printer cursor and to specify the number of graphics characters that will follow. Happily, C is not fanatical about formatting integers with extra spaces, so no width parameter is required.

```
fprintf( stdprn, "\x1B*r1A\x1B*b%dW",
         MaxX/8 );
```

Now the printer is expecting a string of *MaxX/8* graphics characters and two loops, the first from *0* to *MaxX/8* and the second from *0* to *7*, read a series of screen pixels, creating a graphics character describing each eight pixels and sending the final character to the printer.

```
for( i=0; i<MaxX/8; i++ )
{
    m = 0;
    for( k=0; k<8; k++ )
    {
        m <<= 1;
        if( getpixel( i*8+k, j ) ) m++;
    }
    fprintf( stdprn, "%c", m );
}
```

When these two loops are completed and the current row of pixels has been mapped to the printer, the *graph_ends* string is sent, then the loop continues with the next row of pixels.

```
    fprintf( stdprn, "%s", graph_ends );
  }
} break;
```

In the Landscape mode, the initial setup is much the same except that a resolution of 75 dpi is selected and the printer line spacing is adjusted accordingly.

```
case LANDSCAPE:
{
    xprint = 1000.0;
    yprint = 1000.0;
    strcpy( resolution, "75" );
```

```
prstep = 9.6 * AspR;
fprintf( stdprn, "%s%sR", graph_init, resolution );
```

The main loop, however, runs from screen left to screen right and the graphics strings will be created by reading a column of screen pixels instead of a row. Since *MaxY* may not be an even multiple of eight (EGA supports a vertical resolution of 350 pixels), *MaxY+4* is used to set the number of graphics characters that will be sent. Otherwise, a few rows at the bottom of the screen may not be mapped to the printer.

```
for( j=0; j<MaxX; j++ )
{
    fprintf( stdprn, "\x1B&a%-*.1fh%-*.1fV",
                format( xprint ), xprint,
                format( yprint ), yprint );
    yprint += prstep;
    fprintf( stdprn, "\x1B*r1A\x1B*b%dW",
                (int) ( MaxY+4 ) / 8 );
```

The loop reading the screen pixels, however, does not require the addition to the *MaxY* variable, the <= specification is sufficient to ensure that all of the screen is read. Now, the loop proceeds as previously explained except that the horizontal pixel positions read are at *MaxX–j* where *j* is looping from *0* to *MaxX*. This inversion is necessary; otherwise, the printed result would be a mirror image of the screen.

```
    for( i=0; i<=MaxY/8; i++ )
    {
        m = 0;
        for( k=0; k<8; k++ )
        {
            m <<= 1;
            if( getpixel( MaxX-j, i*8+k ) ) m++;
        }
        fprintf( stdprn, "%c", m );
    }
    fprintf( stdprn, "%s", graph_ends );
}
} break;
```

The third mode is the Greyscale mode. This operates almost exactly the same as the Landscape mode except that a resolution of 300 dpi is used and each screen pixel is mapped to a 4x4 greyscale image.

```
case GREYSCALE:
{
   xprint = 1000.0;
   yprint = 1000.0;
   strcpy( resolution, "300" );
   prstep = 2.4 * AspR;
   fprintf( stdprn, "%s%sR", graph_init, resolution );
```

The greyscale mapping is accomplished by adding a loop to read each screen pixel four times for four separate print lines.

```
for( j=0; j<=MaxX; j++ )
   for( p=0; p<4; p++ )
   {
      fprintf( stdprn, "\x1B&a%-*.1fh%-*.1fV",
               format( xprint ), xprint,
               format( yprint ), yprint );
      yprint += prstep;
```

Because only two screen pixels are read for each graphics character output to the printer, the length of the graphics string is specified as *MaxY/2* instead of *(MaxY+4)/8*.

```
      fprintf( stdprn, "\x1B*r1A\x1B*b%dW", MaxY/2 );
      for( i=0; i<=MaxY/2; i++ )
      {
         m = 0;
```

And *k* is looped from *0* to *1* while *m* is shifted left four places, then OR'd with the integer value returned by the Grey_Scale function for the current screen pixel.

```
         for( k=0; k<=1; k++ )
         {
            m <<= 4;
            m |= Grey_Scale( p,
                       getpixel( MaxX-j, i*2+k ) );
         }
         fprintf( stdprn, "%c", m );
```

```
      }
      fprintf( stdprn, "%s", graph_ends );
   }
} break;
}                                               /* end of Switch */
```

The final housekeeping, sending a formfeed command and resetting the printer to its default state, is reserved until the switch statement is ended, instead of duplicating this instruction set for each of the three modes.

```
fprintf( stdprn,
      "\x0C\x1B&lO\x1B(8U\x1B(sp10h12vsb3T\x1B&l1H" );
}
```

Selecting Multiple Copies on Output

One convenient option has not been provided in the LJ_Graph utility: the provision to print multiple copies of a screen image. This provision can be simple. Before sending the final command set (the sequence beginning with \x0C) simply include the following command line:

```
fprintf( stdprn, "\x1B&l%dX", Number_Of_Copies );
```

The parameter *Number_Of_Copies* can be any value from *1* to *99* and the laserjet will print the specified quantity from a single download.

The format Function

The format function accepts a double value, returning an integer value to specify the number of integer places for a numerical string. The integer variable *width* begins with a value of *6* providing for four integer places, one decimal character and one place following the decimal.

If the value of *position* is less than 1000, *width* is decremented, then *position* is tested again against values of 100 and 10. The final value for *width* is returned to the calling function.

```
int format( double position )
{
   int width = 6;

   if( position < 1000.0 ) width- -;
   if( position < 100.0 )  width- -;
   if( position < 10.0 )   width- -;
   return( width );
}
```

The Grey_Scale Function

The Grey_Scale function is called with two parameters: *scanline,* which specifies which of the four scan lines is being created for the current pixel; and *palette_entry*, the color palette number read from the current screen pixel.

```
int Grey_Scale( int scanline, int palette_entry )
{
```

The local variable *grey* is initially set to zero. When Grey_Scale is finished, the value in *grey* will be returned to the calling function.

```
    int grey = 0;
```

Provision is made here for a four-step greyscale for use with CGA low-resolution color modes. Since *palette_entry* for CGA modes can only have values from *0* to *3*, only two tests are required for each *scanline* and, if *palette_entry* AND'd with the test value provides a True Boolean result, the variable *grey* is OR'd with the appropriate bit map value.

Notice that the values OR'd with *grey* for each case total 15. If both tests for each case are True, then the *grey* value returned will have all bits set and the plotted value will be a black square. If only one of the tests returns True, one of the two grey-shade values will be returned; if neither returns True, the plotted value will be a blank square for the tested pixel.

```
    if( GraphDriver == CGA )
    { switch( scanline )
      { case 0: { if( palette_entry & 1 ) grey |=  9;
                  if( palette_entry & 2 ) grey |=  6;
                } break;
        case 1: { if( palette_entry & 1 ) grey |=  4;
                  if( palette_entry & 2 ) grey |= 11;
                } break;
        case 2: { if( palette_entry & 1 ) grey |=  2;
                  if( palette_entry & 2 ) grey |= 13;
                } break;
        case 3: { if( palette_entry & 1 ) grey |=  9;
                  if( palette_entry & 2 ) grey |=  6;
                } break;
    }   }
```

If the GraphDriver is not CGA, then the 16-shade grey-scale is created. Again, notice that the sum of the values for each test, except *case 3*, is 15. Since one dot in the greyscale pattern is not used by any of the 16 grey shades, *case 3* omits the value 8, for a total of 7 (bits 4, 2 and 1).

In each test, only one bit in *palette_entry* is used. Look back at Figure 14-5 and notice that the greyscale palettes for 1, 2, 4, and 8 are the critical dot patterns used here and all of the other dot patterns are a combination of these four, allowing a very simple decision tree to create 16 progressive dot patterns.

```
else
{  switch( scanline )
   {  case 0: {  if( palette_entry & 4 ) grey |=  5;
                 if( palette_entry & 8 ) grey |= 10;
              } break;
      case 1: {  if( palette_entry & 1 ) grey |=  2;
                 if( palette_entry & 2 ) grey |=  8;
                 if( palette_entry & 8 ) grey |=  5;
              } break;
      case 2: {  if( palette_entry & 4 ) grey |=  5;
                 if( palette_entry & 8 ) grey |= 10;
              } break;
      case 3: {  if( palette_entry & 2 ) grey |=  2;
                 if( palette_entry & 8 ) grey |=  5;
              } break;
   }  }
```

Next, if the flag variable *Negative* has been set, the bit pattern in *grey* is XOR'd with 0Fh to invert the results. This changes the default greyscale that begins with the lightest pattern for a palette-entry of 0 and proceeds to return the darkest pattern for a palette-entry of 15, to a greyscale that returns a dark greyscale pattern for low palette colors and a blank greyscale pattern for WHITE (palette entry 15).

```
if( Negative ) grey ^= 0x0F;
```

Last, the value in *grey* is returned to the calling function.

```
return( grey );
}
```

The Print_Pause Function

The Print_Pause function is a simple utility to write a screen prompt and wait for a key response to select one of the three output modes supported by LJ_Graphic.

```c
void Print_Pause( int Invert )
{
    char Ch;
    int  Done = 0;
    if( Invert ) Negative = 1; else Negative = 0;
    PromptLine(
        "Enter <P>ortrait, <L>andscape, <G>reyscale"
        " — any other key to exit ..." );
    while( !Done )
    {
        while( kbhit() ) getch();
        Ch = getch();
        switch( toupper(Ch) )
        {
            case 'P' : LJ_Graphic( PORTRAIT );  break;
            case 'L' : LJ_Graphic( LANDSCAPE ); break;
            case 'G' : LJ_Graphic( GREYSCALE ); break;
            default   : Done++;
} } }
```

If you would like to use this prompt utility in another application, several approaches can be used without overwriting the existing screen.

One method is to use the getimage function to save the area of the screen that the prompt will overwrite, then use putimage to restore the original screen before calling LJ_Graphic or exiting.

Another approach is to switch active video pages, write the prompt information on the alternate page, and then return to the original screen.

The PromptLine Function

The PromptLine function should already be familiar. PromptLine is called with a message string, draws a box at the bottom of the screen, centers the message in the box, and returns to the calling function for further action.

```c
void PromptLine( char *msg )
{
    int   height, MaxX = getmaxx(), MaxY = getmaxy();
```

```
    setcolor( getmaxcolor() );
    settextstyle( DEFAULT_FONT, HORIZ_DIR, 1 );
    settextjustify( CENTER_TEXT, TOP_TEXT );
    height = textheight( "H" );
    bar( 0, MaxY-( height+4 ), MaxX, MaxY );
    rectangle( 0, MaxY-( height+4 ), MaxX, MaxY );
    outtextxy( MaxX/2, MaxY-(height+2), msg );
}
```

More on Colors and Color Mapping

Caveat: Color, like beauty, is largely in the eye of the beholder. We may well differ in our perceptions of color and color values. You are perfectly free to rewrite or adapt the following color translation suggestions to better fit your own chromatic perceptions.

True-Color Grey Scale Palettes

In the GREYSCALE option used in LJ_Graph, the greyscale palette was mapped according to the palette item numbers assigned to the screen pixels, and not by the actual screen colors. But, since the default palette colors are already arranged more or less in order of intensity, this is a minor discrepancy in most cases. If you do need a more accurate color to greyscale mapping, there are several possible approaches.

One is to read the palette color values (not the palette item numbers), order the color values assigned to the palette entries and create a color-to-greyscale translation map. The drawback to this approach, unfortunately, is that these color values do not reflect actual color (visual) intensities and a secondary translation table would have to be manually prepared to provide some basis for ordering.

An easier approach is to decipher the palette color values and create an intensity value for each color, then order the color-to-grey mapping according to these intensities. To attempt this, however, some basis is necessary to say which color is more intense than another. Of the three primary colors (red, blue, and green), the human eye perceives green most strongly, red next, and blue the least. A greyscale formula reflecting the perception of the human eye yields: $grey = 0.30 * R + 0.59 * G + 0.11 * B$.

But the EGA/VGA color palette values have two flags for each color, primary Red and secondary red, primary Green and secondary green, and primary Blue and secondary blue, so a formula is needed that can calculate a grey value from six flags (colors) instead of only three.

If the secondary colors are arbitrarily assigned 1/3 of the base value and the primary colors are assigned 2/3, then a new formula yields: *grey = 0.30 * (r + 2 * R) / 3 + 0.59 * (g + 2 * G)/3 + 0.11 * (b + 2 * B)/3.*

Figure 14-7 shows greyscale percentages generated using this formula. The default palette EGA/VGA colors are labeled with the actual color values appearing in the left column.

Figure 14-7: True Color Greyscale Conversion

Value	r	R	g	G	b	B	%	EGA Color	Value	r	R	g	G	b	B	%	EGA Color
0							0	BLACK	11				□	□	□	503	
8					□		37		29		□	□		□	□	507	
1						□	73	BLUE	42	□			□	□		530	
32	□						100		60	□	□	□		□		533	LIGHTRED
9					□	□	110		35	□			□		□	567	
40	□				□		137		53	□	□	□			□	570	
33	□					□	173		18			□	□			590	
16			□				197		6		□		□			593	
4		□					200	RED	43	□			□	□	□	603	
41	□				□	□	210		61	□	□	□		□	□	607	LIGHTMAGENTA
24			□		□		233		26			□	□	□		627	
12		□			□		237		14		□		□	□		630	
17			□			□	270		19			□	□		□	663	
5		□				□	273	MAGENTA	7		□		□		□	667	LIGHTGREY
48	□		□				297		50	□		□	□			690	
36	□	□					300		38	□	□		□			693	
25			□		□	□	307		27			□	□	□	□	700	
13		□			□	□	310		15		□		□	□	□	703	
56	□		□		□		333	DARKGREY	58	□		□	□	□		727	LIGHTGREEN
44	□	□			□		337		46	□	□		□	□		730	
49	□		□			□	370		51	□		□	□		□	763	
37	□	□				□	373		39	□	□		□		□	767	
2				□			393	GREEN	22		□	□	□			790	
20		□	□				397	BROWN	59	□		□	□	□	□	800	LIGHTCYAN
57	□		□		□	□	407	LIGHTBLUE	47	□	□		□	□	□	803	
45	□	□			□	□	410		30		□	□	□	□		827	
10				□	□		430		23		□	□	□		□	863	
28		□	□		□		433		54	□	□	□	□			890	
3				□		□	467	CYAN	31		□	□	□	□	□	900	
21		□	□			□	470		62	□	□	□	□	□		927	YELLOW
34	□			□			493		55	□	□	□	□		□	963	
52	□	□	□				497		63	□	□	□	□	□	□	1000	WHITE

Examining the greyscale order, notice that the sequence of grey values does not match the sequence generated by the color values, nor the sequence of greys generated by the default conversion in the Grey_Scale function. Here the grey sequence is strictly according to perception intensity and DARKGREY falls midway in the low intensity colors between MAGENTA and CYAN—just as might be expected of an average grey tone. Similarly, the LIGHTGREY color falls between the LIGHTMAGENTA and LIGHTGREEN shades and, you might also note, the LIGHTBLUE appears just slightly lighter than BROWN.

As mentioned earlier, there is no hard and fast rule saying that this is the only greyscale conversion formula possible and, if this does not suit your application or perceptions, please feel free to experiment with the conversion formula. One hint: the simplest method of experimentation would be to use a good spreadsheet, create your formula, apply it to the rRgGbB color bits, and have the spreadsheet sort the results for your examination.

```
/*======================================================*/
/*                       EP-GRAPH.I                     */
/* graphics output driver for dot-matrix printers */
/*======================================================*/

#define   PORTRAIT    0
#define   LANDSCAPE   1

void Print_Graph( int Mode, int Direction )
{
    char   m;
    int    i, j, k, Msb, Lsb,
           MaxX = getmaxx(),
           MaxY = getmaxy();

    setviewport( 0, 0, MaxX, MaxY, 0 );
    fprintf( stdprn, "\x1BA%c", 7 );
                              /* sets line spacing to 7/72 inch */
    switch( Direction )
    {
      case PORTRAIT:
      {
          Lsb = MaxX & 0x00FF;          /* MaxX modulo 256   */
          Msb = MaxX >> 8;              /* (int) MaxX / 256  */
          for( j=0; j<=MaxY/8; j++ )
```

```
    {
        fprintf( stdprn, "\x1B*%c%c%c",
                 Mode, Lsb, Msb );
        for( i=0; i<=MaxX; i++ )
        {
            m = 0;
            for( k=0; k<8; k++ )
            {
                m <<= 1;              /* shift m left one bit  */
                if( getpixel( i, j*8+k ) ) m++;
            }                         /* if pixel on, bit on   */
            fprintf( stdprn, "%c", m );
        }
        fprintf( stdprn, "\x0D\x0A" );
    } }                              /* use CR/LF codes vs \n flag */
case LANDSCAPE:
    {
        Lsb = MaxY & 0x00FF;             /* MaxY modulo 256  */
        Msb = MaxY >> 8;                 /* (int) MaxY / 256 */
        for( j=0; j<MaxX; j+=8 )
        {
            fprintf( stdprn, "\x1B*%c%c%c",
                     Mode, Lsb, Msb );
            for( i=MaxY; i>=0; i- - )
            {
                m = 0;
                for( k=0; k<8; k++ )
                {
                    m <<= 1;          /* shift m left one bit  */
                    if( getpixel( j+k, i ) ) m++;
                }                     /* if pixel on, set bit  */
                fprintf( stdprn, "%c", m );
            }
            fprintf( stdprn, "\x0D\x0A" );
    } } }                            /* use CR/LF codes vs \n flag */
    fprintf( stdprn,"\f" );
}                                    /* form feed to advance paper */
                                     /* end EP-GRAPH.I */
```

```
/*===================================================*/
/*                    LJ-GRAPH.I                     */
/*   graphics output driver for laserjet printers    */
/*===================================================*/

void PromptLine( char *msg )
{
   int    height, MaxX = getmaxx(), MaxY = getmaxy();

   setcolor( getmaxcolor() );          /* set color to white  */
   settextstyle( DEFAULT_FONT, HORIZ_DIR, 1 );
   settextjustify( CENTER_TEXT, TOP_TEXT );
   height = textheight( "H" );         /* check current height */
   bar( 0, MaxY-( height+4 ), MaxX, MaxY );
   rectangle( 0, MaxY-( height+4 ), MaxX, MaxY );
   outtextxy( MaxX/2, MaxY-(height+2), msg );
}

#define  PORTRAIT    0        /* definitions for Print_Graph */
#define  LANDSCAPE   1        /* image orientation           */
#define  GREYSCALE   2         /* and color to greyscale      */
int      Negative;            /* flag for grey scale order    */

int format( double position )
{
   int width = 6;

   if( position < 1000.0 ) width- -;
   if( position < 100.0 )  width- -;
   if( position < 10.0 )   width- -;
   return( width );
}

int Grey_Scale( int scanline, int palette_entry )
{
   int grey = 0;
   if( GraphDriver == CGA && GraphMode != CGAHI )
   {
      switch( scanline )
      {
         case 0: {  if( palette_entry & 1 )
                       grey |=  9;          /* sets bits 1.1. */
                    if( palette_entry & 2 )
```

```
                    grey |=  6;        /* sets bits .1.1 */
            } break;
    case 1: {  if( palette_entry & 1 )
                    grey |=  4;        /* sets bits ...1 */
               if( palette_entry & 2 )
                    grey |= 11;        /* sets bits 111. */
            } break;
    case 2: {  if( palette_entry & 1 )
                    grey |=  2;        /* sets bits 1... */
               if( palette_entry & 2 )
                    grey |= 13;        /* sets bits .111 */
            } break;
    case 3: {  if( palette_entry & 1 )
                    grey |=  9;        /* sets bits .1.1 */
               if( palette_entry & 2 )
                    grey |=  6;        /* sets bits 1.1. */
            } break;
}   }
else
{  switch( scanline )
   {
    case 0: {  if( palette_entry & 4 )
                    grey |=  5;        /* sets bits .1.1 */
               if( palette_entry & 8 )
                    grey |= 10;        /* sets bits 1.1. */
            } break;
    case 1: {  if( palette_entry & 1 )
                    grey |=  2;        /* sets bits ..1. */
               if( palette_entry & 2 )
                    grey |=  8;        /* sets bits 1... */
               if( palette_entry & 8 )
                    grey |=  5;        /* sets bits .1.1 */
            } break;
    case 2: {  if( palette_entry & 4 )
                    grey |=  5;        /* sets bits .1.1 */
               if( palette_entry & 8 )
                    grey |= 10;        /* sets bits 1.1. */
            } break;
    case 3: {  if( palette_entry & 2 )
                    grey |=  2;        /* sets bits ..1. */
```

```
                    if( palette_entry & 8 )
                        grey |=  5;          /* sets bits .1.1 */
                } break;
    }   }
    if( Negative ) grey ^= 0x0F;            /* inverts greyscale */
    return( grey );
}

void LJ_Graphic( int Mode )
{
    int    i, j, k, p, q, xasp, yasp,
           MaxX = getmaxx() + 1,
           MaxY = getmaxy() + 1;
    static  char  graph_ends[] = "\x1B*rB";
    static  char  graph_init[] =
           "\x1BE\x1B&l1H\x1B&lO\x1B*pOX\x1B*pOY\x1B*t";
    double  xprint, yprint, prstep, AspR;
    char    m, resolution[3];

    getaspectratio( &xasp, &yasp );
    AspR = (double) xasp / (double) yasp;
    setviewport( 0, 0, MaxX, MaxY, 0 );
    switch( Mode )
    {
       case PORTRAIT:
       {
           xprint = 690.0,            /* initial page positions */
           yprint = 500.0,
           strcpy( resolution, "100" );            /* 100 DPI */
           prstep = 7.2 / AspR;             /* to match screen */
           fprintf( stdprn, "%s%sR",
                   graph_init, resolution );
           for( j=0; j<=MaxY; j++ )
           {
               fprintf( stdprn,  "\x1B&a%-*.1fh%-*.1fV",
                       format( xprint ), xprint,
                       format( yprint ), yprint );
               yprint += prstep;
               fprintf( stdprn, "\x1B*r1A\x1B*b%dW",
                       MaxX/8 );
               for( i=0; i<MaxX/8; i++ )
```

```c
            {
               m = 0;
               for( k=0; k<8; k++ )
               {
                  m <<= 1;              /* shift m left one bit  */
                  if( getpixel( i*8+k, j ) ) m++;
               }                        /* if pixel on, bit on   */
               fprintf( stdprn, "%c", m );
            }
            fprintf( stdprn, "%s", graph_ends );
         }
      } break;

case LANDSCAPE:
{
   xprint = 1000.0;                /* initial page positions */
   yprint = 1000.0;
   strcpy( resolution, "75" );              /* select 75 DPI */
   prstep = 9.6 * AspR;                 /* to match screen */
   fprintf( stdprn, "%s%sR",
            graph_init, resolution );
   for( j=0; j<MaxX; j++ )
   {
      fprintf( stdprn, "\x1B&a%-*.1fh%-*.1fV",
               format( xprint ), xprint,
               format( yprint ), yprint );
      yprint += prstep;
      fprintf( stdprn, "\x1B*r1A\x1B*b%dW",
               (int) ( MaxY+4 ) / 8 );
      for( i=0; i<=MaxY/8; i++ )
      {
         m = 0;
         for( k=0; k<8; k++ )
         {
            m <<= 1;              /* shift m left one bit */
            if( getpixel( MaxX-j, i*8+k ) ) m++;
         }                        /* if pixel, bit on */
         fprintf( stdprn, "%c", m );
      }
      fprintf( stdprn, "%s", graph_ends );
   }
```

```
    }   break;

    case GREYSCALE:
    {
        xprint = 1000.0;                /* initial page positions */
        yprint = 1000.0;
        strcpy( resolution, "300" );                 /* 300 DPI */
        prstep = 2.4 * AspR;            /* match screen image */
        fprintf( stdprn, "%s%sR",
                graph_init, resolution );
        for( j=0; j<=MaxX; j++ )
        for( p=0; p<4; p++ )
        {
            fprintf( stdprn, "\x1B&a%-*.1fh%-*.1fV",
                    format( xprint ), xprint,
                    format( yprint ), yprint );
            yprint += prstep;
            fprintf( stdprn, "\x1B*r1A\x1B*b%dW",
                    MaxY/2 );
            for( i=0; i<=MaxY/2; i++ )
            {
                m = 0;
                for( k=0; k<=1; k++ )
                {
                    m <<= 4;            /* shift m left four bits */
                    m |= Grey_Scale( p,
                            getpixel( MaxX-j, i*2+k ) );
                }
                fprintf( stdprn, "%c", m );
            }
            fprintf( stdprn, "%s", graph_ends );
    } } }
    /* end of Switch */
    fprintf( stdprn,
        "\x0C\x1B&l0\x1B(8U\x1B(sp10h12vsb3T\x1B&l1H" );
                                        /* close operations */
}

void Print_Pause( int Invert )
{
    char Ch;
    int  Done = 0;
```

```
    if( Invert ) Negative = 1; else Negative = 0;
    PromptLine(
        "Enter <P>ortrait, <L>andscape, <G>reyscale"
        " — any other key to exit ..." );
    while( !Done )
    {
        while( kbhit() ) getch();
        Ch = getch();
        switch( toupper(Ch) )
        {
            case 'P': LJ_Graphic( PORTRAIT );  break;
            case 'L': LJ_Graphic( LANDSCAPE ); break;
            case 'G': LJ_Graphic( GREYSCALE ); break;
             default: Done++;
}   }   }
```

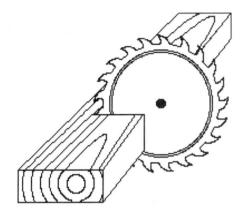

Chapter 15

The Turbo Font Editor

The Font Editor is a utility designed to create or edit stroked fonts for use with Turbo Pascal, Turbo C++, or Turbo Prolog using BGI graphics displays. The Font Editor utility consists of the editor program FE.EXE and nine character fonts: EURO.CHR, GOTH.CHR, LCOM.CHR, LITT.CHR, SANS.CHR, SCRI.CHR, SIMP.CHR, TRIP.CHR, and TSCR.CHR.

The FE Stroked Font Editor is available at no charge on an as is basis to users of Turbo Pascal, Turbo C++, and Turbo Prolog and may be downloaded from Borland International's Compuserve programming forum (use GO BPROGA for Turbo Pascal, use GO BPROGB for Turbo C++ and Turbo Prolog).

Also available from Borland, via Compuserve, are a .BIN to .BGI conversion utility (DFONT.EXE, DFONT.C, and FONT.H) and a .BGI Driver Toolkit (see Appendix D).

The following instructions apply to Font Editor revision 1.0; release date October 1988, copyright Borland International. Future revisions and updates will be available on Borland's Compuserve forum.

Introduction to Stroked Fonts

Stroked fonts define characters as line sequence instructions (strokes) showing the outline composing the specific characters. Alternatively, the standard text font displayed by your computer is a bitmap font with each character defined as a matrix of dots.

The advantage found in stroked fonts is that the characters can be arbitrarily scaled in size and proportions without loss of resolution. Bitmap fonts can also be enlarged, but only in simple multiples of the grid size since they suffer degradation of appearance as they are enlarged.

For example, if a bitmap font is enlarged four times, each dot in the original grid becomes a 4x4 pixel square in the enlargement with resulting jagged steps in appearance (see Figure 15-1).

Figure 15-1: Stroked Versus Bitmap Characters

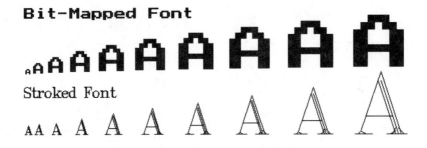

Stroked fonts are not converted to dot patterns (pixels) until the desired font size and output device resolution are known. A stroked font can be sized without suffering in appearance. Also, stroked fonts can be output to devices with quite different resolution (such as 120 dpi dot-matrix printers or 300 dpi laserjet printers) with no stroke resolution loss—see Table 15-1.

The Font Editor can be used to create non-alphabetic or symbol fonts for specialized displays and applications. For example, in Chapter 9, bit images were created for use with the line graph display. Using FE, these same images can be created as a stroked symbol font, much more conveniently that writing bit-by-bit instructions. The resulting symbols can be used not only in the line graph display but in a variety of applications and in any size desired (see Figure 15-2).

Also, several new stroked fonts are available. For details on user-created and new fonts, see *Using Custom Graphics Fonts*.

Figure 15-2: Special Symbol Font Characters (Runic Alphabet)

Table 15-1: Stroked Fonts

Filename	Font	Definition Name	Value
*EURO.CHR	European font	- -	
GOTH.CHR	Gothic font	GOTHIC_FONT[1]	4
*LCOM.CHR	Text (Roman) font	- -	
LITT.CHR	Small font	SMALL_FONT[1]	2
SANS.CHR	Sans-serif font	SANS_SERIF_FONT[1]	3
*SCRI.CHR	Script font	- -	
*SIMP.CHR	Simplex font	- -	
TRIP.CHR	Triplex font	TRIPLEX_FONT[1]	1
*TSCR.CHR	Text italic font	- -	

* new fonts supplied with Font Editor utility
1. Font names and values defined in GRAPHICS.H header file.

System Requirements

The Font Editor is compatible with most systems, but does impose a few minimum requirements:

COMPUTER   Font Editor (FE.EXE) runs on IBM PCs, PC/XTs, PC/ATs, and most compatibles. You must also copy the appropriate .BGI driver (this will be EGAVGA.BGI in most cases) to the same directory as FE.EXE or provide a path in your AUTOEXEC.BAT file to the directory containing the .BGI files.

MOUSE   Font Editor requires a mouse supporting the Microsoft External Mouse Driver Interface (MM protocol). This includes the Microsoft, Mouse Systems, and Logitech bus or serial mice.

If you are using another hardware mouse type, consult your mouse manual for installation instructions. The mouse driver (MOUSE.COM or MOUSE.SYS) must be installed in memory before calling FE. Normally, the mouse is loaded as a DOS device driver by definition in your CON-

FIG.SYS file (DEVICE = MOUSE.SYS) or in your AUTOEXEC.BAT (MOUSE<cr> or MOUSE 2<cr>), depending on the port used)

GRAPHICS: Font Editor also requires an Enhanced Graphics Adapter (EGA) or compatible and a color display. The graphics adapter card must have a minimum of 128K RAM installed.

PLOTTER: (Optional) Font Editor supports hardcopy output to one of the following Hewlett Packard or compatible plotters:

- HP 7470
- HP 7475 (8 1/2 x 11 paper only)
- HP 7440 (Color Pro)

There are two considerations to keep in mind. First, when using a plotter and a serial mouse, two serial ports are required, one for the plotter and one for the mouse. When plotter output is requested, FE will prompt you for the port (COM1 or COM2) for the plotter and will then initialize the indicated serial port. Be sure that you indicate the correct port for plotter or you may find the mouse no longer responding. After the plotter port is selected, FE will ask for initialization parameters, assuming 9600 baud, Even parity, 7 bits, and 1 stop bit. If other settings are desired, the serial port should be initialized using the DOS Mode command.

Second, the most common problem interfacing between an HP plotter and a non-HP computer is in the connecting cable. If you experience any problems, Hewlett-Packard supplies a standard cable for this application, part number HP 17255D, or you can use straight-through RS-232C cabling together with a dummy (null) modem).

General Capabilities

Font Editor edits Borland stroked fonts (files with the .CHR extension shipped with Turbo C++ and Turbo Pascal or fonts supplied with the Font Editor). You can read in fonts, edit individual characters, preview characters on screen or, on a plotter, and save the resulting font back to disk.

Font Editor Display

The Font Editor screen is divided into four major areas. Since each screen reacts slightly different with the mouse, mouse usage will be covered first.

Mouse Conventions

The left and right mouse buttons are treated identically. Two major operations are performed using the mouse with Font Editor: a click, a quick press-and-release of the mouse button when the graphics cursor is positioned on an object to select that object; or a drag, a press-hold-and-move operation used to slide objects or to define an area. When the drag operation is being used, the object sticks to the mouse cursor, moving with the cursor until the button is released.

Area Definition Using the Mouse

The mouse can be used to define an area within the work screen. The location where a mouse button is pressed marks one corner and the diagonally opposite corner is defined when the button is released.

If you define the starting corner erroneously, the error cannot be changed except by starting over (defining a new rectangle). The second corner, however, can be changed by moving the mouse before releasing the mouse button.

Using the Mouse In the Character Window

When the mouse is used in the Character (Edit) window, you will notice that the mouse moves in discrete steps, moving only between indicated intersection points where strokes can start and stop. The spacing of the grid points depends on the Zoom option and also on the size of the font being edited. For example, if you select LITT.CHR (SMALL_FONT), the grid points will be widely spaced (a 12x10 point grid) while selecting SANS.CHR (SANS_SERIF_FONT) will show a tightly spaced grid (a 44x33 point grid),

Escape from Plotter Output

Pressing any mouse button during a plotter output terminates the graphics plotter dump. This may, however, require you to hold the mouse button down for several seconds until the button status is recognized. Plotting will not halt immediately but will continue until the drawing commands in its internal buffer are completed.

The Font Editor Menu

When using Font Editor, a series of menus is displayed as a line of text across the top of the screen for selection by mouse click.

Some items in the menu, such as *Load* and *Save*, perform a single function and, when the function is completed, display the same menu. Other items, such as *Edit*, display a new menu. All menus except the initial menu contain the item *Exit* which will return you the previous menu.

The *Quit* item in the main menu returns to DOS. If changes have been made to the current font, a *Save* prompt will appear before exiting.

Selecting a Character for Editing

When FE is first called, a menu shows all of the .CHR fonts in the current directory. The first step is to use the mouse to select a font for editing. After selection, the display will shift to the edit screen. The font directory can also be called by selecting *Load* from the menu options across the top of the screen.

At the right of the edit screen, a large rectangular area shows a 256-character display (using the extended ASCII character set, not the font currently being edited). Clicking on any character within this box selects this character for edit, displaying the current font's equivalent character in the Edit Window as a series of strokes and below the selection box as it would appear on screen with a size definition of 1. Characters can also be selected for edit by keyboard entry.

Within the selection window, the characters displayed appear in green if the current font contains a stroked character definition or in red if no stroked image has been defined for this character. The characters 00h (null), 20h (space), and FFh appear as blanks, but can be selected and defined as font characters.

The currently selected character is highlighted in the window (as bright green or bright red).

The Character Window

The character window is the large rectangular area on the left half of the screen (see Figure 15-3) where character editing takes place. The Font Editor will display the strokes comprising a selected character. An existing character may be edited or a new character created using the mouse to delete elements or add new lines in this window.

The vertical line along the left side of the grid shows the left edge of the character. Four horizontal lines, beginning at the top, show the height of a capital character (A, B, C, etc), the height of a lowercase character (a, c, e, etc.), the baseline and the descender depth (as for g, j, or y).

Character Width and Spacing

Notice the small triangle along the baseline to the right in Figure 15-3. This marker shows the beginning position for the next character (the inter-character spacing). The character width can be changed by dragging the triangle to a new position.

Kerning, the practice used by typesetters where inter-character spacing is adjusted to allow specific character pairs to fit together, is not supported

per se, however, character widths can be adjusted to create tightly or
loosely spaced fonts as required.

Figure 15-3: Edit Window Display

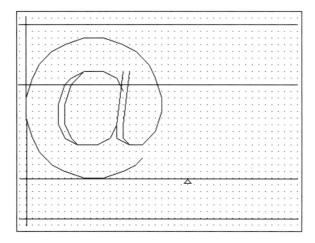

Editing a Character

Character strokes are added or deleted by moving the mouse cursor to the
desired starting point, pressing the button, and dragging to the desired end
point. If no stroke connected these points previously, then a new stroke is
added. If one did exist, then it is deleted.

Curves are not supported. Instead, curves and bends are created as a
series of strokes as shown in Figure 15-3. Drawing a line where there was
none before will add a stroke to the character definition. Drawing a line on
top of an existing line erases the bottom line from the character definition
(leaving no line).

Combinations of adding and deleting strokes can be performed with a
single line. For example, drawing a new stroke in the middle of an existing
line erases that portion of the line, leaving two other lines corresponding
to the end portions that were not drawn over.

The Small Character

The area in the lower right-hand corner of the screen displays a small
version of the current character (as would be displayed on the screen with
a character size of 1). Note: the Small Character display is not affected by
additions or deletions in the Edit window until the Update option is

exercised. This area is for information only; nothing is mouse-selectable here.

The Update Selector Box

Changes—additions or deletions—to the currently edited character are not added to the stroke definition until specifically instructed by clicking on the *Update* option shown above the selection box.

While editing a character, the changes made to a character are saved in a edit buffer. To make the edits permanent, the mouse is used to select the *Update* option, writing the edit buffer to the actual character.

Clicking on the current character in the selection box will bring up a prompt asking if the strokes are to be added (or subtracted) from the current character. Clicking on a new character will display the same prompt before the new selection is displayed in the edit window.

The edit actions on characters only affect the edit image, *not* the character stroke data. For example, suppose several lines are added to a character but the character is not updated. Now, if the Edit option is selected from the menu and used to move the character, only the information in the character buffer will be effected but the new lines added to the character image will not be moved. This applies to all of the edit functions, including move, flip, flop, reverse, shift, cut, and copy.

Editing Tools

This section gives a brief description of the Font Editor tools—see the *Command Reference* section for detailed descriptions of these commands.

Single Strokes

Single strokes can be added or deleted from a character image by moving the mouse cursor into the character window and performing a drag operation between the grid points where the stroke should be added or deleted. As the mouse is dragged, a line appears between the start point and the mouse cursor—a process known as *rubber banding* because the line appears to stretch or shrink to follow the cursor.

Drawing over an existing stroke, deletes the line or, drawing over a portion of an existing line, deletes only a portion of the line. Also, if the mouse cursor is moved outside the character window while rubber banding a line the stroke will be canceled.

Groups of Strokes

Since many characters share the same stroke groups, groups of strokes can be manipulated as a single object using the Edit/Clipboard commands. For example, the strokes defining the left hand part of a "c" will probably be the same as those in the left-hand part of a "d."

The tools available in the Clipboard menu allow selection of a group of strokes from a character to be used again in that character or in another character. Cut and Copy move a group of characters into a holding buffer (the Clipboard). Cut removes the strokes from the current character, while Copy leaves the originals undisturbed.

Strokes are selected for Clipboard by rubber banding a rectangle around the strokes. Note that both end points of a given stroke must be completely inside the rectangle in order to be selected for a Cut or Copy.

The strokes in Clipboard are pasted into a character by selecting the Paste option which adds the contents to the character window. The strokes can be moved using a drag operation.

Paste does not empty Clipboard; the next paste operation will find the same strokes. Cut and Copy always change the contents of the Clipboard. Delete operates like Cut, except that the deleted strokes are not placed in Clipboard, just discarded. Move is similar to a combined Cut and Paste operation, except that the contents of Clipboard are not altered.

The contents of the Clipboard buffer can also be rotated using the commands under Edit/Flip to flip the contents upside down (horizontal axis) or right and left (vertical axis).

Whole Characters

Special techniques are provided for manipulating whole characters.

- **CopyChar** (Edit menu) allows you to copy from one character within a single font to another, duplicating the selected character strokes as a new character. For example, after creating a "c," the "c" could be copied to "d" and edited to create the new character without repeating the strokes used for the "c."
- **Flip** (Edit menu) allows you to flip a character upside down or right/left or both.
- **Shift** (Edit menu) allows you to move a whole character right, left, up, or down.

For example, the characters, b, d, p, and q are usually just flipped versions of one another. You can draw one and use CopyChar and Flip to make the other three.

Whole Fonts

The commands under Global allow you to perform operations on the entire font. These are primarily concerned with intercharacter spacing and, usually, will be used as a part of the final editing process of a font.

- LeftSpace will move every character in the font so that its left-most part is the specified distance from the left margin (the dark solid vertical line in the character window).
- RghtSpace will set the character spacing marker of every character in the font to the distance specified to the right of the right-most stroke of each character.
- BaseLine will shift every character up or down by the same amount so that the base line corresponds to zero.
- Copy will allow selection of another font, copying characters from it into the current work font. Many characters, such as the graphic characters, will not change from one font to another and the Copy option saves the trouble of recreating these.

Font Editor Command Reference

In this section, the Font Editor menu commands and functions are described in detail.

Load   Loads an existing font file into Font Editor. A large rectangle will be draw on the screen. There are two mouse sensitive areas within this rectangle: the file selector area and the file prompt line.

Clicking on the file prompt line will allow you to enter a new filename for loading and may include a new path. If the path/filename does not exist, you will be warned. If you confirm that the file does not exist, the file will be created and will become the default output file when the font is saved.

The file selector area contains a list of all of the files with the extension .CHR on the current drive/directory. As the mouse cursor is moved over these, the filenames will appear on the file prompt line. Clicking on one of these names will select the current file for load.

Show   The tools under Show simply show the appearance of the selected font but do not operate on or change the font.

Font   Shows all of the currently defined characters on the monitor and is also useful for a quick check of the intercharacter spacing. Overlapping characters or gaps between characters will indicate errors in intercharacter spacing.

String   Allows you to type a string of characters for display. Sometimes it is important to see two special characters together to determine the proper appearance and spacing. When a line becomes full, display will continue on the next line or the Enter key can be used to force a new line. When the bottom of the screen is reached, the display does not scroll.

The Escape key is used to exit the String mode.

Plotter   Draws the current font on an HP plotter. See the section on Optional Hardware for a discussion of connecting the plotter.

When you select this tool, you will be asked if the plotter is COM1 or COM2. Font Editor must have the serial port on the PC configured to be able to communicate with the plotter. You may either let FE set the serial port to 9600 baud, Even parity, 7 data bits, and 1 stop bit (in which case the DIP switches on your plotter must be set for this configuration) or you may select NO to make FE skip this step.

If FE does not initialize the plotter's serial port, you must have issued the DOS Mode command prior to starting FE to match your plotter's switch settings. If you're using a serial mouse, be careful not to choose the serial port to which your mouse is connected.

Finally, you'll be asked to confirm plot. Have the paper loaded and the plotter ready before selecting YES. If you start plotting and want to stop before the plot is complete, press and hold a mouse button until the screen clears. Your plotter output will be labeled with the name of the file from which it came, and the page number. In the case of multiple page plots, FE will stop at the end of each page to allow you to load a new piece of paper.

Exit   Returns you to the main menu.

Global   These commands operate on an entire font, unlike most other commands which operate on a single character or stroke.

LeftSpace   Adjusts the space between the left-most stroke of a character and the vertical guide line shown in the character window. Typically, this should be set to zero for all fonts, so that an application which mixes fonts will maintain character spacing between font changes.

RghtSpace   Adjusts the character width mark of all the characters to the set value. The character width value set for each character is the number selected from sub-menu plus the right-most stroke of the character. Therefore, this choice will provide uniform inter-character spacing for a proportionally spaced font.

Typically, this choice is issued for the entire font for proportional spacing, then selected characters, such as the numeric characters and the graphics character symbols which require the same total widths for column lineup, are adjusted individually,

BaseLine   Adjusts each character in the font up or down by the same amount. This option is exercised for an entire font so that all fonts refer to the same baseline value. Thus, an application switching fonts will not have the baseline of the new font shifted up or down from the previous font.

Copy   Selects characters from a different font file. The source font file is selected as under the Load option.

When Copy is selected, you will see two character selector boxes on the screen; the left box corresponding to the source font selected, the right box corresponding to the working font.

Characters are copied individually by clicking on the character desired from the source character box, then clicking on the destination character in the right-hand character box. To quit, select Done in the menu area.

Exit   Returns to the main menu.

Edit   Provides tools for editing whole characters or groups of strokes. The Clipboard functions under this heading are of particular importance.

CopyChar   Allows intra-font copying of characters by selecting source and destination characters within the working font. If a character already exists where you selected the destination character, then you will be asked if that character should be replaced.

Flip   Allows flipping either the current character or the contents of Clipboard. Characters are flipped within the space they occupy. For example, if a character only occupies the lower portion of the character cell, then the results, after flipping it vertically, will only occupy the lower portion of the character cell. The Shift option can be used to change positions. The results of flipping the Clipboard will not be visible until it is pasted into the Edit window.

Shift   Moves a character one dot in any direction. It does not modify the inter-character spacing.

ShowAlso   Superimposes another character over the character currently being edited. The superimposed character's strokes and width marker are shown in red where strokes match the edit character or in green where they do not coincide.

The superimposed character will remain in the edit window until Update is executed or a new edit character is selected.

Clipboard   Contains all the tools for working on groups of strokes. The Cut, Copy, and Paste options work by reading and writing a buffer area called the Clipboard. Move and Delete do not use the Clipboard.

Strokes are selected from the current character by rubber banding a rectangle around them. One corner of the rectangle is defined by the location where you press a mouse button, the diagonally opposite corner is defined by the position where the mouse button is released. Remember, both end points of a stroke must lie completely within the rectangle in order to be selected.

For the Move and Paste options, when a region has been defined, the strokes contained in the region are copied within the window, to the right of the character width marker. The upper-left corner of the strokes will be attached to the mouse cursor while a mouse button is pressed and will stay attached until the button is released.

Cut   Removes the selected strokes from the current character, placing them in the Clipboard. The previous contents of Clipboard are lost.

Copy   Copies the selected strokes from the current character to the clip board without changing the current character. The previous contents of Clipboard are lost.

Paste   Copies the contents of the Clipboard to the current character. The contents of the Clipboard are not changed.

Move   Moves the selected strokes to a new location: the equivalent of a Cut and Paste operation except that the contents (if any) of the Clipboard are not changed.

Delete   Cuts the selected strokes from the current character; is equivalent to a Cut except that the contents of the Clipboard are not changed.

Exit   Returns to the Edit menu.

Exit   Returns to the Main menu.

Save   Writes the current font data to an output file. Save works like the Load command, drawing a large rectangle on the screen containing two mouse sensitive areas: the file selector area and the file prompt line.

Clicking on the file prompt line allows entry of a new filename and may include a new path. You will be warned if the filename entered does not exits. If you confirm that the file does not exist, the file will be created.

The file selector area contains a list of all of the files on the current drive/directory with the extension .CHR. As the mouse cursor is moved over this list, each filename will appear on the file prompt line. Clicking on one of these names will select the current destination file.

Window   Controls the character editing window display. These options do not change the characters, only the way that they are displayed.

The default values shown are set automatically when a font file is loaded. If Font Editor is called without selecting an initial font file (by bypassing Load) these values must be set.

Zoom Out   Reduces the magnification used to display the character in the Edit window. Magnification is automatically set to show all characters in the character window as large as possible when the font file is loaded.

Zoom In   Increases the magnification used to display the character in the Edit window. Magnification is automatically set to show all characters in the character window as large as possible when the font file is loaded.

Magnification may be increased so that characters are larger than the window—parts of characters that would be outside the window are clipped to the window limits. This is useful while working on lowercase letters or the strokes that make up the serifs of a serif font.

Origin   Allows positioning the origin guideline anywhere within the character editing window.

While, for most fonts, this is drawn underneath the baseline guideline and won't be visible, it is still movable. Move the origin guideline towards the top of the window and zoom in to work on descending strokes or move the origin guideline to the bottom of the window to work on uppercase letters.

d-ht   Sets the descender height guideline in the character editing window. This has no effect on the character, character edits, or display of the character in the window. It is for your convenience.

b-ht   Sets the baseline height guideline in the character editing window. This has no effect on the character, character edits, or display of the character in the window. It is for your convenience.

x-ht   Positions the x-height guideline (lowercase height) in the character editing window. This has no effect on the character, character edits, or display of the character in the window. It is for your convenience.

c-ht Positions the character height guideline (uppercase height) in the character editing window. This has no effect on the character, character edits, or display of the character in the window. It is for your convenience.

ShowMovs Shows each *move, draw, draw, ...* sequence in a different color so that some notion of how the character is being stroked can be gained. The sequence of colors shows the order in which strokes are generated.

This option defaults to off. Turning this option on may produce disquieting results when drawing in the character editing window. Its use is not recommended (but is interesting, if somewhat garish).

Grid Shows the grid of points in the character editing on which stokes can begin and end. This option defaults on.

Exit Returns to the Main menu.

Quit Returns to DOS; you will be asked if you want to save any edits.

Beginning a New Font from Scratch

Here are a few considerations for the user who wishes to start a new font from scratch. To begin a new font, start Font Editor and select a new font filename. The screen will show a character window with no characters defined (all character choices will be displayed in red). The four global parameters for the font are determined automatically by the font editor when a file is loaded or saved. These parameters are the Base Height, the Capital Height, the Descender Height, and the Lowercase Height (or x Height). The values for these are determined by examining the characters that a typographer would use to determine the same information.

Capital Height This value is determined by examining the E Ligature character (144 decimal). This is the tallest of the European characters. If this character is undefined, the capitol M is used as the capital height. If neither of these characters are defined, the value will default to 40 (of a maximum +/-64).

Base Height This value is determined by examining the E Ligature or the capital M. This value is used as the origin for the other three dimensions. If neither of these characters are defined, the value will default to 0 (of a maximum of +/-64).

Descender Height This value is determined be examining the lowercase q. If the lowercase q is undefined, the value will default to -7 (of a maximum of +/-64).

Lowercase Height (or x Height)   This value is determined by examining the lowercase x. If the lowercase x is undefined, the value will default to the Capitol Height divided by two.

To define the size and placement of the characters in the font, it is best to define the "M," "q," "x," and E Ligature (if desired) as the first characters. The next time the font is loaded, the character dimensions will be used to define the size and placement of the character window for the font.

If you are defining a special symbol font, these parameters may or may not be relevant but, in most cases, as a minimum, the Base Height should be defined.

Using Custom Fonts

The original fonts supplied with Turbo C++ (or Turbo Pascal) are built-in the BGI Graphics library. Unlike the original fonts, however, user-created fonts (and the five new fonts supplied with the Turbo Font Editor) cannot be referenced directly but must first be installed in the internal font table.

The installuserfont function (Turbo C version 2.0 or later) is supplied for this purpose and returns a font ID number which can be subsequently used with settextstyle to identify the font.

The NEWFONTS.C demo program (at the end of this chapter) installs the five new fonts supplied with the Turbo Font Editor and prints a brief message to the screen with each font (see Figure 15-4).

Identifying the Fonts

The original fonts are identified by constant names in the GRAPHICS.H header file. For convenience and to provide compatibility, the new fonts are also identified by font names but, since no library constants exist for these, the font names are declared as variables with initial values of 0.

```
int   LARGE_FONT = 0,          /* EURO.CHR */
      ROMAN_FONT = 0,          /* LCOM.CHR */
      SIMPLEX_FONT = 0,        /* SIMP.CHR */
      ITALIC_FONT = 0,         /* TSCR.CHR */
      SCRIPT_FONT = 0;         /* SCRI.CHR */
```

An Install_Font Utility

Now, since the possibility always exists that the .CHR file required for a particular font may exist, a simple Install_Font function can be used.

Install_Font is called with the path/filename for the font desired and returns an integer identifying the entry in the internal font table. If the .CHR file for a specified font is not found, Install_Font can display a

Figure 15-4: New Graphics Character Fonts

9 ABCDEFGHIJKL Large
8 ABCDEFGHIJKL Roman
7 *ABCDEFGHIJKL Italic*
6 ABCDEFGHIJKL Simplex
5 *ABCDEFGHIJKL Script*

message and, instead of returning a negative error code, returns a zero value which provides a simpler Boolean test than the graphics error code.

```
int Install_Font( char *font_name )
{
    int  font_number;

    font_number = installuserfont( font_name );
    if( font_number == 0 )
    {                          /* put error message on screen */
        return( 0 );
    }
    else return( font_number );
}
```

Loading Several Fonts

If more than one font is required, the simplest route is to assign all the fonts needed at one time. The integer values returned are assigned to the font variable names (LARGE_FONT, ROMAN_FONT, etc.).

This does not require any excessive memory expenditure, only the font names are installed and the font information itself is loaded into memory only when the font is actually assigned using the settextstyle function.

```
void Load_Fonts()
{
    LARGE_FONT    = Install_Font( "EURO.CHR" );
    ROMAN_FONT    = Install_Font( "LCOM.CHR" );
    ITALIC_FONT   = Install_Font( "TSCR.CHR" );
```

```
    SCRIPT_FONT  = Install_Font( "SCRI.CHR" );
    SIMPLEX_FONT = Install_Font( "SIMP.CHR" );
}
```

Short and simple, that's it. Between the Turbo Font Editor and the preceding utility procedures, there's a world of possibilities for special displays and graphics features.

BGI Stroke File Format

The structure of Borland .CHR (stroked font) file begins at offset 00h with a header:

```
HeaderSize     equ     080h
DataSize       equ     (size of font file)
descr          equ     "Triplex font"
fname          equ     "TRIP"
MajorVersion   equ     1
MinorVersion   equ     0
db     'PK',8,8
db     'BGI ',descr,' V'
db     MajorVersion + '0'
db     (MinorVersion / 10) + '0', (MinorVersion mod 10) + '0'
db     ' - 19 October 1987', 0Dh, 0Ah
db     0,1Ah                              ; null & ctrl-Z = end
dw     HeaderSize                         ; size of header
db     fname                              ; font name
dw     DataSize                           ; font file size
db     MajorVersion,MinorVersion          ; version #'s
db     1,0                                ; minimal version #'s
db     (HeaderSize - $) DUP (0)           ; pad out to header size
```

The data for the file begins at offset 80h:

```
80h      '+'     flags stroke file type
81h-82h          number chars in font file (n)
83h              undefined
84h              ASCII value of first char in file
85h..86h         offset to stroke definitions (8+3n)
87h              scan flag (normally 0)
88h              distance from origin to top of capital
89h              distance from origin to baseline
90h              distance from origin to bottom descender
91h..95h         undefined
96h              offsets to individual character definitions
```

96h + 2n   width table (one word per character)
96h + 3n   start of character definitions

The individual character definitions consist of a variable number of words describing the operations required to render each character. Each word consists of an (x,y) coordinate pair and a two-bit op-code, encoded as shown in Tables 15-2 and 15-3.

Table 15-2: Extended Op-codes

Byte 1	7	6..5..4..3..2..1..0 *bit #*
	op1	<7-bit signed X coord>
Byte 2	7	6..5..4..3..2..1..0 *bit #*
	op2	<7-bit signed Y coord>

Table 15-3: Op-codes

op1	op2	Meaning
0	0	End of character definition
1	0	Move the pointer to (x,y)
1	1	Draw from current pointer to (x,y)

```
/*================================*/
/*            NEWFONTS.C          */
/* Using New Turbo .CHR Alphabets */
/*================================*/

#ifdef __TINY__
#error Graphics demos will not run in the tiny model.
#endif

#include <conio.h>
#include <stdio.h>
#include <stdlib.h>
#include <stdarg.h>
#include <graphics.h>
#include <fcntl.h>
#include ''gprint.i''

int    GraphDriver;
int    GraphMode;
int    ErrorCode = 0;
int    LARGE_FONT = 0,          /* EURO.CHR — install required */
```

```
        ROMAN_FONT = 0,          /* LCOM.CHR — install required */
        SIMPLEX_FONT = 0,        /* SIMP.CHR — install required */
        ITALIC_FONT = 0,         /* TSCR.CHR — install required */
        SCRIPT_FONT = 0;         /* SCRI.CHR — install required */

void Initialize()
{
   GraphDriver = DETECT;
   initgraph( &GraphDriver, &GraphMode, "C:\\TC\\BGI" );
   ErrorCode = graphresult();
   if ( ErrorCode != grOk )
   {
      printf(" Graphics System Error: %s\n",
            grapherrormsg( ErrorCode ) );
      exit( 1 );
   }
}

void Pause()
{
   if( kbhit() ) getch();
   getch();
}

int Install_Font( char *font_name )
{
   int   font_number;

   font_number = installuserfont( font_name );
   if( font_number <= 0 )
   {
      gprintxy( 10, 10, "%s not loaded", font_name );
      Pause();
      return( 0 );
   }
   else return( font_number );
}

void Display_Alphabet( int font, int vpos, char *name )
{
   settextstyle( font, HORIZ_DIR, 4 );
   gprintxy( 50, vpos, "ABCDEFGHIJKL %s", name );
```

```
}

void Load_Fonts()
{
   LARGE_FONT    = Install_Font( "EURO.CHR" );
   ROMAN_FONT    = Install_Font( "LCOM.CHR" );
   ITALIC_FONT   = Install_Font( "TSCR.CHR" );
   SCRIPT_FONT   = Install_Font( "SCRI.CHR" );
   SIMPLEX_FONT  = Install_Font( "SIMP.CHR" );
}

void Show_New_Fonts()
{
   Load_Fonts();
   setcolor(WHITE);
   settextjustify( LEFT_TEXT, TOP_TEXT );
   Display_Alphabet( LARGE_FONT,     20, "Large"   );
   Display_Alphabet( ROMAN_FONT,     80, "Roman"   );
   Display_Alphabet( ITALIC_FONT,   120, "Italic"  );
   Display_Alphabet( SCRIPT_FONT,   160, "Script"  );
   Display_Alphabet( SIMPLEX_FONT,  200, "Simplex" );
}

main()
{
   Initialize();
   cleardevice();
   Show_New_Fonts();
   Pause();
   closegraph();
}
```

Part Three

Object-Oriented Graphics in Turbo C++

While object-oriented programming is hardly limited to graphics applications, graphics are prime territory for object programming. Objects can provide new and powerful graphic capablities that, using conventional programming practices, would be too awkward and too complex for convenient inclusion in most programs.

In Part Three, a variety of graphics objects will be created, beginning with an object-mouse interface and then moving on to screen button objects, scrollbars, and interactive icon objects.

Utilities programs will be demonstrated; including MOUSEPTR, a graphic mouse pointer editor providing interactive design for custom pointer designs; and ICONEDIT which provides a convenient means to design full-color icon images. Additional demo programs will illustrate the use of the various graphic objects.

This book is not an introduction to object-oriented programming and the following chapters do not comprise a primer for C++ programming practices. If you are not familiar with object-oriented programming and need more complete instructions for C++ practices, my companion volume, *Turbo C++ Programming, An Object-Oriented Approach*, is available from Addison-Wesley Publishing Company and provides extensive instruction in object-oriented programming as well as showing variations and more detailed explanations of several of the programs included in this section.

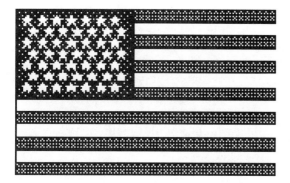

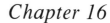

Chapter 16

A Graphics Mouse Object

When an input device is required with a graphics display (except text graphics) the obvious choice is to use the mouse as the primary selection mechanism and the cursor keys as a secondary device.

There are two alternatives for employing a mouse: first, by reading the mouse output codes as an analog of the cursor keys; and second, by directly incorporating a mouse interface in your program and interpreting mouse events directly.

Reading Mouse Events as Cursor Keys

This method uses the default mouse interface (the MOUSE.COM or MOUSE.SYS driver) supplied with the physical mouse hardware and requires little or no special provision by the programmer. When the mouse is moved left, the system receives the two codes (scan and char codes) *00h, 48h,* just as if the left arrow key had been pressed. Similarly, the left mouse button normally returns the same code (*0Dh*) as pressing the *Enter* key on the keyboard.

However, with a Logitech Mouse (and many others), these key response codes can be reassigned or even interpreted as macro instructions (see your mouse manual for details) and it can be difficult to ensure that the appropriate and desired responses will always be returned by the mouse software.

An Object Mouse Interface

For most graphics applications, indirectly interpreting the mouse input (treating the mouse as a keyboard analog) is unreliable or unsatisfactory for several reasons: the mouse movement and key responses may not be assigned correctly, the information returned is less complete than can be read directly from the mouse, little or no control can be exercised over the mouse parameters and, last, the program loop time may produce too much delay in responding to the mouse movement.

For these reasons, most graphics applications seek to exercise a direct interface with the mouse device, allowing the program to set mouse parameters and to read mouse events and position directly.

But, to assume direct control and communication with the mouse, the optimum approach is to create a mouse object which provides methods to:

- restrict mouse movement to a specific screen area
- read the mouse screen position directly
- change the mouse response rates and adjust vertical and horizontal mouse to screen movement ratios
- read mouse keys as both make and break events and test individual key-down status
- select graphics mouse cursors or create new graphics mouse cursor patterns
- selectively hide or display the mouse cursor

Most of these capabilities will be demonstrated in the MOUSEPTR.CPP program in this chapter.

Mouse Types

The object-mouse interface is provided as an include file, MOUSE.I, in this chapter. This mouse interface method can be used with both graphics and text applications.

To begin, there are currently two basic types of mice in use: the Microsoft (two-button) mouse and the Logitech (three-button) mouse. While mice with a variety of trademarks are available, most will conform to one of these two standards.

The basic Microsoft mouse supports 16 mouse functions (functions 0..15) and has two buttons each producing a make and a break response or capable of being read as pressed or released. The Logitech mouse supports all features of the Microsoft mouse, but adds two additional mouse functions (functions 16 and 19) and a third (middle) button.

The procedures in MOUSE.I include both the Microsoft and Logitech mouse functions and the MOUSEPTR.CPP program will operate with either type of mouse though the third button and functions 16 and 19 will not be supported by all Microsoft mice.

Later versions of both the Microsoft and Logitech mouse drivers have added additional interrupt functions and special capabilities but none of these are essential in any form and are not included here.

These mouse procedures do presume the presence of two items: a hardware mouse and a mouse device driver, both of which are supplied by the mouse manufacturer or vendor. The hardware mouse may be either a serial or bus mouse and the mouse device driver may be either MOUSE.COM or MOUSE.SYS (normally both device drivers are supplied with each mouse).

When creating an object unit for use either by yourself or for distribution and use by other parties, it is helpful to provide descriptive documentation listing what functions are available via the unit, the parameters required to call these functions, and any data structures that are used by the object unit and are available to the calling program. For the MOUSE.I unit, sample documentation appears in Appendix B.

The Case of the Bashful Mouse

If you are using VGA or higher resolution graphics, and the mouse pointer does not appear in the graphics application, the problem may be in your mouse driver and can be cured by installing a newer driver package. The problem can be tested, however, by using Turbo C++'s setgraphmode command to select a lower-resolution graphics mode.

For example, using VGA graphics with a vertical resolution of 480 pixels, the graphics mouse cursor does not appear on screen, but when using the *setgraphmode(1)* command to select medium resolution VGA graphics with a 350 vertical resolution, the mouse cursor does appear. If so, contact Microsoft, Logitech, or your mouse supplier to obtain a new version mouse driver or purchase one of the new "HiRes" mice. With the Logitech mouse, mouse driver version 4.0 or later supports all VGA resolutions.

Using an Object Include File

Object include files are called in precisely the same manner as conventional include files:

```
#include "mouse.i"
```

By convention, quotes are used in the include declaration in place of the familiar angle brackets to designate a custom library file rather than a header file referencing a stock library. But there is nothing hard and fast about this convention and, if you prefer, there is nothing preventing use of the angle brackets in place of the quote marks.

However, there are a few other differences as well. For one, object methods are not directly accessible but must be referenced through specific object instances which, normally, are declared in the main program or in subprocedures using the objects.

Object include files may often contain structure definitions, constants, or even object instances (see MOUSE.I which includes defined instances of GMouse and TMouse) for general use by applications using the object.

In MOUSE.I, the type definitions declared by the unit are available to the applications using the unit:

```
typedef struct
    {  unsigned  flag,
                 button,
                 xaxis, yaxis;
    }  mouse_event;

typedef struct
    {  unsigned  int
           ScreenMask[16],
           CursorMask[16],
           xkey, ykey;
    }  g_cursor;
```

Two Buttons Versus Three

The mouse object provides compatibility for both two- and three-button mice, principally by providing definitions for all three buttons:

```
#define ButtonL  = 0;
#define ButtonR  = 1;
#define ButtonM  = 2;
```

If you have worked with OS/2 Presentation Manager, the mouse buttons are defined under OS/2 as 1-2-3, from left to right (with a system option to reverse the order for southpaws). Conventional mouse button ordering, however, began when computer mice had only two buttons—left and right (and some had only one)—thus, the third (middle) button is out of order and is numbered 2. For two-button mice the third, middle, button is not available. Two other constants are provided for general use: SOFTWARE and HARDWARE which are used to set the cursor in text mode.

```
#define SOFTWARE = 0;
#define HARDWARE = 1;
```

Four additional constants which are provided for general convenience:

```
#define  FALSE     0
#define  TRUE      1
#define  OFF       0
#define  ON        1
```

Graphics Mouse Cursors

Graphic mouse cursors images consist of two bit-images—the screen mask and the cursor mask—each a 16 by 16 array that is combined with the existing graphics screen image as shown in Table 16-1.

Table 16-1: Screen and Cursor Mask Effects

Screen Mask Bit	Cursor Mask Bit	Display Bit
0	0	0
0	1	1
1	0	UNAFFECTED
1	1	INVERTED

Five graphics cursors are predefined in the mouse unit for use with graphics mouse applications. The Arrow cursor (see Figure 16-1) is an angled arrow similar to the default graphics cursor. The Check cursor is a check mark with the hot spot at the base of the angle. The Cross cursor is a circle with crosshairs marking a centered hot spot. The Glove cursor is a hand image with the hot spot at the tip of the extended index finger and, last, the Ibeam cursor duplicates the popular vertical bar marker used with graphics text applications. The hot spot for the Ibeam cursor is centered roughly on the vertical bar.

All of the graphics cursor images are available to applications using the mouse unit and are defined as follows:

```
static  g_cursor  ARROW =
        {  0x1FFF, 0x0FFF, 0x07FF, 0x03FF,    // screen mask
           0x01FF, 0x00FF, 0x007F, 0x003F,
           0x001F, 0x003F, 0x01FF, 0x01FF,
           0xE0FF, 0xF0FF, 0xF8FF, 0xF8FF,
```

```
0x0000, 0x4000, 0x6000, 0x7000,        // cursor mask
0x7800, 0x7C00, 0x7E00, 0x7F00,
0x7F80, 0x7C00, 0x4C00, 0x0600,
0x0600, 0x0300, 0x0300, 0x0000,
0x0001, 0x0001  };                     // hot spot coordinates
```

Figure 16-1: The Graphics Arrow Cursor

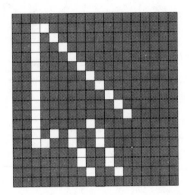

Left, the default (Arrow) graphics cursor is shown against a matching background. Against a contrasting background, only the cursor mask image would appear.

Below (left and right), the screen mask and cursor mask are shown separately.

Screen Mask

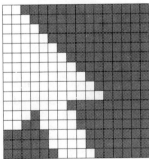

Cursor Mask

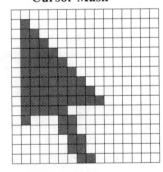

The Screen Mask image is AND'd with the existing screen image before the CursorMask image is XOR's with the result. This ensures that the mouse pointer is visible against any background. At the same time, the existing screen image is protected and—when the graphics cursor is moved or hidden—is restored unchanged.

The MOUSEPTR program creates an ASCII text file following this same format and can be imported directly to any Turbo C or C++ program listing or added to the MOUSE.I unit source listings.

The Object Definitions

The object definitions begin with a general mouse object type, Mouse, which contains 14 methods belonging to the Mouse object:

```
class Mouse
{
   int     Mview;

   protected:
      Mouse();
      ~Mouse();
   public:
      static mouse_event far *Mevents;

      Mmovement *Mmotion();
      Mresult    *Mreset();
      Mstatus    Mpos();
      Mstatus    Mpressed( int button );
      Mstatus    Mreleased( int button );
      void Mshow( int showstat );
      void Mmoveto( int xaxis, int yaxis );
      void Mxlimit( int min_x, int max_x );
      void Mylimit( int min_y, int max_y );
      void Mmove_ratio( int xsize, int ysize );
      void Mspeed( int speed );
      void Mconceal( int left, int top,
                     int right, int bottom );
};
```

The Mouse object type is the base object type containing methods that are common to all mouse objects. Notice, however, that the Mouse object does not contain any data elements, unlike most object examples thus far—only methods which return data structures. Also, the Mouse object is not intended to be called by any applications. Instead, two descendant object types, that will actually be used by applications, are declared, beginning with the GMouse object type (which adds three new procedures, one private, two public, that are specific to graphics mouse applications):

```
class GMouse : public Mouse
{
   private:
      void set_cursor( int xaxis,
                       int yaxis,
                       unsigned mask_Seg,
                       unsigned mask_Ofs );
   public:
      void Set_Cursor( g_cursor ThisCursor );
      void Mlightpen( int set );
};
```

The TMouse object type (text mouse) is also a descendant of the Mouse type, adding two text specific procedures:

```
class TMouse : public Mouse
{
   public:
      void Set_Cursor( int cursor_type,
                       unsigned s_start,
                       unsigned s_stop  );
      void Mlightpen( int set );
};
```

The GMouse and TMouse object types each include Mlightpen methods to support the rare, but still occasional, applications that require lightpen support for either graphics or text applications.

Method Implementations

The object methods defined in the object declaration also require specific implementation. That is, the code specific to each procedure or function, and any types, constants, variables, or local procedures or functions that are private to specific methods and, therefore, not directly available to the application using the object:

```
Mouse::Mouse()    {   }

Mouse::~Mouse()   {   }
```

The Mouse object is provided with constructor and destructor methods which are the first two methods implemented, even though neither has any actual code provided. Still, these implementations must be provided, either here or in the declaration, before the object can be compiled.

The Reset Function

The Mouse implementations begin with the Mreset method which calls the mouse driver, resetting the driver to default conditions, and returning a mouse status argument in the AX register (–1 if mouse present, 0 if not available). The argument is tested and, if the mouse is present, the mouse cursor is turned on.

The BX register returns the button count (2 or 3) for the mouse and both results are returned in the *Mresult* data structure.

```
Mresult *Mouse::Mreset()
{
    static Mresult   m;

    Mview = OFF;
    inreg.x.ax = 0;
    call_mouse;
    m.present = outreg.x.ax;
    m.buttons = outreg.x.bx;
    if( m.present ) Mshow( TRUE );
    return ( &m );
}
```

The Mshow Method

The Mshow method is used to turn the mouse cursor on and off by calling mouse functions 1 and 2, respectively.

Any time a screen update is being executed in an area which may include the mouse cursor, the mouse cursor should be turned off before repainting the screen and restored afterwards. Otherwise, the effects can be surprising, but not desirable. If you would like to see examples caused by omission, comment out the body of this procedure and run the MousePtr program:

```
void Mouse::Mshow( int showstat )
{
    if( showstat )
    {
        inreg.x.ax = 1;                    // mouse function 1  //
        if( !Mview ) call_mouse;           // show mouse cursor //
        Mview = ON;
```

```
    }
    else
    {
        inreg.x.ax = 2;                              // mouse function 2  //
        if( Mview ) call_mouse;                      // hide mouse cursor //
        Mview = OFF;
}   }
```

Mouse functions 1 and 2 have been combined here in a single method to provide a convenience and safety which is lacking in the original functions. Using the original functions, multiple calls to hide the mouse cursor require multiple calls before the cursor is restored (and vice versa). Alternatively, the Mshow method permits the hide and show cursor functions to be called only once, thus ensuring that a single call can always be depended on to reverse the cursor state.

Note that hiding the mouse cursor does not affect tracking operations or button operations—the mouse position is tracked even if the mouse is invisible.

The Mpos Method

The Mpos method reports the mouse cursor position and the status of the mouse buttons. Position coordinates are always reported in pixels.

The *button_status* element (in *Mstatus*) is an integer value with the three least-significant bits indicating the current status of the left, right and, if present, middle buttons. The corresponding bits in *button_status* (starting with bit 0) will be set if the button is down or clear if the button is up:

```
Mstatus Mouse::Mpos()
{                       // returns pointer to Mstatus structure with //
                        // mouse cursor position and button status   //
    static Mstatus  m;

    inreg.x.ax = 3;                              // mouse function 3 //
    call_mouse;
    m.button_status = outreg.x.bx;               // button status    //
    m.xaxis = outreg.x.cx;                       // xaxis coordinate //
    m.yaxis = outreg.x.dx;                       // yaxis coordinate //
    return (m);
}
```

The Mmoveto Method

The Mmoveto method is used to move the mouse cursor to a specific location on the screen. The coordinates used are always absolute screen coordinates in pixels. In text modes, pixel coordinates are still used, but the coordinates are rounded off to position the cursor to the nearest character cell indicated by the pixel coordinates (for example with an 8x8 text display, x/y pixel coordinates of 80/25 would correspond to the 11th column and 4th row of the screen).

```
void Mouse::Mmoveto( int xaxis, int yaxis )
{                                  // mouse cursor to new position //
    inreg.x.ax = 4;                       // mouse function 4 //
    inreg.x.cx = xaxis;
    inreg.x.dx = yaxis;
    call_mouse;
}
```

The Mpressed Method

The Mpressed method reports the current status of all of the buttons, a count of the number of times the requested button has been pressed (since the last call to Mpressed for this button), and the mouse coordinates when the requested button was last pressed:

```
Mstatus Mouse::Mpressed( int button )
{
    static Mstatus  m;

    inreg.x.ax = 5;
    inreg.x.bx = button;
    call_mouse;
    m.button_status = outreg.x.ax;
    m.button_count = outreg.x.bx;
    m.xaxis = outreg.x.cx;
    m.yaxis = outreg.x.dx;
    return (m);
}
```

The Mreleased Method

The Mreleased method is the equivalent of Mpressed except for reporting the number of times the requested button was released:

```
Mstatus Mouse::Mreleased( int button )
{
    static Mstatus  m;

    inreg.x.ax = 6;
    inreg.x.bx = button;
    call_mouse;
    m.button_status = outreg.x.ax;
    m.button_count = outreg.x.bx;
    m.xaxis = outreg.x.cx;
    m.yaxis = outreg.x.dx;
    return (m);
}
```

The Mxlimit and Mylimit Methods

The Mxlimit and Mylimit methods establish screen limits (in pixels) for the mouse movement. This is particularly important when using higher resolution graphics because the default limits may not include the entire screen and, if it does not, portions of the screen cannot be reached with the mouse.

When restricting the mouse to a portion of the screen, if an application is using an exit button as demonstrated in the MousePtr program, either ensure that an alternate exit procedure is supplied or that some method of reaching the exit button is always available:

```
void Mouse::Mxlimit( int min_x, int max_x )
{
    inreg.x.ax = 7;                         // mouse function 7 //
    inreg.x.cx = min_x;
    inreg.x.dx = max_x;
    call_mouse;
}

void Mouse::Mylimit( int min_y, int max_y )
{                                   // sets vertical boundaries //
    inreg.x.ax = 8;                         // mouse function 8 //
    inreg.x.cx = min_y;
    inreg.x.dx = max_y;
    call_mouse;
}
```

The Mxlimit and Mylimit methods could also be combined in a single method accepting four arguments.

The Mmotion Method

The Mmotion method returns a total horizontal and vertical step count since the last call to Mmotion. For a normal mouse, the step count varies from a low of $1/100$ inch increments (100 mickeys/inch) for older mice to $1/200$ inch (200 mickeys/inch) for more modern mice and $1/320$ inch increments (320 mickeys/inch) for a HiRes mouse.

Movement step counts are always within the range −32768..32767, a positive value indicating a left to right horizontal motion or, vertically, a motion towards the user (assuming the cable is pointed away from the user). Horizontal and vertical step counts are reset to zero after this call:

```
Mmovement* Mouse::Mmotion()
{
    static Mmovement  m;

    inreg.x.ax = 11;
    call_mouse;
    m.x_count = _CX;
    m.y_count = _DX;
    return (&m);
}
```

Since the mouse graphics or text cursors are updated automatically, Mmotion is not required to control the screen presentation, but may be used for special applications.

Refer also to the Mmove_ratio and Mspeed functions.

The Mmove_ratio Method

The Mmove_ratio method controls the ratio of physical mouse movement to screen cursor movement with the x- and y-axis arguments (*xsize* and *ysize*) expressed as the number of mickeys (units of mouse motion) required to cover eight pixels on the screen. Allowable values are 1 to 32,767 mickeys, but the appropriate values are dependent on the number of mickeys per inch reported by the physical mouse: values which may be 100, 200, or 320 mickeys per inch depending on the mouse hardware.

Default values are 8 mickeys/8 pixels horizontal and 16 mickeys/8 pixels vertical. For a mouse reporting 200 mickeys/inch, this requires 3.2 inches horizontally and 2.0 inches vertically to cover a 640x200 pixel screen:

```
void Mouse::Mmove_ratio( int xsize, int ysize )
{
   inreg.x.ax = 15;
   inreg.x.cx = xsize;
   inreg.x.dx = ysize;
   call_mouse;
}
```

The Mspeed Method

The Mspeed method establishes a threshold speed (in physical mouse velocity units, mickeys/second) above which the mouse driver adds an acceleration component, allowing fast movements with the mouse to move the cursor further than slow movements.

The acceleration component varies according to the mouse driver installed. For some drivers, acceleration is a constant multiplier, usually a factor of two, while other drivers, including the Logitech mouse, use variable acceleration with multiplier values increasing on an acceleration curve:

```
void Mouse::Mspeed( int speed )
{
   inreg.x.ax = 19;
   inreg.x.dx = speed;
   call_mouse;
}
```

The threshold value can be any value in the range 0..7FFFh with an average value in the range of 300 mickeys/second. Acceleration can be disabled by setting a high threshold (7FFFh) or restored by setting a low or zero threshold.

The Mconceal Method

The Mconceal method designates a rectangular area of the screen where the mouse cursor will automatically be hidden and is used principally to guard an area of the screen that will be repainted:

```
void Mouse::Mconceal( int left, int top,
                      int right, int bottom )
{
   inreg.x.ax = 16;
   inreg.x.cx = left;
   inreg.x.dx = top;
```

```
   inreg.x.si = right;
   inreg.x.di = bottom;
   call_mouse;
}
```

The mouse cursor is automatically hidden if it is in or moves into the area designated, but the Mconceal function is temporary, functioning by decrementing the mouse counter in the same manner as a call to the Mshow(FALSE) function.

The area set by calling Mconceal will be cleared and the mouse cursor enabled over the entire screen by calling Mshow(TRUE).

The GMouse Method Implementations

The GMouse implementation adds three graphics-specific methods to the general mouse functions inherited from the Mouse object type. Two of these new methods are public (accessible to applications using the object) but the third is private and can only be called by another object method.

```
class GMouse : public Mouse
{
   private:                            // graphic cursor shape    //
      void set_cursor( int xaxis,
                       int yaxis,
                       unsigned mask_Seg,
                       unsigned mask_Ofs );
   public:
      void Set_Cursor( g_cursor ThisCursor );
      void Mlightpen( int set );
};
```

The set_cursor Method

The set_cursor method is private and cannot be called directly by an application. It is called, indirectly, through the Set_Cursor method. The set_cursor method is the actual mechanism for changing the graphics mouse cursor and is called with the *x*- and *y*-axis coordinates for the cursor's hot spot and the segment and offset address of the cursor image.

```
void GMouse::set_cursor( int xaxis, int yaxis,
                         unsigned mask_Seg,
                         unsigned mask_Ofs )

{
```

```
    struct SREGS  seg;

    inreg.x.ax = 9;
    inreg.x.bx = xaxis;
    inreg.x.cx = yaxis;
    inreg.x.dx = mask_Ofs;
    seg.es     = mask_Seg;
    int86x( 0x33, &inreg, &outreg, &seg );
}
```

The Set_Cursor Method

The Set_Cursor method loads a new cursor screen and mask, making it the active graphics mouse pointer:

```
void GMouse::Set_Cursor( g_cursor ThisCursor )
{
    set_cursor( ThisCursor.xkey,
                ThisCursor.ykey,
                _DS,
                (unsigned) ThisCursor.ScreenMask );
}
```

The selected graphics cursor may be one of the predefined cursors supplied with the mouse unit (MOUSE.I) or may be a cursor defined by the application program.

The Set_Cursor method (public) is used by applications to call the set_cursor method (private) for the actual operation but provides the simplicity of changing cursors with a single argument identifying the cursor image name, instead of having to specify the offset, segment, and hot spot coordinates for the cursor image.

The Mlightpen Methods

While lightpens are relatively scarce, a few applications do continue to use these, and the mouse driver package offers a pair of functions supporting lightpen emulation.

Two methods have been created, one for the GMouse object and the other for the TMouse object type. Both implement the lightpen functions in exactly the same manner:

```
void GMouse::Mlightpen( int set )
{
    if( set ) inreg.x.ax = 13;
```

```
      else  inreg.x.ax = 14;
   call_mouse;
}
```

Light pen emulation is turned off by default. When enabled, simultaneous down states of both the right and left buttons emulate the pen-down state and release of both buttons emulates the pen-up state.

The TMouse Methods

While three functions were added to create a graphics mouse object descended from the general mouse object, to do the same for the text mouse, only two procedures are provided, paralleling two of the graphic mouse procedures: Set_Cursor, a method for setting the text cursor type (see Figure 16-1), and Mlightpen, supporting lightpen emulation as previously discussed. Table 16-2 shows the text cursor size settings.

```
class TMouse : public Mouse
{
   public:
      void Set_Cursor( int cursor_type,
                       unsigned s_start,
                       unsigned s_stop  );
      void Mlightpen( int set );
};
```

While the Set_Cursor method has the same name as the GMouse function, this version is implemented in an entirely different manner. Strictly speaking, however, this is not an example of polymorphism because both the GMouse and TMouse are descended from Mouse and not from each other (these are siblings, not descendants).

The Set_Cursor Method (Text Version)

The text version of the Set_Cursor method can be used to select either hardware or software cursors and set the cursor parameters:

```
void TMouse::Set_Cursor( int cursor_type,
                         unsigned s_start,
                         unsigned s_stop  )
{
   inreg.x.ax = 10;
   inreg.x.bx = cursor_type;
   inreg.x.cx = s_start;
```

```
    inreg.x.dx = s_stop;
    call_mouse;
}
```

The hardware cursor uses the video controller to create the cursor with the arguments (*c1* and *c2*) identifying the start and stop scan lines for the cursor. The number of scan lines in a character cell is determined by the hardware video controller (and monitor), but as a general rule, for monochrome systems the range is 0..7 and for CGA the range is 0..14, top to bottom.

Table 16-2: Text Cursor Size Settings

Video Type (Mode)	Monochrome (07h)	Text (00-03h)
DEFAULT START/STOP	9h / 0Ah	06h / 07h
BLOCK START/STOP	00h / 0Ah	00h / 0Bh

In general, however, a start scan line of six and a stop scan line of seven will produce an underline cursor. A start scan line of two and a stop scan line of five or six produces a block cursor and works well even on high resolution VGA systems.

The software cursor is slightly more complicated. Using the software cursor, the *c1* and *c2* parameters create a character or character attributes which are, respectively, ANDed and XORed with the existing screen character. The *c1* parameter (screen mask) is ANDed with the existing screen character and attributes at the mouse cursor location, determining which elements are preserved. Next, the *c2* parameter (cursor mask) is XORed with the results of the previous operation, determining which characteristics are changed.

In actual practice, a screen mask value of $7F00 might be used to preserve the color attributes, while a cursor mask value of $8018 would establish a blinking up-arrow cursor or $0018 for a non-blinking up arrow. In either case the existing foreground and background color attributes are preserved. In the same fashion, a screen mask of $0000 and a cursor mask of $FFFF will produce a flashing white block cursor. See Table 16-3 for more information.

As a general rule, the eight least-significant bits of the screen mask should be either $..00 or $..FF; with the former preferred.

Table 16-3: Software Cursor Parameter Format

Bit	Description
0..7	Extended ASCII character code
8..10	Foreground color
11	Intensity: 1 = high, 0 = medium
12..14	Background color
15	Blinking (1) or non-blinking (0)

The Mouse Pointer Utility

A mouse cursor editor (MOUSEPTR.CPP) is the second example in this chapter. It is program providing both a useful utility to create mouse cursor images and a means of demonstrating the use of the mouse unit.

While MOUSEPTR could have been created as an object-oriented program, this utility is written largely in conventional C format, aside from calls to the object-oriented mouse unit. This is done for two reasons: first, to avoid complicated explanations which will appear later and, second, because portions of the code used in this program will serve to contrast the object-oriented graphics button structures that will be created in Chapter 17. You are, however, welcome and invited to practice object-oriented programming by revising the MOUSEPTR program using the object-oriented button utilities that will be presented shortly.

The MOUSEPTR program is generally self-explanatory and provides two grid structures for editing the screen and cursor masks to create a mouse pointer image. Naturally, editing is accomplished using the mouse to toggle squares in the grids or to select the option buttons below the grids. In brief, the options listed in Tables 16-4 and 16-5 are provided.

Table 16-4: MOUSEPTR Cursor Mask Option Buttons

Cursor Mask Options	Description
Clear	Reset all bits in the cursor mask grid to FALSE (zero).
Invert	Reverse all bits in the cursor mask grid.
Copy to Screen	Copies the cursor mask grid to the screen mask grid.

Table 16-5: MOUSEPTR General Mask Options

General Options	Description
Invert	Reverse all bits in the screen mask grid.

General Options	Description
Make from Cursor	Creates a screen mask grid image from the cursor mask grid. For each point in the screen mask grid, if the corresponding point in the cursor mask grid or any adjacent point in the cursor mask grid is TRUE, the screen mask grid point is FALSE.
Set Hotspot	The next point selected in either the screen or cursor mask grids will be the hot spot for the mouse cursor and will appear in red on both grids. Any existing hot spot is cleared.
Use Pointer	Makes the edited cursor image the active mouse pointer on the screen.
Arrow Pointer	Restores the arrow mouse pointer.
Save Pointer	Saves the current screen and cursor grid images to an ASCII file using hexadecimal format. The output file can be imported directly for use by any Turbo C or C++ program. The current directory is used and the filename extension .CUR is automatically supplied.
Exit	Exits from the program. No safety features are supplied to prevent accidental exits.

The control options affect both the screen and cursor masks.

The .CUR File Format

The mouse cursor image is saved in an ASCII format that is suitable for direct inclusion in any program using the MOUSE.I unit:

```
static  g_cursor  ARROW =                       // screen mask //
      {   0x1FFF, 0x0FFF, 0x07FF, 0x03FF,
          0x01FF, 0x00FF, 0x007F, 0x003F,
          0x001F, 0x003F, 0x01FF, 0x01FF,
          0xE0FF, 0xF0FF, 0xF8FF, 0xF8FF,
                                                // cursor mask //
          0x0000, 0x4000, 0x6000, 0x7000,
          0x7800, 0x7C00, 0x7E00, 0x7F00,
          0x7F80, 0x7C00, 0x4C00, 0x0600,
          0x0600, 0x0300, 0x0300, 0x0000,
          0x0001, 0x0001  };                    // xkey, ykey //
```

All values are written in hexadecimal format, simplifying any manual editing or revision that might be desired. The *xkey* and *ykey* values are written as word values though these are actually only integer values (and never exceed 0x000F). Conversion is handled automatically by Turbo C++.

Conventional Style Button Operations

The MOUSEPTR utility is operated by the series of button controls previously listed, but these are buttons only in a limited sense. An outline and

label are written to the screen with a separate function arbitrarily matching
the mouse pointer location coordinates at the time that a mouse button is
pressed to the corresponding screen images. The screen and cursor grids
are treated in a similar fashion.

In Chapter 17, this dichotomy will be resolved in an object type named
Button. Also, images, screen positions, and control responses will be
merged into a single control object.

The Button object type can be used to replace a large part of the
programming instructions in the MOUSEPTR utility program, replacing
not only the screen, cursor, and general control buttons, but also replacing
the screen and cursor grids with arrays of blank buttons.

For the moment, however, the topic is the conventional or non-object-
oriented control structure that begins by using the gmouse object (type
GMouse) to enable graphics mouse operations:

```
Result = gmouse.Mreset();
if( Result->present )
{
    do {
```

Within the loop, only the left mouse button is used and the loop begins
by calling Mpressed to test for a left button pressed event:

```
Position = gmouse.Mpressed( ButtonL );
if( Position.button_count )
{
```

If the returned button_count is not zero, the next step is to decide where
the mouse cursor was located when the button was pressed. This is accomplished with nested *if* statements.

```
if( TPos( Position.yaxis, 30, 270 ) )
{                            // screen or cursor grids //
    if( TPos( Position.xaxis,  15, 255 ) )
       ScreenSet( Position.xaxis,
                  Position.yaxis );
    if( TPos( Position.xaxis, 384, 624 ) )
       CursorSet( Position.xaxis,
                  Position.yaxis );
} else
if( TPos( Position.yaxis, 280, 300 ) )
                         // screen or cursor commands //
```

```
          {                                 // screen mask items //
             if( TPos( Position.xaxis,   15,   75 ) )
                ClearScreen(); else
             if( TPos( Position.xaxis,   85,  145 ) )
                InvertScreen(); else
             if( TPos( Position.xaxis,  155,  295 ) )
                ScreenFromCursor(); else
                                            // cursor mask items //
             if( TPos( Position.xaxis,  364,  484 ) )
                CursorToScreen(); else
             if( TPos( Position.xaxis,  494,  554 ) )
                InvertCursor(); else
             if( TPos( Position.xaxis,  564,  624 ) )
                ClearCursor();
          } else
          if( TPos( Position.yaxis, 320, 340 ) )
          {                               // general command options //
             if( TPos( Position.xaxis,   15,  125 ) )
                UseNewCursor(); else
             if( TPos( Position.xaxis,  140,  250 ) )
                gmouse.Set_Cursor( ARROW ); else
             if( TPos( Position.xaxis,  265,  375 ) )
                SetHotSpot(); else
             if( TPos( Position.xaxis,  390,  500 ) )
                SavePointer(); else
             if( TPos( Position.xaxis,  515,  625 ) )
                Exit = TRUE;
      } } }
      while( !Exit );
   }
```

While this response structure does work well it has a serious deficiency. A popular adage holds that "if it works, don't fix it!" But sometimes what works in one situation does not work in all situations. The coding used in this example is a case in point. For an EGA or higher resolution graphics system, the MOUSEPTR program works just fine, but, for a CGA video, extensive conversions would have to be made before the image grids and the control buttons could fit within a 200-pixel vertical resolution.

While it is possible to write formulas to provide adaptation to different vertical (and horizontal) resolutions for the screen images, it is also be necessary to have a series of variables associated with each of these screen elements and to assign screen coordinate values to each corresponding to the video resolution in use. In conventional programming, however, this is awkward and unwieldy. This is also an excellent example of where and how object-oriented programming provides tremendous advantages, as will be shown in Chapter 17.

Summary

In this chapter, an object-mouse was created as an include file, MOUSE.I, and is used in examples to provide general mouse control. Before proceeding further, you should have a working mouse unit, containing both the graphics and text mouse object methods, compiled and ready for use.

Either the MOUSEPTR program (following) or the button, scrollbar, and icon demo programs in subsequent chapters can be used to test the object-mouse:

```
//=========================================================//
// MOUSE.I: Turbo C++ source code for mouse interface //
//   object. #include dos.h before this #include to   //
//   define the register set to pass args to driver   //
//=========================================================//

#include <dos.h>
#include <stddef.h>

#define   call_mouse int86(0x33, &inreg, &outreg)
                   // interrupt call for mouse device driver //
#define   EVENTMASK  0x54
#define   lower (x, y)  (x < y) ? x : y
#define   upper (x, y)  (x > y) ? x : y
#define   ButtonL    0
#define   ButtonR    1
#define   ButtonM    2
#define   SOFTWARE   0                    // text cursor types //
#define   HARDWARE   1
#define   FALSE      0
#define   TRUE       1
#define   OFF        0
#define   ON         1

union  REGS  inreg, outreg;              // static registers //

typedef struct {  int present,           // TRUE if present //
```

```
                        buttons;            // # of buttons      //
               }   Mresult;

typedef struct
    { int button_status,        // bits 0-2 on if button down //
          button_count,         // # times button was clicked //
          xaxis, yaxis;         // mouse cursor position       //
    }  Mstatus;

typedef struct
    { int x_count,              // net horizontal movement //
          y_count;              // net vertical movement   //
    }  Mmovement;               // returned by mMotion     //

typedef struct
    { unsigned  flag,                    // mouse event record //
               button,
               xaxis, yaxis;
    }  mouse_event;

typedef struct              // graphics cursor descriptor //
    { unsigned  int
        ScreenMask[16],
        CursorMask[16],
        xkey, ykey;
    }  g_cursor;

static  g_cursor  ARROW =                    // screen mask //
        {  0x1FFF, 0x0FFF, 0x07FF, 0x03FF,
           0x01FF, 0x00FF, 0x007F, 0x003F,
           0x001F, 0x003F, 0x01FF, 0x01FF,
           0xE0FF, 0xF0FF, 0xF8FF, 0xF8FF,
                                             // cursor mask //
           0x0000, 0x4000, 0x6000, 0x7000,
           0x7800, 0x7C00, 0x7E00, 0x7F00,
           0x7F80, 0x7C00, 0x4C00, 0x0600,
           0x0600, 0x0300, 0x0300, 0x0000,
           0x0001, 0x0001  };                // xkey, ykey  //

static  g_cursor CHECK =                     // screen mask //
        {  0xFFF0, 0xFFE0, 0xFFC0, 0xFF81,
           0xFF03, 0x0607, 0x000F, 0x001F,
           0x803F, 0xC07F, 0xE0FF, 0xF1FF,
```

```
                0xFFFF,  0xFFFF,  0xFFFF,  0xFFFF,
                                                            // cursor mask //
                0x0000,  0x0006,  0x000C,  0x0018,
                0x0030,  0x0060,  0x70C0,  0x3980,
                0x1F00,  0x0E00,  0x0400,  0x0000,
                0x0000,  0x0000,  0x0000,  0x0000,
                0x0005,  0x000A  };                         // xkey, ykey  //

static  g_cursor CROSS =                                    // screen mask //
          {  0xF01F,  0xE00F,  0xC007,  0x8003,
             0x0441,  0x0C61,  0x0381,  0x0381,
             0x0381,  0x0C61,  0x0441,  0x8003,
             0xC007,  0xE00F,  0xF01F,  0xFFFF,
                                                            // cursor mask //
             0x0000,  0x07C0,  0x0920,  0x1110,
             0x2108,  0x4004,  0x4004,  0x783C,
             0x4004,  0x4004,  0x2108,  0x1110,
             0x0920,  0x07C0,  0x0000,  0x0000,
             0x0007,  0x0007  };                            // xkey, ykey  //

static  g_cursor GLOVE =                                    // screen mask //
          {  0xF3FF,  0xE1FF,  0xE1FF,  0xE1FF,
             0xE1FF,  0xE049,  0xE000,  0x8000,
             0x0000,  0x0000,  0x07FC,  0x07F8,
             0x9FF9,  0x8FF1,  0xC003,  0xE007,
                                                            // cursor mask //
             0x0C00,  0x1200,  0x1200,  0x1200,
             0x1200,  0x13B6,  0x1249,  0x7249,
             0x9249,  0x9001,  0x9001,  0x8001,
             0x4002,  0x4002,  0x2004,  0x1FF8,
             0x0004,  0x0000  };                            // xkey, ykey  //

static  g_cursor IBEAM =                                    // screen mask //
          {  0xF39F,  0xFD7F,  0xFEFF,  0xFEFF,
             0xFEFF,  0xFEFF,  0xFEFF,  0xFEFF,
             0xFEFF,  0xFEFF,  0xFEFF,  0xFEFF,
             0xFEFF,  0xFEFF,  0xFD7F,  0xF39F,
                                                            // cursor mask //
             0x0C60,  0x0280,  0x0100,  0x0100,
             0x0100,  0x0100,  0x0100,  0x0100,
             0x0100,  0x0100,  0x0100,  0x0100,
             0x0100,  0x0100,  0x0280,  0x0C60,
```

```
          0x0007, 0x0008 };                    // xkey, ykey  //

class Mouse
{
   int     Mview;                    // mouse cursor status flag //

   protected:
      Mouse();                       // constructor method    //
      ~Mouse();                      // destructor method     //
   public:
      static mouse_event far *Mevents;
                       // Global far ptr to mouse event record //

      Mmovement *Mmotion();          // net cursor motion     //
      Mresult   *Mreset();
      Mstatus   Mpos();
      Mstatus   Mpressed( int button );
      Mstatus   Mreleased( int button );
      void Mshow( int showstat );
      void Mmoveto( int xaxis, int yaxis );
      void Mxlimit( int min_x, int max_x );
      void Mylimit( int min_y, int max_y );
      void Mmove_ratio( int xsize, int ysize );
      void Mspeed( int speed );
      void Mconceal( int left, int top,
                     int right, int bottom );
};

class GMouse : public Mouse
{
   private:                          // graphic cursor shape   //
      void set_cursor( int xaxis,
                       int yaxis,
                       unsigned mask_Seg,
                       unsigned mask_Ofs );
   public:
      void Set_Cursor( g_cursor ThisCursor );
      void Mlightpen( int set );
};

class TMouse : public Mouse
{
```

```
   public:
                                      // text cursor shape        //
      void Set_Cursor( int cursor_type,
                       unsigned s_start,
                       unsigned s_stop  );
      void Mlightpen( int set );
};


//========================================================//

//   implementation of the standard mouse functions    //
//========================================================//


Mouse::Mouse()
{
}

Mouse::~Mouse()
{
}

        // resets mouse default status, returns pointer to  //
        // Mresult structure indicating if mouse installed  //
        // and, if present, number of buttons - always call //
        // during initialization                            //
Mresult *Mouse::Mreset()
{
   static Mresult  m;

   Mview = OFF;
   inreg.x.ax = 0;                         // mouse function 0 //
   call_mouse;
   m.present = outreg.x.ax;
   m.buttons = outreg.x.bx;
   if( m.present ) Mshow( TRUE );
   return ( &m );
}

void Mouse::Mshow( int showstat )
{
   if( showstat )
   {
```

```
      inreg.x.ax = 1;                   // mouse function 1   //
      if( !Mview ) call_mouse;          // show mouse cursor  //
      Mview = ON;
   }
   else
   {
      inreg.x.ax = 2;                   // mouse function 2   //
      if( Mview ) call_mouse;           // hide mouse cursor  //
      Mview = OFF;
}  }

Mstatus Mouse::Mpos()
{                   // returns pointer to Mstatus structure with //
                    // mouse cursor position and button status   //
   static Mstatus  m;

   inreg.x.ax = 3;                      // mouse function 3 //
   call_mouse;
   m.button_status = outreg.x.bx;       // button status      //
   m.xaxis = outreg.x.cx;               // xaxis coordinate //
   m.yaxis = outreg.x.dx;               // yaxis coordinate //
   return (m);
}

void Mouse::Mmoveto( int xaxis, int yaxis )
{                               // mouse cursor to new position //
   inreg.x.ax = 4;                      // mouse function 4 //
   inreg.x.cx = xaxis;
   inreg.x.dx = yaxis;
   call_mouse;
}

       // return button pressed info; current status (up/dn), //
       // times pressed since last call, cursor position at   //
       // last press - resets count and position info         //
       //          button 0 - left, 1 - right, 2 - center     //
Mstatus Mouse::Mpressed( int button )
{
   static Mstatus  m;

   inreg.x.ax = 5;                      // mouse function 5   //
   inreg.x.bx = button;                 // request for button //
   call_mouse;
```

```
        m.button_status = outreg.x.ax;
        m.button_count = outreg.x.bx;
        m.xaxis = outreg.x.cx;
        m.yaxis = outreg.x.dx;
        return (m);
}

Mstatus Mouse::Mreleased( int button )
{                       // returns release info about button //
        static Mstatus  m;

        inreg.x.ax = 6;                     // mouse function 6    //
        inreg.x.bx = button;                // request for button  //
        call_mouse;
        m.button_status = outreg.x.ax;
        m.button_count = outreg.x.bx;
        m.xaxis = outreg.x.cx;
        m.yaxis = outreg.x.dx;
        return (m);
}


        // Set min / max horizontal range for cursor. Moves  //
        // cursor inside range if outside when called. Swaps //
        // values if min_x and max_x are reversed.           //
void Mouse::Mxlimit( int min_x, int max_x )
{
        inreg.x.ax = 7;                         // mouse function 7 //
        inreg.x.cx = min_x;
        inreg.x.dx = max_x;
        call_mouse;
}

void Mouse::Mylimit( int min_y, int max_y )
{                               // sets vertical boundaries //
        inreg.x.ax = 8;                     // mouse function 8 //
        inreg.x.cx = min_y;
        inreg.x.dx = max_y;
        call_mouse;
}

void GMouse::set_cursor( int xaxis, int yaxis,
                         unsigned mask_Seg,
                         unsigned mask_Ofs )
```

```
{                                    // Sets graphic cursor shape //
   struct SREGS   seg;

   inreg.x.ax = 9;                          // mouse function 9 //
   inreg.x.bx = xaxis;             // xaxis cursor hot spot //
   inreg.x.cx = yaxis;             // yaxis cursor hot spot //
   inreg.x.dx = mask_Ofs;
   seg.es     = mask_Seg;
   int86x( 0x33, &inreg, &outreg, &seg );
}

      // set text cursor type, 0 = software, 1 = hardware  //
      // software cursor, arg1 and arg2 are the screen and //
      //    cursor masks.                                  //
      // hardware cursor, arg1 and arg2 specify scan line  //
      //    start/stop - i.e. cursor shape.                //
void TMouse::Set_Cursor( int cursor_type,
                         unsigned s_start,
                         unsigned s_stop  )
{
   inreg.x.ax = 10;                      // mouse function 10 //
   inreg.x.bx = cursor_type;
   inreg.x.cx = s_start;
   inreg.x.dx = s_stop;
   call_mouse;
}

Mmovement* Mouse::Mmotion()
{            // reports net cursor motion since last call //
   static Mmovement   m;

   inreg.x.ax = 11;                      // mouse function 11  //
   call_mouse;
   m.x_count = _CX;                      // net xaxis movement //
   m.y_count = _DX;                      // net yaxis movement //
   return (&m);
}

void GMouse::Mlightpen( int set )
{
   if( set ) inreg.x.ax = 13;            // function 13  ON //
      else   inreg.x.ax = 14;            // function 14 OFF //
   call_mouse;
```

```
}

void TMouse::Mlightpen( int set )
{
    if( set )  inreg.x.ax = 13;            // function 13  ON //
         else  inreg.x.ax = 14;            // function 14 OFF //
    call_mouse;
}

void Mouse::Mmove_ratio( int xsize, int ysize )
{                  // motion-to-pixel ratio with ratio R/8 //
    inreg.x.ax = 15;                       // Default 16 vert //
    inreg.x.cx = xsize;                    //           8 horiz //
    inreg.x.dx = ysize;
    call_mouse;
}

void Mouse::Mconceal( int left, int top,
                      int right, int bottom )
{                              // area where mouse hidden //
    inreg.x.ax = 16;                     // use for scr update //
    inreg.x.cx = left;
    inreg.x.dx = top;
    inreg.x.si = right;
    inreg.x.di = bottom;
    call_mouse;
}

void Mouse::Mspeed( int speed )
{                              // sets speed threshold   //
    inreg.x.ax = 19;           // in mickeys/second for  //
    inreg.x.dx = speed;        // for accelerated mouse //
    call_mouse;                // movement response     //
}

void GMouse::Set_Cursor( g_cursor ThisCursor )
{
    set_cursor( ThisCursor.xkey,
                ThisCursor.ykey,
                _DS,
                (unsigned) ThisCursor.ScreenMask );
}
```

```
      // type definitions for use by applications //

GMouse   gmouse;
TMouse   tmouse;


              //=====================================//
              //            MOUSEPTR.CPP             //
              //   Demo program for Mouse Object     //
              // and utility to create mouse cursor  //
              //=====================================//

#ifdef __TINY__
#error Graphics demos will not run in the tiny model
#endif

#include <conio.h>
#include <stdio.h>
#include <stdlib.h>
#include <stdarg.h>
#include <graphics.h>
#include <string.h>
#include "mouse.i"

Mstatus    Position;
g_cursor   NewCursor;
int        Buttons, XIndex, YIndex, HotSpotX = 0,
           HotSpotY = 0, HotSpotSelect, Screen[16][16],
           Cursor[16][16];

int TPos( int TP, int Low, int High )
{
    return( ( TP >= Low ) && ( TP <= High ) );
}

void BoxItem( int x, int y, int w, int h, char* text )
{
    settextjustify( CENTER_TEXT, CENTER_TEXT );
    rectangle( x, y, x+w, y+h );
    outtextxy( x+(w/2), y+(h/2), text );
}

void FillSquare( int x1, int y1, int x2, int y2,
```

```
                  int FillStyle,  int Color )
{
   int  outline[10];

   outline[0] = outline[6] = outline[8] = x1;
   outline[2] = outline[4] = x2;
   outline[1] = outline[3] = outline[9] = y1;
   outline[5] = outline[7] = y2;
   setfillstyle( FillStyle, Color );
   fillpoly( 5, outline );
}

void EraseSquare( int x1, int y1, int x2, int y2 )
{
   FillSquare( x1, y1, x2, y2, EMPTY_FILL, 0 );
}

void Beep()
{
   sound( 220 ); delay( 100 ); nosound();
                 delay(  50 );
   sound( 440 ); delay( 100 ); nosound();
}

void MakeCursor()
{
   int    i, j;
   unsigned int TBit;

   NewCursor.xkey = HotSpotX;
   NewCursor.ykey = HotSpotY;
   for( i=0; i<=15; i++ )
   {
      NewCursor.ScreenMask[i] = 0x0000;
      NewCursor.CursorMask[i] = 0x0000;
      for( j=0; j<=15; j++ )
      {
         NewCursor.CursorMask[i] <<= 1;
         if( Cursor[j][i] ) NewCursor.CursorMask[i]++;
         NewCursor.ScreenMask[i] <<= 1;
         if( Screen[j][i] ) NewCursor.ScreenMask[i]++;
} } }
```

```
void UseNewCursor()
{
   MakeCursor();
   gmouse.Mshow( FALSE );
   gmouse.Set_Cursor( NewCursor );
   gmouse.Mshow( TRUE );
}

void PaintScreen( int X, int Y )
{
   int Color = WHITE;

   if ( ( X == HotSpotX ) && ( Y == HotSpotY ) )
      Color = LIGHTRED;
   gmouse.Mshow( FALSE );
   if( Screen[X][Y] )
      FillSquare( X*15+18, Y*15+33, X*15+27, Y*15+42,
                  SOLID_FILL, Color );
   else
   {
      EraseSquare( X*15+15, Y*15+30, X*15+30, Y*15+45 );
      FillSquare(  X*15+15, Y*15+30, X*15+30, Y*15+45,
                   CLOSE_DOT_FILL, Color );
   }
   gmouse.Mshow( TRUE );
   setcolor( WHITE );
}

void PaintCursor( int X, int Y )
{
   int Color = WHITE;

   if( ( X == HotSpotX ) && ( Y == HotSpotY ) )
      Color = LIGHTRED;
   gmouse.Mshow( FALSE );
   if( Cursor[X][Y] )
      FillSquare( (X+1) * 15 + 369, (Y+2) * 15,
                  (X+2) * 15 + 366, (Y+3) * 15 - 3,
                  SOLID_FILL, Color );
   else
      FillSquare( (X+1) * 15 + 369, (Y+2) * 15,
                  (X+2) * 15 + 369, (Y+3) * 15,
```

```
                    CLOSE_DOT_FILL, Color );
   gmouse.Mshow( TRUE );
   setcolor( WHITE );
}

void HotSpotComplete()
{
   PaintCursor( HotSpotX, HotSpotY );
   PaintScreen( HotSpotX, HotSpotY );
   gmouse.Mshow( FALSE );
   HotSpotSelect = FALSE;
   setcolor( WHITE );
   settextjustify( CENTER_TEXT, CENTER_TEXT );
   BoxItem( 265, 320, 110, 20, "Set Hotspot" );
   gmouse.Mshow( TRUE );
}

void SetHotSpot()
{
   int X, Y;

   X = HotSpotX;
   Y = HotSpotY;
   HotSpotX = -1;
   HotSpotY = -1;
   PaintCursor( X, Y );
   PaintScreen( X, Y );
   gmouse.Mshow( FALSE );
   HotSpotSelect = TRUE;
   setcolor( RED );
   settextjustify( CENTER_TEXT, CENTER_TEXT );
   BoxItem( 265, 320, 110, 20, "Set Hotspot" );
   setcolor( WHITE );
   gmouse.Mshow( TRUE );
}

void ScreenLayout()
{
   int i, j;

   settextjustify( CENTER_TEXT, CENTER_TEXT );
   outtextxy( 135, 20, "Screen Mask" );
```

```
        outtextxy( 504, 20, "Cursor Mask" );
        HotSpotComplete();
                       // screen mask items //
        BoxItem(  15, 280,  60, 20, "Clear" );
        BoxItem(  85, 280,  60, 20, "Invert" );
        BoxItem( 155, 280, 140, 20, "Make from Cursor" );
                       // cursor mask items //
        BoxItem( 564, 280,  60, 20, "Clear" );
        BoxItem( 494, 280,  60, 20, "Invert" );
        BoxItem( 344, 280, 140, 20, "Copy to Screen" );
                       // control options //
        BoxItem(  15, 320, 110, 20, "Use Pointer" );
        BoxItem( 140, 320, 110, 20, "Arrow Pointer" );
        BoxItem( 265, 320, 110, 20, "Set Hotspot" );
        BoxItem( 390, 320, 110, 20, "Save Pointer" );
        BoxItem( 515, 320, 110, 20, "Exit" );
        for( i=0; i<=15; i++ )
            for( j=0; j<=15; j++ )
            {
                Screen[i][j] = FALSE;
                PaintScreen( i, j );
                Cursor[i][j] = FALSE;
                PaintCursor( i, j );
    }        }

void ClearScreen()
{
    int  i, j;

    for( i=0; i<=15; i++ )
        for( j=0; j<=15; j++ )
            if( Screen[i][j] )
            {
                Screen[i][j] = FALSE;
                PaintScreen( i, j );
    }        }

void ClearCursor()
{
    int  i, j;

    for( i=0; i<=15; i++ )
```

```
        for( j=0;  j<=15;  j++ )
           if( Cursor[i][j] )
           {
              Cursor[i][j] = FALSE;
              PaintCursor( i, j );
}           }

void InvertScreen()
{
   int  i, j;

   for( i=0;  i<=15;  i++ )
      for( j=0;  j<=15;  j++ )
      {
         if( Screen[i][j] ) Screen[i][j] = FALSE;
                       else Screen[i][j] = TRUE;
         PaintScreen( i, j );
}      }

void InvertCursor()
{
   int i, j;

   for( i=0;  i<=15;  i++ )
      for( j=0;  j<=15;  j++ )
      {
         if( Cursor[i][j] ) Cursor[i][j] = FALSE;
                       else Cursor[i][j] = TRUE;
         PaintCursor( i, j );
}      }

void ScreenSet( int xaxis, int yaxis )
{
   int x, y;

   x = ( xaxis / 15 ) - 1;
   y = ( yaxis / 15 ) - 2;
   if( HotSpotSelect )
   {
      HotSpotX = x;
      HotSpotY = y;
      HotSpotComplete();
   }
```

```
      else
      {
         if( Screen[x][y] ) Screen[x][y] = FALSE;
                      else Screen[x][y] = TRUE;
         PaintScreen( x, y );
}   }

void CursorSet( int xaxis, int yaxis )
{
   int x, y;

   x = ( xaxis - 384 ) / 15;
   y = ( yaxis / 15 ) - 2;
   if( HotSpotSelect )
   {
      HotSpotX = x;
      HotSpotY = y;
      HotSpotComplete();
   }
   else
   {
      if( Cursor[x][y] ) Cursor[x][y] = FALSE;
                   else Cursor[x][y] = TRUE;
      PaintCursor( x, y );
}   }

void CursorToScreen()
{
   int i, j;

   for( i=0; i<=15; i++ )
      for( j=0; j<=15; j++ )
      {
         Screen[i][j] = Cursor[i][j];
         PaintScreen( i, j );
}      }

void ScreenFromCursor()
{
   int i, j, x, y, Test;

   for( i=0; i<=15; i++ )
      for( j=0; j<=15; j++ )
```

```
            {
                Test = TRUE;
                for( x=-1; x<=1; x++ )
                    for( y =-1; y<=1; y++ )
                        if( ( TPos( i+x, 0, 15 ) ) &&
                              ( TPos( j+y, 0, 15 ) ) &&
                              ( Cursor[i+x][j+y] ) ) Test = FALSE;
                Screen[i][j] = Test;
                PaintScreen( i, j );
}        }

int SavePointer()
{
    int  i, Done = FALSE;
    char Ch, CursorName[8]="", FileName[12]="";
    FILE *CF;

    strcpy( CursorName, "........" );
    setviewport( 269, 0, 369, 42, TRUE );
    settextjustify( CENTER_TEXT, CENTER_TEXT );
    gmouse.Set_Cursor( IBEAM );
    gmouse.Mmoveto( 277, 30 );
    i = 0;
    do
    {
        gmouse.Mshow( FALSE );
        clearviewport();
        setcolor( LIGHTRED );
        rectangle( 0, 0, 100, 40 );
        outtextxy( 50, 10, "Save As" );
        outtextxy( 50, 20, "File Name?" );
        outtextxy( 50, 30, CursorName);
        gmouse.Mmoveto( 277+i*8,30 );
        gmouse.Mshow( TRUE );
        Ch = getch();
        if( Ch == 0x0D ) Done = TRUE;
        else if( ( Ch == 0x08 ) && ( i > 1 ) ) i-=2;
        else if( i > 7 ) { Beep(); i--; }
        else CursorName[i] = Ch;
        i++;
    }
```

```
while( !Done );
gmouse.Set_Cursor( ARROW );
gmouse.Mshow( FALSE );
clearviewport();
setviewport( 0, 0, getmaxx(), getmaxy(), TRUE );
gmouse.Mshow( TRUE );
for( i=7; i>=0; i- )
{
    if( CursorName[i] == '.' ) CursorName[i] = '\0';
    if( CursorName[i] == ' ' ) CursorName[i] = '\0';
}
if( strlen( CursorName ) == 0 ) { Beep(); return(0); }
MakeCursor();
strcpy( FileName, CursorName );
strcat( FileName, ".CUR" );
outtextxy( 320, 10, FileName );
CF = fopen( FileName, "w" );
fprintf( CF, "static  g_cursor %s = \n", CursorName );
fprintf( CF,
    "            { 0x%04X, 0x%04X, 0x%04X, 0x%04X,\n",
    NewCursor.ScreenMask[0], NewCursor.ScreenMask[1],
    NewCursor.ScreenMask[2], NewCursor.ScreenMask[3] );
for( i=1; i<=3; i++ )
    fprintf( CF,
        "              0x%04X, 0x%04X, 0x%04X, 0x%04X,\n",
        NewCursor.ScreenMask[i*4],
        NewCursor.ScreenMask[i*4+1],
        NewCursor.ScreenMask[i*4+2],
        NewCursor.ScreenMask[i*4+3] );
for( i=0; i<=3; i++ )
    fprintf( CF,
        "              0x%04X, 0x%04X, 0x%04X, 0x%04X,\n",
        NewCursor.CursorMask[i*4],
        NewCursor.CursorMask[i*4+1],
        NewCursor.CursorMask[i*4+2],
        NewCursor.CursorMask[i*4+3] );
fprintf( CF, "              0x%04X, 0x%04X };\n",
        NewCursor.xkey,  NewCursor.ykey );
fprintf( CF, "\n" );
fclose( CF );
```

```
        return( 1 );
}

main()
{
    int GDriver = DETECT, GMode, GError,
        Exit = FALSE, i, j;
    Mresult* Result;

    initgraph( &GDriver, &GMode, "C:\\TC\\BGI" );
    GError = graphresult();
    if( GError != grOk )
    {
        printf( "Graphics error: %s\n",
                grapherrormsg(GError) );
        printf( "Program aborted...\n" );
        exit(1);
    }
    cleardevice();
    ScreenLayout();
    Result = gmouse.Mreset();
    setwritemode( COPY_PUT );
    if( Result->present )
    {
        do
        {
            Position = gmouse.Mpressed( ButtonL );
            if( Position.button_count )
            {
                if( TPos( Position.yaxis, 30, 270 ) )
                {                       // screen or cursor grids //
                    if( TPos( Position.xaxis,  15, 255 ) )
                        ScreenSet( Position.xaxis,
                                   Position.yaxis );
                    if( TPos( Position.xaxis, 384, 624 ) )
                        CursorSet( Position.xaxis,
                                   Position.yaxis );
                } else
                if( TPos( Position.yaxis, 280, 300 ) )
                                    // screen or cursor commands //
                                           // screen mask items //
                {
```

```
            if( TPos( Position.xaxis,  15,  75 ) )
               ClearScreen(); else
            if( TPos( Position.xaxis,  85, 145 ) )
               InvertScreen(); else
            if( TPos( Position.xaxis, 155, 295 ) )
               ScreenFromCursor(); else
                                          // cursor mask items //
            if( TPos( Position.xaxis, 364, 484 ) )
               CursorToScreen(); else
            if( TPos( Position.xaxis, 494, 554 ) )
               InvertCursor(); else
            if( TPos( Position.xaxis, 564, 624 ) )
               ClearCursor();
         } else
         if( TPos( Position.yaxis, 320, 340 ) )
         {                            // general command options //
            if( TPos( Position.xaxis,  15, 125 ) )
               UseNewCursor(); else
            if( TPos( Position.xaxis, 140, 250 ) )
               gmouse.Set_Cursor( ARROW ); else
            if( TPos( Position.xaxis, 265, 375 ) )
               SetHotSpot(); else
            if( TPos( Position.xaxis, 390, 500 ) )
               SavePointer(); else
            if( TPos( Position.xaxis, 515, 625 ) )
               Exit = TRUE;
      } } }
      while( !Exit );
   }
   tmouse.Mreset();
   tmouse.Set_Cursor( HARDWARE, 11, 12 );
   Beep();
}
```

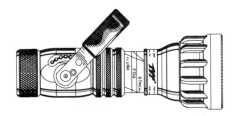

Chapter 17

Buttons, Scrollbars, and Control Objects

A natural consequence of graphics programming and a graphics mouse is to provide your applications with graphics controls.

As a first step in this direction, in Chapter 16, the GraphicMouse object was demonstrated by the MOUSEPTR utility in which a number of screen controls were mouse-operated. Each of these control buttons, however, required specific code to create the button image, to write a label to each button box, and to test the mouse coordinates each time a button was pressed to decide which control had been selected.

Any changes in the layout of the screen could only be accomplished by changing every program element that applied to each control element changed. In brief, both creating the program and revising the program entailed laborious attention to detail as well as presenting considerable opportunity for error. Of course, when any opportunity for error exists, the guiding principles of the universe become actively engaged to ensure that such an error will occur.

There are also ways of reducing the probabilities of error without giving up graphics controls. Since the amount of work required to create these controls can also be reduced or eliminated by creating graphic control objects instead of individual graphic controls, suddenly graphics controls become even more convenient than conventional application controls.

Graphic Control Objects

The object-oriented programming extensions provided by Turbo C++ offer a variety of conveniences for the programmer. One area where the conveniences are most impressive (if only in the visual sense) is in creating graphic control objects.

For graphics applications, a control object has to fill five major criteria and should be able to:

- create and maintain its own screen display
- change size and position if required
- change appearance as appropriate to its function (buttons, for example, change visual state to indicate a mouse hit or selection state)
- respond to a mouse event directly or indirectly (the minimum requirement is that an object must be able to test the mouse event coordinates against its own position and size and report a hit when it occurs)
- erase itself from the screen and, if required, remove itself from memory

Other tasks and capabilities will also be assigned to graphic control objects, but these five are the absolute minimums that will be demanded of any graphics control. These are also the tasks which, in conventional programming, are the hardest to accomplish and require the major portion of the programmer's time (both in developing an application and subsequently in revising and debugging the program).

With a graphic control object, however, only one instance of a specific object type requires the programmer's attention—the first one created. Once the first instance of an object has been created and debugged, any number of clones of the object can be created—with differences, duplications, and variations as required—but without each instance requiring repetitive debugging and problem solving.

Creating a new object type descended from a working object requires much less time and work than writing a new feature using conventional programming since much of the task is inherited from the ancestor object and does not require laborious repetition. It also avoids the probability of additional errors.

If any additional inducement is required once a graphic control object unit has been created, the graphic controls can be used simply as if these were extensions to Turbo Pascal (which, in effect, they are).

Creating Graphic Control Objects

The graphic control unit (GCONTROL.TPU) will provide four object types though only three of these are actually control objects: Button, Radiobutton, and ScrollBar. The fourth object type, VueMeter, is a graphics analog of an older tuning or metering device popular in electronics applications before the days of digital displays.

Before discussing the graphics control objects, however, the GControl unit uses three other units: Crt, Graph, and Mouse. The first two are standard units supplied by Turbo Pascal, while the third unit, Mouse.TPU supplies the various mouse object types.

An ancestor object type, Point, provides the primal ancestor for the other object types.

The Point Object Type

The Point object is provided as a generic ancestor for all graphic objects, supplying the basic position and color variables, a reference variable for restoring viewport settings, and a variety of methods that will be needed by most descendant object types. (The Point object type is neither illustrated nor demonstrated.)

```
class Point
{
   protected:
      int    x, y, Color;
      viewporttype VRef;
   public:
      Point();
      void Move( int PtX, int PtY );
      virtual void Draw();
      void Create( int PtX, int PtY, int C );
      void RestoreViewport();
      void SetColor( int C );
      virtual void SetLoc( int PtX, int PtY );
      virtual void Erase();
      int  GetColor();
      int  GetX();
      int  GetY();
};
```

The real reason for Point appearing as a separate type, Point's data elements declared as protected, and Point's methods as public is so the Point variables and methods can be used. They can be used not only by the current object types but also by other descendant object types that may be created by calling on GCONTROL.OBJ without necessarily having the source code for the unit.

If you are not familiar with how descendant object types are created, a more complete explanation is provided in Turbo C++ Programming: An Object-Oriented Approach, also available from Addison-Wesley Publishing Company.

Point::Point()

The Point object type is supplied with a variety of basic methods, beginning with the constructor method, Point::Point, which is used to initialize a Point object instance. Each descendant object type will have its own, different initialization procedure providing the handling required by each.

```
Point::Point()
{
    getviewsettings( &VRef );
}
```

In this case, the Point method does nothing except to save the viewport settings that are in effect at the time the object is created.

Point::Create()

The Create method for the Point object is called with three parameters, the first two specifying screen location and the third setting the color. It concludes by calling the Draw method.

```
void Point::Create( int PtX, int PtY, int C )
{
    SetLoc( PtX, PtY );
    Color = C;
    Draw();
}
```

Point::Move()

The Move method accepts only two coordinate parameters and moves an existing object from its present location by calling the Erase method, changing the position coordinates by calling SetLoc, and then calling the Draw method to recreate the object at its new location.

```
void Point::Move( int PtX, int PtY )
{
    Erase();
    SetLoc( PtX, PtY );
    Draw();
}
```

Point::Draw()

The Draw method requires no parameters and simply draws the object on the screen using the object instance's position and color parameters. Normally the Draw method would only be called by other object methods. It might be called directly by an application if, for example, some other process had overwritten the object image and it was necessary to restore the screen image.

```
void Point::Draw()
{
    putpixel( x, y, Color );
}
```

Point::RestoreViewPort()

Many, if not all, graphic objects will use Turbo C++'s setviewport procedure to establish local viewport settings during various screen operation. The object types created here, before establishing their own viewport settings, save the viewport parameters that existed when the object was first created and, when their tasks are completed, call the RestoreViewPort method to reset the original viewport parameters stored in *VRef*.

```
void Point::RestoreViewport()
{
    setviewport( VRef.left,   VRef.top,
                 VRef.right, VRef.bottom, VRef.clip );
}
```

Point::SetColor()

The SetColor method provides a means of changing the color of an instance of Point by reassigning the Color parameter and then calling the Draw method.

```
void Point::SetColor( int C )
{
    Color = C;
    Draw();
}
```

Point::SetLoc()

The SetLoc method simply changes the location coordinates of an object and will be inherited by all descendant object types.

```
void Point::SetLoc( int PtX, int PtY )
{
    x = PtX + VRef.left;
    y = PtY + VRef.top;
}
```

As defined, the SetLoc method does nothing except to set the location coordinates as an offset relative to the viewport origin. It is called by the Create and Move methods both of Point and of all descendants including the ScrollBar object class which redefines this method but explicitly calls the Point ancestor method as well.

Point::Erase()

The Erase method uses a local integer to save the current instance's Color value, then changes the color to the background color before calling the Draw method to erase the screen image and, finally, resets the Color variable to the saved value.

```
void Point::Erase()
{
    int Temp;

    Temp = Color;
    Color = getbkcolor();
    Draw();
    Color = Temp;
}
```

Three function methods, GetColor, GetX, and GetY return object instance values to the calling application.

```
int  Point::GetColor()    {  return( Color );    }
```

```
int  Point::GetX()  {  return( x + VRef.left );  }

int  Point::GetY()  {  return( y + VRef.top );  }
```

In the case of the latter two functions, the object instance values are corrected for the viewport settings to return the same values that were the original parameters, or their effective equivalents if the object's position has changed since it was created. In effect, the coordinate system under which an object is created remains valid for all method calls to the object—a provision that makes the object independent of any viewport changes and greatly simplifies the object's operations.

As mentioned, the Point object type is not really intended for direct use by an application, particularly since each object consists of one screen pixel but requires several bytes for its definition. As a means of manipulating single pixels, this is simply not efficient (but it is an effective ancestor type for more complicated objects).

Mouse Access

Because two static instances of mouse objects, gmouse which is graphic and tmouse which is a text version, have been declared in the MOUSE.I file, the graphic objects defined here are able to interact autonomously with the mouse instead of relying on the application to supply mouse event and position information.

The *tmouse* instance is supplied, of course, so that the mouse can be reset to text mode operation before the program exits (see CTRLTEST.CPP for an example).

The Button Object Type

The Button object type is the basic graphic control object and provides the screen analog of a physical button. An instance of button may have any of three button styles (see Figure 17-1) that are defined as:

```
ButtonType = ( Rounded, Square, ThreeD );
```

The Button object is a direct descendant of the Point object type and, therefore, inherits the position, color, and viewport setting variables as well as Point's methods. Button adds several new variables:

```
Exist, State, Rotate : boolean;
DblClkTime, FontSize, TypeFace, SizeX, SizeY : integer;
ThisButton : ButtonType;
BtnTxt : STR40;
```

Figure 17-1: Three Button Object Styles

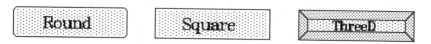

ThisButton, of course, describes the button's style and the *SizeX* and *SizeY* variables are also obvious while the *BtnTxt* variable is the label string displayed on the button.

The Boolean *State* determines whether the button is selected or not and offers visual feedback in the form of a color inversion. The *Exist* and *Rotate* flags are primarily internal and will be discussed later. Likewise, *FontSize* is usually set by the object itself while *TypeFace* is the screen font style used to label the button.

The variable *DblClkTime* is a sampling delay for a mouse double-click selection.

Button Methods

The Button object type defines nearly two dozen methods in addition to the methods inherited from the Point object type.

If this sounds like a great deal of fuss for a simple button object, remember that simply because methods are defined does not mean that you are forced to use all of them. Also, Turbo C++'s smart linking only includes procedures in the compiled .EXE that are actually used. Simply because methods are provided in the object unit does not mean they will be included as fact in the .EXE program. In this case, this plethora of methods is defined simply to provide complete access to all of Button's characteristics and capabilities. They're there but you don't have to use them! Unless, of course, you need them—in which case, their absence would be the irritation and not their presence.

Button::Button()

The first method, as always, is the constructor method, Button::Button, which is essential for dynamic object instances.

```
Button::Button()
{
    Rotate = FALSE;
    SetTypeSize( 2 );
    SetTypeFace( TRIPLEX_FONT );
}
```

In this case, the constructor has not been overloaded to supply two versions. Here only the default constructor method has been defined and it initializes the button orientation, typesize, and font, but does not draw the actual button. If desired, an overloaded constructor could be defined as:

```
Button::Button( int PtX, int PtY, int Width,
                int Height, int C, char* Text )
{
    SetTypeSize( 2 );
    SetTypeFace( TRIPLEX_FONT );
    Create( int PtX, int PtY, int Width,
            int Height, int C, char* Text )
}
```

Button::Create()

To finish the task of initializing a Button instance, the Button::Create method is provided.

```
void Button::Create( int PtX, int PtY, int Width,
                     int Height, int C, char* Text )
{
    getviewsettings( &VRef );
    setviewport( 0, 0, getmaxx(), getmaxy(), TRUE );
    settextjustify( CENTER_TEXT, CENTER_TEXT );
    SetLoc( PtX, PtY );
```

The Create method begins by calling several other Button methods to assign the various parameters. At the same time, some conditions are set by default, such as the text justification settings and the *Width* and *Height* are given minimum default values.

```
if( Width < 20 ) SizeX = 20;       else SizeX = Width;
if( Height < 20 ) SizeY = 20;      else SizeY = Height;
if( SizeY > SizeX ) Rotate = TRUE; else Rotate = FALSE;
```

The *Rotate* flag is determined by relationship between the horizontal and vertical button sizes. If the button is taller than it is wide, then *Rotate* is set so that the button label will be written vertically, not horizontally.

Last, the button *Color* is set, *State* is initialized as FALSE, the text label is set and, finally, the button itself is written to the screen by calling the Draw method.

```
    Color  = C;
    State  = FALSE;
    strcpy( BtnTxt, Text );
    Draw();
}
```

Button::~Button()

The next Button method is the destructor method. With static instances of Button, the destructor method is essentially redundant because the Erase method can be called directly to delete an object's screen image. However, when dynamic objects are used, a destructor method is vital to permit disposal of memory when the object is no longer needed.

```
Button::~Button()
{
    Erase();
}
```

But the destructor method is also explicitly defined with an instruction to call the Erase method so that when an object instance is terminated by scope, its image will also be removed from the screen.

Button::Draw()

The Draw method creates the object's screen image. Since the Button object can have three different styles as well as varying sizes and label orientations, the Draw method is moderately complex and also tracks several preexisting conditions, such as color and viewport settings, so that these can be restored to their previous settings when the image is completed.

```
void Button::Draw()
{
    int     i, radius = 6, offset = 3, AlignX, AlignY;
    Outline RectArr;
```

Before anything is drawn, the graphic mouse interface object is called to turn off the mouse cursor, regardless of where the cursor may be on the screen, so that the mouse cursor does not interfere with the new screen image.

```
    gmouse.Mshow( FALSE );
```

Next, a new viewport is created to limit drawing operations to the image area required for the button. It sets the text justification and drawing color.

```
setviewport( x, y, x+SizeX, y+SizeY, TRUE );
settextjustify( CENTER_TEXT, CENTER_TEXT );
setcolor( Color );
```

For the Square button style, drawing the button image is quite simple and requires only calling the rectangle function.

```
switch( ThisButton )
{
   case SQUARE:
   { rectangle( 0,  0,  SizeX, SizeY );
      break;                                    }
```

The button instance label will be added later.

For the THREE_D button style, the drawing operations are slightly more complicated, requiring an outer rectangle, shading, an inner rectangle and, finally, four lines to complete the 3-D image.

```
   case THREE_D:                            // ThreeD Outline //
   { rectangle( 0, 0, SizeX, SizeY );
      RectArr[0] = RectArr[2] = RectArr[8] =
      RectArr[1] = RectArr[7] = RectArr[9] = 1;
      RectArr[4] = RectArr[6] = SizeX-1;
      RectArr[3] = RectArr[5] = SizeY-1;
      setfillstyle( CLOSE_DOT_FILL, Color );
      setlinestyle( USERBIT_LINE, 0, NORM_WIDTH );
      fillpoly( 5, RectArr );
      setlinestyle( SOLID_LINE, 0, NORM_WIDTH );
      rectangle( 2*radius, 2*radius, SizeX-2*radius,
                 SizeY-2*radius );
      line( 0, 0, 2*radius, 2*radius );
      line( 0, SizeY, 2*radius, SizeY-2*radius );
      line( SizeX, 0, SizeX-2*radius, 2*radius );
      line( SizeX, SizeY, SizeX-2*radius,
            SizeY-2*radius );
      break;
   }
```

The default case, Rounded, is the most complex of all because the button outline is built up from four partial arcs for the corners and then four lines to complete the sides.

```
case ROUNDED:
{                                           // draw corners //
   arc( SizeX-radius, radius, 0, 90, radius );
   arc( radius, radius, 90, 180, radius );
   arc( radius, SizeY-radius, 180, 270, radius );
   arc( SizeX-radius, SizeY-radius, 270, 360, radius );
                                            // draw sides   //
   line( radius, 0, SizeX-radius, 0 );
   line( radius, SizeY, SizeX-radius, SizeY );
   line( 0, radius, 0, SizeY-radius );
   line( SizeX, radius, SizeX, SizeY-radius );
} }
```

Next, a separate case statement is used to fill RectArr with the coordinates for the center of each button style.

```
switch( ThisButton )                        // fill button  //
{   case SQUARE:
   case ROUNDED:
   {  RectArr[0] = RectArr[2] = RectArr[8] =
      RectArr[1] = RectArr[7] = RectArr[9] = offset;
      RectArr[4] = RectArr[6] = SizeX-offset;
      RectArr[3] = RectArr[5] = SizeY-offset;      break;
   }
   case THREE_D:
   {  RectArr[0] = RectArr[2] = RectArr[8] =
      RectArr[1] = RectArr[7] = RectArr[9] = 2*radius+1;
      RectArr[4] = RectArr[6] = SizeX-2*radius-1;
      RectArr[3] = RectArr[5] = SizeY-2*radius-1;
} }
```

Then the actual fill is executed according to the button *State*, using the fillpoly procedure with a blank line style to outline the filled area.

```
if( State ) setfillstyle( SOLID_FILL, Color );
        else setfillstyle( CLOSE_DOT_FILL, Color );
setlinestyle( USERBIT_LINE, 0, NORM_WIDTH );
fillpoly( 5, RectArr );
```

```
setlinestyle( SOLID_LINE, 0, NORM_WIDTH );
                            // adjust fonts and string to fit //
```

After the button image is completed, the button's label still needs to be drawn but, before drawing the text string, the text direction (*TextDir*) has to be determined.

```
settextstyle( TypeFace, Rotate, FontSize );
AlignX = (SizeX/2)-3;
AlignY = (SizeY/2)-3;
```

Finally, if the button *State* is set, then the label needs to be drawn in the background color instead of the button color.

```
if( State ) setcolor( getbkcolor() );
outtextxy( AlignX, AlignY, BtnTxt );
if( State ) setcolor( Color );
RestoreViewport();
gmouse.Mshow( TRUE );
}
```

The remainder of the process is simply housekeeping, restoring the original viewport settings, making the mouse cursor visible again, and restoring the original drawing color.

Button::Erase()

The Erase method doesn't bother with the Draw method but simply resets the viewport before using the ClearViewPort command to erase the screen image. Please note, the mouse cursor is still turned off before the screen is cleared and turned on afterwards.

```
void Button::Erase()
{
   gmouse.Mshow( FALSE );
   setviewport( x, y, x+SizeX, y+SizeY, TRUE );
   clearviewport();
   RestoreViewport();
   gmouse.Mshow( TRUE );
}
```

Button::ButtonHit()

The ButtonHit method is central to all graphic control objects and returns an integer (Boolean) result to the calling application, confirming button selection by a mouse hit.

```
int Button::ButtonHit()
{
   Mstatus  P = gmouse.Mpressed( ButtonL );
```

A couple of different approaches are possible in creating the ButtonHit method. One option is to pass mouse coordinates to the ButtonHit method but this should be rejected because it is unnecessarily awkward.

Instead, when the ButtonHit method is asked for a check, ButtonHit itself calls gmouse to request mouse button status and coordinates.

Four Boolean tests are AND'd to satisfy an *if* conditional to determine if this is a valid hit event.

```
if( ( P.xaxis >= x ) && ( P.xaxis <= x+SizeX ) &&
    ( P.yaxis >= y ) && ( P.yaxis <= y+SizeY ) )
```

If this is a hit, then the Invert method is called to change the screen image before reporting the results back to the calling application.

```
   {
      Invert();
      return( TRUE );
   }
   return( FALSE );
}
```

Of course, if a hit has not occurred, a FALSE result is returned by default.

The remaining methods provided for the Button object, are largely self-explanatory and will not be discussed in any detail here.

The RadioButton Object Type

The RadioButton object type is a circular button and is often used in groups where only one button from a set may be selected at any time. However, provisions for canceling set RadioButtons when a new button is selected are not included in the object type itself but must be handled by the application. A selection of RadioButton objects appear in Figure 17-2.

The RadioButton object type, as a descendant of the Button object type, inherits a variety of variables though not all of these, nor all of the inherited methods, will be used by nor are applicable to the RadioButton type.

Instead, the RadioButton adds two new integer variables, *Outline*, which will be the outline color for this button type, and *Radius* which is the size of the button.

RadioButton::RadioButton()

RadioButton is provided with an overloaded constructor method for both default and parameter initializers in the same fashion as the Button object type.

```
RadioButton::RadioButton() {  }

RadioButton::RadioButton( int PtX, int PtY,
                          int C, int R, char* Text )
{
   Create( PtX, PtY, C, R, Text );
}
```

The second constructor method simply calls the Create method to pass along the parameter list but is assigned no explicit tasks of its own.

RadioButton::~RadioButton()

Again for the reasons cited for the Button object, the destructor method is supplied with an instruction to call the Erase method before the object instance is terminated.

```
RadioButton::~RadioButton() {  Erase();  }
```

RadioButton::Create()

The RadioButton Create method is called with location parameters, button color and radius, and a text string that is nominally limited to 10 characters length.

```
void RadioButton::Create( int PtX, int PtY,
                          int C, int R, char* Text )
{
   getviewsettings( &VRef );
   settextjustify( CENTER_TEXT, CENTER_TEXT );
   SetLoc( PtX, PtY );
   Radius = R;
```

After preserving the viewport settings and initiating the position and radius variables, Init assigns the outline color by ORing the color parameter with 08h so that the outline color always has the intensity bit set. If you are using a variant color palette, this provision may need to be altered.

```
Outline = C | 0x08;
Color = C;
State = FALSE;
strcpy( BtnTxt, Text );
Draw();
}
```

The *Color*, *State*, *Exist*, and *BtnTxt* variables are set before calling the Draw method.

RadioButton::Draw()

The Draw method is redefined because, obviously, the RadioButton object requires a different set of drawing instructions to create a different shape. Also, with RadioButton, the *x,y* coordinates are center coordinates for the button image instead of corner coordinates for a rectangular button.

```
void RadioButton::Draw()
{
    int XAsp, YAsp, i, OldColor = getcolor();

    RestoreViewport();
    getaspectratio( &XAsp, &YAsp );
    setcolor( Outline );
    gmouse.Mshow( FALSE );
```

The current color and viewport settings are preserved and the mouse pointer hidden before the object's image is drawn. Then the appropriate fill style is selected together with the proper color to show the RadioButton instance's *State*.

```
    if( State ) setfillstyle( SOLID_FILL, Color );
    else        setfillstyle( INTERLEAVE_FILL, Color );
    fillellipse( x, y, Radius,
                 Radius * (double) ( XAsp / YAsp ) );
```

When the fillellipse function is called to draw the button image, with corrections for the screen aspect ratio, the button outline is drawn using the *Outline* color and filled with pattern and button color.

Instances of the RadioButton object type are too small to contain a text label so the *BtnTxt* label is written, centered, below the button image before the mouse pointer and the original drawing colors are restored.

```
    settextstyle( DEFAULT_FONT, HORIZ_DIR, 1 );
    outtextxy( x, y + Radius + 10, BtnTxt );
    gmouse.Mshow( TRUE );
    setcolor( OldColor );
}
```

RadioButton::Erase()

For the Button object type, the Erase method used the viewport settings and ClearViewport to erase the button image. This could be used for the RadioButton as well but is not, in this case, the most practical means because the button label may be omitted in order to space button closely or may be included with wider spacing. Therefore, to erase a RadioButton, the Erase method operates in a different fashion, changing both *Color* and *Outline* to the background drawing color and then calling the Draw method to cancel the screen image.

```
void RadioButton::Erase()
{
    int OldColor = Color;

    Color = getbkcolor();
    Outline = Color;
    Draw();
    Color = OldColor;
    Outline = OldColor | 0x08;
}
```

After Draw is finished, the original color values are restored so the RadioButton can be recreated at a new location if necessary.

RadioButton::ButtonHit()

The ButtonHit method for the RadioButton object type is also different.

```
int  RadioButton::ButtonHit()
{
    int  OffX, OffY;

    Mstatus  P = gmouse.Mpressed( ButtonL );
    OffX = abs( P.xaxis - x );
    OffY = abs( P.yaxis - y );
```

In this case, the mouse coordinates are converted to an offset from the RadioButton's center position—an offset that is calculated as an absolute distance instead of a signed value.

Comparing the offset distance as a hypotenuse length against the button radius has a tendency (when the values are large because the mouse is not close to the button) to create a floating point error. Therefore, two offset tests are made to decide first if the mouse event is close to the button tested.

```
if( ( OffX < 2 * Radius ) && ( OffY < 2 * Radius ) )
```

If the mouse event is at least in the immediate vicinity of the button, then a test is made to decide if the button was actually hit.

```
    if( hypot( OffX, OffY ) < Radius )
    {
        Invert();
        return( TRUE );
    }
    return( FALSE );
}
```

If a hit did occur, then the button's state is set TRUE and the results reported to the calling application.

With RadioButton controls, buttons cannot be deselected with a mouse hit. Instead, any other button which as been selected is turned off, using the inherited SetState method, only when a new button is turned on—just like the station selector on your car radio. However, since the object class does not know how many instances of RadioButton exist, it's up to the application to take care of turning off the radio buttons as demonstrated in CTRLTEST.CPP.

The two additional RadioButton methods, SetRadius and GetRadius, should be self-explanatory.

The ScrollBar Object Type

The third control object type provided by the GControl unit is the ScrollBar object which is probably also the most familiar graphics control device of all since this is used, in one form or another, by virtually every graphics application which requires a display extending beyond the physical limits of a single screen.

In this example, the scrollbars have square end pads and a square thumbpad that can be mouse manipulated to control the position parameters of the calling application. In other implementations, the thumbpad might be variable in width to show not only a position within a range but to also show what portion of the total range was shown by the current display. This latter embellishment, however, is left as an exercise for the readers who are invited to create their own scrollbars with whatever revisions and features appeal to their applications. Two scrollbars, horizontal and vertical, appear in Figure 17-2 on page 399.

For the present, a new enumerated type is declared for use with scrollbars: HitType.

```
typedef enum { NO_HIT, RIGHT, UP, HBAR,
               VBAR, LEFT, DOWN } HitType;
```

The ScrollBar object type is declared as a descendant of Button, inheriting all the object variables and methods declared by its ancestors, Point and Button, but again, declaring several new variables.

```
class ScrollBar : public Button
{
    private:
        int  LineColor, SPos, Step, ScrollMove;
```

The *ScrollMove* variable determines the orientation, vertical or horizontal, of each ScrollBar instance. The *LineColor* variable is the drawing color for the object image, *SPos* is the position of the thumbpad within the scrollbar and *Step* is an incremental value for the thumbpad movement.

ScrollBar::ScrollBar()

The ScrollBar object class is provided with an overloaded constructor method but, this time, the default constructor method does accomplish something beyond simply initializing the object instance.

```
ScrollBar::ScrollBar()
{
    x = y = SizeX = SizeY = Color =
    LineColor = SPos = Step = ScrollMove = 0;
}
```

If ScrollBar is initialized without parameters, all of the variable elements are set to zero as a precaution. Or, if a parameter list is supplied, then the Create method is called.

```
ScrollBar::ScrollBar( int PtX, int PtY, int Size,
                      int C1, int C2, int Orientation )
```

```
{
    Create( PtX, PtY, Size, C1, C2, Orientation );
}
```

ScrollBar::Create()

This Create method is similar to previous examples and creates a ScrollBar instance with a specified location—*PtX* and *PtY*, length (*Size*), outline, and image colors (*C1* and *C2*), and *Orientation*.

```
void ScrollBar::Create( int PtX, int PtY, int Size,
                        int C1, int C2, int Orientation )
{
    getviewsettings( &VRef );
    if( Size < 100 ) Size = 100;
```

In this case, the width will be set arbitrarily as 20 pixels and a minimum length (*Size*) of 100 pixels.

The initial thumbpad position is at either the left or the top of the scrollbar (depending on the orientation) and is offset from the physical end by 21 pixels (the bar width) to leave room for the endpad.

```
    ScrollMove = Orientation;
    SPos = 21;
    Step = Size / 100;
```

The value for Step will be initialized as 100 units over the full scrollbar length, providing 100-step adjustment. The length of the scrollbar, however, is not fixed at this point because it will be adjusted, if necessary, to fit within the viewport. This is also an area where very short scrollbars might require revisions in the algorithm but, for the present, the simpler if less adaptable algorithm is used.

SizeX and *SizeY* are adjusted according to the horizontal or vertical orientation and the inherited *PtX* and *PtY* variables are adjusted, if necessary, to provide space for the final scrollbar size.

```
    switch( ScrollMove )
    {
      case VERT_DIR:
      {
        SizeX = 20;
        SizeY = Size;
        while( PtX + SizeX > VRef.right ) PtX- -;
```

```
        break;
    }
    case HORIZ_DIR:
    {
        SizeX = Size;
        SizeY = 20;
        while( PtY + SizeY > VRef.bottom ) PtY- -;
    }  }
```

Notice that the *Step* size is not adjusted further even if the scrollbar length has changed—a factor which you might wish to revise if your application has different requirements. Be sure that you have a minimum *Step* of one pixel or it may be very hard to move.

```
    SetLoc( PtX, PtY );
    LineColor = C1;
    Color = C2;
    Draw();
}
```

Create ends by calling the Draw method.

ScrollBar::Draw()

This version of the Draw method calls several other methods which are private to ScrollBar, beginning with SetOutline to create the scrollbar outline as a solid bar, then erasing the center of the bar.

```
void ScrollBar::Draw()
{
    int  OldColor = getcolor();

    SetOutline();
```

Next, arrows are drawn at the ends of the bar and, last, the thumbpad is created.

```
    SetArrows();
    SetThumbPad();
    setcolor( OldColor );
}
```

The actual processes involved in drawing the scrollbar image are quite conventional and may be seen in the program listing.

ScrollBar::ScrollHit()

The Boolean ButtonHit method used previously is hardly sufficient for use with a ScrollBar object because the application may need to know where a mouse hit occurred in order to respond appropriately. Therefore, the a ScrollHit method returns a HitType reporting whether the mouse hit occurred at one of the endpads (and which), at the thumbpad, or somewhere along the scrollbar.

```
HitType ScrollBar::ScrollHit()
{
   HitType   Result = NO_HIT;
   int       NPos = 0;

   Mstatus   P = gmouse.Mpressed( ButtonL );
```

Like the previous control objects, the ScrollHit method queries the mouse directly for the mouse button status and mouse cursor position, using a series of Boolean tests to determine where the mouse hit occurred.

```
switch( ScrollMove )
{
   case VERT_DIR:
      if( ( P.xaxis >= x ) && ( P.xaxis <= x+20 ) &&
          ( P.yaxis >= y ) )
         if( P.yaxis <= y+20 )         Result = UP;
         else
         if( P.yaxis <= y+SizeY-31 ) Result = VBAR;
         else
         if( P.yaxis <= y+SizeY )      Result = DOWN;
         break;
   case HORIZ_DIR:
      if( ( P.yaxis >= y ) && ( P.yaxis <= y+20 ) &&
          ( P.xaxis >= x ) )
         if( P.xaxis <= x+20 )         Result = LEFT;
         else
         if( P.xaxis <= x+SizeX-31 ) Result = HBAR;
         else
         if( P.xaxis <= x+SizeX )      Result = RIGHT;
}
```

After the hit test is completed, if a valid hit has occurred, the thumbpad position is updated according to the hit type. Of course, if no hit has occurred, this is reported immediately.

```
if( Result == NO_HIT ) return( Result );
switch( Result )
{
    case   LEFT:
    case     UP: NPos = SPos-Step;                  break;
    case  RIGHT:
    case   DOWN: NPos = SPos+Step;                  break;
    case   HBAR: NPos = P.xaxis - ( x + 10 );  break;
    case   VBAR: NPos = P.yaxis - ( y + 10 );
}
```

Two precautionary tests are executed to ensure that the updated position remains valid.

```
if( NPos < 21 ) NPos = 21;
switch( Result )
{
    case   LEFT:
    case  RIGHT: if( NPos > SizeX-41 ) NPos = SizeX-41;
                 break;
    case     UP:
    case   DOWN: if( NPos > SizeY-41 ) NPos = SizeY-41;
}
```

Finally, after a new thumbpad position (*NPos*) has been verified, the mouse cursor is turned off, the existing thumbpad is erased, the new position assigned, and a new thumbpad is image created before the mouse cursor is restored.

```
    gmouse.Mshow( FALSE );
    EraseThumbPad();
    SPos = NPos;
    SetThumbPad();
    gmouse.Mshow( TRUE );
    return( Result );
}
```

This is another example, like Button and RadioButton, where the control object acts extensively on its own before reporting results back to the calling application. Thus, only after the ScrollBar has taken care of updating its own image and requirement, the hit results are returned to the calling application.

This is also one of the strengths of graphic control objects—their ability to act autonomously—limited, of course, to the extent of the programmer's provisions.

The ScrollHit method's capabilities, of course, do not extend to controlling the calling application which has to execute its own response to changes in the scrollbar's thumbpad position.

ScrollBar::GetPosition()

A ScrollBar hit event is probably not, by itself, enough information for the calling application to decide what response to take. Therefore, the GetPosition method returns the scrollbar's thumbpad location.

```
int ScrollBar::GetPosition()   {  return( SPos );   }
```

The thumbpad position also may or may not mean much to the application because this is a position relative to the scrollbar, but means nothing in absolute terms.

ScrollBar::GetPercent()

There's a simpler method of retrieving a relative position report from a scrollbar object—the GetPercent method which returns a integer percentage according to the position of the thumbpad along the scrollbar.

```
int ScrollBar::GetPercent()
{
   switch( ScrollMove )
   {  case HORIZ_DIR:
         return( 100*(double)(SPos-21)/(double)(SizeX-41));
      case VERT_DIR:
         return( 100*(double)(SPos-21)/(double)(SizeY-41));
}  }
```

This is information that the calling application can use for whatever purposes it may need, as will be shown presently in the CTRLTEST demo.

The VueMeter Object Type

The VueMeter is not a graphics control object, per se, but is a simple metering device modeled after a popular electronic device from the ages predating solid state instruments and digital readouts. It displays a pie-sector, analog meter with a range of 0 to 360 degrees. An example of a VueMeter object appears in Figure 17-2.

The VueMeter object type is a descendant of the RadioButton type and declares a single integer object variable, *Closure*, which is the degree of closure of the meter together with a couple of specialized methods to control the degree of opening or closure.

Since the VueMeter object does not have any special features, in object-oriented graphics terms, that have not been demonstrated already, this final object type is left as an exercise for your experimentation.

Other Meter Objects

A variety of other meter objects are also possible, ranging from the "catseye" tuning meters that appeared in a variety of applications in early radio and electronics equipment to the conventional "moving needle" meters that have been used in VOM equipment, auto dashboards and various other applications for a century or more.

Figure 17-2: The Graphics Control Object Demo

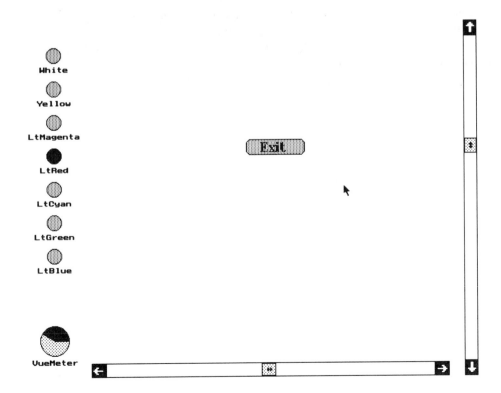

Perhaps these sound like antiques, but the scrollbar objects are simply visual analogs of slidebar potentiometers and the button objects analogs of physical button switches.

The reasons for using any of these objects are because visual analogs of non-digital instruments are frequently still easier to understand, if less precise, than digital displays. I won't recommend using these for every application but, occasionally, these may well be preferable to more conventional digital displays.

In the CTRLTEST demo the analog VueMeter will be demonstrated in one, very simple, application.

The CtrlTest Demonstration

The CtrlTest demo program is a simple example employing two ScrollBar objects for position, eight RadioButtons for colors, and one VueMeter totaling the percentage positions of the two ScrollBars. It also uses a single Button object that is positioned by the scrollbars, changes color in response to the radio buttons, and terminates the demo when clicked by the mouse pointer.

The CtrlTest demo uses the mouse object appearing earlier and the graphic control objects (GCONTROL.I) created in this chapter.

Once these library sources are provided, the CtrlTest demo itself is extremely simple, consisting of several object variable declarations and the main procedure—with no subprocedures.

The variable declarations, however, deserve a few comments:

```
Mstatus        Position;
```

The *Position* variable provides mouse access, but please note, no mouse object is declared by the program because MOUSE.I has already provided the mouse object declaration.

GCONTROL cannot declare the specific object instances that the program will use, only the object types. Thus, in CTRLTEST's declarations, the actual object instances which will be used are defined as:

```
ScrollBar      HScroll, VScroll;
VueMeter       CatsEye;
RadioButton    RButton[7];
Button         ExitButton;
```

The two scrollbar instances are declared with specific names but the RadioButton instances are declared as an array of object instances.

The demo program begins by calling the graphic mouse Mreset method to enable the mouse for graphics operation and tests the returned value to be sure that the mouse is present before proceeding.

```
if( !gmouse.Mreset() ) exit(1);
```

Next, the various object instances require individual initialization. Since all of these are static instances, the default constructor methods (without parameters) have already been called implicitly, therefore the Create methods are called now with the parameter lists establishing each object.

```
for( i=RMin; i<=RMax; i++ )
   RButton[i].Create( 50, 360-(45*i), i+9, 10,
                      ColorStr[i] );
CatsEye.Create( 50, getmaxy()-50, LIGHTRED, 20,
                "VueMeter" );
```

Before setting up the two scrollbars, the active window is reduced to exclude the left-hand side of the screen where the RadioButtons and VueMeter are located and the viewport settings saved using the *VRef* variable.

```
setviewport( 100, 0, getmaxx(), getmaxy(), TRUE );
getviewsettings( &VRef );
HScroll.Create( 0, getmaxy(), VRef.right-VRef.left-40,
                GREEN, LIGHTGREEN, HORIZ_DIR );
VScroll.Create( getmaxx()-VRef.left-20, 0, getmaxy(),
                GREEN, LIGHTGREEN, VERT_DIR );
```

The ScrollBar position and size parameters are expressed in terms of the current viewport settings rather than attempting to figure out what integer values should be used.

In like fashion, the Button::Create method is called with two parameters reported by the ScrollBar instances.

```
ExitButton.SetButtonType( ROUNDED );
ExitButton.Create( HScroll.GetPosition()-20,
                   VScroll.GetPosition(),
                   80, 20, LIGHTRED, "Exit" );
```

Remember, each of these control object instances includes a record of the viewport settings when it was created and will reset the default viewport to these parameters. The VueMeter and RadioButton instances lie outside the viewport created for the scrollbars and *ExitButton* but establish their own viewport settings when they are actively being redrawn.

```
RButton[3].SetState( TRUE );
```

As one last task before starting the real work, the RadioButton for the initial color selection (LIGHTRED) is turned on.

The main program simply loops waiting for *ExitButton* to report a hit event but, while waiting, executes another *do..while* loop which continues until a left mouse button release event occurs.

```
do
{
    Position = gmouse.Mpressed( ButtonL );
    if( Position.button_count )
    {
```

The first event tested is the status of the left mouse button. If down, then ExitButton is called to test for a hit that will terminate the loop.

```
Exit = ExitButton.ButtonHit();
if( !Exit )
do
{
```

If it isn't time to exit, then the scrollbars are queried for a hit and, depending on the hit type, the application could take some specific action.

```
MoveButton = FALSE;
switch( HScroll.ScrollHit() )
{
    case LEFT:
    case HBAR:
    case RIGHT: MoveButton = TRUE;
}
switch( VScroll.ScrollHit() )
{
    case UP:
    case VBAR:
    case DOWN: MoveButton = TRUE;
}
```

For demonstration purposes, the only action taken is to set *MoveButton* as TRUE so that the next step can update the ExitButton position and the CatsEye setting.

```
if( MoveButton )
{
    ExitButton.Move( HScroll.GetPosition()-20,
                     VScroll.GetPosition() );
    CatsEye.Select(
        (double) HScroll.GetPercent()/100*180 +
        (double) VScroll.GetPercent()/100*180 );
}
```

If either scrollbar has reported a hit of any kind then the ExitButton.Move and the CatsEye.Select methods are called with the two scrollbars' GetPosition methods as parameters. In effect, the several objects are being told to talk to each other and work things out among themselves. After all, as long as they can talk the same language, why should the application bother acting as an interpreter?

If no scrollbar hit has occurred, the remaining possibility is that one of the RadioButton instances has been hit so another loop is used to poll these.

```
else for( i=RMin; i<=RMax; i++ )
        if( RButton[i].ButtonHit() )
        {
            for( j=RMin; j<=RMax; j++ )
                RButton[j].SetState( FALSE );
```

If any of the radio buttons report a hit, an inner loop is used to ensure that all of these are turned off, since one of these may already be on when this happens.

Afterwards, the selected radio button is turned on before ExitButton and CatsEye's SetColor methods are told to ask RButton[i] for a new color setting.

```
            RButton[i].SetState( TRUE );
            ExitButton.SetColor(
                RButton[i].GetColor() );
            CatsEye.SetColor(
                RButton[i].GetColor() );
        }
```

Once a button down event has initiated the test loop, this inner loop continues until a button release event occurs to signal that the mouse button is no longer being held down.

```
        Position = gmouse.Mreleased( ButtonL );
    }
    while( !Position.button_count );
}  }
while( !Exit );
```

The program ends by closing the graphics mode and resetting the system mouse to text mode by initializing the text mouse object. Depending on the mouse software and system in use, this may or may not be necessary, but it is certainly common courtesy to always do so.

```
closegraph();
tmouse.Mreset();
}
```

Summary

The graphics control objects created in GCONTROL.I demonstrate the basic requirements of interactive objects. These can be used as is in other applications or as the basis for your own custom control objects.

The MOUSE and GCONTROL units will be used again in Chapter 18 to create icon images that are also mouse-interactive, though in a different fashion.

```
//===============================================//
//  Graphic Controls object file == GCONTROL.I   //
//===============================================//

#include <math.h>
// #include <graphics.h>
// #include "mouse.i"

typedef enum { ROUNDED, SQUARE, THREE_D } ButtonType;
typedef enum { NO_HIT, RIGHT, UP, HBAR,
               VBAR, LEFT, DOWN } HitType;
typedef int  Outline[10];

class Point
{
```

```
   protected:
      int    x, y, Color;
      viewporttype VRef;
   public:
      Point();
      void Move( int PtX, int PtY );
      virtual void Draw();
      void Create( int PtX, int PtY, int C );
      void RestoreViewport();
      void SetColor( int C );
      virtual void SetLoc( int PtX, int PtY );
      virtual void Erase();
      int  GetColor();
      int  GetX();
      int  GetY();
};

class Button : public Point
{
   protected:
      int             State, Rotate, FontSize,
                      TypeFace, SizeX, SizeY;
      ButtonType   ThisButton;
      char           BtnTxt[40];
   public:
      Button();
      ~Button();
      virtual void Draw();
      void Create( int PtX, int PtY, int Width,
                   int Height, int C, char* Text );
      virtual void Erase();
      void Invert();
      virtual void Move( int PtX, int PtY );
      void SetColor( int C );
      void SetState( int BState );
      void SetLabel( char* Text );
      void SetButtonType( ButtonType WhatType );
      void SetTypeSize( int TxtSize );
      void SetTypeFace( int TxtFont );
      int  GetWidth();
      int  GetHeight();
```

```cpp
        int  GetState();
        int  GetTextSize();
        int  ButtonHit();
        ButtonType  GetType();
};

class RadioButton : public Button
{
   protected:
      int Outline, Radius;
   public:
      RadioButton();
      RadioButton( int PtX, int PtY, int C,
                   int R, char* Text );
      ~RadioButton();
      void Create( int PtX, int PtY, int C,
                   int R, char* Text );
      void Draw();
      void Erase();
      void SetRadius( int R );
      int  GetRadius();
      int  ButtonHit();
};

class VueMeter : public RadioButton
{
      int Closure;
   public:
      VueMeter();
      VueMeter( int PtX, int PtY,
                int C, int R, char* Text );
      ~VueMeter();
      void Create( int PtX, int PtY,
                   int C, int R, char* Text );
      void Draw();
      void Erase();
      void Select( int Degree );
      void Close( int Degree );
      void Open( int Degree );
};

class ScrollBar : public Button
```

```
{
   private:
      int  LineColor, SPos, Step, ScrollMove;
   public:
      ScrollBar();                        // constructor method //
      ScrollBar( int PtX, int PtY, int Size,
                 int C1, int C2, int Orientation );
      ~ScrollBar();                       // destructor method  //
      void Create( int PtX, int PtY, int Size,
                 int C1, int C2, int Orientation );
      virtual void SetLoc( int PtX, int PtY );
      HitType  ScrollHit();
      int  GetPosition();
      int  GetDirection();
      int  GetPercent();
   private:
      virtual void Draw();
      virtual void Erase();
      void SetOutline();
      void SetArrows();
      void SetThumbPad();
      void EraseThumbPad();
};


      //=======================================//
      // implementation for object type Point //
      //=======================================//

Point::Point()
{
   getviewsettings( &VRef );
}

void Point::SetLoc( int PtX, int PtY )
{
   x = PtX + VRef.left;
   y = PtY + VRef.top;
}

void Point::Draw()
{
```

```
      putpixel( x, y, Color );
}

void Point::RestoreViewport()
{
   setviewport( VRef.left,  VRef.top,
                VRef.right, VRef.bottom, VRef.clip );
}

void Point::Create( int PtX, int PtY, int C )
{
   SetLoc( PtX, PtY );
   Color = C;
   Draw();
}

void Point::Erase()
{
   int Temp;

   Temp = Color;
   Color = getbkcolor();
   Draw();
   Color = Temp;
}

void Point::Move( int PtX, int PtY )
{
   Erase();
   SetLoc( PtX, PtY );
   Draw();
}

void Point::SetColor( int C )
{
   Color = C;
   Draw();
}

int  Point::GetColor()  {  return( Color );  }

int  Point::GetX()  {  return( x + VRef.left );  }

int  Point::GetY()  {  return( y + VRef.top );  }
```

```
//========================================//
// implementation for object type Button //
//========================================//

Button::Button()
{
   Rotate = FALSE;
   SetTypeSize( 2 );
   SetTypeFace( TRIPLEX_FONT );
}

Button::~Button()
{
   Erase();
}

void Button::Draw()
{
   int      i, radius = 6, offset = 3, AlignX, AlignY;
   Outline RectArr;

   gmouse.Mshow( FALSE );
   setviewport( x, y, x+SizeX, y+SizeY, TRUE );
   setcolor( Color );
   switch( ThisButton )
   {
      case SQUARE:
      {  rectangle( 0,  0,  SizeX, SizeY );
         break;                                   }
      case THREE_D:                            // ThreeD Outline //
      {  rectangle( 0, 0, SizeX, SizeY );
         RectArr[0] = RectArr[2] = RectArr[8] =
         RectArr[1] = RectArr[7] = RectArr[9] = 1;
         RectArr[4] = RectArr[6] = SizeX-1;
         RectArr[3] = RectArr[5] = SizeY-1;
         setfillstyle( CLOSE_DOT_FILL, Color );
         setlinestyle( USERBIT_LINE, 0, NORM_WIDTH );
         fillpoly( 5, RectArr );
         setlinestyle( SOLID_LINE, 0, NORM_WIDTH );
         rectangle( 2*radius, 2*radius, SizeX-2*radius,
                    SizeY-2*radius );
         line( 0, 0, 2*radius, 2*radius );
```

```
                  line( 0, SizeY, 2*radius, SizeY-2*radius );
                  line( SizeX, 0, SizeX-2*radius, 2*radius );
                  line( SizeX, SizeY, SizeX-2*radius,
                        SizeY-2*radius );
                  break;
              }
          case ROUNDED:
              {                                        // draw corners //
                  arc( SizeX-radius, radius, 0, 90, radius );
                  arc( radius, radius, 90, 180, radius );
                  arc( radius, SizeY-radius, 180, 270, radius );
                  arc( SizeX-radius, SizeY-radius, 270, 360, radius );
                                                      // draw sides     //
                  line( radius, 0, SizeX-radius, 0 );
                  line( radius, SizeY, SizeX-radius, SizeY );
                  line( 0, radius, 0, SizeY-radius );
                  line( SizeX, radius, SizeX, SizeY-radius );
      }  }
      switch( ThisButton )                             // fill button   //
      {  case SQUARE:
         case ROUNDED:
          {  RectArr[0] = RectArr[2] = RectArr[8] =
             RectArr[1] = RectArr[7] = RectArr[9] = offset;
             RectArr[4] = RectArr[6] = SizeX-offset;
             RectArr[3] = RectArr[5] = SizeY-offset;       break;
          }
          case THREE_D:
          {  RectArr[0] = RectArr[2] = RectArr[8] =
             RectArr[1] = RectArr[7] = RectArr[9] = 2*radius+1;
             RectArr[4] = RectArr[6] = SizeX-2*radius-1;
             RectArr[3] = RectArr[5] = SizeY-2*radius-1;
      }  }
      if( State ) setfillstyle( SOLID_FILL, Color );
             else setfillstyle( CLOSE_DOT_FILL, Color );
      setlinestyle( USERBIT_LINE, 0, NORM_WIDTH );
      fillpoly( 5, RectArr );
      setlinestyle( SOLID_LINE, 0, NORM_WIDTH );
                                  // adjust fonts and string to fit //
      settextstyle( TypeFace, Rotate, FontSize );
      AlignX = (SizeX/2)-3;
      AlignY = (SizeY/2)-3;
```

```
      if( State ) setcolor( getbkcolor() );
      outtextxy( AlignX, AlignY, BtnTxt );
      if( State ) setcolor( Color );
      RestoreViewport();
      gmouse.Mshow( TRUE );
}

void Button::Create( int PtX, int PtY, int Width,
                     int Height, int C, char* Text )
{
   getviewsettings( &VRef );
   setviewport( 0, 0, getmaxx(), getmaxy(), TRUE );
   settextjustify( CENTER_TEXT, CENTER_TEXT );
   SetLoc( PtX, PtY );
   if( Width < 20 ) SizeX = 20;        else SizeX = Width;
   if( Height < 20 ) SizeY = 20;       else SizeY = Height;
   if( SizeY > SizeX ) Rotate = TRUE; else Rotate = FALSE;
   Color = C;
   State = FALSE;
   strcpy( BtnTxt, Text );
   Draw();
}

void Button::Erase()
{
   gmouse.Mshow( FALSE );
   setviewport( x, y, x+SizeX, y+SizeY, TRUE );
   clearviewport();
   RestoreViewport();
   gmouse.Mshow( TRUE );
}

void Button::Move( int PtX, int PtY )
{
   Erase();
   SetLoc( PtX, PtY );
   Draw();
}

void Button::SetLabel( char* Text )
{
   strcpy( BtnTxt, Text );
```

```
    Draw();
}

void Button::SetColor( int C )
{
    Color = C;
    Draw();
}

void Button::SetState( int BState )
{
    if( State != BState ) Invert();
}

void Button::SetTypeSize( int TxtSize )
{
    FontSize = TxtSize;
}

void Button::SetTypeFace( int TxtFont )
{
    TypeFace = TxtFont;
}

void Button::SetButtonType( ButtonType WhatType )
{
    ThisButton = WhatType;
}

void Button::Invert()
{
    if( State ) State = FALSE;  else State = TRUE;
    Draw();
}

int Button::GetWidth()          { return( SizeX ); }

int Button::GetHeight()         { return( SizeY ); }

int Button::GetState()          { return( State ); }

int Button::GetTextSize()       { return( FontSize ); }

ButtonType Button::GetType() { return( ThisButton ); }
```

```
int Button::ButtonHit()
{
   Mstatus  P = gmouse.Mpressed( ButtonL );
   if( ( P.xaxis >= x ) && ( P.xaxis <= x+SizeX ) &&
       ( P.yaxis >= y ) && ( P.yaxis <= y+SizeY ) )
   {
      Invert();
      return( TRUE );
   }
   return( FALSE );
}


   //=============================================//
   // implementation for object type RadioButton //
   //=============================================//

RadioButton::RadioButton() {   }

RadioButton::RadioButton( int PtX, int PtY,
                          int C, int R, char* Text )
{
   Create( PtX, PtY, C, R, Text );
}

RadioButton::~RadioButton() {   Erase();   }

void RadioButton::Create( int PtX, int PtY,
                          int C, int R, char* Text )
{
   getviewsettings( &VRef );
   settextjustify( CENTER_TEXT, CENTER_TEXT );
   SetLoc( PtX, PtY );
   Radius = R;
   Outline = C | 0x08;
   Color = C;
   State = FALSE;
   strcpy( BtnTxt, Text );
   Draw();
}

void RadioButton::Draw()
{
```

```
   int XAsp, YAsp, i, OldColor = getcolor();

   RestoreViewport();
   getaspectratio( &XAsp, &YAsp );
   setcolor( Outline );
   gmouse.Mshow( FALSE );
   if( State ) setfillstyle( SOLID_FILL, Color );
   else         setfillstyle( INTERLEAVE_FILL, Color );
   fillellipse( x, y, Radius,
                Radius * (double) ( XAsp / YAsp ) );
   settextstyle( DEFAULT_FONT, HORIZ_DIR, 1 );
   outtextxy( x, y + Radius + 10, BtnTxt );
   gmouse.Mshow( TRUE );
   setcolor( OldColor );
}

void RadioButton::Erase()
{
   int OldColor = Color;

   Color = getbkcolor();
   Outline = Color;
   Draw();
   Color = OldColor;
   Outline = OldColor | 0x08;
}

void RadioButton::SetRadius( int R )  {  Radius = R;  }

int  RadioButton::GetRadius()  {  return( Radius );  }

int  RadioButton::ButtonHit()
{
   int  OffX, OffY;

   Mstatus  P = gmouse.Mpressed( ButtonL );
   OffX = abs( P.xaxis - x );
   OffY = abs( P.yaxis - y );

   if( ( OffX < 2 * Radius ) && ( OffY < 2 * Radius ) )
      if( hypot( OffX, OffY ) < Radius )
      {
         Invert();
```

```
                return( TRUE );
            }
        return( FALSE );
    }


        //=========================================//
        // implementation for object type VueMeter //
        //=========================================//

VueMeter::VueMeter()   {  }

VueMeter::VueMeter( int PtX, int PtY,
                    int C, int R, char* Text )
{
    Create( PtX, PtY, C, R, Text );
}

VueMeter::~VueMeter()   {  Erase();   }

void VueMeter::Create( int PtX, int PtY,
                       int C, int R, char* Text )
{
    getviewsettings( &VRef );
    settextjustify( CENTER_TEXT, CENTER_TEXT );
    SetLoc( PtX, PtY );
    Radius = R;
    Color = C;
    Closure = 1;
    strcpy( BtnTxt, Text );
    Draw();
}

void VueMeter::Draw()
{
    int  XAsp, YAsp;

    RestoreViewport();
    getaspectratio( &XAsp, &YAsp );
    if( Closure < 0 )   Closure = 0;
    if( Closure > 360 ) Closure = 360;
    gmouse.Mshow( FALSE );
    setcolor( Color );
```

```
   setfillstyle( SOLID_FILL, Color );
   sector( x, y, 0, Closure, Radius,
           Radius * (double) ( XAsp / YAsp ) );
   settextstyle( DEFAULT_FONT, HORIZ_DIR, 1 );
   settextjustify( CENTER_TEXT, CENTER_TEXT );
   outtextxy( x, y + Radius + 10, BtnTxt );
   setcolor( WHITE );
   setfillstyle( CLOSE_DOT_FILL, Color );
   if( Closure < 360 )
      sector( x, y, Closure, 360, Radius,
              Radius * (double) ( XAsp / YAsp ) );
   gmouse.Mshow( TRUE );
}

void VueMeter::Erase()
{
   int  XAsp, YAsp;

   getaspectratio( &XAsp, &YAsp );
   gmouse.Mshow( FALSE );
   setcolor( getbkcolor() );
   setfillstyle( SOLID_FILL, getbkcolor() );
   sector( x, y, 0, 360, Radius,
           Radius * (double) ( XAsp / YAsp ) );
   settextstyle( DEFAULT_FONT, HORIZ_DIR, 1 );
   settextjustify( CENTER_TEXT, CENTER_TEXT );
   outtextxy( x, y + Radius + 10, BtnTxt );
   setcolor( WHITE );
   gmouse.Mshow( TRUE );
}

void VueMeter::Select( int Degree )
{
   Closure = Degree;
   Draw();
}

void VueMeter::Close( int Degree )
{
   Closure += Degree;
   Draw();
}
```

```
void VueMeter::Open( int Degree )
{
   Closure -= Degree;
   Draw();
}


      //=========================================//
      // implementation for object type ScrollBar //
      //=========================================//

ScrollBar::ScrollBar()
{
   x = y = SizeX = SizeY = Color =
   LineColor = SPos = Step = ScrollMove = 0;
}

ScrollBar::ScrollBar( int PtX, int PtY, int Size,
                      int C1, int C2, int Orientation )
{
   Create( PtX, PtY, Size, C1, C2, Orientation );
}

ScrollBar::~ScrollBar()  {  Erase();  }

void ScrollBar::Create( int PtX, int PtY, int Size,
                        int C1, int C2, int Orientation )
{
   getviewsettings( &VRef );
   if( Size < 100 ) Size = 100;
   ScrollMove = Orientation;
   SPos = 21;
   Step = Size / 100;
   switch( ScrollMove )
   {
     case VERT_DIR:
     {
        SizeX = 20;
        SizeY = Size;
        while( PtX + SizeX > VRef.right ) PtX- -;
        break;
     }
```

```
            case HORIZ_DIR:
            {
                SizeX = Size;
                SizeY = 20;
                while( PtY + SizeY > VRef.bottom ) PtY- -;
        }   }
    SetLoc( PtX, PtY );
    LineColor = C1;
    Color = C2;
    Draw();
}

void ScrollBar::SetLoc( int PtX, int PtY )
{
    Point::SetLoc( PtX, PtY );
    while( ( x + SizeX ) > VRef.right )   SizeX- -;
    while( ( y + SizeY ) > VRef.bottom ) SizeY- -;
}

void ScrollBar::EraseThumbPad()
{
    switch( ScrollMove )
    {
        case VERT_DIR:
            setviewport( x+2, y+SPos, x+18, y+SPos+19, TRUE );
            break;
        case HORIZ_DIR:
            setviewport( x+SPos, y+2, x+SPos+19, y+18, TRUE );
    }
    clearviewport();
    RestoreViewport();
}

void ScrollBar::SetThumbPad()
{
    Outline RectArr;
    int     OldColor = getcolor();

    setviewport( x, y, x+SizeX, y+SizeY, TRUE );
    setcolor( LineColor );
    setfillstyle( CLOSE_DOT_FILL, Color );
    switch( ScrollMove )
```

```
   {
      case VERT_DIR:
      {
         RectArr[0] = RectArr[2] = RectArr[8] = 2;
         RectArr[1] = RectArr[7] = RectArr[9] = SPos;
         RectArr[4] = RectArr[6] = 18;
         RectArr[3] = RectArr[5] = SPos+19;
         break;
      }
      case HORIZ_DIR:
      {
         RectArr[0] = RectArr[2] = RectArr[8] = SPos;
         RectArr[1] = RectArr[7] = RectArr[9] = 2;
         RectArr[4] = RectArr[6] = SPos+19;
         RectArr[3] = RectArr[5] = 19;
   }  }
   fillpoly( 5, RectArr );
   setcolor( OldColor );
   RestoreViewport();
}

void ScrollBar::SetOutline()
{
   Outline RectArr;

   setcolor( LineColor );
   setviewport( x, y, x+SizeX, y+SizeY, TRUE );
   RectArr[0] = RectArr[2] = RectArr[8] = 1;
   RectArr[1] = RectArr[7] = RectArr[9] = 1;
   RectArr[4] = RectArr[6] = SizeX-1;
   RectArr[3] = RectArr[5] = SizeY-1;
   setfillstyle( SOLID_FILL, Color );
   setlinestyle( SOLID_LINE, 0, NORM_WIDTH );
   fillpoly( 5, RectArr );
                                 // clear center of bar //
   setfillstyle( SOLID_FILL, getbkcolor() );
   switch( ScrollMove )
   {
      case VERT_DIR:
      {
         RectArr[1] = RectArr[7] = RectArr[9] = 21;
```

```
             RectArr[3] = RectArr[5] = SizeY-21;
             break;
          }
          case HORIZ_DIR:
          {
             RectArr[0] = RectArr[2] = RectArr[8] = 21;
             RectArr[4] = RectArr[6] = SizeX-21;
    }  }
    fillpoly( 5, RectArr );
}

void ScrollBar::SetArrows()
{
    setcolor( getbkcolor() );
    setlinestyle( SOLID_LINE, 0, THICK_WIDTH );
    switch( ScrollMove )
    {   case VERT_DIR:
       {
          line( 10, 4,   4, 12 );
          line( 10, 4, 16, 12 );
          line( 10, 4, 10, 16 );
          line( 10, SizeY-4,   4, SizeY-12 );
          line( 10, SizeY-4, 16, SizeY-12 );
          line( 10, SizeY-4, 10, SizeY-16 );
          break;
       }
       case HORIZ_DIR:
       {
          line( 4, 10, 12,   4 );
          line( 4, 10, 12, 16 );
          line( 4, 10, 16, 10 );
          line( SizeX-4, 10, SizeX-12,   4 );
          line( SizeX-4, 10, SizeX-12, 16 );
          line( SizeX-4, 10, SizeX-16, 10 );
    }  }
    setlinestyle( SOLID_LINE, 0, NORM_WIDTH );
}

void ScrollBar::Draw()
{
    int  OldColor = getcolor();
```

```
      SetOutline();                        // scrollbar outline  //
      SetArrows();                         // scrollbar arrows   //
      SetThumbPad();                       // draw thumbpad      //
      setcolor( OldColor );                // restore orig color //
}

void ScrollBar::Erase()
{
   gmouse.Mshow( FALSE );
   setviewport( x, y, x+SizeX, y+SizeY, TRUE );
   clearviewport();
   RestoreViewport();
   gmouse.Mshow( TRUE );
}

HitType ScrollBar::ScrollHit()
{
   HitType  Result = NO_HIT;
   int      NPos = 0;

   Mstatus  P = gmouse.Mpressed( ButtonL );
   switch( ScrollMove )
   {
      case VERT_DIR:
         if( ( P.xaxis >= x ) && ( P.xaxis <= x+20 ) &&
             ( P.yaxis >= y ) )
            if( P.yaxis <= y+20 )         Result = UP;
            else
            if( P.yaxis <= y+SizeY-31 ) Result = VBAR;
            else
            if( P.yaxis <= y+SizeY )      Result = DOWN;
            break;
      case HORIZ_DIR:
         if( ( P.yaxis >= y ) && ( P.yaxis <= y+20 ) &&
             ( P.xaxis >= x ) )
            if( P.xaxis <= x+20 )         Result = LEFT;
            else
            if( P.xaxis <= x+SizeX-31 ) Result = HBAR;
            else
            if( P.xaxis <= x+SizeX )      Result = RIGHT;
   }
   if( Result == NO_HIT ) return( Result );
```

```
   switch( Result )
   {
      case  LEFT:
      case    UP: NPos = SPos-Step;                 break;
      case RIGHT:
      case  DOWN: NPos = SPos+Step;                 break;
      case  HBAR: NPos = P.xaxis - ( x + 10 );  break;
      case  VBAR: NPos = P.yaxis - ( y + 10 );
   }
   if( NPos < 21 ) NPos = 21;
   switch( Result )
   {
      case  LEFT:
      case RIGHT: if( NPos > SizeX-41 ) NPos = SizeX-41;
                  break;
      case    UP:
      case  DOWN: if( NPos > SizeY-41 ) NPos = SizeY-41;
   }
   gmouse.Mshow( FALSE );
   EraseThumbPad();
   SPos = NPos;
   SetThumbPad();
   gmouse.Mshow( TRUE );
   return( Result );
}

int ScrollBar::GetPosition()   {  return( SPos );   }

int ScrollBar::GetDirection()  {  return( ScrollMove );   }

int ScrollBar::GetPercent()
{
   switch( ScrollMove )
   {  case HORIZ_DIR:
         return( 100*(double)(SPos-21)/(double)(SizeX-41));
      case VERT_DIR:
         return( 100*(double)(SPos-21)/(double)(SizeY-41));
}  }

      //=========== end of methods =============//
```

```
//============================//
//        GCONTROL.CPP        //
//    Graphic Control Test    //
//============================//

#include <conio.h>
#include <stdio.h>
#include <stdlib.h>
#include <stdarg.h>
#include <string.h>
#include <graphics.h>

#include "mouse.i"                          // mouse object //
#include "gcontrol.i"           // button and scrollbar objects //

char* const ColorStr[] = { "LtBlue", "LtGreen", "LtCyan",
                "LtRed", "LtMagenta", "Yellow", "White" };
int   const RMin = 0, RMax = 6;

main()
{
   Mstatus        Position;
   int            Exit = FALSE, MoveButton, i, j,
                  GDriver = DETECT, GMode, GError;
   viewporttype   VRef;
   ScrollBar      HScroll, VScroll;
   VueMeter       CatsEye;
   RadioButton    RButton[7];
   Button         ExitButton;

   initgraph( &GDriver, &GMode, "C:\\TC\\BGI" );
   GError = graphresult();
   if( GError )
   {
      printf( "Graphics error: %s\n",
              grapherrormsg( GError ) );
      printf( "Program aborted...\n" );
      exit(1);
   }
   if( !gmouse.Mreset() ) exit(1);
   cleardevice();
   for( i=RMin; i<=RMax; i++ )
```

```
      RButton[i].Create( 50, 360-(45*i), i+9, 10,
                         ColorStr[i] );
CatsEye.Create( 50, getmaxy()-50, LIGHTRED, 20,
                "VueMeter" );
setviewport( 100, 0, getmaxx(), getmaxy(), TRUE );
getviewsettings( &VRef );
HScroll.Create( 0, getmaxy(), VRef.right-VRef.left-40,
                GREEN, LIGHTGREEN, HORIZ_DIR );
VScroll.Create( getmaxx()-VRef.left-20, 0, getmaxy(),
                GREEN, LIGHTGREEN, VERT_DIR );
ExitButton.SetButtonType( ROUNDED );
ExitButton.Create( HScroll.GetPosition()-20,
                   VScroll.GetPosition(),
                   80, 20, LIGHTRED, "Exit" );
RButton[3].SetState( TRUE );
do
{
   Position = gmouse.Mpressed( ButtonL );
   if( Position.button_count )
   {
      Exit = ExitButton.ButtonHit();
      if( !Exit )
      do
      {
         MoveButton = FALSE;
         switch( HScroll.ScrollHit() )
         {
            case LEFT:
            case HBAR:
            case RIGHT: MoveButton = TRUE;
         }
         switch( VScroll.ScrollHit() )
         {
            case UP:
            case VBAR:
            case DOWN: MoveButton = TRUE;
         }
         if( MoveButton )
         {
            ExitButton.Move( HScroll.GetPosition()-20,
```

```
                              VScroll.GetPosition() );
            CatsEye.Select(
               (double) HScroll.GetPercent()/100*180 +
               (double) VScroll.GetPercent()/100*180 );
         }
         else for( i=RMin; i<=RMax; i++ )
               if( RButton[i].ButtonHit() )
               {
                  for( j=RMin; j<=RMax; j++ )
                     RButton[j].SetState( FALSE );
                  RButton[i].SetState( TRUE );
                  ExitButton.SetColor(
                     RButton[i].GetColor() );
                  CatsEye.SetColor(
                     RButton[i].GetColor() );
               }
         Position = gmouse.Mreleased( ButtonL );
      }
      while( !Position.button_count );
   }  }
   while( !Exit );
   closegraph();          // restore text mode and ...      //
   tmouse.Mreset();       // reset mouse for text operation //
}
```

Chapter 18

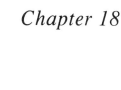

Graphic Icon Objects

With the increasing popularity of graphics applications many programs (and programmers) have abandoned text menus and labeled buttons in favor of icon-based applications like those pioneered by the Apple computers, Microsoft Windows, and Presentation Manager.

In many cases, such as the Apple Macintosh, where text labels appear almost as if they were afterthoughts, graphic icons have been taken to extremes, which many consider more hindrance than help. In other cases, such as Presentation Manager, icons appear principally in an informative capacity rather than as the primary interactive element.

Regardless of your likes or dislikes, icons are a natural element in graphic programming and can be used in whatever fashions your preferences and applications dictate.

If you find icons intensely distasteful or irritating, then you are under no obligation to use them. If you find them an irritant, then those using your applications are likely to find your employment of them irritating.

Take or leave icons as you wish, but remember these are a valid element of graphics programming and will appear more often in the future.

Creating Icon Images

Icons can serve as screen symbols and as buttons to summon or control applications or subprocedures. Since control buttons have already been shown in other demonstrations, this chapter will be concerned first with the images used for icons and, second, with a simple demo where the mouse maneuvers the icon around the screen.

For the business line graph, the symbols used were created in various ways: by defining bit maps, by drawing images, and so on. For general applications, a more versatile and consistent method of creating icons and bit images is required. Hence, the IconEdit utility.

The IconEdit Utility

The IconEdit utility provides a simple bit-map editor that can create icon images up to 32 pixels square in monochrome or color, can save and retrieve images from disk, and can invert images or change color to monochrome.

Most graphics systems using icons have used monochrome icons even though some, such as the Macintosh, allow colors to be assigned to icons. Multicolor icons, however, are relatively uncommon even though color monitors are increasingly common. In the case of this icon editor, multicolor icons are supported or monochrome icons may be created with a color specified. The monochrome icons, of course, require less memory both as disk files and in RAM.

The size limitations (32x32) are arbitrary and can easily be increased, though some screen rearrangements will be necessary. In most cases, however, a 32-bit square image is more than sufficient while smaller sizes are frequently preferred. Smaller image sizes are readily available through vertical and horizontal size options. In general, when creating an icon, you should start with the default (large) image size and then reduce the grid size after the image is completed.

The IconEdit utility requires the Mouse and GControl utilities created in previous chapters. If you do not have these already, both should be completed before attempting to create the IconEdit program or before running the IconDemo program. All of these, together with the other programs and units created in this book, are available on a program disk available from Addison-Wesley Publishing (please see the coupon at the back of this book).

The IconEdit utility is not very complex and provides a drawing grid and various option and color buttons. The mouse draws on the grid using the selected color when the left button is down or using the background color when the right button is down. Otherwise, the drawing program is essentially self-explanatory. See Figure 18-1 for a picture of the Icon Editor

A few comments on how icons are saved as files is in order.

Figure 18-1: The Icon Editor

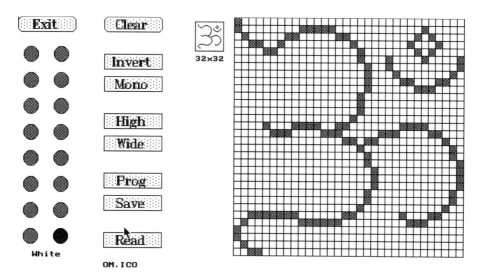

OM.ICO

The Icon Image Files

The SaveImage procedure is used to save a created icon bit image as a disk file. The file save procedure begins with a pair of tests to determine if the icon image can be saved in a monochrome format or if a multicolor format is required.

Before testing for either condition, the first two bytes written to the output file are the horizontal and vertical sizes of the icon image. With this done, the first test is to retrieve the state of the MonoBtn button. If this is set (TRUE) then the image will be saved as monochrome.

```
CFlag = !MonoBtn.GetState();
```

If *CFlag* is not set by the first test, a second test is executed by checking the entire *image* array to decide if more than one color is present by setting the *C1* variable to the first non-background color entry encountered and then comparing all subsequent non-background entries against this color value. If a second color entry is encountered, then multicolor is assumed and *CFlag* is set as TRUE.

```
if( CFlag )
{
    CFlag = FALSE;
    for( i=0; i<=HSize; i++ )
```

```
    for( j=0; j<=VSize; j++ )
        if( Image[i][j] )
            if( !C1 ) C1 = Image[i][j];
            else
            if( C1 != Image[i][j] )
                CFlag = TRUE;

}
```

If the icon image is color then the third byte written to the output file is the multicolor flag, *C2*, with the value FFh.

```
if( CFlag )
{
    write( handle, &C2, 1 );
```

For a multicolor icon, pairs of pixels are combined as two four-bit color values (0..15 or 00h..0Fh) creating one, eight-bit file byte. While this is only minimal image encoding, a 16 color, 32 by 32 pixel icon requires only 515 bytes to store versus slightly over one kilobyte without encoding.

```
    for( i=0; i<=HSize; i++ )
    {
        C2 = k = 0;
        for( j=0; j<=VSize; j++ )
        {
            k++;
            C2 <<= 4;
            C2 += Image[i][j];
            if( k==2 )
            {
                k = 0;
                write( handle, &C2, 1 );
        } }
        if( k )
        {
            C2 <<= 4;
            write( handle, &C2, 1 );
} } }
```

For a monochrome icon, the third file byte is the active palette color (00h..0Fh). Note, this color is simply the currently selected working color, not the color used to create the icon image. By selecting different drawing colors before saving an icon image to file, the icon can be saved in a different color than it was drawn and, depending on whether you find this useful or a nuisance, you may consider it a bug or a feature.

```
    else
    {
        write( handle, &ActiveColor, 1 );
```

For a monochrome icon, after writing a single byte to establish the color used, the image itself is stored as an array of Boolean bits with eight true/false bits per file byte.

```
    for( i=0; i<=HSize; i++ )
        for( j=0; j<=3; j++ )
            if( j*8 <= VSize )
            {
                C2 = 0;
                for( k=0; k<=7; k++ ) C2 <<= 1;
                if( j*8+k <= VSize )
                    if( Image[i][j*8+k] ) C2++;
                write( handle, &C2, 1 );
    }           }
```

Note that each row of pixels in the icon image begins a new file byte even if the vertical size of the image is not a multiple of eight bits. While this is not the absolute optimum for data compression, this does simplify encoding and decoding and a 32 by 32 icon requires only 67 bytes versus 515 bytes for a multicolor icon.

Of course, depending on system parameters, file size minimums may result in 256 to 1,024 bytes being allocated to store a 67 byte icon image. You may wish to consider combining several icon data sets into a single file. This, however, is left as an exercise for the reader's ingenuity.

The Icon Object

The icon object type is defined in the demo program ICONEDIT.CPP. but could be included in the GCONTROL unit or even redefined as a descendant of the Button object type. Unlike previous object types, however, the icon object type is not created as a separate unit and supplies only minimal object methods, but it may be elaborated as desired.

Figure 18-2 shows the IconDemo program which loads four icon images from disk files and supplies a single exit button. For demonstration purposes, you'll have to create an icon images and alter the filenames to match.

Figure 18-2: Demonstrating Icons

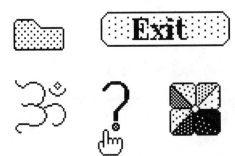

At present, all that can be done with the icons shown is to drag the images around the screen using the mouse. Icon selection could also be supplied by implementing a double-click feature and using this to chain other operations.

The Icon object is similar to the Button object demonstrated previously and, at this point, should be generally self-explanatory.

```
//=======================//
//      ICONEDIT.CPP       //
//    Icon_Image_Editor    //
//=======================//

#include <conio.h>
#include <fcntl.h>
#include <io.h>
#include <stdio.h>
#include <stdlib.h>
#include <stdarg.h>
#include <string.h>
#include <graphics.h>
#include <\sys\stat.h>

#include "mouse.i"
#include "gprint.i"
#include "gcontrol.i"

typedef  int  Outline[10];

Mstatus        Position;                        // mouse position //
```

```
palettetype    OrgPalette;
viewporttype   VRef;

int    ActiveColor = WHITE, HSize = 31, VSize = 31, i, j,
       GridColor = BLUE, PixColor, GDriver, GMode, GError;
unsigned int   Image[32][32];
Button         ExtBtn,  ClrBtn,  HighBtn, WideBtn,
               MonoBtn, InvBtn, SaveBtn, ReadBtn;
RadioButton    RButton[16];

void FillSquare( int x, int y, int FillStyle, int Color )
{
   int   OrgColor = getcolor();
   Outline   outline;

   setcolor( GridColor );
   outline[0] = outline[6] = outline[8] = x;
   outline[1] = outline[3] = outline[9] = y;
   outline[2] = outline[4] = x+10;
   outline[5] = outline[7] = y+10;
   setfillstyle( FillStyle, Color );
   fillpoly( 5, outline );
   setcolor( OrgColor );
}

void Beep()
{
   sound( 220 ); delay( 100 ); nosound();
                 delay(  50 );
   sound( 440 ); delay( 100 ); nosound();
}

void PaintGrid()
{
   char * Temp1, Temp2;

   setcolor( WHITE );
   gmouse.Mshow( FALSE );
   setviewport( 246, 06, 286, 86, TRUE );
   clearviewport();
   rectangle( 0, 0, HSize+8, VSize+8 );
   settextjustify( CENTER_TEXT, CENTER_TEXT );
   settextstyle( DEFAULT_FONT, HORIZ_DIR, 1 );
```

```
      gprintxy( 20, 50, "%2dx%2d", HSize, VSize );

      setviewport( 300, 0, getmaxx(), getmaxy(), TRUE );
      clearviewport();
      setviewport( 0, 0, getmaxx(), getmaxy(), TRUE );

      for( i=0; i<=HSize; i++ )
         for( j=0; j<=VSize; j++ )
         {
            FillSquare( i*10+300, j*10,
                        INTERLEAVE_FILL, Image[i][j] );
            putpixel( 250+i, 10+j, Image[i][j] );
         }
      gmouse.Mshow( TRUE );
}

void NoteColor()
{
   char*  const  ColorNames[] =
      { "Black", "Blue", "Green", "Cyan", "Red", "Magenta",
        "Brown", "LightGray", "DarkGray",  "LightBlue",
        "LightGreen", "LightCyan", "LightRed", "LtMagenta",
        "Yellow", "White" };

   setviewport( 0, 310, 80, 330, TRUE );
   setcolor( ActiveColor );
   settextstyle( DEFAULT_FONT, HORIZ_DIR, 1 );
   settextjustify( CENTER_TEXT, CENTER_TEXT );
   clearviewport();
   outtextxy( 40, 10, ColorNames[ActiveColor] );
   setviewport( 0, 0, getmaxx(), getmaxy(), TRUE );
}

void ClearImage()
{
   int  i, j;

   for( i=0; i<=HSize; i++ )
      for( j=0; j<=VSize; j++ )
         Image[i][j] = 0;
   PaintGrid();
   ClrBtn.SetState( FALSE );
   if( InvBtn.GetState() ) InvBtn.SetState( FALSE );
```

```
}

void InvertImage()
{
   int  i, j;

   for( i=0; i<=HSize; i++ )
      for( j=0; j<=VSize; j++ )
         Image[i][j] ^= 0x0F;              // XOR'd with 0Fh //
   PaintGrid();
}

void Monochrome()
{
   int  i, j;

   if( InvBtn.GetState() )
   {
       for( i=0; i<=HSize; i++ )
          for( j=0; j<=VSize; j++ )
             Image[i][j] &= 0x0F;
       PaintGrid();
   }
   if( MonoBtn.GetState() )
   {
       getpalette( &OrgPalette );
       for( i=1; i<=15; i++ )
          setpalette( i, OrgPalette.colors[ ActiveColor ] );
   } else setallpalette( &OrgPalette );
   delay( 100 );
}

int  ReadSize()
{
   char  Ch, TempStr[4] = "";
   int   Done = FALSE;

   settextjustify( LEFT_TEXT, TOP_TEXT );
   settextstyle( DEFAULT_FONT, HORIZ_DIR, 1 );
   setviewport( 120, 330, getmaxx(), 340, TRUE );
   while( !Done )
   {
      clearviewport();
```

```
         gprintxy( 1, 1, "Size (10..32): %s", TempStr );
         Ch = getch();
         if( Ch == 0x0D ) Done = TRUE;
         else
         if( ( Ch >= '0' ) && ( Ch <= '9' ) )
            strncat( TempStr, &Ch, 1 );
      }
   clearviewport();
   setviewport( 0, 0, getmaxx(), getmaxy(), TRUE );
   return( atoi( TempStr ) );
}

void SetWidth()
{
   int  Result = ReadSize();

   if( ( Result < 10 ) || ( Result > 32 ) ) Beep();
   else
   {
      HSize = Result-1;
      PaintGrid();
   }
   WideBtn.SetState( FALSE );
}

void SetHeight()
{
   int  Result = ReadSize();

   if( ( Result < 10 ) || ( Result > 32 ) ) Beep();
   else
   {
      VSize = Result-1;
      PaintGrid();
   }
   HighBtn.SetState( FALSE );
}

char* ReadName( char* Note )
{
   char  Ch, TempStr[20] = "";
   int   Done = FALSE;
```

```
      setcolor( WHITE );
      settextjustify( LEFT_TEXT, TOP_TEXT );
      settextstyle( DEFAULT_FONT, HORIZ_DIR, 1 );
      setviewport( 120, 330, getmaxx(), 340, TRUE );
      while( !Done )
      {
         clearviewport();
         gprintxy( 1, 1, "%s%s", Note, TempStr );
         Ch = getch();
         if( Ch == 0x0D ) Done = TRUE;
         else
         if( ( ( Ch >= '0' ) && ( Ch <= '9' ) ) ||
             ( ( Ch >= 'A' ) && ( Ch <= 'Z' ) ) ||
             ( ( Ch >= 'a' ) && ( Ch <= 'z' ) ) ||
               ( Ch == '.' ) ) strncat( TempStr, &Ch, 1 );
      }
      clearviewport();
      setviewport( 0, 0, getmaxx(), getmaxy(), TRUE );
      return( TempStr );
}

void ReportError( char* ErrMsg )
{
      settextjustify( LEFT_TEXT, TOP_TEXT );
      settextstyle( DEFAULT_FONT, HORIZ_DIR, 1 );
      setviewport( 120, 330, getmaxx(), 350, TRUE );
      clearviewport();
      setcolor( LIGHTRED );
      outtextxy( 1, 1, ErrMsg );
      setcolor( WHITE );
      getch();
      clearviewport();
      setviewport( 0, 0, getmaxx(), getmaxy(), TRUE );
}

void SaveImage()
{
      unsigned int  C1 = 0, C2 = 0xFF;
      int   i, j, k, handle, CFlag = FALSE;
      char  FileName[14];

      strcpy( FileName, ReadName( "Write Image: " ) );
```

```
if( FileName == "" )
{
   Beep();
   SaveBtn.SetState( FALSE );
   return;
}
outtextxy( 120, 330, FileName );
if( ( handle = open( FileName,
                     O_CREAT | O_TRUNC | O_BINARY,
                     S_IREAD | S_IWRITE ) ) == - 1 )
{
   ReportError( "Cannot open output file" );
   return;
}
write( handle, &HSize, 1 );
write( handle, &VSize, 1 );
CFlag = !MonoBtn.GetState();
if( CFlag )
{
   CFlag = FALSE;
   for( i=0; i<=HSize; i++ )
      for( j=0; j<=VSize; j++ )
         if( Image[i][j] )
            if( !C1 ) C1 = Image[i][j];
            else
            if( C1 != Image[i][j] )
               CFlag = TRUE;
}
if( CFlag )
{                                          // multicolor Image //
   write( handle, &C2, 1 );                // multicolor flag  //
   for( i=0; i<=HSize; i++ )
   {
      C2 = k = 0;
      for( j=0; j<=VSize; j++ )
      {
         k++;
         C2 <<= 4;
         C2 += Image[i][j];
         if( k==2 )
```

```
              {
                  k = 0;
                  write( handle, &C2, 1 );
              }  }
              if( k )
              {
                  C2 <<= 4;
                  write( handle, &C2, 1 );
      }  }  }
      else
      {                                      // monochrome Image //
         write( handle, &ActiveColor, 1 );  // palette color     //
         for( i=0; i<=HSize; i++ )
            for( j=0; j<=3; j++ )
               if( j*8 <= VSize )
               {
                   C2 = 0;
                   for( k=0; k<=7; k++ ) C2 <<= 1;
                   if( j*8+k <= VSize )
                       if( Image[i][j*8+k] ) C2++;
                   write( handle, &C2, 1 );
      }          }
      close( handle );
      SaveBtn.SetState( FALSE );
}

void ReadImage()
{
   unsigned  int  C1 = 0, C2 = 0;
   int     i, j, k, handle;
   char*  FileName;

   strcpy( FileName, ReadName( "Read Image: " ) );
   if( FileName == "" )
   {
      Beep();
      ReadBtn.SetState( FALSE );
      return;
   }
   outtextxy( 120, 330, FileName );
   if( ( handle =
```

```
            open( FileName, O_RDONLY | O_BINARY ) ) == -1 )
   {
      ReportError( "Cannot open input file" );
      return;
   }
   read( handle, &HSize, 1 );
   read( handle, &VSize, 1 );
   read( handle, &C1, 1 );
   if( C1 == 0xFF )
   {                                        // multicolor Image //
      for( i=0; i<=HSize; i++ )
         for( j=0; j<=VSize/2; j++ )
         {
            read( handle, &C2, 1 );
            Image[i][j*2] = C2 >> 4;
            if( VSize >= j*2+1 )
               Image[i][j*2+1] = C2 & 0x0F;
   }     }
   else
   {                                        // monochrome Image //
      for( i=0; i<=HSize; i++ )
         for( j=0; j<=3; j++ )
            if( j*8 <= VSize )
            {
               read( handle, &C2, 1 );
               for( k=0; k<=7; k++ )
               {
                  if( j*8+k <= VSize )
                     if( C2 & 0x80 )  Image[i][j*8+k] = C1;
                     else             Image[i][j*8+k] = 0;
                  C2 <<= 1;
   }          }  }
   close( handle );
   PaintGrid();
   ReadBtn.SetState( FALSE );
}

main()
{
   Mstatus  Mevent;
   int      Exit = FALSE;
```

```
GDriver = DETECT;
initgraph( &GDriver, &GMode, "C:\\TP\\BGI" );
GError = graphresult();
if( GError != grOk )
{
   printf( "Graphics error: %s\n",
           grapherrormsg( GError ) );
   printf( "Program aborted..." );
   exit(1);
}
if( !gmouse.Mreset() ) exit(1);
cleardevice();


     //======================================//
     //    setup graphic control objects    //
     //======================================//

for( i=0; i<=7; i++ )
   RButton[i].Create( 18, 50+35*i,      i, 10, "" );
for( i=8; i<=15; i++ )
   RButton[i].Create( 60, 50+35*(i-8), i, 10, "" );
ExtBtn.SetAll( ROUNDED,   1,   1, 80, 20,
                 LIGHTRED,   "Exit"  );
ClrBtn.SetAll( ROUNDED, 120,   1, 80, 20,
                 LIGHTRED,   "Clear" );
InvBtn.SetAll( ROUNDED, 120,  50, 80, 20,
                 LIGHTGREEN, "Invert" );
MonoBtn.SetAll( SQUARE, 120,  80, 80, 20,
                 LIGHTGREEN, "Mono"  );
HighBtn.SetAll( SQUARE, 120, 130, 80, 20,
                 YELLOW,     "High"  );
WideBtn.SetAll( SQUARE, 120, 160, 80, 20,
                 YELLOW,     "Wide"  );
SaveBtn.SetAll( SQUARE, 120, 210, 80, 20,
                 LIGHTCYAN,  "Save"  );
ReadBtn.SetAll( SQUARE, 120, 240, 80, 20,
                 LIGHTCYAN,  "Read"  );

NoteColor();
RButton[ActiveColor].SetState( TRUE );
for( i=0; i<=HSize; i++ )
```

```
        for( j=0; j<=VSize; j++ )
            Image[i][j] = 0;
PaintGrid();

                //==========================//
                //     start edit program    //
                //==========================//

while( !Exit )
{
   Mevent = gmouse.Mpos();
   Exit = ExtBtn.ButtonHit();
   if( Mevent.button_status & 0x07 )
   do
   {
      if( Mevent.xaxis < 120 )
      {
         for( i=0; i<=15; i++ )
            if( RButton[i].ButtonHit() )
            {
               gmouse.Mshow( FALSE );
               for( j=0; j<=15; j++ )
                  RButton[j].SetState( FALSE );
               RButton[i].SetState( TRUE );
               ActiveColor = i;
               NoteColor();
               gmouse.Mshow( TRUE );
      }       }
      else
      if( Mevent.xaxis < 250 )
      {
         if( ClrBtn.ButtonHit() )  ClearImage();
         if( InvBtn.ButtonHit() )  InvertImage();
         if( MonoBtn.ButtonHit() ) Monochrome();
         if( HighBtn.ButtonHit() ) SetHeight();
         if( WideBtn.ButtonHit() ) SetWidth();
         if( SaveBtn.ButtonHit() ) SaveImage();
         if( ReadBtn.ButtonHit() ) ReadImage();
      }
      else
      {
```

```
            PixColor = ActiveColor;
            if( Mevent.button_status & 0x02 )
               PixColor = BLACK;
            i = ( Mevent.xaxis - 300 ) / 10;
            j = Mevent.yaxis / 10;
            if( ( i >= 0 ) && ( i <= HSize ) &&
                ( j >= 0 ) && ( j <= VSize ) )
               if( Image[i][j] != PixColor )
               {
                   gmouse.Mshow( FALSE );
                   Image[i][j] = PixColor;
                   FillSquare( i*10+300, j*10,
                               INTERLEAVE_FILL, PixColor );
                   putpixel( 250+i, 10+j, PixColor );
                   gmouse.Mshow( TRUE );
          }       }
        Mevent = gmouse.Mpos(); // get mouse button status //
    }                           // continue if any button down //
    while( Mevent.button_status );
  }
  closegraph();                 // restore text mode and ...        //
  tmouse.Mreset();              // reset mouse for text operation //
}


          //=============================//
          //          ICONTEST.CPP        //
          //   Icon Object Demo Program   //
          //=============================//

#include <conio.h>
#include <fcntl.h>
#include <io.h>
#include <stdio.h>
#include <stdlib.h>
#include <string.h>
#include <graphics.h>
#include <\sys\stat.h>

#include "mouse.i"
#include "gprint.i"
```

```
#include "gcontrol.i"

class Icon
{
      void  *ImgPtr;
      int   X, Y, XOfs, YOfs, HSize, VSize, State;
   public:
      Icon();
      ~Icon();
      void Create( char* FileName );
      void Show( int Status );
      void MoveTo( int XPos, int YPos );
      void Drag();
      int  MouseSelect();
};

Icon::Icon()
{
   HSize = VSize = XOfs = YOfs = X = Y = 0;
}

Icon::~Icon()
{
   if( State ) Show( FALSE );
   free( ImgPtr );
}

void Icon::Create( char* FileName )
{
   unsigned  int  C1 = 0, C2 = 0;
   int  i, j, k, handle;

   if( ( handle =
         open( FileName, O_RDONLY | O_BINARY ) ) == -1 )
   {
      gprintxy( 200, 200,
               "Cannot open %s as input file", FileName );
      getch();
      return;
   }
   read( handle, &HSize, 1 );
   read( handle, &VSize, 1 );
```

```
   read( handle, &C1, 1 );
   if( C1 == 0xFF )
   {                                         // multicolor Image //
      for( i=0; i<=HSize; i++ )
         for( j=0; j<=VSize/2; j++ )
         {
            read( handle, &C2, 1 );
            putpixel( i, j*2, C2 >> 4 );
            if( VSize >= j*2+1 )
               putpixel( i, j*2+1, C2 & 0x0F );
   }       }
   else
   {                                         // monochrome Image //
      for( i=0; i<=HSize; i++ )
         for( j=0; j<=3; j++ )
            if( j*8 <= VSize )
            {
               read( handle, &C2, 1 );
               for( k=0; k<=7; k++ )
               {
                  if( j*8+k <= VSize )
                  if( C2 & 0x80 ) putpixel( i, j*8+k, C1 );
                  else            putpixel( i, j*8+k, 0 );
                  C2 <<= 1;
   }       } }
   close( handle );
   ImgPtr = malloc( (unsigned)
                    imagesize( 0, 0, HSize, VSize ) );
   getimage( 0, 0, HSize, VSize, ImgPtr );
   putimage( 0, 0, ImgPtr, XOR_PUT );
   State = FALSE;
}

void Icon::Show( int Status )
{
   if( Status != State )
   {
      gmouse.Mshow( FALSE );
      putimage( X, Y, ImgPtr, XOR_PUT );
      State = !State;
      gmouse.Mshow( TRUE );
```

```
}   }

void Icon::MoveTo( int XPos, int YPos )
{
   if( State ) putimage( X, Y, ImgPtr, XOR_PUT );
   X = XPos;
   Y = YPos;
   putimage( X, Y, ImgPtr, XOR_PUT );
   State = TRUE;
}

int   Icon::MouseSelect()
{
   Mstatus   Mevent = gmouse.Mpos();

   if( ( Mevent.xaxis >= X ) && ( Mevent.xaxis <= X+HSize ) &&
       ( Mevent.yaxis >= Y ) && ( Mevent.yaxis <= Y+VSize ) )
   {
      XOfs = MouseX - X;            // icon position relative //
      YOfs = MouseY - Y;            // to mouse cursor hotspot //
      Drag();
      return( TRUE );
   }
   return( FALSE );
}

void Icon::Drag()
{
   Mstatus   Mevent;
   int       XPos, YPos, XOld = -1, YOld = -1, Done = FALSE;

   Mevent = gmouse.Mreleased( ButtonL );  // clear releases //
   Show( FALSE );                          // hide objects   //
   gmouse.Set_Cursor( GLOVE );
   do
   {
      Mevent = gmouse.Mpos();
      XPos = Mevent.xaxis;
      YPos = Mevent.yaxis;
      if( ( XPos != XOld ) || ( YPos != YOld ) )
      {
         gmouse.Mshow( FALSE );
```

```
         putimage( XPos-XOfs, YPos-YOfs, ImgPtr, XOR_PUT );
         putimage( XOld-XOfs, YOld-YOfs, ImgPtr, XOR_PUT );
         gmouse.Mshow( TRUE );
         XOld = XPos;
         YOld = YPos;
      }
      Mevent = gmouse.Mreleased( ButtonL );
      Done = Mevent.button_count; // test for release event //
   }
   while( !Done );
   X = XPos-XOfs;            // update object coordinates //
   Y = YPos-YOfs;                  // to the final position   //
   gmouse.Set_Cursor( ARROW );  // restore mouse cursor        //
}

   //======= end of Icon object definition ========//

void main()
{
   int     i, GDriver = DETECT, GMode, GError;
   Mstatus Mevent;
   Button  ExitButton;
   Icon    PixImage[4];

   initgraph( &GDriver, &GMode, "C:\\TP\\BGI" );
   GError = graphresult();
   if( GError != grOk )
   {
      printf( "Graphics error: %s\n",
              grapherrormsg( GError ) );
      printf( "Program aborted..." );
      exit(1);
   }
   if( !gmouse.Mreset() ) exit(1);
   cleardevice();
   PixImage[0].Create( "FILEFLDR.ICO" );
   PixImage[1].Create( "OM.ICO" );
   PixImage[2].Create( "QUESTION.ICO" );
   PixImage[3].Create( "RAINBOW3.ICO" );
   for( i=0; i<=3; i++ )
      PixImage[i].MoveTo( 40 * i + 60, 200 );
   ExitButton.SetAll( ROUNDED, getmaxx()-80, 1,
```

```
                        80, 20, LIGHTRED, "Exit" );
gmouse.Mshow( TRUE );


        //===========================//
        //     start demo program    //
        //===========================//

while( !ExitButton.ButtonHit() )
{
   Mevent = gmouse.Mpressed( ButtonL );
   if( Mevent.button_count  )
      for( i=0; i<=3; i++ )
         if( PixImage[i].MouseSelect() ) /* ??? */;
}                             //===========================//
closegraph();                // restore text mode and ... //
tmouse.Mreset();             // reset mouse for text ops  //
}                            //===========================//
```

Part Four

Fractals and Other Strange Phenomena

Most of the applications and demonstrations shown have been more or less practical in nature (with the possible exception of the animation chapter). But graphics are not limited to conventional applications and there are strange and fascinating realms in mathematics that are best explored through the medium of the computer.

Such explorations might be carried out unassisted, however, this would be rather like attempting to find the head waters of the Amazon by wading up stream—it could be done, but why?

In this section, I'll offer instructions and plans for more reliable vehicles of exploration to take you into the realms of fractals, strange attractors, and other mysteries in the worlds of mathematic curiosity. This is a world where your voyages are limited only by your imagination.

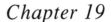

Chapter 19

On the Shores of Fractal Seas

The shores of the fractal seas comprise a strange and wonderful land uncharted by explorers with canoes and native guides but mapped and sounded by mathematicians, travelled via the repetitious labors of a computer chip, and drawn in bits of light and shadow on computer screens.

These strange lands are neither imaginary nor fantasy. They are very real. So real, in fact, that the fractal universe appears to form the very root and basis of our own, more familiar universe. To be less poetic and more accurate, the same equations in which we find these strange worlds also govern more commonplace elements of our universe ranging from the crystal structures of minerals (and snow flakes and proteins) to the delicate tracery of a fern and the complex labyrinth of our circulatory structures.

In this chapter, partially due to space and subject limitations, I will offer directions for entry to only a few of these fascinating realms and will not attempt to provide a detailed explanation for either the mathematics behind these excursions nor their relevance to the larger physical universe. I will offer a few suggestions for finding guidebooks and additional information for the interested explorer.

Many of these realms remain unknown land and I offer no surety against your entrapment in a maze of wonderment nor warranty for your eventual sane and sound return to the mundane cosmos. Hic draconis![1]

The Fractal Universe

The now-ubiquitous term *fractal* was first coined by Benoit B. Mandelbrot to denote the fact that, in reality, the dimension of a surface (in the mundane world) or of an equation (in the mathematic world) was often determined by how it was measured. To use a physical example, if you measure the coastline of the state of Maine using a yardstick which is 10 miles in length, you will arrive at a certain numerical result.

But, if you now repeat your survey a second time—this time using a one-mile unit of measure—you will derive a second result, one which is fractionally larger than the first. A third survey, using a mere $^1/10$-mile yardstick, will yield a third, still greater, result and a fourth survey—now reducing the incremental measurement to a true 36-inch yard—yields a fourth figure greater than its predecessors.

In like fashion, as you continue to decrease the size of the unit of measure, your survey includes smaller and smaller irregularities as you sum the length of this irregular boundary and, predictably, L_1 is less than L_2 is less than L_3 . . . L_{n-1} is less than L_n.

However, no matter how small your increment of measure becomes—even when you reach the point of tracing the irregularities of individual bits of sand—we can also say that L_n is less than twice L_1. The length has not increased without bounds.

This assertion is easily proven and may be accepted as valid. However, please remember this figure of magnitude—2—because this will be used further in testing fractal explorations.

The Mandelbrot Set

The Mandelbrot set is probably the most famous fractal landscape currently explored and has been featured (usually in full color) in scholarly journals, *Scientific American*, and *Time* as well as countless less prestigious publications. While Benoit Mandelbrot was not the first to discover this fascinating land—its shores had previously been sighted by mathematicians Robert Brooks and J. Peter Matelski—Mandelbrot was the first to make a

---

1 Here there be dragons.

detailed exploration and, therefore, is indelibly appended to the maps of this realm.

The Mandelbrot set is an equation lying in the realm of numbers between –2.0 and +0.5 longitude and –1.25 and +1.25 latitude and is dominated by a large fractal sea with bays, inlets, and tributaries as shown in Figure 19-1.

As with many lands, the most interesting regions are those immediately surrounding the sea. They offer irregular terrain and, most certainly, fitting my earlier description of the difficulties in precisely measuring the coastline of Maine.

In this case, no attempt will be made to measure a coastline. Instead, the "coastline" is a mathematical artifice, though a very real one, created by recursively examining a relatively simple equation: $Zn+1 = Zn2 + C$, where C is the value of each point (the longitude and latitude of the point) and Z1 is zero for each point (an initial value).

In this landscape, however, while longitude is measured in real numbers, the latitude lies along the imaginary axis and, therefore, all latitudinal values are denoted by the letter *i* which, to mathematicians, indicates the square root of minus 1—an "imaginary" number.

To mathematicians, imaginary numbers are numbers that have, in the conventional sense, the strange property that, when squared, produce negative results. If this bothers you and seems to go against all that is rational and real, I will sincerely suggest you stop reading now; things will get stranger before we're done.

In conventional terms, if a positive number is squared (multiplied by itself), the result is a positive number. In like fashion, if a negative number is squared, the result is also a positive number. Thus, both 2^2 and -2^2 yield 4. With imaginary numbers, however, $2i^2$ or $-2i^2$ both yield the result –4, while the square root of –4 is an imaginary number with the value $+/-2i$.

Using imaginary numbers for the axis of latitude is no less real than the Mandelbrot set itself. Remember, each time the value for the latitude is squared, the results will be negative—regardless of the sign of the original value—but will no longer be imaginary. At the same time, an imaginary number multiplied by a real number always produces an imaginary result.

Now, with this brief excursion into the theory of mathematics out of the way, I'll return to the formula used to explore the Mandelbrot set. Beginning at an arbitrary position within the set, using the point coordinates –0.6 and 0.4*i* for my example, the first value calculated is simply:

$$1) \quad Z_0 = (\,0\,)^2 - 0.6 + 0.4i$$
$$= -0.6 + 0.4i$$

Figure 19-1: The Mandelbrot Set

Approximate area shown in Figure 19-2.

In the second step the result of the first calculation becomes the first term of the equation while the original point coordinates remain as the constant term in the equation.

2) $Z_1 = (-0.6 + 0.4i)^2 - 0.6 + 0.4i$
    $= 0.36 - 0.48i - 0.16 - 0.6 + 0.4i$
    $= -0.4 - 0.08i$

I will also calculate a distance between the current position, $-0.4 - 0.08i$ and the graph zero point, yielding the result 0.407921561... as long as this distance is not equal to or greater than 2.0 (remember, I mentioned earlier that this value would be important, the why will be covered in a moment), I will continue the calculations recursively, producing the third term as:

3) $Z_2 = (-0.4 - 0.08i)^2 - 0.6 + 0.4i$

Again, the distance calculated is: 0.178283369..., which is still much less than 2.0 (but don't assume that the distance is always getting smaller).

Two End-Points

With the recursive formula used for the Mandelbrot set, each point calculated will tend to one of two end-points. First, after X-number of recursions, the distance result will exceed 2.0 and, after this point, the distance will continue to increase indefinitely. Second, after an X-number of recursions, the distance result will still be less than 2.0 and can be expected to continue to remain less than 2.0.

In the second instance, when distance never reaches nor exceeds 2.0—and I've chosen 100 recursions as a practical limit—the point can be said to lie within the fractal sea, the broad blank areas which form the dominate feature of the Mandelbrot set. In this case, I can say that the point has a fractal dimension that is less than 2 and, arbitrarily, this point is assigned a sea level color value (i.e., is part of the fractal sea).

It's the first instance, when distance eventually exceeds 2.0, that determines the features of the landscape surrounding the fractal sea and makes the Mandelbrot set most interesting. Each time the recursive distance reaches the breakpoint, the "altitude" of the landscape, at that point, is determined by the number of recursions required to reach this point. For example, if the breakpoint is reached on the third recursion, the altitude is 3 and the point is plotted in the corresponding color. In other terms, the altitude is a measure of how fast each point, except those at sea level, approaches infinity. The results are a complex map of colors showing the contours of a fractal landscape.

There's more. If you examine Figure 19-1 or 19-2 (or, better yet, your own color version), you will find that the fractal sea has many bays and tributaries along its shores. If you magnify (recalculate) any of these areas (as done in Figure 19-2), you will also find that all areas of the fractal sea, when viewed at a sufficiently large scale, are contiguous. There are no isolated areas and, as any area is enlarged, you will also find that the same principal features shown in Figure 19-1 repeat themselves in smaller and smaller scale throughout the Mandelbrot set, but always remain joined together with the larger scale features.

Implementing The Mandelbrot Set

The program MANDEL.C provides a basic implementation of the Mandelbrot set and shows the entire area from longitude −2.0 to +0.5 and latitude −1.25 to +1.25. Viewing smaller areas of the set (and in greater detail) can be provided simply by changing the XOrg, XMax, YOrg, and YMax values. The rest of the mapping procedure will adjust to accommodate the values chosen though, if desired at higher magnifications, you may also increase the Limit value beyond 100.

Warning, plotting the Mandelbrot set is and increasing the value of Limit can increase the plotting times. Also, a math co-processor can assist in reducing calculation times.

MANDEL.C is brief and fairly straightforward. The only complexity is found in the algorithm required to provide the reiterative calculation for the complex expression: $(x + y)^2$.

```
XTemp = ( XIter * XIter )
      - ( YIter * YIter ) + XPos;
YIter = 2 * ( XIter * YIter ) + YPos;
XIter = XTemp;
```

Within the calculations, *XTemp* is used to store initial results temporarily because both variable arguments are used in calculating each result and the original values must be available for each calculation.

Figure 19-2: Magnification of the Mandelbrot Set

The second calculation is simpler, using the *hypot* function to return a real value for the absolute distance from the arbitrary zero point (X-axis = 0, Y-axis = 0).

```
if( hypot( fabs( XIter ),
           fabs( YIter ) ) >= 2.0 )
     Done++;
```

Note that the *fabs* (float absolute) function is used to ensure only positive values are passed to *hypot* as arguments—thus avoiding a float error.

The calculation process is quite simple, but due to the number of points calculated, also requires quite a bit of time to generate a complete Mandelbrot Set. The presence of a co-processor will speed things up as will a fast CPU, however, even under ideal circumstances, this is not a rapid process.

The Henon Curve

In addition to fractal landscapes, a variety of other curious entities inhabit the mathematic universe. One of these is the Henon curve, an example of a wondrous mathematic creature known as a *strange attractor*.

Like the Mandelbrot set, the Henon attractor also uses a simple recursive formula and, at first glance, appears to be plotting a series of scattered dots. As the process continues, however, you will see that these scattered points actually form a complex curve as shown in Figure 19-3—rather as if some strange force continually impelled these seemingly random points to gather together in a coherent pattern. Hence, the name, strange attractor.

The Henon Curve is also like the Mandelbrot set in that any portion of the curve can be magnified to show increasingly greater detail and what may appear initially to be a single thread, under magnification, becomes a skein of threads and/or loops and curves as shown in Figure 19-4.

The formula for the Henon Attractor is expressed as:

$$X = Y + 1 - 1.4 * X^2$$
$$Y = 0.3 * X$$

Warning: as magnification increases, it may be necessary to increase the number of reiterations in order to plot enough points for the details to become clear.

Figure 19-3: The Henon Attractor

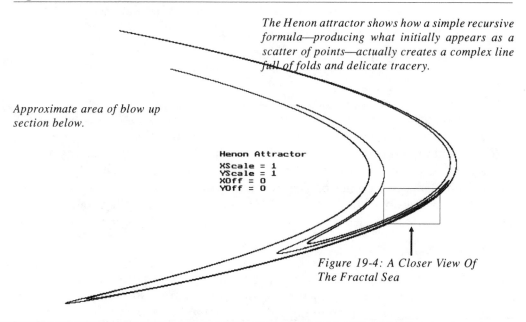

The Henon attractor shows how a simple recursive formula—producing what initially appears as a scatter of points—actually creates a complex line full of folds and delicate tracery.

Approximate area of blow up section below.

Henon Attractor
XScale = 1
YScale = 1
XOff = 0
YOff = 0

Figure 19-4: A Closer View Of The Fractal Sea

Figure 19-4: The Henon Attractor—A Section Blow-up

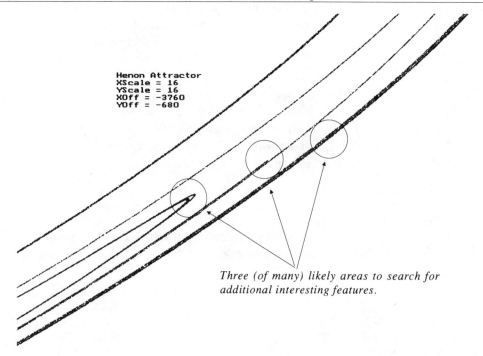

Henon Attractor
XScale = 16
YScale = 16
XOff = -3760
YOff = -680

Three (of many) likely areas to search for additional interesting features.

The Malthusian Curve

Some years ago, while playing with the Henon Attractor, I began looking at other recursive formulas and investigating their properties in a similar manner. There are quite a variety of recursive formulas, many of which are worth looking at. One of the formulas I tried was the Malthusian Growth formula which, supposedly, calculates the growth of a population through successive generations and is expressed as:

$$P_{n+1} = R * P_n * (1 - P_n)$$

where R is the rate of growth for successive generations of the population.

For practical purposes of calculating population growth, I suspect this formula is an over simplification, but mathematically, it is also interesting because the Malthusian Curve is another strange attractor or, more correctly, a family of strange attractors, but also with some fractal characteristics and some fascinating discontinuities as well.

Leaving the practical aspects aside[2], by plotting changes in *R* for values in the range 2.3 to 3.8 and calculating several thousand generations at each value, a series of curves are produced with each value of *R* creating a single, complex curve after (approximately) the first seven generations.

The values plotted for the first few generations calculated at each *R* can be seen in Figure 19-5 as a series of strokes beginning at the lower left corner and show the initial generations before the values enter the proximity of the strange attractor. Once the proximity of the strange attractor is reached, however, all subsequent points—for each given value of *R*—will appear somewhere along the curve defined by the attractor. Figure 19-6 provides a second view of the same set of attractors, primarily because differing views reveal details that may have been hidden earlier.

As with the previous examples, the Malthusian Curve is best understood by watching its generation (preferably on a high-resolution, color monitor) rather than by examining a black-and-white reproduction of the end result.

You should also notice that there are several points (values of *R*) where the strange attractor quite suddenly changes form and shape. Within the final series of attractors, the group forming the broad, sweeping curve, several further discontinuities can observed where specific values of *R* do

2 These are being investigated by at least one qualified Professor at Chiang Mai University and are certainly beyond my explanation.

Figure 19-5: Malthusian Flux

Both graphs are created by plotting populations at different rates of growth. Several catastrophic discontinuities are obvious even on the scale used here while other features become visible only as the scale increases or when a different view is selected.

Figure 19-6: Malthusian Flux

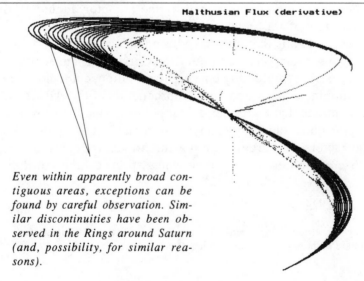

Even within apparently broad contiguous areas, exceptions can be found by careful observation. Similar discontinuities have been observed in the Rings around Saturn (and, possibility, for similar reasons).

not create continuous curves, but only a few selected points. These points follow the same general shape as the adjacent attractors.

In these latter cases, one possibility is that these regions may be artifacts of the machine, products of the calculations interacting with the limitations of the CPU and the algorithms used. This particular possibility is left for others to investigate and to prove or disprove. I may also be quite wrong in suggesting this, but it would certainly be an error not to mention it.

This brings me to my final excursion into the world of the mathematically strange.

Hic Draconis

The Dragon Curve is an interesting fractal pattern that begins as a straight line, but in each successive generation, exhibits a fractal dimension equal to the square root of 2. For example, after any two generations, the dimension (length) of the line is precisely doubled though the absolute distance between the begin and end points always remains constant.

Figure 19-7 shows a Dragon Curve in the 1st, 2nd, 3rd, and 12th generations as created by the algorithm in DRAGON.C. There are two points which you should realize about each of the figures shown.

First, the Dragon Curve is composed entirely of line segments, all of which are individually equal in length and always meet at 90° angles. And, second, the Dragon Curve is always a single continuous line which does not, at any point, cross itself (though vertices may and do coincide).

With these two cautions firmly in mind, you may enjoy attempting to trace the length of the curve.

On the other hand, if you would like a less taxing approach, simply modify the source program (DRAGON.C) to provide a brief time delay after each segment in drawn and then watch how it's done.

Arabesque

The Dragon Curve algorithm, with one minor change, also generates a second interesting pattern which I've titled Arabesque. To produce this second fractal pattern, simply comment out the instruction:

```
sign *= -1;
```

and adjust the y-axis position as necessary.

Figure 19-7: The Dragon Curve

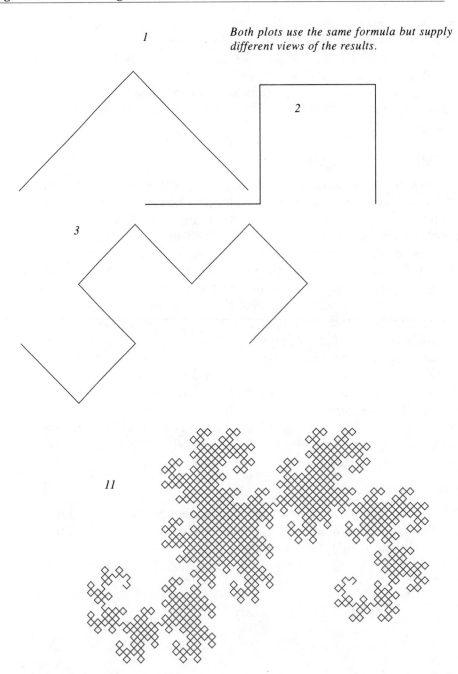

Both plots use the same formula but supply different views of the results.

Summary

The subject of fractal is entirely too extensive to be covered in any detail in a single chapter or even in a single book. Here, I've been able to provide a brief glimpse into a fascinating world filled with strange and wonderful detail. However, a variety of sources are available to provide at least a few maps and suggestions for further exploration, some of which are:

Mandelbrot Explorer

The Mandelbrot Explorer is a software program together with a series of stored Mandelbrot images that can be used to convenient explore different areas with in the Mandelbrot set. Requires MS-DOS 2.0 or later and EGA or VGA. Available from:

Peter Garrison
1613 Altivo Way
Los Angeles, CA 90026
(213) 665-1397

Chaos—Making a New Science

Chaos, by James Gleick, is available from Penguin Books in both hardback and paperback. It is an excellent introduction and guide not only to the world of fractal mathematics, but also to the science of chaotic systems and chaotic behavior and how these mathematic entities have very real effects in the physical universe. Complete with numerous color plates, this volume is highly recommended and contains an extensive bibliography of further references.

Chaos

Chaos, edited by Arun V. Holden, published by Princeton University Press, in an international collection of mathematical and technical papers dealing with chaotic systems, strange attractors, and fractal dimensions. While fascinating and informative—a fair knowledge of mathematics is required—this volume is not recommended for the casually curious. It will be greatly appreciated by those with the appropriate background and a modicum of patience.

The Science of Fractal Images

Fractal Images, edited by Peitgen and Saupe is published by Springer-Verlag and contains extensive color illustrations as well as notes and explana-

tions from a variety of sources. This volume falls somewhere between a
"coffee table" edition and an illustrated textbook.

```
//=====================//
//        DRAGON.C         //
//=====================//

#ifdef __TINY__
#error Graphics demos will not run in the tiny model.
#endif

#include <conio.h>
#include <stdio.h>
#include <stdlib.h>
#include <stdarg.h>
#include <graphics.h>

int  GraphDriver, GraphMode, ErrorCode,
     xaxis[4098], yaxis[4098], step, sign;

void Initialize()
{
   GraphDriver = DETECT;
   initgraph( &GraphDriver, &GraphMode, "C:\\TC\\BGI" );
   ErrorCode = graphresult();
   if( ErrorCode != grOk )
   {
       printf( "Graphics System Error: %s\n",
               grapherrormsg( ErrorCode ) );
       exit( 1 );
} }

void Pause()
{
   while( kbhit() ) getch();
   getch();
}

void Generate_Dragon( int color )
{
    int i, j, dx, dy;

    j = step / 2;
```

```
   setcolor( color );
   for( i=1; i<=4096; i+=step )
   {
      dx = xaxis[step+i] - xaxis[i];
      dy = yaxis[step+i] - yaxis[i];
      sign *= -1;                    /* comment out for Arabesque */
      xaxis[i+j] = xaxis[i] + ( dx + ( dy * sign ) ) / 2;
      yaxis[i+j] = yaxis[i] + ( dy - ( dx * sign ) ) / 2;
      if( color != 0 )
      {
         line( xaxis[i],        yaxis[i],
               xaxis[i+j],      yaxis[i+j]      );
         line( xaxis[i+j],      yaxis[i+j],
               xaxis[i+step], yaxis[i+step] );
} } }
void main()
{
   int  i;

   step = 4096;
   sign = -1;
   Initialize();
   xaxis[1] = getmaxx() / 4;
   xaxis[4097] = 3 * getmaxx() / 4;
   yaxis[1] = yaxis[4097] = 2 * getmaxy() / 3;
   setcolor( BLUE );
   line( xaxis[1], yaxis[1], xaxis[4097], yaxis[4097] );
   delay( 1000 );
   for( i=1; i<=13; i++ )
   {
      clearviewport();
      outtextxy( 1, 10, "Fractal Dragon Curve" );
      Generate_Dragon( i );
      step /= 2;
      delay( 1000 );
   }
   Pause();
   closegraph();
}
```

```
//=====================//
//        HENON.C         //
//=====================//

#ifdef __TINY__
#error Graphics demos will not run in the tiny model.
#endif

#include <conio.h>
#include <stdio.h>
#include <stdlib.h>
#include <stdarg.h>
#include <graphics.h>

#include "gprint.i"

int     GraphDriver, GraphMode, MaxColors,
        ErrorCode, MaxX, MaxY;
double  XScale, YScale, XOff, YOff;

void Initialize()
{
   GraphDriver = DETECT;
   initgraph( &GraphDriver, &GraphMode, "C:\\TC\\BGI" );
   ErrorCode = graphresult();
   if( ErrorCode != grOk )
   {
      printf( "Graphics System Error: %s\n",
               grapherrormsg( ErrorCode ) );
      exit( 1 );
   }
   MaxX = getmaxx();
   MaxY = getmaxy();
}

void Pause()
{
   while( kbhit() ) getch();
   getch();
}

void StrangeAttractor()
{
```

```
int     a, i, Color, XPos, YPos;
double  Xold, Xnew, Yold, Ynew,
        Xmax, Xmin, Ymax, Ymin;


        //==============================//
        //        Henon Attractor       //
        //  x = y + 1 - ( 1.4 * x * x ) //
        //  y = 0.3 * x                 //
        //==============================//

Xold = Xnew = Yold = Ynew = 0;

for( Color=1; Color<=15; Color++ )
   for( i=1; i<=0x00FF; i++ )
   {
      Xnew = Yold + 1 - ( 1.4 * Xold * Xold );
      Ynew = 0.3 * Xold;
      XPos = ( Xnew * MaxX/3 * XScale )
             + MaxX/2 + XOff;
      YPos = ( Ynew * MaxY   * YScale )
             + MaxY/2 + YOff;
      if( ( XPos >= 0 ) && ( XPos <= MaxX ) &&
          ( YPos >= 0 ) && ( YPos <= MaxY ) )
         putpixel( XPos, YPos, Color );
      Yold = Ynew;
      Xold = Xnew;
   }
gprintxy( 10, 110, "Henon Attractor" );
gprintxy( 10, 120, "XScale = %5.2f", XScale );
gprintxy( 10, 130, "YScale = %5.2f", YScale );
gprintxy( 10, 140, "  XOff = %8.5f", XOff );
gprintxy( 10, 150, "  YOff = %8.5f", YOff );
}

void main()
{
   Initialize();
   cleardevice();
   XScale = 1;                    // values to adjust scale //
   YScale = 1;
   XOff = 0;                      // and screen position    //
```

```
   YOff = 0;
   StrangeAttractor();
   Pause();
   closegraph();
}
```

```
           //=====================//
           //      MALTHUS1.C      //
           //=====================//
```

```
#ifdef __TINY__
#error Graphics demos will not run in the tiny model.
#endif

#include <conio.h>
#include <stdio.h>
#include <stdlib.h>
#include <stdarg.h>
#include <graphics.h>

int   GraphDriver, GraphMode, MaxColors, MaxX, MaxY,
      MaxGen = 0x00FF, ErrorCode;

void Initialize()
{
   GraphDriver = DETECT;
   initgraph( &GraphDriver, &GraphMode, "C:\\TC\\BGI" );
   ErrorCode = graphresult();
   if( ErrorCode != grOk )
   {
      printf( "Graphics System Error: %s\n",
              grapherrormsg( ErrorCode ) );
      exit( 1 );
   }
   MaxX = getmaxx();
   MaxY = getmaxy();
}

void StrangeAttractor()
{
   int     i, j, k, l, Color, Count, X, Y;
   double  PopOld, PopNew, Rate;
```

```
//======================================//
//      Malthusean Population Growth     //
//           Pn+1 = R * ( Pn - Pn^2 )    //
//======================================//
    PopNew = 0.0;
    Rate = 2.3;
    Color = BLACK;
    for( j=1; j<=151; j++ )
    {
        Color++;
        if( Color >= WHITE ) Color = BLUE;
        Count = 0;
        Rate +=  0.01;                      // increment Rate   //
        PopOld = 0.01;                      // reset Population //
        for( i=1; i<=MaxGen; i++ )
        {
            PopNew = Rate * ( PopOld * ( 1 - PopOld ) );
            X = PopOld * MaxX;
            Y = MaxY - ( PopNew * MaxY );
            putpixel( X, Y, Color );
            if( PopOld == PopNew ) Count++;
                else                 Count = 0;
            if( Count > 10 ) i = MaxGen;        // break loop //
            PopOld = PopNew;
    }  }
    outtextxy( 10, 10, "Malthusian Flux" );
}
void Pause()
{
    while( kbhit() ) getch();
    getch();
}
main()
{
    Initialize();
    cleardevice();
    StrangeAttractor();
    Pause();
    closegraph();
}
```

```
//=====================//
//     MALTHUS2.C      //
//=====================//

#ifdef __TINY__
#error Graphics demos will not run in the tiny model.
#endif

#include <conio.h>
#include <stdio.h>
#include <stdlib.h>
#include <stdarg.h>
#include <graphics.h>

#include "gprint.i"

int    GraphDriver, GraphMode, MaxColors,
       MaxX, MaxY, ErrorCode;

void Initialize()
{
   GraphDriver = DETECT;
   initgraph( &GraphDriver, &GraphMode, "C:\\TC\\BGI" );
   ErrorCode = graphresult();
   if( ErrorCode != grOk )
   {
      printf( "Graphics System Error: %s\n",
              grapherrormsg( ErrorCode ) );
      exit( 1 );
   }
   MaxX = getmaxx();
   MaxY = getmaxy();
}

void StrangeAttractor()
{
   int     i, j, k, l, Color, Count;
   double  PopOld, PopNew, X, Y, Rate;

   PopOld = PopNew = 0.0;
   Rate = 2.3;
   Y = 0;
   for( j=1; j<=15; j++ )
```

```
    {
        Color++;
        if( Color > WHITE ) Color = BLUE;
        for( k=1; k<=10; k++ )
        {
            Count = 0;
            Rate  = Rate + 0.01;
            PopOld = 0.01;
            for( i=1; i<=1000; i++ )
            {
                PopNew = Rate * ( PopOld * ( 1 - PopOld ) );
                X = PopNew - PopOld;
                putpixel( ( X * MaxX / 2 ) + MaxX / 2,
                          ( MaxY / 2 ) - ( Y * MaxY / 2 ),
                          Color );
                if( PopOld == PopNew ) Count++;
                    else                   Count = 0;
                if( Count > 100 ) i = 10000;
                PopOld = PopNew;
                Y = X;
        } } }
        outtextxy( 10, 10, "Malthusian Flux" );
    }

void Pause()
{
    while( kbhit() ) getch();
    getch();
}

main()
{
    Initialize();
    cleardevice();
    StrangeAttractor();
    Pause();
    closegraph();
}
```

```
//===================//
//       MANDEL.C      //
//===================//

#ifdef __TINY__
#error Graphics demos will not run in the tiny model.
#endif

#include <conio.h>
#include <stdio.h>
#include <stdlib.h>
#include <stdarg.h>
#include <graphics.h>
#include <math.h>

int    GraphDriver, GraphMode, ErrorCode;

void Initialize()
{
   GraphDriver = DETECT;
   initgraph( &GraphDriver, &GraphMode, "C:\\TC\\BGI" );
   ErrorCode = graphresult();
   if( ErrorCode != grOk )
   {
      printf( "Graphics System Error: %s\n",
              grapherrormsg( ErrorCode ) );
      exit( 1 );
   }  }

void Pause()
{
   while( kbhit() ) getch();
   getch();
}

int    XSize, YSize, Limit, i, j, Steps, Done;
double XStep, YStep, XPos, YPos, XOrg, YOrg,
       XMax, YMax, XIter, YIter, XTemp;

main()
{                              //===== Mandelbrot Area =====//
   Initialize();               //                            //
   XSize = getmaxx();          //              -1.25         //
```

```
YSize = getmaxy();              //                  ^              //
Limit = 100;                    //                  |              //
                                //   -2.0  <- - + - -> +0.5        //
XOrg = -2.0;                    //                  |              //
YOrg = -1.25;                   //                  v              //
XMax =  0.5;                    //                +1.25            //
YMax =  1.25;                   //                                 //
                                //=============================//
XStep = ( XMax - XOrg ) / XSize;
YStep = ( YMax - YOrg ) / YSize;
for( i=0; i<=XSize; i++ )
   for( j=0; j<=YSize; j++ )
   {                            // initialize value for position //
      XPos = XOrg + i * XStep;
      YPos = YOrg + j * YStep;
      XIter = 0.0;              // zero the beginning values //
      YIter = 0.0;
      Done = Steps = 0;         // zero flag and step value  //
      while( !Done )
      {
         XTemp = ( XIter * XIter )
               - ( YIter * YIter ) + XPos;
         YIter = 2 * ( XIter * YIter ) + YPos;
         XIter = XTemp;
         Steps++;
         if( hypot(fabs(XIter),fabs(YIter)) >= 2.0 )
            Done++;
         if( Steps >= Limit ) Done++;
         if( kbhit() )                    // break out of loops //
         {
            i = XSize;
            j = YSize;
            Done++;
         } }
      if( Steps < Limit ) putpixel( i, j, Steps );
   }
Pause();
closegraph();
}
```

Graphics Functions

arc

```
int  xcenter, ycenter, startangle, endangle, radius;
arc( xcenter, ycenter, startangle, endangle, radius );
```

Draws circular arc; startangle and endangle are in degrees (0..360); *xcenter*, *ycenter*, and *radius* in pixels.

bar

```
int  left, top, right, bottom;
bar( left, top, right, bottom );
```

Draws a filled-in rectangular bar using current fill pattern and color. For an outlined bar, use bar3d with depth zero.

bar3d

```
int  left, top, right, bottom, depth, topflag;
bar3d( left, top, right, bottom, depth, topflag );
```

Outlines a three-dimensional rectangular bar using current line style and color, then fills in results using current fill pattern and color. The bar's depth is given in pixels (normally about 25 percent of width). If the *topflag* parameter is zero, no top is added, allowing bars to be stacked.

circle

```
int  xcenter, ycenter, radius;
circle( xcenter, ycenter, radius );
```

Draws a circle using current color, centered at coordinates given with specified radius (in pixels).

cleardevice

```
cleardevice();
```

Erases the entire graphics screen, moves the current position (CP) to home (0,0).

clearviewport

```
clearviewport();
```

Erases the current viewport (graphics window), moving current position (CP) to home position (0,0) within the viewport setting.

closegraph

```
closegraph();
```

Uses _graphfreemem to deallocate memory reserved for graphics system and restores screen to text mode detected when initgraph was called.

detectgraph

```
int     graphdriver, graphmode;
detectgraph( &graphdriver, &graphmode );
```

Normally called by initgraph, detectgraph checks the hardware and returns values for the graphics driver and highest valid mode.

drawpoly

```
int  points;
int  poly[] = { 100,100, 200,100, 200,200, 100,200, 100,100 };
drawpoly( points, poly );
```

Draws the outline of a polygon using current color setting; *points* gives the number of vertices for the polygon; *poly* points to a sequence of integer pairs, each pair defining the *x,y* coordinates of one vertex of the polygon. In order to draw a closed figure with *n* vertices, *points* = *n+1* and the *nth* (final) coordinate pair is equal to the *0th* (first) coordinate pair.

If an error occurs, graphresult returns –6.

ellipse

```
int  xcenter, ycenter, startangle,
     endangle, xradius, yradius;
ellipse( xcenter, ycenter, startangle,
         endangle, xradius, yradius );
```

Draws an elliptical arc centered at (x,y) with separate x-axis and y-axis radii. The start and end angles are given in degrees. For a complete (closed) ellipse, use a start angle of 0 and an end angle of 360. Uses current color.

farmalloc

```
void far *bitimage;
int  xleft, ytop, xright, ybottom;
bitimage = farmalloc(
                imagesize( xleft, ytop, xright, ybottom ) );
```

Allocates memory for a pixel image (or other application), returning a pointer to the memory location. Use farmalloc for small data models and include <alloc.h> header file to allocate a far pointer.

fillellipse

```
int  xcenter, ycenter, xradius, yradius;
fillellipse( xcenter, ycenter, xradius, yradius );
```

(Turbo C version 2.0 or later) The fillellipse function draws an ellipse using *xcenter, ycenter* as the center point and *xradius, yradius* as the horizontal and vertical axes, filling the ellipse with the current fill color and fill pattern. Unlike the ellipse function, start and end angle arguments are not supported and an elliptical arc cannot be drawn.

fillpoly

```
int  points;
int  poly[] = { 100,100, 200,100, 200,200,
```

```
                    100,200, 100,100 };
fillpoly( points, poly );
```

Draws and fills a polygon using current fill style and color settings; *points* gives the number of vertices for the polygon; *poly* points to a sequence of integer pairs, each pair defining the *x,y* coordinates of one vertex of the polygon. In order to draw a closed figure with *n* vertices, *points* = *n+1* and the *nth* (final) coordinate pair is equal to the *0th* (first) coordinate pair.

If an error occurs, graphresult returns –6.

floodfill

```
int  xpoint, ypoint, bordercolor;
floodfill( xpoint, ypoint, bordercolor );
```

Fills a bounded (enclosed) region defined by the specified *bordercolor*, beginning at (x,y), a point within the area to be filled and using the current fill pattern and color. If the start point is outside a bounded region, the exterior will be filled. If a break occurs in the line defining the region, then the fill will leak.

For future compatibility, fillpoly is recommended where possible instead of floodfill. If an error occurs, graphresult will return a value of –7.

getarccoords

```
struct  arccoordstype   arcinfo;
getarccoords( &arcinfo );
```

Returns the coordinates of the last call to arc. The structure *arccoordstype* is defined in GRAPHICS.H as:

```
struct  arccoordstype { int x, y;
                        int xstart, ystart, xend, yend;  };
```

This structure defines the center point (x,y), the starting point (xstart,ystart), and the end point (xend,yend) of the arc. These values can be used to draw chords or other lines meeting the ends of the arc and are used by the pieslice function.

getaspectratio

```
int  xasp, yasp;
getaspectratio( &xasp, &yasp );
```

Returns x- and y-axis aspects. The aspect ratio is calculated as *xasp/yasp* and is used as a scaling factor by the arc, circle, and pieslice routines to make circles on the screen appear round.

Each graphics driver and graphics mode has an associated aspect ratio determined by the relative height and width of the pixels. For example, with the VGA graphics system, where each pixel is square, xasp = yasp and the aspect ratio is 1. The y aspect factor is normalized to 10,000 and, in general, xasp <= 10,000 (most pixels are taller than they are wide).

getbkcolor

```
int   backcolor = getbkcolor();
```

Returns current background color setting.

getcolor

```
int   forecolor = getcolor();
```

Returns current foreground color setting.

getdrivername

```
char   *driver_name;
driver_name = getdrivername();
```

The getdrivername function returns a pointer to a string identifying the current graphics driver.

getfillpattern

```
char   fillpatterninfo[8];
getfillpattern( &fillpatterninfo );
```

Copies a user-defined fill pattern to memory.

getfillsettings

```
struct   fillsettingtype fillinfo;
getfillsettings( &fillinfo );
```

Returns information about current fill pattern. The structure *fillsettingtype* is defined in GRAPHICS.H as:

```
struct   fillsettingtype { int pattern;
                           int color;    };
```

getgraphmode

```
int   modenow;
modenow = getgraphmode();
```

Returns the current graphics mode set by initgraph or setgraphmode.

getimage

```
include <alloc.h>
void   far   *bitimage;
int    xleft, ytop, xright, ybottom;
bitimage = farmalloc(
                imagesize( xleft, ytop, xright, ybottom ) );
getimage( xleft, ytop, xright, ybottom, bitimage );
```

Saves bit image from specified region into memory. The four integer parameters define the area to be saved. Use imagesize to get memory requirements, then allocate memory for image storage (memory allocation must be less than 64K). For compatibility with small data models, instead of malloc, the farmalloc function is used allocate memory but alloc.h must be included.

getlinesettings

```
struct   linesettingstype   lineinfo;
getlinesettings( &lineinfo );
```

Fills *lineinfo* with the current line style, pattern (*upattern*)and thickness. The structure *linesettingstype* is defined in GRAPHICS.H as:

```
struct   linesettingstype { int linestyle;
                            unsigned upattern;
                            int thickness;      };
```

getmaxcolor

```
int  MaxColors = getmaxcolor() + 1;
```

Returns the maximum valid color (palette size -1) for the current graphics mode.

getmaxx

```
int   MaxX = getmaxx();
```

Returns the maximum x-axis screen coordinate (max CP) for the current graphics driver and mode.

getmaxy

```
int  MaxY = getmaxy();
```

Returns the maximum x-axis screen coordinate (max CP) for the current graphics driver and mode.

getmodename

```
char  *mode_name;
mode_name = getmodename();
```

The getmodename function returns a pointer to a string identifying the current graphics mode.

getmoderange

```
int  graphdriver, lomode, himode;
getmoderange( graphdriver, &lomode, &himode );
```

Provides the lowest and highest valid mode values for the specified *graphdriver*. If the *graphdriver* specified is invalid, *lomode* and *himode* return set to −1.

getpalette

```
struct  palettetype      palette;
getpalette( &palette );
```

Fills *palette* with current palette information (settings). The structure *palettetype* is defined in GRAPHICS.H as:

```
struct  palettetype { unsigned char size;
                      signed char colors[MAXCOLORS + 1]; };
```

palette.size gives the number of colors valid for the current graphics driver and mode, *palette.color* is an array of *size* of bytes containing the color numbers for each entry in the palette.

getpixel

```
int  x, y;
color = getpixel( x, y );
```

Returns the color value of the indicated pixel at (*x,y*).

gettextsettings

```
struct   textsettingstype    textinfo;
gettextsettings( &textinfo );
```

Fills *textinfo* with the current text font, direction, size and horizontal and vertical justification. The structure *textsettingstype* is defined in GRAPH-ICS.H as:

```
struct   textsettingstype {   int font;   int direction;
                              int charsize;
                              int horiz; int vert;          };
```

getviewsettings

```
struct   viewporttype    viewport;
getviewsettings( &viewport );
```

Fills *viewport* with graphics window coordinates and clipping flag. The structure *viewporttype* is defined in GRAPHICS.H as:

```
struct   viewporttype   {   int left, top, right, bottom;
                            int clipflag;   };
```

The viewport's corners appear as absolute screen coordinates. If *clipflag* is non-zero, all lines will be truncated at the margins of the current viewport; otherwise, line drawings will extend across the entire screen.

getx

```
int   xpos = getx();
```

Returns the current position x coordinate (CPX) relative to the viewport.

gety

```
int      ypos = gety();
```

Returns the current position y coordinate (CPY) relative to the viewport.

gprintf   *(not included in GRAPHICS.LIB)*

```
include <stdarg.h>
void gprintf( int *xloc, int *yloc, char *fmt, ... )
{
```

```
va_list  argptr;
char     workstr[140];
struct   textsettingstype   textinfo;

gettextsettings( &textinfo );
va_start( argptr, format );
vsprintf( workstr, fmt, argptr );
outtextxy( *xloc, *yloc, workstr );
if( textinfo.direction == HORIZ_DIR )
     *yloc += textheight( workstr ) + 2;
else *xloc += textheight( workstr ) + 2;
va_end( argptr );
}
```

The length of the *fmt* argument should not exceed 140.

The gprintf routine is the graphics equivalent of printf. This routine is not included in the GRAPHICS.LIB. It must be entered by the programmer.

Text output is handled in both horizontal and vertical orientations. In horizontal orientation, the x-axis CP remains unchanged while the y-axis CP is moved down by the height of the workstring plus two pixels. In vertical orientation, the x-axis CP is incremented by the width of the string plus two pixels while the y-axis CP is not altered; otherwise, the actual text output is handled by outtextxy; see text for further notes.

gprintxy   *(not included in GRAPHICS.LIB)*

```
void gprintxy( xloc, yloc, fmtstr, ... )
```

The gprintxy routine works as per gprintf but accepts coordinate arguments directly and does not return an adjusted screen position for next string output. This routine is not included in the GRAPHICS.LIB but must be entered by the programmer.

graphdefaults

```
graphdefaults();
```

Resets all graphic settings to the default values; including restoring viewport to entire screen, setting CP to (0,0), resetting default palette, background and drawing colors, default fill style and pattern, default text font, and justification.

grapherrormsg

```
char    *ErrMsg = grapherrormsg( ErrorCode );
```

Returns a pointer to the string indicated by the ErrorCode.

_graphfreemem

```
unsigned size;
int       *memptr;
_graphfreemem( &memptr, size );
```

Normally _graphfreemem is called by closegraph to deallocate the memory reserved for drivers, fonts, and internal buffers. By default, _graphfreemem calls the free function, but custom memory management can be created by defining a new _graphfreemem.

_graphgetmem

```
unsigned  size;
_graphgetmem( size );
```

Normally _graphgetmem is called by initgraph to allocate memory space for graphic drivers, graphic character fonts, and internal buffers. By default, _graphgetmem uses the malloc function to set memory allocation but custom memory management can be created by defining a new _graphgetmem function.

graphresult

```
int  ErrorCode = graphresult();
```

Returns an error code for the last failed graphics operation.

imagesize

```
unsigned  size = imagesize(ulx, uly, lrx, lry);
```

Returns the size in bytes required to store the bit image according to the size specified. If the size required for the image is greater than 64Kbytes, a value of –1 (0xFFFF) is returned.

initgraph

```
int  graphdriver = DETECT, graphmode;
char *driverpath;
initgraph( &graphdriver, &graphmode, driverpath );
```

Initializes graphics system by loading graphics driver and putting system in graphics mode. When *graphdriver* is set to DETECT (0), detectgraph is called to test the system's graphics adapter and select the highest resolution mode valid. If not graphics hardware is detected, *graphdriver* is set to –2 and graphresult will also return –2.

A common error occurs in setting pathstring as:

```
char *driverpath = "C:\TURBOC\BGI";
```

instead of

```
char *driverpath = "C:\\TURBOC\\BGI";
```

A specific *graphdriver* can also be assigned. The *driverpath* must specify the directory where the .BGI drivers and .CHR fonts are located.

installuserdriver

```
driver = installuserdriver( "DRIVER", detect_driver() );
```

The installuserdriver allows installation of a custom or vendor-added device driver to the BGI internal table.

installuserfont

```
int  USER_FONT = 0;
USER_FONT = installuserfont( "\\FontPath\\FontName.CHR" );
```

The installuserfont function loads a .CHR (stroked) font which is not built into the BGI system, returning an font ID number which can be passed to settextstyle to select the font. Up to 20 external fonts can be installed at any time. If the internal font table is full, a value of -11 (*grError*) is returned.

line

```
int xstart, ystart, xend, yend;
line( xstart, ystart, xend, yend );
```

Draws a line between the points specified using the current color, line style, and thickness without changing the current position (CP).

linerel

```
int xdev, ydev;
linerel( xdev, ydev );
```

Draws a line from the current position to another point separated from CP by the distance *xdev*, *ydev*; uses the current color, line style, and thickness and updates CP to the new position.

lineto

```
int  x, y;
lineto(x,y);
```

Draws a line from the current position to the point specified by (*x,y*), using the current color, line style, and thickness. Resets CP to (*x,y*). S

malloc

```
void  *bitimage;
int   xleft, ytop, xright, ybottom;
bitimage = malloc(
             imagesize( xleft, ytop, xright, ybottom ) );
```

Allocates memory for a pixel image (or other application), returning a pointer to the memory location.

moverel

```
int  xdev, ydev;
moverel( xdev, ydev );
```

Moves CP the relative distance specified by (*xdev,ydev*).

moveto

```
int     x, y;
moveto( x, y );
```

Moves CP to the absolute point specified by (*x,y*).

outtext

```
outtext( "Display string for viewport" );
```

Displays string in viewport (graphics window) beginning at CP, using current font, color, charsize, direction and text justification. If horizontal justification is LEFT_TEXT and direction is HORIZ_DIR, CP's x-axis coordinate is advanced by *textwidth(textstring)*—otherwise CP is not altered.

outtextxy

```
int  x, y;
outtextxy( x, y, "Display string for viewport" );
```

Displays string in viewport (graphics window) beginning at position specified by (*x,y*), using current font, color, charsize, direction, and text justification. CP's coordinates are not changed.

pieslice

```
int  xcenter, ycenter, startangle, endangle, radius;
pieslice( xcenter, ycenter, startangle, endangle, radius );
```

Draws and fills in a pie slice, centered at (*xcenter,ycenter*) through the arc specified by the start and end angles (in degrees). The pie slice is outlined in the current drawing color, then filled using the current fill pattern and color.

putimage

```
void  far *bitimage;
int   xleft, ytop, ops;
putimage( xleft, ytop, bitimage, ops );
```

Writes a previously saved bit image to the screen with the upper-left corner of the image appearing at (*xleft,ytop*). The *ops* parameter controls how each image pixel (color) is combined with the existing screen pixels.

putpixel

```
int  xpos, ypos, color;
putpixel( xpos, ypos, color );
```

Sets the pixel specified by (*xpos,ypos*) to the color indicated.

rectangle

```
int  xleft, ytop, xright, ybottom;
rectangle( xleft, ytop, xright, ybottom );
```

Draws a rectangle in the current line style, thickness, and color.

registerbgidriver and registerfarbgidriver

```
int  GraphicDriver;
if ( registerbgidriver( GraphicDriver ) < 0 ) exit(1);
```

The registerbgidriver function is used to register a linked-in graphics driver. If the specified graphics driver is not found, a negative error code is returned; otherwise, the internal driver number is returned. The registerfarbgidriver should not be called unless the /F option is used with the BGIOBJ.EXE utility.

registerbgifont and registerfarbgifont

```
int   GraphicFont;
if( registerbgifont( GraphicFont ) < 0 ) exit(1);
```

The registerbgifont function is used to register a linked stroked font character set. If the specified font is not found, a negative error code is returned; otherwise, the registered font number is returned. The registerfarbgidriver should not be called unless the /F option is used with the BGIOBJ.EXE utility.

restorecrtmode

```
restorecrtmode();
```

Resets video to text mode detected by initgraph. May be used with setgraphmode to switch back and forth between graphics and text modes.

sector

```
int   xcenter, ycenter, startangle,
      endangle, xradius, yradius;
sector( xcenter, ycenter, startangle,
        endangle, xradius, yradius );
```

The sector function creates an elliptical arc, draws lines from the end points to the center point and then fills in the completed figure. The sector outline is drawn using the current drawing color and current line style for the radius lines, then filled using the current fill pattern and fill color (see floodfill). Screen aspect ratio adjustment is automatic.

setactivepage

```
int   pagenum;
setactivepage( pagenum );
```

Selects graphics page *pagenum* for output. This may or may not the active visual page (see setvisualpage) but all graphics output will be directed to this page. Only EGA, VGA, and Hercules graphics cards currently support multiple graphics (or text) pages. Useful for animation.

setallpalette

```
struct  palettetype  newpalette;
setallpalette( &newpalette );
```

Makes *newpalette* the current palette. All color changes are effected immediately. The colors for *newpalette* must be assigned using setpalette.

setbkcolor

```
int  backcolor;
setbkcolor( backcolor );
```

The argument *backcolor* can be a name or value.

setcolor

```
int  forecolor;
setcolor( forecolor );
```

Sets the current drawing color using *palette.color[forecolor]*.

setfillpattern

```
int  color;
char diamond[8] = {  0x10, 0x38, 0x7C, 0xFE,
                     0x7C, 0x38, 0x10, 0x00 };
setfillpattern( &diamond, color );
```

Selects an 8x8 user-defined fill pattern. The *diamond* pattern is a sequence of 8 bytes, each byte corresponding to 8 pixels in the pattern. One bits turn on pixel, zero bits turn off pixel. The example pattern *diamond* creates a small 7x7 diamond pattern with a one-pixel border at right and bottom.

setfillstyle

```
setfillstyle( SOLID_FILL, GREEN );
```

Sets current fill pattern and color.

All patterns except EMPTY_FILL use the current fill color. Note: pattern 12 (USER_FILL) can only be called *after* setfillpattern has established the user-defined fill pattern.

setgraphbufsize

```
unsigned  bufsize, oldbufsize;
oldbufsize = setgraphbufsize( bufsize );
```

Several of graphics routines use a memory buffer created by initgraph via _graphgetmem. The default size is 4 kilobytes (4,096 bytes), but it can be decreased to save space or increased if more buffer memory is required. The setgraphbufsize function must be called *before* calling initgraph.

setgraphmode

```
int  graphmode;
setgraphmode( graphmode );
```

Resets system from text mode to graphics mode, clearing the screen. Graphics mode must have been previously initialized by initgraph.

setlinestyle

```
unsigned  linepattern;
int  style, width;
setlinestyle( style, linepattern, width );
```

Sets current line width and style. Note: a line width of 2 can also be assigned, but any value greater than three results in a graphics error and causes the line style and width to be set to the default settings.

setpalette

```
int  palette_index, color;
setpalette( palette_index, color );
```

With any of the 320x200 pixel video graphics modes (CGA, MCGA or AT&T), color selections are limited to predefined 4-color palettes: C0, C1, C2 and C3. In each palette, the background color (index 0) can be user defined but colors 1..3 cannot be changed. In other graphics modes, all colors can be redefined. These symbolic color constants are defined in GRAPHICS.H.

The IBM-8514 graphics card and IBM8514 driver support a color palette of 256 colors from a total of 262,144 (256K) color values. No symbolic constants are defined for this driver, but the IBM-8514 card can also emulate VGA modes (as IBM8514LO but the VGA driver is recommended for better compatibility—see initgraph). Each color is defined by three six-bit values for the Red, Green, and Blue components.

setrbgpalette

```
int   colornum, valuered, valueblue, valuegreen;
setrbgpalette( colornum, valuered, valueblue, valuegreen );
```

The setrbgpalette routine is provided for use with the IBM8514 driver. The *colornum* argument sets the palette color (0..255) to be defined by the *valuered*, *valueblue*, and *valuegreen* arguments. Only the six most significant bits of the low byte of each color argument are used (values from 0 to 252 in steps of 4. Arguments of 252, 253, 254, and 255 are treated identically since the 6 most significant bits are the same).

The other palette manipulation routines in the graphics library are not valid with the IBM8514 driver in IBM8514HI (1023x768 pixel) mode. This includes setallpalette, setpalette, and getpalette. Also, the floodfill routine is not valid with this driver and mode.

settextjustify

```
int hjustify, vjustify;
settextjustify( hjustify, vjustify );
```

Sets horizontal and vertical text justification. Default settings are LEFT_TEXT, TOP_TEXT (0,2).

When justification is set as *LEFT_TEXT* and *direction = HORIZ_DIR*, the current position's *x* setting is advanced after a call to outtext or gprintf by textwidth(string).

settextstyle

```
int   font, direction, charsize;
settextstyle( font, direction, charsize );
```

Sets current graphics text characteristics according to *font*, *direction*, and *charsize* selected.

Normally, only one font is kept in memory at any time but multiple fonts can be linked using the BGIOBJ utility. Except for DEFAULT_FONT which is built into the graphics system, the .CHR files for the selected font must be in the directory or subdirectory indicated by initgraph as driverpath or linked and registered using registerbgifont.

Graphics Text Direction is horizontal by default but can be set to vertical (rotated 90° counterclockwise).

For bit-mapped font(s): *charsize* may be 0..10. Zero and one display 8x8 pixel rectangles, 2 = 16x16 pixel rectangle, etc., up to 10 times normal size.

For stroked fonts: *charsize = 0* magnifies the stroked font by the default factor of 4 or by the user-defined size factors set by setusercharsize. A maximum magnification of 10 is valid.

If invalid values are passed to settextjustify, graphresult will return –11 (*general error*) and the current text settings will remain unchanged.

setusercharsize

```
int   xmult, xdiv, ymult, ydiv;
setusercharsize( xmult, xdiv, ymult, ydiv );
```

Provides user-defined character magnification for stroked fonts. These values are active only if settextstyle is called to set *charsize = 0*. The scaled width is defined as *xmult/xdiv*; the scaled height is defined as *ymult/ydiv*.

setviewport

```
int   xleft, ytop, xright, ybottom, clipflag;
setviewport( xleft, ytop, xright, ybottom, clipflag );
```

The viewport's coordinates are absolute screen coordinates. If *clipflag* is non-zero, all lines will be truncated at the viewport margins; otherwise, line drawings will extend across the entire screen.

setvisualpage

```
int   pagenum;
setvisualpage( pagenum );
```

Selects graphics page *pagenum* for active visual page and ay not the active graphics page (see setactivepage). Only EGA, VGA, and Hercules graphics cards currently support multiple graphics (or text) pages. Useful for animation.

setwritemode

```
int   writemode;
setwritemode( writemode );
```

The setwritemode function sets the screen writing mode for line drawing in graphics modes. Two constants are defined for *writemode*: COPY_PUT = 0 (default) and XOR_PUT = 1

Note: setwritemode currently works only with line, linerel, lineto, rectangle, and drawpoly.

textheight

```
int  charheight = textheight( "H" );
```

Returns the height of a string in pixels, using the current font size, scaling factors, and text direction. This may be the height of a single character or be the height of an entire string.

textwidth

```
int  charwidth = textwidth( "H" );
```

Returns the width of a string in pixels, using the current font size, scaling factors and text direction. This may be the width of a single character or be the width of an entire string.

Mouse and Turtle Functions

Mouse Structure Definitions

Mresult

```
struct { int  present,               /* TRUE if mouse present */
             buttons;                /* # of buttons on mouse */
       }   Mresult;
```

Mstatus

```
struct { int  button_status,    /* bits 0-2 on if button down */
             button_count,      /* # times button was clicked */
             xaxis, yaxis;      /* mouse cursor position */
       }   Mstatus;
```

Mmovement

```
struct { int x_count,                /* net horizontal movement */
             y_count;                /* net vertical movement   */
       }   Mmovement;
```

mouse_event

```
struct { unsigned flag,                /* mouse event record   */
                  button,              /* button(s) pressed    */
```

```
                    xaxis, yaxis;        /* cursor position    */
        }   mouse_event;
```

g_cursor

```
struct { unsigned int
            ScreenMask[16],        /* screen mask descriptor */
            CursorMask[16],        /* cursor mask descriptor */
            xkey, ykey;             /* cursor hot spot     */
        }   g_cursor;
```

Mouse Functions

Mreset

```
    Mresult  m;
        m = Mreset();
```

Resets mouse default status, returns pointer to Mresult structure containing information indicating if mouse installed and, if present, number of buttons. Always call during initialization.

Mshow

```
        Mshow( ON );
        Mshow( OFF );
```

Turns mouse cursor on (visible) or off (hidden). Cursor state does not affect mouse tracking, only screen image visibility. Cursor image should be concealed during screen update operations.

*Mpos

```
    m_status  m;
        m = Mpos();
```

Calls mouse function 3, returning pointer to *Mstatus* structure containing current mouse cursor position and button status.

Mmoveto

```
    int  xaxis, yaxis;
        Mmoveto( xaxis, yaxis );
```

Calls mouse function 4, moving move mouse cursor to defined position.

*Mpressed

```
Mstatus   m;
    m = Mpressed( ButtonL );
```

Calls mouse function 5 for information on specified button. Returns a pointer to the *Mstatus* structure containing the current status of the button specified (up or down), the number of times the button was pressed since last call, and the cursor position the last time the button was pressed. Resets the count and position information. ButtonL (0) is left, ButtonR (1) is right, and ButtonM (2) is the center (three-button mice only).

*Mreleased

```
Mstatus   m;
    m = Mreleased( ButtonL );
```

Calls mouse function 6 for information on specified button. Returns a pointer to the *Mstatus* structure containing the current status of the button specified (up or down), the number of times the button was pressed since last call, and the cursor position the last time the button was pressed. Resets the count and position information. ButtonL (0) is left, ButtonR (1) is right, and ButtonM (2) is the center (three-button mice only).

Mxlimit

```
int   x_min, x_max;
    Mxlimit( x_min, x_max );
```

Uses mouse function 7 to set horizontal mouse boundaries, limiting screen mouse movement. If mouse cursor is outside of this range, the cursor is moved inside the boundary specified. If *x_min* is larger than *x_max*, values are swapped.

Mylimit

```
int   y_min, y_max;
    Mylimit( y_min, y_max );
```

Uses mouse function 8 to set vertical mouse boundaries, limiting screen mouse movement. If mouse cursor is outside of this range, the cursor is moved inside the boundary specified. If *y_min* is larger than *y_max*, values are swapped.

*Mmotion

```
Mmovement   m;
    m = Mmotion();
```

Uses mouse function 11, returning pointer to *Mmovement* structure reporting net cursor motion since last call to this function.

Mmove_ratio

```
int  xstep, ystep;
    Mmove_ratio( xstep, ystep );
```

Uses mouse function 15 to set mouse movement to pixel (cursor) motion ratio. Default values are 16 vertical, 8 horizontal.

Mspeed

```
int  speed;
    Mspeed( speed );
```

Calls mouse function 19, setting a speed threshold (in mickies/second) for accelerated cursor movement. A normal setting is 300 mickies/second (012Ch); maximum is 32,767 mickies/second (7FFFh).

Set_Cursor   (text mouse)

```
unsigned  s_start, s_stop;
    Set_Cursor( HARDWARE, s_start, s_stop );
```

Uses mouse function 10 to set text cursor type (SOFTWARE = 0, HARDWARE = 1). For software cursor, s_start and s_stop are the screen and cursor masks. For hardware cursor, s_start and s_stop specify scan line start/stop, that is, cursor shape.

Set_Cursor   (graphic mouse)

```
gcursor  ThisCursor;
    Set_Cursor( ThisCursor );
    Set_Cursor( GLOVE );
```

Selects graphics mouse cursor by calling private *set_cursor* method with extended parameter syntax.

Turtle Functions

back

```
int   distance;
    forward( distance );
```

Moves turtle specified distance in one-pixel steps. Movement is opposite current turtle direction; if pen is down, draws a line using current drawing color.

create_turtle

```
create_turtle();
```

Creates turtle cursor image, normally called only by init_turtle function.

clear_turtle_screen

```
clear_turtle_screen();
```

Clears turtle screen and resets turtle cursor to home position.

correct_direction

```
int   angle;
    correct_direction( &angle );
```

Restricts angle to 0..360 degree range.

drawstr

```
char   logostr[] = instruction_string;
int    scale;
    drawstr( scale, logostr );
```

Deciphers instruction string to draw character, figure, or logo using turtle graphics. Scale acts as multiplier setting size of figure drawn.

If the instruction string is longer than 150 characters, the figure will be truncated.

forward

```
int   distance;
    forward( distance );
```

Moves turtle specified distance in one-pixel steps. Movement is in current turtle direction; if pen is down, draws a line using current drawing color.

heading

```
int  angle;
   angle = heading();
```

Returns the current turtle heading.

hide_turtle

```
      hide_turtle();
```

If turtle cursor is visible, hides cursor.

home

```
      home();
```

Resets turtle cursor to turtle home position (normally at the center of the turtle window).

init_turtle

```
      init_turtle();
```

Calls create_turtle to generate turtle cursor, reads video aspect ratio and screen size, sets up initial turtle window and home position, and sets default turtle values and flags. Defaults include: pen color equals maximum valid color for video mode; turtle cursor visible; turtle delay zero (fast turtle); screen wrap off; pen down; and turtle heading NORTH.

no_wrap

```
      no_wrap();
```

Turns off turtle screen wrap. Allows turtle movement outside of turtle window but drawing is restricted to window area.

pen_down

```
      pen_down();
```

Puts turtle pen down in drawing position. Turtle movement will draw a line using current pen color.

pen_up

```
pen_up();
```

Raises turtle pen, allowing movement without drawing.

rsin

```
double   sin_angle;
int      angle;
   sin_angle = rsin( angle );
```

Returns the sine of an angle in degrees.

rcos

```
double   cos_angle;
int      angle;
   cos_angle = rcos( angle );
```

Returns the cosine of an angle in degrees.

set_heading

```
int  degrees;
   set_heading( degrees );
```

Sets turtle heading in degrees. Angles are corrected to 0..360 degree range.

set_pen_color

```
int  color;
   set_pen_color( color );
```

Sets current turtle-draw color. Argument is checked against valid color range. Color can be passed as 0 to erase.

set_position

```
int  xaxis, yaxis;
   set_position( xaxis, yaxis );
```

Sets turtle cursor to position specified. Coordinates are relative to turtle home position (normally center of turtle window).

show_turtle

```
    show_turtle();
```

If turtle cursor is not visible, restores cursor image at current position.

step_turtle

```
  int   xstep, ystep;
    step_turtle( xstep, ystep );
```

Moves turtle cursor, drawing if the pen is down and turtle is within turtle window. Adjusts position at window limits if screen wrap is in effect.

turn_left

```
  int   degrees;
    turn_left( degrees );
```

Turns turtle heading to left number of degrees specified. Resulting angle is in 0..360 degree range. A negative argument turns turtle heading to right.

turn_right

```
  int   degrees;
    turn_right( degrees );
```

Turns turtle heading to right number of degrees specified. Resulting angle is in 0..360 degree range. A negative argument turns turtle heading to left.

turtle_window

```
  int   xcenter, ycenter;
  int   xwidth, yheight;
    turtle_window( xcenter, ycenter, xwidth, yheight );
```

Sets turtle window with center at absolute screen coordinates *xcenter,ycenter*. The window will be *xwidth* pixels wide, *yheight* pixels high unless margins exceed physical screen limits. A three-pixel margin is reserved at top and left for the turtle cursor image requirements. The turtle cursor is set to the home position.

turtle_where

```
    if( turtle_where() ) ...
```

Returns TRUE (1) if turtle cursor is within the turtle window.

turtle_delay

```
int   timeout;
    turtle_delay( timeout );
```

Sets turtle speed using time delay executed between turtle steps.

wrap

```
wrap()
```

Turns off turtle wrap, allowing turtle cursor to move outside of turtle window.

xcor

```
int   xaxis;
    xaxis = xcor();
```

Returns the turtle cursor x-axis position (relative to the home position).

ycor

```
int   yaxis;
    yaxis = ycor();
```

Returns the turtle cursor y-axis position (relative to the home position).

The BGI Driver Toolkit

Creating Device Drivers for the Borland Graphics Interface

The BGI Driver Toolkit is available at no charge on an "as is" basis to registered users of Turbo Pascal, Turbo C++, and Turbo Prolog and may be downloaded from Borland International's languages forum on the CompuServe network. The BGI Driver Toolkit also includes a .BIN to .BGI conversion utility (DFONT.EXE, DFONT.C, and FONT.H) and a debug driver.

Also available from Borland, via Compuserve, are the Turbo Font Editor (see Chapter 17) with nine graphics character fonts: EURO.CHR, GOTH.CHR, LCOM.CHR, LITT.CHR, SANS.CHR, SCRI.CHR, SIMP.CHR, TRIP.CHR, and TSCR.CHR; and a new VGA 256-color .BGI driver (see Appendix E). Future revisions and updates will be available on Borland's Compuserve forum.

The BGI Driver Toolkit

Copyright (c) 1988 Borland International
Revision 1
September 15, 1988

Introduction

The Borland Graphics Interface (BGI) is a fast, compact, and device-independent software package for graphics development built into the Turbo Pascal, Turbo C++, and Turbo Prolog language products. Device independence is achieved via loadable device-specific drivers called from a common kernel. This document describes basic BGI functionality, as well as the steps necessary to create new device drivers. Accompanying this document are files containing sample code (see Table C-1) and other pertinent information.

Table C-1: Sample Code Files

Filename	File Description
BH.C	BGI loader header building program source
BH.EXE	BGI loader header building program
DEVICE.INC	Structure and macro definition file
DEBVECT.ASM	Vector table for sample (DEBUG) driver
DEBUG.C	Main module for sample driver
MAKEFILE	Build file
BUILD.BAT	A batch file for MAKE-phobics
TEST.C	C program demonstrating how to register and load a new device driver.
DFONT.EXE	A .BIN to .BGI conversion utility
DFONT.C	C source code for the conversion utility
FONT.H	Header file used by DFONT

BGI Run-time Architecture

Programs produced by Borland languages create graphics via two entities acting in concert: the generic BGI kernel and a device-specific driver. Typically, an application built with a Borland compiler will include several device driver files on the distribution disk (extension .BGI) so that the program can run on various types of screens and printers. Graphics requests (for example, draw line and draw bar, etc.) are sent by the application to the BGI kernel, which in turn makes requests of the device driver to actually manipulate the hardware.

A BGI device driver is a binary image; that is, a sequence of bytes without symbols or other linking information. The driver begins with a short header, followed by a vector table containing the entry points to the functions inside. The balance of the driver comprises the code and data required to manipulate the target graphics hardware.

All code and data references in the driver must be near (small model, offset only), and the entire driver, both code and data, must fit within 64K.

In use, the device driver can count on its being loaded on a paragraph boundary. The BGI kernel uses a register-based calling convention to communicate with the device driver (described in detail briefly).

BGI Graphics Model

When considering the functions list below, keep in mind that BGI performs most drawing operations using an implicit drawing or tracing color (COLOR), fill color (FILLCOLOR), and pattern (FILLPATTERN). For example, the PIESLICE call accepts no pattern or color information, but instead uses the previously set COLOR value to trace the edge of the slice, and the previously set FILLCOLOR and FILLPATTERN values for the interior.

For efficiency, many operations take place at the position of the current pointer, or CP. For example, the LINE routine accepts only a single (x,y) coordinate pair, using the CP as the starting point of the line and the passed coordinate pair as the ending point. Many functions (LINE, to name one) affect CP, and the MOVE function can be used to explicitly adjust CP. The BGI coordinate system places the origin (pixel 0,0) at the upper left-hand corner of the screen.

Header Section

The device header section, which must be at the beginning of the device driver, is built using macro BGI defined in file DEVICE.INC. The BGI macro takes the name of the device driver to be built as an argument. For example, a driver named DEBUG would begin as shown here:

```
CSEG    SEGMENT PARA PUBLIC 'CODE'   ; any segment naming may be used
        ASSUME DS:CSEG, CS:CSEG       ; cs=ds
        CODESEG
        INCLUDE DEVICE.INC            ; include the device.inc file
        BGI     DEBUG                 ; declare the device header section
```

The device header section declares a special entry point known as EMULATE. If the action of a device driver vector is not supported by the hardware of a device, the vector entry should contain the entry EMULATE. This will be patched at load-time to contain a jump to the kernel's emulation routine. These routines will emulate the action of the vector by breaking down the request into simpler primitives. For example, if the hardware has functionality to draw polygons, the polygon vector will contain the address of the routine to dispatch the polygon data to the hardware and would appear as follows:

```
        dw    offset    POLYGON       ; Vector to the Polygon Routine
```

If, as is often the case, the hardware doesn't have the functionality to display polygons, the vector would instead contain the EMULATE vector:

```
        dw              EMULATE       ; Polygon functions must be emulated
```

The kernel has emulation support (as shown in Table C-2) for the following vectors:

Table C-2: Vector Emulation Support

Vector	Support
POLYGON	Rendering polygons
BARFILL	Filling rectangles
PATBAR	Pattern filling of rectangles
ARC	Elliptical arc rendering
PIESLICE	Elliptical pie slices
FILLED_ELLIPSE	Filled ellipses
SYMBOLS	Line marking symbols
FILLSTYLE	Solid filling styles
TSTYLE	Text drawing styles
TEXT	Hardware text rendering
TEXTSIZ	Scaling of hardware text

The Driver Status Table

BGI requires that each driver contain a Driver Status Table (DST) to determine the basic characteristics of the device which the driver addresses. As an example, the DST for a CGA display is shown here:

```
STATUS      STRUC
STAT        DB      0           ; Current Device Status (0 = No Errors)
DEVTYP      DB      0           ; Device Type Identifier (must be 0)
XRES        DW      639         ; Device Full Resolution in X Direction
YRES        DW      199         ; Device Full Resolution in Y Direction
XEFRES      DW      639         ; Device Effective X Resolution
YEFRES      DW      199         ; Device Effective Y Resolution
XINCH       DW      9000        ; Device X Size in inches*1000
YINCH       DW      7000        ; Device Y Size in inches*1000
ASPEC       DW      4500        ; Aspect Ratio = (y_size/x_size) * 10000
            DB      8h
            DB      8h          ; for compatibility, use these values
            DB      90h
            DB      90h
STATUS      ENDS
```

The BGI interface provides a system for reporting errors to the BGI kernel and to the higher level code developed using Borland's language packages. This is done using the STAT field of the Driver Status Table. This field should be filled in by the driver code if an error is detected during the execution of the device installation (INSTALL).

The next field in the Device Status Table, DEVTYP, describes the class of the device which the driver controls; for screen devices, this value is always 0.

The next four fields, XRES, YRES, XEFRES, and YEFRES contain the number of pixels available to BGI on this device in the horizontal and vertical dimensions, minus one. For screen devices, XRES=XEFRES and YRES=YEFRES. The XINCH and YINCH fields are the number of inches horizontally and vertically into which the device's pixels are mapped, times 1,000. These fields in conjunction with XRES and YRES permit device resolution (DPI, or dots per inch) calculation.

$$\text{Horizontal resolution (DPI)} = (XRES+1) / (XINCH/1000)$$
$$\text{Vertical resolution (DPI)} = (YRES+1) / (YINCH/1000)$$

The ASPEC (aspect ratio) field is effectively a multiplier/divisor pair (the divisor is always 10,000) which is applied to Y coordinate values to produce aspect-ratio adjusted images (for example, round circles). For example, an ASPEC field of 4,500 implies that the application will have to transform Y coordinates by the ratio: 4,500/10,000 when drawing circles to that device if it expects them to be round. Individual monitor variations may require an additional adjustment by the application.

The Device Driver Vector Table

The routines in the device driver are accessed via a vector table. This table is at the beginning of the driver and contains 16-bit offsets to subroutines and configuration tables within the driver. The format of the vector table is shown below.

VECTOR_TABLE:

DW	INSTALL	; Driver initialization and installation
DW	INIT	; Initialize device for output
DW	CLEAR	; Clear graphics device; get fresh screen
DW	POST	; Exit from graphics mode, unload plotter, etc.
DW	MOVE	; Move Current Pointer (CP) to (X,Y)
DW	DRAW	; Draw Line from (CP) to (X,Y)
DW	VECT	; Draw line from (X0,Y0) to (X1,Y1)
DW	POLY	; Define polygon

```
        DW      BAR                 ; Filled rectangle from (CP) to (X,Y)
        DW      PATBAR              ; Patterned rectangle from (X,Y) to (X1,Y1)
        DW      ARC                 ; Define ARC
        DW      PIESLICE            ; Define an elliptical pie slice
        DW      FILLED_ELLIPSE      ; Draw a filled ellipse
        DW      PALETTE             ; Load a palette entry
        DW      ALLPALETTE          ; Load the full palette
        DW      COLOR               ; Set current drawing color/background
        DW      FILLSTYLE           ; Filling control and style
        DW      LINESTYLE           ; Line drawing style control
        DW      TEXTSTYLE           ; Hardware Font control
        DW      TEXT                ; Hardware Draw text at (CP)
        DW      TEXTSIZ             ; Hardware Font size query
        DW      FLOODFILL           ; Fill a bounded region
        DW      GETPIX              ; Read a pixel from (X,Y)
        DW      PUTPIX              ; Write a pixel to (X,Y)
        DW      BITMAPUTIL          ; Bitmap Size query function
        DW      SAVEBITMAP          ; BITBLT from screen to system memory
        DW      RESTOREBITMAP       ; BITBLT from system memory to screen
        DW      SETCLIP             ; Define a clipping rectangle
        DW      COLOR_QUERY         ; Color Table Information Query
        DW      RESERVED            ; Reserved for Borland's use (0)
        DW      SYMBOL              ; Draw a Graphics Symbol
;
;       32 additional vectors are reserved for Borland's future use.
;
        DW      RESERVED            ; Reserved for Borland's use (1)
        DW      RESERVED            ; Reserved for Borland's use (2)
        DW      RESERVED            ; Reserved for Borland's use (3)

                .

                .

                .

        DW      RESERVED            ; Reserved for Borland's use (30)
        DW      RESERVED            ; Reserved for Borland's use (31)
        DW      RESERVED            ; Reserved for Borland's use (32)
;
;       Any vectors following this block may be used by
;       independent device driver developers as they see fit.
;
```

Vector Descriptions

The following information describes the input, output, and function of each of the functions accessed through the device vector table.

```
DW        offset    INSTALL      ; device driver installation
```

The kernel calls the INSTALL vector to prepare the device driver for use. A function code is passed in AL. The following function codes are defined:

Install Device

—>Install Device: AL = 00
Input: CL = Mode Number for device
                         CH = Auto-Detect maximum device number
Return: ES:BX —> Device Status Table
                         (see STATUS structure, preceding)

The Install Device function is intended to inform the driver of the operating parameters which will be used. The device should not be switched to graphics mode (see INIT). On input, CL contains the mode in which the device will operate, and CH contains the maximum device number that will be used. An example of the use of the maximum device number is a graphics board with four modes, the last two of which require extended hardware. The Auto-Detect routine would check for the additional hardware, and if it is not present, would set the Maximum Device Number to limit entering the modes requiring the additional hardware.

The return value from the Install Device function is a pointer to a Device Status Table (described earlier).

Mode Query

—>Mode Query: AL = 001h
Input: Nothing
Return: CX   The number of modes supported by this device

The Mode Query function is used to inquire the maximum number of modes supported by this device driver. This value is effected by the setting of the Auto-Detect Maximum Device Number as set in the Install Device function described above.

Mode Names

—>Mode Names: AL = 002h
Input: CX   The mode number for the query.
Return: ES:BX —> a Pascal string containing the name

The Mode Names function is used to inquire the ASCII form of the mode number present in CX. The return value in ES:BX points to a Pascal string describing the given mode.

A Pascal, or _length_, string is a string in which the first byte of data is the number of characters in the string, followed by the string data itself. To ease access to these strings from C, the strings should be followed by a zero byte, although this zero byte should not be included in the string length. The following is an example of this format:

```
NAME:    db    16, '1280 x 1024 Mode', 0
```

INIT

```
DW         offset         INIT    ; Initialize device for output
Input:     ES:BX                  —> Device Information Table
Return:    Nothing
```

This vector is used to change an already INSTALLed device from text mode to graphics mode. This vector should also initialize any default palettes and drawing mode information as required. The input to this vector is a device information table (DIT). The format of the DIT is shown below and contains the background color and an initialization flag. If the device requires additional information at INIT-time, these values can be appended to the DIT. There in no return value for this function. If an error occurs during device initialization, the STAT field of the Device Status Table should be loaded with the appropriate error value.

```
;          Device Information Table definition
struct     DIT
DB         0                  ; Background color for initializing screen
DB         0                  ; Init flag; 0A5h = don't init;
                              ;   anything else = init
DB         64 dup 0           ; Reserved for Borland's future use
                              ; additional user information here
DIT        ends
```

CLEAR

```
DW         offset  CLEAR         ; Clear the graphics device
Input:     Nothing
Return:    Nothing
```

This vector is used to clear the graphics device to a known state. In the case of a CRT device, the screen is cleared. In the case of a printer or plotter, the paper is advanced, and pens are returned to station.

POST

DW	offset POST	; Exit from graphics mode
Input:	Nothing	
Return:	Nothing	

This routine is used to close the graphics system. In the case of graphics screens or printers, the mode should be returned to text mode. For plotters, the paper should be unloaded and the pens should return to station.

MOVE

DW	offset MOVE	; Move the current drawing pointer
Input:	AX	the new CP x coordinate
	BX	the new CP y coordinate
Return:	Nothing	

Sets the Driver's current pointer (CP) to (AX,BX). This function is used prior to any of the TEXT, ARC, SYMBOL, DRAW, FLOODFILL, BAR, or PIESLICE routines to set the position where drawing is to take place.

DRAW

DW	offset DRAW	; Draw a line from the (CP) to (X,Y)
Input:	AX	the ending x coordinate for the line
	BX	the ending y coordinate for the line
Return:	Nothing	

Draw a line from the CP to (X,Y). The current LINESTYLE setting is used. The current pointer (CP) is updated to the line's endpoint.

VECT

DW	VECT	; Draw line from (X1,Y1) to (X2,Y2)
Input:	AX	X1; The beginning X coordinate for the line
	BX	Y1; The beginning Y coordinate for the line
	CX	X2; The ending X coordinate for the line
	DX	Y2; The ending Y coordinate for the line
Return:	Nothing	

Draw a line from the (X1,Y1) to (X2,Y2). The current LINESTYLE setting is used to draw the line. Note: CP is *not* changed by this vector.

POLY

DW	POLY	; Define polygon.
Input:	ES:BX	—> polygon
	CX = number of points in polygon	

	AX = 6	outline polygon in current color
	AX = 7	outline and fill polygon in current color, fill color and fill pattern
	AX = 8	fill polygon in current fill color and fill pattern
Return:	Nothing	

The polygon entry point is usually EMULATEd. Users with hardware capable of accepting polygon data in a single operation should contact Borland's technical support department for more information.

BAR

DW	BAR	; fill and outline rectangle (CP),(X,Y)
Input:	AX	X — right edge of rectangle
	BX	Y — bottom edge of rectangle
	CX	3D = width of 3D bar (ht = .75 * wdt); 0 = no 3D effect
	DX	3D bar top flag; if CX <> 0 and DX = 0, draw a top
Return:	Nothing	

Fill and outline a bar (rectangle), using the current COLOR, FILLCOLOR, and FILLPATERN. The current pointer defines the upper left corner of the rectangle and (X,Y) is lower, right. An optional 3-D shadow effect (intended for business graphics programs) is obtained by making CX nonzero. DX serves as a flag indicating whether a top should be drawn on the bar.

PATBAR

DW	PATBAR	; fill rectangle (X1,Y1), (X2,Y2)
Input:	AX	X1 — the rectangle's left coordinate
	BX	Y1 — the rectangle's top coordinate
	CX	X2 — the rectangle's right coordinate
	DX	Y2 — the rectangle's bottom coordinate
Return:	Nothing	

Fill (but don't outline) the indicated rectangle with the current fill pattern and fill color.

ARC

DW	ARC	; Draw an elliptical arc
Input:	AX	Starting angle of the arc in degrees (0..360)
	BX	Ending angle of the arc in degrees (0..360)

	CX	X radius of the elliptical arc
	DX	Y radius of the elliptical arc
Return:	Nothing	

ARC draws an elliptical arc using the (CP) as the center point of the arc, from the given start angle to the given end angle. To get circular arcs, the application (not the driver) must adjust the Y radius as follows: *YRAD :=* *XRAD * (ASPEC / 10000)* where ASPEC is the aspect value stored in the DST.

PIESLICE

DW	PIESLICE	; Draw an elliptical pie slice
Input:	AX	Starting angle of the slice in degrees (0..360)
	BX	Ending angle of the slice in degrees (0..360)
	CX	X radius of the elliptical slice
	DX	Y radius of the elliptical slice
Return:	Nothing	

PIESLICE draws a filled elliptical pie slice (or wedge) using CP as the center of the slice, from the given start angle to the given end angle. The current FILLPATTERN and FILLCOLOR is used to fill the slice and it is outlined in the current COLOR. To get circular pie slices the application (not the driver) must adjust the Y radius as follows: *YRAD := XRAD * ASPEC/10000* where ASPEC is the aspect value stored in the driver's DST.

FILLED_ELLIPSE

DW	FILLED_ELLIPSE	; Draw a filled ellipse at (CP)
Input:	AX	X Radius of the ellipse
	BX	Y Radius of the ellipse
Return:	Nothing	

This vector is used to draw a filled ellipse. The center point of the ellipse is assumed to be at the current pointer (CP). The AX Register contains the X Radius of the ellipse, and the BX Register contains the Y Radius of the ellipse.

PALETTE

DW	PALETTE	; Load a color entry into the Palette
Input:	AX	The index number and function code for load
	BX	The color value to load into the palette
Return:	Nothing	

The PALETTE vector is used to load single entries into the palette. The register AX contains the function code for the load action and the index of the color table entry to be loaded. The upper two bits of AX determine the action to be taken. The table below tabulates the actions. If the control bits are 00, the color table index in (AX AND 03FFFh) is loaded with the value in BX. If the control bits are 10, the color table index in (AX AND 03FFFh) is loaded with the RGB value in (Red=BX, Green=CX, and Blue=DX). If the control bits are 11, the color table entry for the background is loaded with the value in BX.

ALLPALETTE

DW	ALLPALETTE	; Load the full palette
Input:	ES:BX	—> array of palette entries
Return:	Nothing	

The ALLPALETTE routine loads the entire palette in one driver call. The register pair ES:BX points to the table of values to be loaded into the palette. The number of entries is determined by the color entries in the Driver Status Table. The background color is not explicitly loaded with this command.

COLOR

DW	COLOR	; Load the current drawing color.
Input:	AL	Index number of the current drawing color
	AH	Index number of the fill color
Return:	Nothing	

The COLOR vector is used to determine the current drawing color. The value in AL is the index into the palette of the new current drawing color. The value in the AH register is the color index of the new fill color. All primitives are drawn with the current drawing color until the color is changed. The fill color is used for the interior color for the bar, polygon, pie slice, and floodfill primitives.

FILLSTYLE

DW	FILLSTYLE	; Set the filling pattern
Input:	AL	Primary fill pattern number
	ES:BX	If the pattern number is 0FFh, this points to user-defined pattern mask.
Return:	Nothing	

Set the fill pattern for drawing. The fill pattern is used to fill all bounded regions (BAR, POLY, and PIESLICE).

In the case of a user-defined fill pattern, the register pair ES:BX point to 8 bytes of data arranged as a 8x8 bit pattern to be used for the fill pattern.

LINESTYLE

DW	LINESTYLE	; Set the line drawing pattern
Input:	AL	Line pattern number
	BX	User defined line drawing pattern
	CX	Line width for drawing
Return:	Nothing	

Set the current line drawing style and the width of the line. The line width is either one pixel or three pixels.

If the value in AL is four, the user is defining a line style in the BX register. If the value in AL is not four, then the value in register BX is ignored.

TEXTSTYLE

DW	TEXTSTYLE	; Hardware text style control
Input:	AL	Hardware font number
	AH	Hardware font orientation
		0 = Normal, 1 = 90 Degree, 2 = Down
	BX	Desired X Character size *
	CX	Desired Y Character size *
Return:	BX	Closest X Character size available *
	CX	Closest Y Character size available *
		* in graphics units

The TEXTSTYLE vector is used to define the attributes of the hardware font for output. The parameters that are affected are the selection of which hardware font to be used, the orientation of the font for output, and the desired height and width of the font output. All subsequent text will be drawn using these attributes.

If the desired size is not supported by the current device, the closest available match to the desired size should be used. The return value from this function gives the dimensions of the font (in pixels) which will actually be used.

For example, if the desired font is 8x10 pixels and the device supports 8x8 and 16x16 fonts, the closest match will be the 8x8. The output of the function will be BX = 8, and CX = 8.

TEXT

DW	TEXT	; Hardware text output at (CP)
Input:	ES:BX	—> ASCII text of the string
	CX	The length (in characters) of the string.
	AL	Horizontal Justification Point
		0 = Left, 1 = Center, 2 = Right
	AH	Vertical Justification Point
		0 = Bottom, 1 = Center, 2 = Top
Return:	BX	The width of the string in graphics units.
	CX	The height of the string in graphics units.

This function is used to send hardware text to the output device. The text is output to the device beginning at the (CP). The placement of the text with respect to the (CP) is determined by the two bytes in AX. The value in AL is the horizontal justification flag. If the value is 0, the (CP) defines the left-most edge of the text string, if the value is 1, the (CP) defines the center of the text string, and if the value is 2, the (CP) defines the right-most edge of the text string. The value in AH is the vertical justification flag. If the value is 0, the (CP) defines the bottom edge of the text string, if the value is 1, the (CP) defines the center of the text string, and if the value is 2, the (CP) defines the top edge of the text string.

TEXTSIZ

DW	TEXTSIZ	; Determine the height and width of text
		; strings in graphics units.
Input:	ES:BX	—> ASCII text of the string
	CX	The length (in characters) of the string.
Return:	BX	The width of the string in graphics units.
	CX	The height of the string in graphics units.

This function is used to determine the actual physical length and width of a text string. The current text attributes (set by TEXTSTYLE) are used to determine the actual dimensions of a string without displaying it. The application can thereby determine how a specific string will fit and reduce or increase the font size as required. There is *no* graphics output for this vector. If an error occurs during length calculation, the STAT field of the Device Status Record should be marked with the device error code.

FLOODFILL

DW	FLOODFILL	; Fill a bounded region using a flood fill
Input:	AX	The *x* coordinate for the seed point

	BX	The *y* coordinate for the seed point
	CL	The boundary color for the Flood Fill
Return:	Nothing	(Errors are returned in Device Status STAT field)

This function is called to fill a bounded region on bitmap devices. The (*X*,*Y*) input coordinate is used as the seed point for the flood fill. (CP) becomes the seed point. The current FILLPATTERN is used to flood the region.

GETPIXEL

DW	GETPIXEL	; Read a pixel from the graphics screen
Input:	AX	The *x* coordinate for the seed point
	BX	The *y* coordinate for the seed point
Return:	DL	The color index of the screen pixel read

GETPIXEL reads the color index value of a single pixel from the graphics screen. The color index value is returned in the DL register.

PUTPIXEL

DW	PUTPIXEL	; Write a pixel to the graphics screen
Input:	AX	The *x* coordinate for the seed point
	BX	The *y* coordinate for the seed point
	DL	The color index of the pixel read from the screen
Return:	Nothing	

PUTPIXEL writes a single pixel with the color index value contained in the DL register.

BITMAPUTIL

DW	BITMAPUTIL	; Bitmap Utilities Function Table
Input:	Nothing	
Return:	ES:BX	—> BitMap Utility Table.

The BITMAPUTIL vector loads a pointer into ES:BX which is the base of a table defining special case entry points used for pixel manipulation. These functions are currently only called by the ellipse emulation routines that are in the BGI kernel. If the device driver does not use emulation for ellipses, this entry does not have to be implemented. This entry was provided since some hardware requires additional commands to enter and exit pixel mode, thus adding overhead to the GETPIXEL and SETPIXEL vectors. This overhead affected the drawing speed of the ellipse emulation routines. These entry points are provided so that the ellipse emulation routines can enter pixel mode and remain in pixel mode, for the duration of the ellipse rendering process.

The format of the BITMAPUTIL table is as follows:

```
DW        offset  GOTOGRAPHIC
                      ; Enter pixel mode on the graphics hardware
DW        offset  EXITGRAPHIC
                      ; Leave pixel mode on the graphics hardware
DW        offset  PUTPIXEL
                      ; Write a pixel to the graphics hardware
DW        offset  GETPIXEL
                      ; Read a pixel from the graphics hardware
DW        offset  GETPIXBYTE
                      ; Return a word containing the pixel depth
DW        offset  SET_DRAW_PAGE
                      ; Select page in which to draw primitives
DW        offset  SET_VISUAL_PAGE
                      ; Set the page to be displayed
DW        offset  SET_WRITE_MODE
                      ; XOR Line Drawing Control
```

The parameters of these functions are as follows:

```
    GOTOGRAPHIC            ; Enter pixel mode on the graphics hardware
```

This function is used to enter the special Pixel Graphics mode:

```
    EXITGRAPHIC           ; Leave pixel mode on the graphics hardware
```

This function is used to leave the special Pixel Graphics mode:

```
    PUTPIXEL              ; Write a pixel to the graphics hardware
```

This function has the same format as the PUTPIXEL entry described previously:

```
    GETPIXEL             ; Read a pixel from the graphics hardware
```

This function has the same format as the GETPIXEL entry described previously:

```
    GETPIXBYTE           ; Return a word containing the pixel depth
```

This function returns the number of bits per pixel (color depth) of the graphics hardware in the AX register:

SET_DRAW_PAGE   ; Select alternate output graphics pages (if any)

This function takes the desired page number in the AL register and selects alternate graphics pages for output of graphics primitives:

SET_VISUAL_PAGE   ; Select the visible alternate graphics pages (if any)

This function takes the desired page number in the AL register and selects alternate graphics for displaying on the screen:

SET_WRITE_MODE   ; XOR Line drawing mode control.

XOR Mode is selected if the value in AX is one, and disabled if the value in AX is zero.

SAVEBITMAP

DW	SAVEBITMAP	; Write from screen to system memory
Input:	ES:BX	—> write buffer in system memory
	SI	Starting X coordinate of screen block
	DI	Starting Y coordinate of screen block
	CX	Ending X coordinate of screen block
	DX	Ending Y coordinate of screen block
Return:	Nothing	

The SAVEBITMAP routine is a block copy routine which copies screen pixels from a defined rectangle as specified by (SI,DI)–(CX,DX) to the system memory.

RESTOREBITMAP

DW	RESTOREBITMAP	; Write system memory to the screen.
Input:	ES:BX	—> buffer in system memory
	SI	Starting X coordinate of screen block
	DI	Starting Y coordinate of screen block
	CX	Ending X coordinate of screen block
	DX	Ending Y coordinate of screen block
	AL	Write mode for block writing
Return:	Nothing	

The RESTOREBITMAP vector is used to load screen pixels from the system memory. The routine reads a stream of bytes from the system memory into the rectangle defined by (SI,DI)–(CX,DX). The value in the AL register defines the mode that is used for the write.

SETCLIP

DW	SETCLIP	; Define a clipping rectangle
Input:	AX	Upper Left X coordinate of clipping rectangle
	BX	Upper Left Y coordinate of clipping rectangle
	CX	Lower Right X coordinate clipping rectangle
	DX	Lower Right Y coordinate clipping rectangle
Return:	Nothing	

The SETCLIP vector defines a rectangular clipping region on the screen. The registers (AX,BX)–(CX,DX) define the clipping region.

COLOR_QUERY

DW	offset COLOR_QUERY; Device Color Information Query

This vector is used to inquire the color capabilities of a given piece of hardware. A function code is passed into the driver in AL.

—>	Color Table Size	AL = 000h
Input:	None:	
Return:	BX	The size of the color lookup table.
	CX	The maximum color number allowed.

The COLOR TABLE SIZE query is used to determine the maximum number of colors supported by the hardware. The value returned in the BX register is the number of color entries in the color lookup table. The value returned in the CX register is the highest number for a color value. This value is usually the value in BX minus one, however there can be exceptions.

—>	Default Color Table	AL = 001h
Input:	Nothing	
Return:	ES:BX	—> default color table for the device

The DEFAULT COLOR TABLE function is used to determine the color table values for the default (power-up) color table. The format of this table is a byte containing the number of valid entries, followed by the given number of bytes of color information.

SYMBOL

DW	SYMBOL	; Draw a graphics symbol at (CP)
Input:	AL	Code number of symbol (see following)
Return:	Nothing	

This vector is used to write a symbol (or marker—an indicator for representing points on a line graph) to the output device. The symbol is written at the current pointer (CP).

Device Driver Construction Particulars

The source code for a sample, albeit unusual, BGI device driver is included with this Toolkit to assist developers in creating their own. The demonstration driver is provided in two files, DEBVECT.ASM and DEBUG.C. ThisDebugdriver doesn't actually draw graphics, but instead simply sends descriptive messages to the console screen (via DOS function call 9) upon receiving commands. Instead of simply playing back commands, your own driver would be structured similarly, but would access control ports and screen memory to perform each function.

Cookbook

1. Compile or assemble the files required.
2. Link the files together, making sure that the device vector table is the first module within the link.
3. Run EXE2BIN on the resulting .EXE or .COM file to produce a .BIN file. There should be no relocation fixups required.
4. Run program BH (provided with the toolkit) on the .BIN file to produce the .BGI file.

The resulting driver is now ready for testing. Examine the file TEST.C for an example of installing, loading, and calling a newly-created device driver.

Examples

```
; To call any BGI function from assembly language include the structure below and
; use the CALLBGI macro.
CALLBGI   MACRO   P
        MOV         SI,$&P                  ; Put opcode in (SI)
        CALL        CS:DWORD PTR BGI_ADD     ; BGI_ADD points to driver
        ENDM

; e.g., to draw a line from (10,15) to (200,300):
        MOV         AX, 10
        MOV         BX, 15
        MOV         CX, 200
        MOV         DX, 300
```

```
        CALLBGI VECT

; To index any item in the status table include the status table structures below
and
; use the BGISTAT macro.
BGISTAT   MACRO   P                     ; get ES:<SI> —> BGI STATUS
    LES  SI, CS:DWORD PTR STABLE    ; get location of status to SI
    ADD SI, $&P                     ; offset to correct location
    ENDM

; e.g., to obtain the aspect ratio of a device:
    BGISTAT ASPEC
    MOV     AX, ES:[SI]             ; (AX) = Y/X *10000
```

Appendix D

A VGA 256-Color .BGI Driver

In addition to the Font Editor utility and the custom .BGI package, Borland has provided a new VGA driver (VGA256.BGI) that supports the full VGA color resolution with a 256-hue palette employing the Hue-Saturation-Intensity (HSI) color model.

Available from Borland's languages forum on Compuserve, the VGA utility package consists of five programs: the VGA256.BGI driver, the HSI.EXE and HSI.PAS color hue demonstration, VGADEMO.EXE, and VGADEMO.PAS.

The VGADEMO is the principal demonstration (and does work on non-VGA systems though without the full range of 256 colors). The VGADEMO program includes demonstrations of several graphics functions that were new to Turbo C version 2.0 (or Turbo Pascal version 5.0), including the setaspectratio, fillellipse, sector, and setwritemode functions. The 256 Color and SetRGBPalette demos, of course, will only execute correctly on systems with VGA or compatible video cards. On an EGA system, for example, these two demo segments execute but are restricted to the EGAVGA default palette of 16 colors.

Of interest to the programmer, in the HSI or VGADEMO programs, are the VGASetAllPalette procedure and the DetectVGA256 function. While the source codes for both demo programs are written in Pascal, C programmers should have little difficulty converting these for C++ applications.

Appendix E

The Graphic Character Fonts

Ten graphics character fonts are shown following. Fonts 0..4 are graphics character fonts distributed with Turbo C, Turbo Pascal, and Turbo Prolog. Fonts 5..9 are provided with the Turbo Font Editor (see Chapter 17).

The font illustrations following were created by writing each font to the screen (VGA—640x480) as shown, then capturing the screen image as a .PCX file. Each font was created as two separate images, then recombined to provide a single font illustration.

The exact appearance of each font will vary depending on screen resolution and character magnification. For example, in EGA modes, note characters B0h..B2h which may show some distortion toward the bottom of the character where the stroke instructions "slip" slightly as they are mapped to the pixel image. This is normal and expected and is usually not visually apparent on the screen.

Also, the overall appearance of the characters on screen is generally smoother—due to tendency of illuminated pixels to visually "melt" together—than they appear on paper.

The versions of fonts 1..4 shown in Table E-1 are the expanded versions of the original distribution fonts as distributed with the Turbo Font Editor utility.

Table E-1: Graphics Character Fonts

Font	Font Name	Type
0	DEFAULT_FONT	Bit-mapped
1	TRIPLEX_FONT	Stroked
2	SMALL_FONT	Stroked
3	SANS_SERIF_FONT	Stroked
4	GOTHIC_FONT	Stroked
5	SCRIPT_FONT	Stroked
6	SIMPLEX_FONT	Stroked
7	ITALIC_FONT	Stroked
8	ROMAN_FONT	Stroked
9	LARGE_FONT	Stroked

	0	1	2	3	4	5	6	7	8	9	A	B	C	D	E	F
0		☺	☻	♥	♦	♣	♠	•	◘	○	◙	♂	♀	♪	♫	☼
1	►	◄	↕	‼	¶	§	▬	↨	↑	↓	→	←	∟	↔	▲	▼
2		!	"	#	$	%	&	'	(	)	*	+	,	–	.	/
3	0	1	2	3	4	5	6	7	8	9	:	;	<	=	>	?
4	@	A	B	C	D	E	F	G	H	I	J	K	L	M	N	O
5	P	Q	R	S	T	U	V	W	X	Y	Z	[	\	]	^	_
6	`	a	b	c	d	e	f	g	h	i	j	k	l	m	n	o
7	p	q	r	s	t	u	v	w	x	y	z	{	|	}	~	⌂
8	Ç	ü	é	â	ä	à	å	ç	ê	ë	è	ï	î	ì	Ä	Å
9	É	æ	Æ	ô	ö	ò	û	ù	ÿ	Ö	Ü	¢	£	¥	₧	ƒ
A	á	í	ó	ú	ñ	Ñ	ª	º	¿	⌐	¬	½	¼	¡	«	»
B	░	▒	▓	│	┤	╡	╢	╖	╕	╣	║	╗	╝	╜	╛	┐
C	└	┴	┬	├	─	┼	╞	╟	╚	╔	╩	╦	╠	═	╬	╧
D	╨	╤	╥	╙	╘	╒	╓	╫	╪	┘	┌	█	▄	▌	▐	▀
E	α	ß	Γ	π	Σ	σ	µ	τ	Φ	Θ	Ω	δ	∞	φ	ε	∩
F	≡	±	≥	≤	⌠	⌡	÷	≈	°	∙	·	√	ⁿ	²	■	

Font Number: 0 — DEFAULT_FONT — Bit-mapped

Source File: (built-in to GRAPHICS.LIB) — Size = 3

	0	1	2	3	4	5	6	7	8	9	A	B	C	D	E	F
0																
1																
2		!	"	#	$	%	&	'	(	)	*	+	,	−	.	/
3	0	1	2	3	4	5	6	7	8	9	:	;	<	=	>	?
4	@	A	B	C	D	E	F	G	H	I	J	K	L	M	N	O
5	P	Q	R	S	T	U	V	W	X	Y	Z	[	\	]	^	_
6	`	a	b	c	d	e	f	g	h	i	j	k	l	m	n	o
7	p	q	r	s	t	u	v	w	x	y	z	{	|	}	~	△
8	Ç	ü	é	â	ä	à	å	ç	ê	ë	è	ï	î	ì	Ä	Å
9	É	æ	Æ	ô	ö	ò	û	ù	ÿ	Ö	Ü	ø	£	Ø	₧	ƒ
A	á	í	ó	ú	ñ	Ñ	ª	º	¿	⌐	¬	½	¼	¡	«	»
B	░	▓	▒	│	┤	╡	╢	╖	╕	╣	║	╗	╝	╜	╛	┐
C	└	┴	┬	├	─	┼	╞	╟	╚	╔	╩	╦	╠	═	╬	╧
D	╨	╤	╥	╙	╘	╒	╓	╫	╪	┘	┌	█	▄	▌	▐	▀
E	α	ß	Γ	π	Σ	σ	µ	γ	Φ	Θ	Ω	δ	∞	ø	∈	∩
F	≡	±	≥	≤	⌠	⌡	÷	≈	°	∙	·	√	ⁿ	²	■	

Font Number: 1 — *TRIPLEX_FONT* — Stroked

Source File: TRIP.CHR — Size = 3

	0	1	2	3	4	5	6	7	8	9	A	B	C	D	E	F
0																
1																
2		!		#	$	٪	&	'	(	)	*	+	,	−	.	/
3	0	1	2	3	4	5	6	7	8	9	:	;	<	=	>	?
4	@	A	B	C	D	E	F	G	H	I	J	K	L	M	N	O
5	P	Q	R	S	T	U	V	W	X	Y	Z	[	\	]	^	_
6	`	a	b	c	d	e	f	g	h	i	j	k	l	m	n	o
7	p	q	r	s	t	u	v	w	x	y	z	{	|	}	~	△
8	Ç	ü	é	â	ä	à	å	ç	ê	ë	è	ï	î	ì	Ä	Å
9	É	æ	Æ	ô	ö	ò	û	ù	ÿ	Ö	Ü	ø	£	Ø	₧	ƒ
A	á	í	ó	ú	ñ	Ñ	ª	º	¿	⌐	¬	½	¼	¡	«	»
B	▦	▩	▨	│	┤	╡	╢	╖	╕	╣	║	╗	╝	╜	╛	┐
C	└	┴	┬	├	─	┼	╞	╟	╚	╔	╩	╦	╠	═	╬	╧
D	╨	╤	╥	╙	╘	╒	╓	╫	╪	┘	┌	█	▄	▌	▐	▀
E	α	β	Γ	π	Σ	σ	µ	γ	Φ	Θ	Ω	δ	∞	ø	∈	∩
F	≡	±	≥	≤	⌠	⌡	÷	≈	°	∙	·	√	ⁿ	²	▪	

Font Number: 2 — SMALL_FONT — Stroked

Source File: LITT.CHR — Size = 7

	0	1	2	3	4	5	6	7	8	9	A	B	C	D	E	F
0																
1																
2		!	"	#	$	%	&	'	(	)	*	+	,	−	.	/
3	0	1	2	3	4	5	6	7	8	9	:	;	<	=	>	?
4	@	A	B	C	D	E	F	G	H	I	J	K	L	M	N	O
5	P	Q	R	S	T	U	V	W	X	Y	Z	[	\	]	^	_
6	'	a	b	c	d	e	f	g	h	i	j	k	l	m	n	o
7	p	q	r	s	t	u	v	w	x	y	z	{	|	}	~	△
8	Ç	ü	é	â	ä	å	à	ç	ê	ë	è	ï	î	ì	Ä	Å
9	É	œ	Æ	ô	ö	ò	û	ù	ÿ	Ö	Ü	ø	£	Ø	₧	ƒ
A	á	í	ó	ú	ñ	Ñ	ª	º	¿	⌐	¬	½	¼	¡	«	»
B	▒	▓	▒	│	┤	╡	╢	╖	╕	╣	║	╗	╝	╜	╛	┐
C	└	┴	┬	├	─	┼	╞	╟	╚	╔	╩	╦	╠	═	╬	╧
D	╨	╤	╥	╙	╘	╒	╓	╫	╪	┘	┌	█	▄	▌	▐	▀
E	α	ß	Γ	π	Σ	σ	µ	γ	Φ	Θ	Ω	δ	∞	ø	∈	∩
F	≡	±	≥	≤	⌠	⌡	÷	≈	°	•	·	√	ⁿ	²	■	

Font Number: 3 — SANS_SERIF_FONT — Stroked

Source File: SANS.CHR — Size = 3

	0	1	2	3	4	5	6	7	8	9	A	B	C	D	E	F
0																
1																
2		!	"	#	$	%	&	'	(	)	*	+	,	−	.	/
3	0	1	2	3	4	5	6	7	8	9	:	;	<	=	>	?
4	@	A	B	C	D	E	F	G	H	I	J	K	L	M	N	O
5	P	Q	R	S	T	U	V	W	X	Y	Z	[	\	]	^	_
6	`	a	b	c	d	e	f	g	h	i	j	k	l	m	n	o
7	p	q	r	s	t	u	v	w	x	y	z	{	|	}	~	△
8	Ç	ü	é	â	ä	à	å	ç	ê	ë	è	ï	î	ì	Ä	Â
9	É	æ	Æ	ô	ö	ò	û	ù	ÿ	Ö	Ü	ø	£	Ø	₧	ƒ
A	á	í	ó	ú	ñ	Ñ	ª	º	¿	⌐	¬	½	¼	¡	«	»
B	▓	▓	▓	│	┤	╡	╢	╖	╕	╣	║	╗	╝	╜	╛	┐
C	└	┴	┬	├	─	┼	╞	╟	╚	╔	╩	╦	╠	═	╬	╧
D	╨	╤	╥	╙	╘	╒	╓	╫	╪	┘	┌	█	▄	▌	▐	▀
E	α	ß	Γ	π	Σ	σ	µ	τ	Θ	Ω	δ	∞	ø	ε	∩	
F	≡	±	≥	≤	⌠	⌡	÷	≈	°	∙	·	√	ⁿ	²	■	

Font Number: 4 — GOTHIC_FONT — Stroked[1]

Source File: GOTH.CHR — Size = 3

	0	1	2	3	4	5	6	7	8	9	A	B	C	D	E	F
0																
1																
2		!	"	#	$	%	&	'	(	)	*	+	,	—	.	/
3	0	1	2	3	4	5	6	7	8	9	:	;	<	=	>	?
4	@	A	B	C	D	E	F	G	H	I	J	K	L	M	N	O
5	P	Q	R	S	T	U	V	W	X	Y	Z	[	\	]	^	_
6	'	a	b	c	d	e	f	g	h	i	j	k	l	m	n	o
7	p	q	r	s	t	u	v	w	x	y	z	{	|	}	~	△
8	Ç	ü	é	â	ä	à	å	ç	ê	ë	è	ï	î	ì	Ä	Å
9	É	æ	Æ	ô	ö	ò	û	ù	ÿ	Ö	Ü	¢	£	¥	₧	ƒ
A	á	í	ó	ú	ñ	Ñ	ª	º	¿	⌐	¬	½	¼	¡	«	»
B	▒	▓	▒	│	┤	╡	╢	╖	╕	╣	║	╗	╝	╜	╛	┐
C	└	┴	┬	├	─	┼	╞	╟	╚	╔	╩	╦	╠	═	╬	╧
D	╨	╤	╥	╙	╘	╒	╓	╫	╪	┘	┌	█	▄	▌	▐	▀
E	α	β	Γ	π	Σ	σ	µ	τ	Φ	Θ	Ω	δ	∞	φ	Є	∩
F	≡	±	≥	≤	⌠	⌡	÷	≈	°	∙	·	√	ⁿ	²	■	

Font Number: 5 — SCRIPT_FONT[1] — Stroked

Source File: SCRI.CHR — Size = 3

	0	1	2	3	4	5	6	7	8	9	A	B	C	D	E	F
0																
1																
2		!	"	#	$	%	&	'	(	)	*	+	,	—	.	/
3	0	1	2	3	4	5	6	7	8	9	:	;	<	=	>	?
4	@	A	B	C	D	E	F	G	H	I	J	K	L	M	N	O
5	P	Q	R	S	T	U	V	W	X	Y	Z	[	\	]	^	_
6	'	a	b	c	d	e	f	g	h	i	j	k	l	m	n	o
7	p	q	r	s	t	u	v	w	x	y	z	{	|	}	~	△
8	Ç	ü	é	â	ä	à	å	ç	ê	ë	è	ï	î	ì	Ä	Å
9	É	œ	Æ	ô	ö	ò	û	ù	ÿ	Ö	Ü	ø	£	Ø	₧	ƒ
A	á	í	ó	ú	ñ	Ñ	ª	º	¿	⌐	¬	½	¼	¡	«	»
B	▓	▓	▓	│	┤	╡	╢	╖	╕	╣	║	╗	╝	╜	╛	┐
C	└	┴	┬	├	─	┼	╞	╟	╚	╔	╩	╦	╠	═	╬	╧
D	╨	╤	╥	╙	╘	╒	╓	╫	╪	┘	┌	█	▄	▌	▐	▀
E	α	β	Γ	π	Σ	σ	µ	τ	Φ	Θ	Ω	δ	∞	ø	∈	∩
F	≡	±	≥	≤	⌠	⌡	÷	≈	°	∙	·	√	ⁿ	²	■	

Font Number: 6 — *SIMPLEX_FONT*[1] — *Stroked*

Source File: SIMP.CHR — Size = 3

	0	1	2	3	4	5	6	7	8	9	A	B	C	D	E	F
0																
1																
2		!	"	#	$	%	&	'	(	)	*	+	,	−	.	/
3	0	1	2	3	4	5	6	7	8	9	:	;	<	=	>	?
4	@	A	B	C	D	E	F	G	H	I	J	K	L	M	N	O
5	P	Q	R	S	T	U	V	W	X	Y	Z	[	\	]	^	_
6	'	a	b	c	d	e	f	g	h	i	j	k	l	m	n	o
7	p	q	r	s	t	u	v	w	x	y	z	{	|	}	~	△
8	Ç	ü	é	â	ä	à	å	ç	ê	ë	è	ï	î	ì	Ä	Å
9	É	æ	Æ	ô	ö	ò	û	ù	ÿ	Ö	Ü	ø	£	Ø	₧	ƒ
A	á	í	ó	ú	ñ	Ñ	ª	º	¿	⌐	¬	½	¼	¡	«	»
B	░	▓	▒	│	┤	╡	╢	╖	╕	╣	║	╗	╝	╜	╛	┐
C	└	┴	┬	├	─	┼	╞	╟	╚	╔	╩	╦	╠	═	╬	╧
D	╨	╤	╥	╙	╘	╒	╓	╫	╪	┘	┌	█	▄	▌	▐	▀
E	α	ß	Γ	π	Σ	σ	µ	τ	Φ	Θ	Ω	δ	∞	φ	ε	∩
F	≡	±	≥	≤	⌠	⌡	÷	≈	°	∙	·	√	ⁿ	²	■	

Font Number: 7 — ITALIC_FONT[1] — Stroked

Source File: TSCR.CHR — Size = 3

	0	1	2	3	4	5	6	7	8	9	A	B	C	D	E	F
0																
1																
2		!	"	#	$	%	&	'	(	)	*	+	,	−	.	/
3	0	1	2	3	4	5	6	7	8	9	:	;	<	=	>	?
4	@	A	B	C	D	E	F	G	H	I	J	K	L	M	N	O
5	P	Q	R	S	T	U	V	W	X	Y	Z	[	\	]	^	_
6	'	a	b	c	d	e	f	g	h	i	j	k	l	m	n	o
7	p	q	r	s	t	u	v	w	x	y	z	{	|	}	~	△
8	Ç	ü	é	â	ä	à	á	ç	ê	ë	è	ï	î	ì	Ä	Å
9	É	æ	Æ	ô	ö	ò	û	ù	ÿ	Ö	Ü	ø	£	Ø	₧	ƒ
A	á	í	ó	ú	ñ	Ñ	a	o	¿	⌐	¬	½	¼	¡	«	»
B	▓	▓	▓	│	┤	╡	╢	╖	╕	╣	║	╗	╝	╜	╛	┐
C	└	┴	┬	├	─	┼	╞	╟	╚	╔	╩	╦	╠	═	╬	╧
D	╨	╤	╥	╙	╘	╒	╓	╫	╪	┘	┌	█	▄	▌	▐	▀
E	α	ß	Γ	π	Σ	σ	µ	τ	Φ	Θ	Ω	δ	∞	ø	∈	∩
F	≡	±	≥	≤	⌠	⌡	÷	≈	°	·	·	√	ⁿ	²	■	

Font Number: 8 — ROMAN_FONT[1] — Stroked

Source File: LCOM.CHR — Size = 3

	0	1	2	3	4	5	6	7	8	9	A	B	C	D	E	F
0																
1																
2		!	"	#	$	%	&	'	(	)	*	+	,	−	.	/
3	0	1	2	3	4	5	6	7	8	9	:	;	<	=	>	?
4	@	A	B	C	D	E	F	G	H	I	J	K	L	M	N	O
5	P	Q	R	S	T	U	V	W	X	Y	Z	[	\	]	^	_
6	`	a	b	c	d	e	f	g	h	i	j	k	l	m	n	o
7	p	q	r	s	t	u	v	w	x	y	z	{	|	}	~	△
8	Ç	ü	é	â	ä	à	å	ç	ê	ë	è	ï	î	ì	Ä	Å
9	É	æ	Æ	ô	ö	ò	û	ù	ÿ	Ö	Ü	ø	£	Ø	₧	ƒ
A	á	í	ó	ú	ñ	Ñ	ª	º	¿	⌐	¬	½	¼	¡	«	»
B	░	▒	▓	│	┤	╡	╢	╖	╕	╣	║	╗	╝	╜	╛	┐
C	└	┴	┬	├	─	┼	╞	╟	╚	╔	╩	╦	╠	═	╬	╧
D	╨	╤	╥	╙	╘	╒	╓	╫	╪	┘	┌	█	▄	▌	▐	▀
E	α	ß	Γ	π	Σ	σ	µ	τ	Φ	Θ	Ω	δ	∞	φ	∈	∩
F	≡	±	≥	≤	⌠	⌡	÷	≈	°	∙	·	√	ⁿ	²	■	

Font Number: 9 — LARGE_FONT [1] — Stroked

Source File: EURO.CHR — Size = 1

Note 1: Font numbers and font titles for fonts 5..9 are not predefined. The font numbers shown were arbitrarily assigned by installuserfont in the order each font was assigned to the internal font table while preparing these illustrations. The font names are equally arbitrary but are intended as descriptive mneumonics.